D1535847

THE PLANNING AND DRAFTING

DRAFTING

OF

WILLS AND TRUSTS

FIFTH EDITION

By

THOMAS L. SHAFFER
Robert and Marion Short Professor of Law Emeritus
University of Notre Dame
Supervising Attorney, Notre Dame Legal Aid Clinic

CAROL ANN MOONEY
of the Indiana Bar
President, St. Mary's College
Notre Dame, Indiana

and

AMY JO BOETTCHER
of the Wisconsin Bar

Fifth Edition Revisions by Thomas L. Shaffer

FOUNDATION PRESS

2007

THOMSON
——————*——————™
WEST

© 1972, 1979, 1991, 2001 FOUNDATION PRESS
© 2007 By FOUNDATION PRESS
   395 Hudson Street
   New York, NY 10014
   Phone Toll Free 1–877–888–1330
   Fax (212) 367–6799
   foundation–press.com
Printed in the United States of America

ISBN 978-1-59941-258-0

 TEXT IS PRINTED ON 10% POST CONSUMER RECYCLED PAPER

PREFACE

This is a book for the study of wills, trusts, future interests, and ancillary devices such as powers of attorney and health care agencies (proxies), in a law-office planning context. We hope many students and lawyers will find it interesting to read and useful as a sort of handbook. But our principal purpose is to use the book in teaching–in one or both of two ways:

We think our book can be used as a text, in lieu of or in addition to doctrinal books on the law of wills and trusts. Its bias as a text is that it approaches the subject, chronologically and logically, the way a practicing lawyer approaches it–that is:

– First she meets, interviews, advises, and counsels her client(s).

– Next she considers what law she needs to know.

– Next she makes, with her clients, the planning and drafting decisions necessary to do the job.

– Then she considers what the documents she drafts are to say and how they are to say it.

We also think our book can be used as a course book for combined courses in this field, and in law-school teaching clinics, in a functional way. Part One puts the project in a functional context. The lawyer here begins work with a client. What is that client like? What emotions and biases accompany the visit to a law office? How do lawyers react to clients who come in "to have our wills done"? How can the experience be a growing, human experience for both lawyer and client(s)? Chapter 1, a prelude on counseling, deals with these questions and inserts classroom devices we have used with success in exploring and discussing them. This functional focus continues (in Chapter 2) with special consideration of the skills for probate practice (clients in bereavement), and Chapter 3 concludes with a detailed chapter on interviewing (that chapter, incidentally, introduces clients who form the basis for part of the planning and drafting in Chapter 10).

Part Two deals with tools–the doctrines, distinctions, and devices that are brought to bear in reaching the clients' objectives–in order: wills, trusts, future interests (perpetuities), death taxation, and language in drafting. Part Three then presents (or reviews) an array of clients:

– The "simple will" client who needs exactly what he asks for–to "have my will done"–and who, like wealthier contemporaries, wishes to make general, specific, and charitable legacies.

— Two sets of "non-estate" clients (one the family interviewed in Chapter 3) who need contingent trust arrangements for dependent children, but who are not otherwise wealthy enough to invite tax-oriented draftsmanship. Modern alternatives for this "non-estate planning" make this work almost a complex sub-speciality in itself. This is one of the three longest chapters in the book; in it, we consider, as a necessary category for modern practice, planning for a handicapped child who is likely to remain dependent on parents for the rest of his and their lives (whoever dies last). These clients were interviewed in Chapter 3; Chapter 10 also continues from the first and second editions consideration of a family whose children are not handicapped.

— Chapters 11 and 12 consider elderly clients who do not have enough wealth to require tax-oriented planning and drafting, but who need to consider planning for the disabilities of age as well as planning for distribution after death. Chapter 12 also considers end-of-life decisions for younger clients. (We note that the dying patients in the famous modern cases–Quinlan, Cruzan, Lawrance, Schiavo–were all young women.)

Throughout these chapters we have added exercises, so that the reader can test his understanding. We use these as teaching and testing devices, in lieu of or in addition to traditional case analysis in class and examination questions. They afford opportunity for the exercise of law-office skills as well as opportunity to demonstrate an understanding of the law.

It has seemed best to us to delve into the lives of our clients–to consider all of the more obvious alternatives, and to suggest heavily annotated forms for them. The educational objective is that students consider every step in the process in its functional setting, and locate the step in a coherent scheme of client counseling, good drafting, and sound legal theory. Our forms are offered less to be used for clients than as material for practice and discussion. Most of the forms are annotated in detail, with alternative provisions. The first appendix (Statutory Appendix) provides the text of representative statutes and regulations in several areas of modern reform; these supplement our use of the Uniform Probate Code in the text. The second appendix presents additional clients for planning-drafting assignment and class discussion.

Our friends, colleagues, and spouses have helped with the raw material for this book. For the material carried forward from the earlier four editions, we are grateful to students at Notre Dame, the University of California, Los Angeles, and the University of Virginia; to the late James M. Corcoran, Jr., of the Evanston Bar; to Michael Cunningham, Michael Gahan, and Thomas Botkin, who worked on earlier editions when they were Notre Dame law students; to Mrs. Michael Robert Kessler in Los Angeles, and Nancy Wesolowski and Karlene Hamilton, Linda Harrington and Rebecca Carlton at Notre Dame. Continuing from the third edition to the fourth and fifth, we are grateful to the Notre Dame Class of 1991, and to our research assistants, Susan Bernstein, Al Stashis, Steven Judge, Anna Wollscheid, T.J. Pillari, and Kristopher Ritter; and Nancy Shaffer, George Efta, and Bradley Boettcher, M.D.; and, through it all, we thank the University of Notre Dame for support and encouragement.

T.L.S.
C.A.M.
A.J.B.

Notre Dame, Indiana
November, 1971
July, 1978
October, 1990
August, 2000
January, 2007

*

ACKNOWLEDGMENTS

We are grateful to publishers of material we have written for other purposes which has been adapted for this edition of this book:

Mooney and Wernz, "Planning for a Disabled Child," a study prepared for the Northwestern Mutual Life Insurance Company (1989);

Mooney, Asher, Bass, Hembleton, Krashin and Prensky, "Alzheimer's Disease–Planning for Dementia," 2 Probate and Property 7 (1988);

Mooney, "Discretionary Trusts: An Estate Plan to Supplement Public Assistance for Disabled Persons," 25 Arizona Law Review 939 (1983);

Shaffer, Book Review, 61 Kentucky Law Journal 538 (1971);

Shaffer, "Men and Things: The Liberal Bias Against Property," 57 American Bar Association Journal 123 (1971);

Shaffer, "Confidential Relationship, Undue Influence, and the Psychology of Transference," 45 North Dame Lawyer 197 (1970);

Shaffer, "Modern Fiduciary Powers Statutes," 58 Illinois Bar Journal 654 (1970);

Shaffer, "Fifty Estates in Elkhart County," Res Gestae, September, 1969, p. 22;

Shaffer, "The Overture in a Well-Drawn Will," The Practical Lawyer, January, 1968, page 45; reproduced with the permission of The Practical Lawyer, 4025 Chestnut Street, Philadelphia, PA 19104;

Shaffer, "Non-Residuary Legacies," reprinted from Trusts and Estates, September, 1967, p. 813; copyright Communication Channels, Inc., 461 Eighth Avenue, New York, N.Y. 10001;

Shaffer, "Non-Estate Planning," 42 Notre Dame Lawyer 153 (1966);

Shaffer, "Life Insurance Proceeds in Trusts," Res Gestae, July, 1966, p. 9;

Shaffer, Book Review, 39 Notre Dame Lawyer 356 (1964);

Office Will and Trust Forms, Notre Dame Legal Aid Clinic.

T.L.S.
C.A.M.
A.J.B.

*

For

Notre Dame

Our Mother

*

SUMMARY OF CONTENTS

SUMMARY OF CONTENTS

*

TABLE OF CONTENTS

APPENDICES

*

LIST OF FORMS

*

THE PLANNING

AND

DRAFTING OF WILLS AND TRUSTS

*

Part One

CLIENTS

Chapter 1

PLANNING TOGETHER

This chapter and Chapters 2, 3, and 8 are preludes to the property-settlement practice, the first three dealing with the counseling relationship an office lawyer has with her clients, and Chapter 8 dealing with the philosophy and system behind styles of draftsmanship. We try in this chapter to survey some of the more important findings of Shaffer's early book, *Death, Property, and Lawyers*; of four editions of his and Elkins' Nutshell on legal interviewing and counseling; and of Shaffer's and Redmount's counseling casebook.

The wills-trusts practice is centered in the human relationships of a law office. We find law students ready to explore the implications of that observation, and we find them often surprised at what they learn. The learning community is usually conscious that there is a professional community out there somewhere, but the learning community is often unrealistic in supposing what the professional community is like. The learning community *assumes* a topography for law practice, rather than building one through observation or experience. The late Louis M. Brown, a veteran teacher and practitioner, asked his students in a course in law-office practice, "How much time do you think you, as a lawyer, will spend researching?" Answers, he said, ranged around a mean of about 50 per cent. Professor Brown's observation of lawyers in practice indicated to him that practicing lawyers spend five to ten per cent of their time in research. That real statistic is unsettling for students who assume they will have time in the practice for research and thought on the legal problems of their clients, and it demonstrates the kind of bookish bias we law professors condition into their professional self images.

A. COUNSELING IN THE LAW OFFICE

It would be exciting if we teachers of law-office subjects (wills, trusts, property, taxation, corporations, contracts, commercial law, and others) could experience with our students what the professional community is like, rather than merely asking them to read about it, or, worse, to make the usual assumptions. The object would be to replace guesses about the professional community with interpersonal realities—the fact, for example, that most lawyers spend most of their time in their offices, in one-on-one human encounters. In the property-settlement practice we might turn up some other neglected realities. Another example:

The lawyer's professional law-office world is a small community of lawyer, client, and client's family. It is remote from the political community experienced in other courses, particularly in the "public law" courses. Much of the recent, policy-oriented teaching material in the "estates" field is weakened by the fact that its authors ignore the vast differences between the politics of a national (or even international) community and the politics of an inter-personal, family community. The family, its property, and its economic and social extensions have their own economics, their own social psychology, and their own political implications; these inter-personal dimensions are often not even suggested in policy-oriented discussions of the law of wills, intestate succession, death taxation, property titles, power of attorney, advance directives, and future interests.

The examination community which exercises first tyranny over law students (and this includes both academic examinations and bar examinations) is analytically irrelevant to either the learning community or the professional community. It is worse than that; it is an intrusion into each of them. The real context of law-office practice is not a competitive context; it is a counseling context. Examinations are no preparation for this and are a poor way to evaluate one's promise for it.

The professional community acts in a law office. The material generally available to students is unreal because it is about a litigious community (courts); in fact, the majority of it is about the most remote, most unlikely part of the litigious community (appellate courts). In most law courses (torts, for example, or criminal law, or evidence) the real professional world is a pyramid; the appellate-court world is a tiny speck at the top of the pyramid:

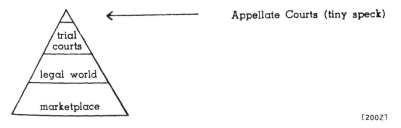

In the property-settlement practice, and other law-office fields (corporations and commercial law), the professional world is a sub-pyramid under the professional-community (litigation) pyramid:

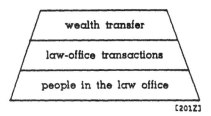

[201Z]

This suggests that we who teach in this field begin and end with enormous obstacles to our own impact on our students and to our students' growth for the practice of law. The obstacle is of our own making. It is we who have produced material for law-office practice that is fashioned from law-office failure (litigation). That would not be so bad if we could say that failure is common in the law office—but it is not—or if all instances of failure came to light, as the physician's failures tend to end up in the mortuary. The fact is that "estates" learning materials based on litigation are unreal, distorted, insignificant, and dysfunctional. There has always been a great deal of formal judicial supervision—litigation in a minimal sense—in the property-settlement practice. But even that formal contact has a diminishing role in modern practice. If the professional wealth-transfer world were a pie, something more than half of it would have to be accounted traditionally outside the law of probate supervision, and only a tiny slice of what remains now involves any amount of realistic litigation:

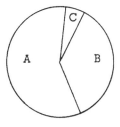

A: Unsupervised wealth transfer
   (joint tenancy, trust interests,
   life insurance)

B: Supervised wealth transfer
   (probate)

C: Litigation in wealth transfer
   (will contest, heirship,
   claims, etc.)
   (tiny slice)

[202Z]

Slice "A" of the pie is growing in modern property-settlement practice, and slices "B" and "C" are shrinking. The use of living trusts, no-administration estates, fringe benefits in employment, and group, governmental, and employer-sponsored insurance programs for retirement and family support are all outside the supervised (probate) wealth-transfer practice. And the increasing expense and trauma of litigation constantly reduces the proportion of serious, non-criminal courtroom combat. Good lawyers in this field regard litigation as failure.

Lawyers who practice property-settlement law do it in a law office, in intimate encounter with one or two other people, often in the presence of emotion, and without much help from books, or professional elders, or the blindfolded woman on top of the courthouse. This professional world is different in three key dimensions from the way our teaching materials might lead a law student to suppose:

The world we teach about is a world built upon *rights and duties;* the world of office practice is a world built upon human *needs and emotions* and is relatively irrational, unsolomonic, and fluid. It is more about what holds people together than it is about what separates them.

The world we teach about is a world that involves lawyers as *advocates;* in the law office world the lawyer is a *manipulator* who knows how to get what clients want with subtle, unpublic, unjudicial consideration of the power structure. The professional ideal in the world law schools traditionally teach about is *mastery*; the professional ideal in the world of practice is *competence;* the difference between the two ideas is the difference between knowing about something and being able to do it.

The world law schools traditionally teach about is, finally, a world in which standards of decision relate more or less to *fairness;* the professional world in property-settlement practice is a world in which the standards of decision relate to *love and hate,* to human persons reaching out to one another or failing to reach out. Standards of decision are less likely to reflect abstract ideas of justice than they are to turn on what Anne Tyler called "errors of aimlessness, passivity ... [and] echoing internal silence." (Tyler is the expert on the family in America, as Mark Twain was the expert on the Mississippi river boat.)

1. LEARNING WITH EXERCISES

An experience-based approach to this subject would begin with concentration on counseling skills, and that means it would postpone—if not forsake—law books. The most important resources for counselor-centered learning are people. The first and best resource in learning about people is oneself; the second best resource in learning about people is other people.

The focus for a counselor-centered beginning to property settlement is the feelings of clients in a law-office, wealth-transfer environment, and how lawyers react to the feelings of clients. The biological (and probably fundamental) center of this world is death. Death is the first item on an agenda for experienced learning in this field: How do you feel about death? How do you talk about it? How do you react to another person's talking about it?

Exercise 1.1

1.1.1. If the reader is willing to give this idea a try, in terms of method and in terms of subject matter, he can get together with one person or half a dozen people who are willing to talk to one another and try it out. (One way to begin building a rapport for a really educational conversation is to talk for a moment or two about how you feel *right now.*) Here are some topics for educational discussion on the *realities* of property-settlement practice:

— One at a time, give the other members of the group your immediate reactions—probably only a word or two—to the word "death." When everyone has reacted, talk about your reactions for a few minutes.

— One at a time—and without discussing it first—complete this sentence: "The age at which people are most afraid of death is ___." After everyone tries an answer to that question, see if the group can agree on an age range in terms of a decade in life—e.g., up to 12; 13–19; 20–29; 30–39, 40–59, 60–79, 80–99.

— One at a time—and without discussing it first—give your answer to two questions: (1) At what age would I like to die? (2) At what age do I think I will die? When everyone has answered, discuss your answers.

1.1.2.   Another way to get at some of these feelings is the Diggory–Rothman questionnaire on values destroyed by death. Without discussing your answer, choose one—only one—of the seven consequences of death they list. When everyone has made a choice, report your choices to the other members of your group and discuss them. This is what Diggory and Rothman asked:

Here are seven consequences of death. Indicate the *one* that seems to you worst, or most distasteful:

A.   I could no longer have any experiences.

B.   I am uncertain as to what might happen to me if there is a life after death.

C.   I am afraid of what might happen to my body after death.

D.   I could no longer care for my dependents.

E.   My death would cause grief to my relatives and friends.

F.   All my plans and projects would come to an end.

G.   The process of dying might be painful.

The second important area of client feelings in the property-settlement practice centers in attitudes toward *property*. Assume a law-office client wants to make a will and that she is a divorced woman, a single parent, the mother of two small children, a young executive, who is buying a house and a car. She is doing all right financially; in Auden's phrase she is "trudging on time to a tidy fortune." Here are some guesses on her feelings:

— She distrusts lawyers (but maybe not—at least not *yet*—her lawyer).

— She says she is concerned about taxes and about the corrosive effect of the probate system.

— She wants, in a vaguely articulated way, to provide for her children "if something happens."

One way to re-structure her feelings is to look at them in terms of:

— *Death:* She wouldn't be here if she weren't thinking about death. You cannot look after your family from the grave.

— *Property:* The part of her which is tied up in things won't die, and that part looms larger than our consider-the-lilies-of-the-field cultural myths admit. It is that part of her—that piece of immortality—which is her lawyer's immediate assignment.

— *Giving:* Why does she give things in her will? (Focus for a moment on "things" literally—some valuable jewelry, an old sports car she values highly, an "heirloom" family Bible.) One possibility is inevitability, but if you can't take it with you, you can nonetheless say who gets it instead. Another possibility is that she gives things to express feelings. Consider such moldy examples as livery of seisin and the provincial French ritual for separating a cow from the spirit of its owner; or such familiar things as "say it with flowers" or "diamonds are forever." A third possibility is convention (and here broaden your focus to include her wealth—life insurance, savings, the family home): She gives at the times and in the ways people usually give things. Wills are an example of conventional giving, and most of their contents are conventional. A final possibility is control. She gives to obtain immortality through property, and she uses property to manipulate people. "Nothing for Mary if she marries a Catholic" is a quaint example. What about: "I want the money used to give the kids [now ages three and five] a college education"?

Another advantage of learning about legal counseling with people instead of with books is that a lawyer may then be able to acknowledge and deal with *the lawyer's* feelings. A young lawyer may react negatively to his client if the client is looked at in economic or social-status terms; viewed that way, the client may be a conventional middle-class snob, and the lawyer may feel like a hypocrite and a cheat if the lawyer pretends to himself and others that he feels warm toward the client. Can I, as a legal counselor, be more useful to this client, and more honest, if I feel his *anxiety* about death, his personal *involvement* with his property, and his *need* to express love despite death and through property? As John Updike says: "Strange people look ugly only for a while, until you begin to fill in those tufty monkey features with a little history and stop seeing their faces and start seeing their lives."

2.   COUNSELOR MODEL

This professional world is a legal-counseling world. Its models and its assumptions are *peculiar* to it, and often they are not well articulated. Contrast the model of the property lawyer in the first chapter of the classic Casner and Leach property casebook with a legal counseling model adapted from the most prevalent theories of counseling as these are found in psychology, personnel guidance, the clergy, and medicine:

The *property lawyer* (Casner and Leach model) keeps a cool head in the midst of personal conflict. She is a person who knows how to think things through. She has a demonstrated capacity for (and confidence in) leadership. She can make her analysis count; she can implement it. Dr. Andrew Watson saw these legal talents in terms of the personality structures which cause students to come to law school in the first place; he generalized them as a passion for order (cool head) and a capacity for oral aggression (leadership). These are self-centered professional concerns: Counselors outside the law, by and large, find them undesirable.

Counselors express a preference, in training and in practice, for client-centered indices of concern. One way to generalize the concerns of the *legal counselor* would be that he seeks a capacity for acceptance (what Carl Rogers called "unconditional positive regard"); for understanding (empathic understanding, not just, or not even, sympathy); and for congruence (awareness of the feelings within himself). These concerns might be summarized as desire for the ability to be personally helpful. In terms of professional concern, the *property lawyer* and the *legal counselor* hardly resemble one another:

Property Lawyer	**Legal Counselor**
Objective analysis (order)	Acceptance (unconditional
Leadership (oral aggression)	positive regard)
	Understanding (empathy)
	Congruence

Both models also operate from a catalogue of professional skills:

The property lawyer is fact conscious; the legal counselor is perceptive (sensitive to verbal and non-verbal signals).

The property lawyer is relevance conscious; the legal counselor is empathic and congruent (he tunes in to feelings, his own and his client's).

The property lawyer is comprehensive (leaves no stone unturned); the legal counselor listens.

The property lawyer exercises foresight; the legal counselor is resilient (she stays in the interpersonal ball game, worries less about what's coming next).

The property lawyer is verbally sophisticated (says things well); the legal counselor is open.

The property lawyer is orally aggressive (wins arguments); the legal counselor summarizes when she talks, and then reflects accurately what she has been listening to.

The property lawyer is thorough; the legal counselor shows care for her client, and tends to build her structures more in terms of the client's vital interests than in terms of a professional mold for the client's affairs.

To summarize a comparison of models in terms of legal skills:

Property Lawyer	**Legal Counselor**
fact conscious	perceptive to verbal and non-verbal signals
relevance conscious	empathic and congruent
comprehensive	listening
foresightful	resilient
verbally sophisticated	open
orally aggressive	accurate in summarizing, reflective
thorough	accepting and caring

Exercise 1.2

1.2.1. An exercise for the property-settlement lawyer might center on self evaluation in terms of these *counselor* skills. We would not recommend an evaluation in negative terms of property-lawyer skills; all of them are obviously useful to a lawyer, and some are vital. Our point is that they are not *adequate* in education, or anywhere else in a world of people. The model they build tends toward an inhumane and unresponsive legal profession.

For this exercise, use a slip of paper for your assessment; don't discuss this with anyone before you do it. Use a scale of from zero to seven on each of the following counselor dimensions.

A. Perceptive (7)   Opaque (0)

B. Empathic (7)   Insensitive (0)
    Empathy means the ability to share the feelings of another person, to really know—feel—how she feels, and to show her that you know.

C. Congruent (7)   Disassociated (0)
    A congruent person is all together. His feelings and actions jibe; you know where he is.

D. Listening (7)   Not listening (0)
    Note that the listener has somehow to commu-

nicate the fact that he is listening.

E. Resilient (7)   Bogged down (0)

A resilient person bounces back and hangs in.

F. Open (7)   Closed (0)

G. Summarizing (7)   Misses boat (0)

A good summarizer reflects accurately and efficiently. He can stop the action, bring conclusions up to date, and move on.

H. Accepting (7)   Judgmental (0)

I. Caring (7)   Unconcerned (0)

Maurice Blauche, wise old guru, in Jacqueline Winspear's novel *Maisie Dobbs* (2003), gives this advice: "Never follow a story with a question, Maisie, not immediately. And remember to acknowledge the storyteller, for in some way even the messenger is affected by the story he brings."

The result of this experience might be a personal assessment and an agenda for experimentation with new behavior, behavior calculated to prepare one effectively for life as a legal counselor. It might be more useful than reading a whole chapter on the Rule Against Perpetuities, even the one in this book.

B. FEELINGS ABOUT DEATH

Feelings about death pervade the practice of law in the office and the courtroom, at least as much as they pervade the theatre or the marketplace. This is nowhere clearer than in the property-settlement practice. We have been curious about feelings on death in three familiar areas of the lawyer's world—three "populations" as the social scientists might describe them: (1) law students discussing their feelings and the feelings of the clients they have in clinical practice or will have later; (2) lawyers and clients in will-interview situations; and (3) judges who decided questions that turned on death attitudes, particularly in federal tax cases involving the old Sec. 2035 of the Internal Revenue Code of 1954 ("gifts in contemplation of death").

1. LAW STUDENTS

Shaffer once tape-recorded an evening's discussion of death by his wife Nancy, along with third-year law students and their spouses. The pedagogical objective was to help students develop sensitivity to the feelings of their clients, but the project also had research value. We found some expectable attitudes toward death among this young, professionally educated group, and we found a few surprises. Here are some examples:

Attitudes toward death are different depending on age. Our participants believed, and even expected, that older people are reconciled to death. Older people, they thought (or expected), accept death with resignation, if not with welcome. "Deaths of grace" was the phrase used by one of the students with respect to his opinion on how his grandparents felt about their deaths. However, other psychological data indicate that old people are not typically reconciled to death, but use the same elaborate devices of defense and evasion young people use. These students reacted initially to the idea of their *own* deaths as catastrophic, inexplicable interferences with nature, as some sort of *mistake*. They seemed to agree with Jerome S. Bruner when he said, "One reads drug advertising with the sense that death must be an error on the part of the consumer." The comparison leads to interesting reflections on the fact that the lawyers we work with are young but many of our clients are not.

Deeper attitudes toward death are ambivalent. One student expressed the general feeling of the group when he said his reflection on his own death gave him "two feelings simultaneously." Our group saw, to Shaffer's mild surprise, many positive aspects in the idea of death. Death was seen as sometimes desirable. Some students said they had thought of death as a pleasant release, an escape, and that this included even romantic images of death by suicide. These fantasies had been common in adolescence. Some thought of death in terms of heroism and the brave confrontation of fate; they talked about the deaths of John F. Kennedy, Martin Luther King, Jr., and Dag Hammarskjold. Death in this mode is not seen as painful; a distinction is made, implicitly, between death and the pain of dying.

It would be desirable to seize death. These young people tended to think of death—as they did, perhaps, of all their problems—as something to be seen to, something to be controlled (solved?). These are *planning* thoughts. (Compare the common use of "estate planning" to describe what a will drafting lawyer does for clients.) These thoughts in our group were not necessarily, or even principally, suicidal. They were more a matter of coming to terms with the possibility of being dead. The students discussed a touching interview Dr. King had the night before he was killed, in which he spoke of his acceptance of death, and of the real possibility of his being assassinated.

Even so, the general reaction to death was defensive. The students and their spouses said they do not like to talk about their own deaths; they think it is more positive—better, in a moral sense—to focus on living. Death is something that inhibits freedom; it makes enjoyable things less enjoyable. One young woman, who was working as an x-ray technician, mentioned giving x-rays to a patient who had terminal cancer, and who knew it. The patient was cheerful, and that seemed anomalous. "He's going to die," she said. "How can he be so happy?" This defensive emotion, and the desire to seize death, tended to blend into a decision that the way to face death was to make life meaningful. The young women in the group decided to keep on keeping on, and talked of Voltaire hoeing his garden, and of St. Francis of Assisi, who said he would live his last day as he lived all of the others. The male law students spoke of the same mood, but used examples from heroic lives (King, Kennedy, Hammarskjold) and great deeds. Both groups seemed to want to seize death—which seemed realistic and robust. They seemed determined to lead useful lives.[1]

2. LAW OFFICE SITUATIONS

The professional encounter with death attitudes that most lawyers meet regularly is in the law office, in the property-settlement practice. Shaffer's research among wills clients and their lawyers suggests several generalizations about the way people handle that delicate topic, and the way we come to terms—or fail to come to terms—with our own attitudes toward death:

Law-office discussion of death is characterized by euphemism and evasion. A lawyer who doubts that generalization might begin by examining the words she uses when talking to a will client about the client's death. Do her words sound as if they would be proper for a funeral parlor? Does she use "expire," or "pass on," or even the awkward illegitimate verb (or noun) "decease," when she means "die" (death)? A common lawyer's interview question is "What if something should happen?" It is somehow more comfortable for us to say it that way than "What if you should die?" or, "What is to happen *when* you die?"

Evasion of death takes many forms in our professional lives. One of the more subtle is the use of gallows humor; this seems especially noticeable among young lawyers. Shaffer: "Here is a remark I caught myself making: I read the client's life-insurance policy, noted the accidental-death rider, and said, 'The best way for you to die would be in an accident.' He laughed, but I doubt that he thought it was funny. Evasion of unpleasantness through wry jokes and pressure-reducing laughter is often mentioned in death research from hospitals. I should not have been surprised to find it in the law office but I was surprised to find that I was the lawyer who used it."

Death is recognized starkly when it involves concern for the support of dependents. Clients who see us for wills seem distinctive compared with other populations when research focuses on cessation of support (material and personal) for dependents as one of the effects of death. In will interviews, the death of the client is treated almost formally, in an unreal

---

1. In some ways this conversational resolution resembled the resolution Dr. Kübler-Ross described in patients reconciled to death, a condition she referred to as hope.

way, *until* the lawyer begins to ask about guardianships and trusts for orphaned minor children, or about methods of care for dependent older people. Then the interview gets intense, because it involves two affect-laden factors:

First, concern for support for dependents is a dominant day-to-day concern in most of our lives. Madison Avenue knows that. ("You want the best for your family." "What's a mother to do?") The life-insurance industry has been built upon support concern. When the sociologist Stouffer set out in the mid-fifties to see if Americans were concerned about espionage, subversion, and communist plots, he uncovered vast, impressive evidence that people are concerned about their families, to the virtual exclusion of everything else. Political concern showed up in fewer than a tenth of his responses, and concern over communism (even at the height of the so-called McCarthy era) in less than one per cent.

The second factor that is involved is death anxiety, which has been shown to be a principal under-the-surface worry in almost all of us, a worry magnified by nuclear weapons, and television commercials against cigarettes and in favor of bran cereal, and newspaper reports of highway accidents. When the two factors are combined, as they are in a will interview on dependent support, the lawyer touches basic, powerful human feelings. Working with young married couples who have children, for example, we find that the whole emotional character of the interview undergoes radical change when lawyer and clients discuss child-care questions.

Usually, when the subject of physical care for children comes up, our young-parent clients have already thought about the subject and respond quickly with the name of a relative. But the effect of their emotional preparation vanishes when the interviewer goes one step further and asks, "What if the guardian you have chosen cannot do it?" The clients become less articulate, flushed, and in some cases cannot answer the question. In one case, a young mother had to leave the room to recover her composure. She said later she had felt physically ill.

We find a similar reaction in two other situations—when questions are asked about alternative disposition if children do not survive, and when it is suggested that the client might want to provide discretionary use of trust funds for the children of the person she has chosen to be her children's guardian. The latter situation seems to provoke a surprise at the thought that the person chosen as guardian (a sister who was married and had children of her own, for instance) had duties and concerns that might interfere with the care of the client's orphaned children.

There seem to be some deeper threads running through this phenomenon—beyond our principal point, that dependent care is the tenderest of all approaches to a client on the subject of her own death. One of the deeper threads seems to be a special anxiety about the loss of environment; it suggests some of Dr. Lifton's work on the survivors of atomic holocaust. The idea is that we come to terms with death by assuming that those around us will continue to live, and will carry out what death prevents us from carrying out. The suggestion that our "supporting persons" will also die—whether the topic is nuclear war or the premature death of a guardian—carries special terror. Another of the deeper threads is, as Sigmund Freud said, that one cannot really imagine his own death. The only way death can become real and manageable is to imagine survival—survival in property, perhaps, or in persons (especially children) who will be around to carry on. The idea was expressed by Dr. Edwin N. Shneidman as a post-self: "The self or ego relates to the core of one's active functioning, his cognitive and emotional masterings and maneuvers in the present life; the *post-self,* on the other hand, refers to the ways in which one might live on, survive, or have some measure of impact or influence after the event of his own physical death."

The point has implications for the property-settlement practice. It involves a circumstance we wills lawyers deal with every day—immortality through property (the "dead hand" as some students put it, confusing present-day images of the grim reaper with the medieval mortmain laws that dealt with church ownership). We prefer to think of manipulation by the dead as a fixation of wealthy patriarchs who create spendthrift trusts and condition future interests on their children not marrying outside the faith. But it is equally present in the young, impecunious client who wants life-insurance used for the college educa-tion of a three-year-old. What is working here is what Dr. Shneidman called "psycho-semantic logic"; Hocking defined it as "the inclusive or reflective self which contemplates the death of the dated, excursive self, and is half able to accept it."

These death feelings suggest a number of thoughts about counseling will clients. Most of them reflect increased sensitivity to the feelings of clients about a broadened area of death anxiety which is present and real and dealt with in the law office—not only death, but also death taxes, the probate system, the care of dependents, the completion of important work, and the fear of disabling disease and old age. This counseling process resembles the dynamics of psychological counseling as they were defined by the great humanistic psychologists Carl Rogers and E.H. Porter: The initial feelings of the client are negative (resentment at the probate system, at taxes, at having to bother with lawyers); the result of good legal counseling is the emergence of positive feelings, a "facilitation" of the client's interest and ability in seizing his own death through planning, through the realistic use of his property personality. As is so often the case in legal counseling, this analysis is not a matter of asking lawyers to enter a new professional activity; it is more a matter of realizing that we are in this activity, as our forebears have been for centuries, and that we should do a good job of it.

3. JUDGES

One of the procedures used in modern "suicidology"—especially in legal situations where suicide is asserted (life insurance, death certification, etc.)—is called the psychological autopsy. The idea is that a psychiatrist or psychologist carefully assembles evidence about the person's behavior before death and determines, as a pathologist might determine cause of death from examining the corpse, what the dead person's motives were.

It occurred to Shaffer, in looking at familiar legal analogues to this psychological procedure, that federal judges performed psychological autopsies after Congress imposed an estate tax on "gifts in contemplation of death" under the old (pre–1976) version of Sec. 2035, Internal Revenue Code of 1954. The Supreme Court decided in 1931 that "contemplation" in the statute calls for an examination of the emotions and attitudes of the dead donor. (*United States v. Wells*, 283 U.S. 102, 1931.) This decision required that lower-court federal judges perform psychological autopsies in most Sec. 2035 cases. There are literally hundreds of reported examples in the federal reports of the forty-year period 1931–1971. They are among the most unusual cases in legal literature.

"The court's inquiry," as Judge Alfred B. Rubin once put it, "is into the mind of the decedent, into that 'heap or collection of different perceptions.' "The law, he said, "seeks an elusive shadow from the recesses of the mind of the deceased," and judges recognize—or at least Judge Rubin recognized—that "decision may result ... from intuition, emotional reaction, and visceral response to the composite picture that results from the images imposed on each other in court by advocates with opposite motives...." (*Fatter v. Usry*, 269 F.Supp. 582, 586–587, E.D.La. 1967.)

Shaffer undertook to compare these hundreds of judicial ventures into the psychological autopsy with recent findings in death psychology. Psychologists came to this field in their science very late. Much of the research dates from Dr. Herman Feifel's two anthologies on the meaning of death. Shaffer had the help of Dr. Feifel and Dr. Robert S. Redmount. (Dr. Redmount has the best of both worlds. He is both a lawyer and a practicing clinical psychologist.) These three decided that some judicial death psychology is incredibly naive, some evasive, and some perceptive and even poetic.

Naive legal ideas. It is almost a rule of law in these cases that one who contemplates death surrenders to it; that a death-contemplating person gives up. The psychological literature indicates that this may not be true, that many persons who know they face death seem to become more peaceful, even more cheerful, than they were before. It is not uncommon in hospitals for the terminally ill patient to console the doctor.

Another judicial idea was that a person does not know death is approaching if the doctor doesn't know it. There is strong clinical evidence, and there is beginning to be some experimental evidence, that death is often foreseen in the tissues. Reports of patients who expect to die in relatively minor surgery, and who do die, despite their surgeons' assurance they will not, are an example.

A third and common idea in the contemplation-of-death opinions is that very active people, especially travelers, do not contemplate death. Classical and modern literary instances—Tolstoy's stories in "Three Deaths," for example, or Frank O'Connor's account of the last days of George Russell—contradict that assumption.

Evasive strategies. Rules on burden of proof in Sec. 2035 cases provided judges easy access to evasion on the disturbing issue of death contemplation. One rule presumed that an assessment of additional estate tax by the Commissioner of Internal Revenue was correct; the taxpayer had to prove it was incorrect. Another rule presumed that any gift made within three years of death was made in contemplation of death; the taxpayer had to overcome that presumption. Scores of cases were decided solely on the burden of proof. A psychological way to express that result is that the evidence left the judge ambivalent about saying that the decedent contemplated death and acted under the influence of that contemplation. Common factual instances which seemed to provoke this judicial evasion were transfers to satisfy "moral obligation"; transfers made while the decedent was suffering grief reaction at the death of someone else (often a spouse); transfers made for manipulative purposes; and transfers which suggested that the decedent was expressing futility—even something like suicide—by transferring property.

Perceptive ideas. Some Sec. 2035 opinions seemed to put federal judges on the frontiers of death psychology. The most perceptive of these involved a recognition that a person probably is in variable relationships with the things he owns—just as a person stands in variable relationships with the people in his life. There is in a person's life, for instance, some property that is *work;* a carpenter's tools are what the carpenter does, and many business people stand in a work relationship to their businesses. Different from property as work is property as *power;* some clients propose to use their property to influence their loved ones, to manipulate them, even after the owner is dead and property will be all that remains of his life. Finally, some property is deeply *personal;* it expresses the person's self; it binds him to other people. Family residential property is often like that; heirlooms and valued collections, animals, and even automobiles, often stand in that way in relationship to their owners.

The most perceptive Sec. 2035 opinions recognize these levels of property-personality, and decide the "contemplation of death" question in reference to this judicial insight. A person might dispose of project property because he wants to retire. He need not be contemplating death.

He might dispose of power property in order to induce loved ones to conform to strongly life-centered wishes. A grandmother who makes transfers to her son so that he will live close by, where she can enjoy her grandchildren, is an example.

But disposition of the third sort of property personality (of tangible personal property for example) is a more final sort of act; it suggests death. It may even suggest what Dr. Karl Menninger called "focal suicide." Some opinions make this sort of perceptive distinction. They seem to transcend the demands of the case and teach lawyers something about clients that is more important than the administration of the tax laws.

Exercise 1.3[2]

1.3.1. Rank-order the following in terms of how they have influenced your present attitudes toward death.

___ Death of a relative

___ Death of a friend

___ Death of an animal

___ Religious upbringing

___ Specific reading (what?)

___ Work or volunteer experience

___ Films

___ Television and radio

___ Conversation

___ Ritual (funerals for example)

___ Drug experience

___ Mystical experience

___ Other (explain)

1.3.2. What were your childhood conceptions of death and dead people?

1.3.3. Describe your first contact or brush with death. (Your earliest memory or recollection of death.) What were your feelings and reactions? What remnants of this experience are in you today?

1.3.4. Discuss the ways in which death was talked about in your family. Was it more or less taboo than, for instance, discussion of sex, finances, etc.?

---

2. An adaptation of the Shneidman Attitude-to-Death survey.

1.3.5. Check those statements (one or more) which apply to your own thoughts about death:

___ It will be wonderful.

___ It holds the promise of a new and better life.

___ All my troubles will be over.

___ I don't think about it.

___ I have nothing to do with the subject.

___ I feel fine and have no reason to think about it.

___ It's the end of everything.

___ Terror overcomes me.

___ I dread the thought of it.

1.3.6. If it were entirely up to you, what would you have done with your body after you die? (Buried, cremated, donated to medical school or science, etc., indifferent.) Why do you make these choices?

1.3.7. Would you be willing to donate your heart for a transplantation (after your death)? To whom? Under what circumstances? How do you feel about having your heart beat in another person?

1.3.8. If you were told that you had a terminal disease and a limited time to live, how would you spend your time until you died? What things would you especially want to do?

1.3.9. If you are married, would you prefer to outlive your spouse or would you prefer that your spouse outlive you? Discuss your reasons.

1.3.10. How would you like to be remembered after your death? (In what ways and by whom?) How much does this matter to you?

C. FEELINGS ABOUT PROPERTY

First, property is something I am. Our favorite image on people and things is Humphrey Bogart on the *African Queen,* chugging down the fetid jungle river with Katherine Hepburn. The boat's ancient steam engine jammed and rattled and scattered hot steam; Bogart jumped up, ran to the boiler and kicked it. And the boiler worked again. Hepburn asked what was the matter with the boiler and Bogart said it was jammed. Hepburn asked him why, and Bogart said one of his helpers left a screw-driver in it one day when he was working on it, and the screw-driver jammed a valve. Hepburn asked why he didn't take it apart and take the screw-driver out. And Bogart said, "You know, I'm gonna do that one of these days. The only reason I ain't done it up to now is I kinda like kickin' her. She's all I got."

Property is a part of what is me. Sartre makes a theoretical case for that proposition: "The quality of being possessed does not indicate a purely external denomination ... ; on the contrary, this quality affects its very depths.... This is the significance of primitive funeral ceremonies where the dead are buried with the objects which belong to them.... The corpse, the cup from which the dead man drank, the knife he used, make a single dead person. The desire to have is at bottom reducible to the desire to be related to a certain object in a certain relation of being.... I draw the collection of my surroundings into being with myself. If they are taken from me, they die as my arm would die if it were severed from me.... The totality of my possessions reflects the totality of my being. I *am* what I have."

Property personality is a common thing in the law of succession—in this culture and others. Consider the astounding respect that is shown for the wishes of a dead person on the disposition of his property. In Tahiti, and in Iowa and Kansas, one reason a person makes a will is in order to prevent fights—because his survivors will not resist what he wants done as much as they will resist what someone else, someone who lacks the dead person's identification with the property, wants. Throughout the law of succession, in all cultures, there lingers this idea that the property is the personality of the dead person. Property is his immortality.

In Allegra Goodman's novel, *Katterskill Falls* (1998), Rav Elijah Kirshner gave his son Jeremy all of his books; half of them had belonged to the Rav's late wife, Jeremy's mother, Sarah. Everything else (two valuable pieces of property in the Catskills and a place in Brooklyn), the Rav gave to his other son Isaiah, the elder son, who, as it turned out, was the Rav's successor in the Hasidic community the story is about (the Kirshners). Jeremy is left bitter about the succession; Isaiah is left bitter about the books. Jeremy after talking to someone else, about another family's tension over succession to property, thinks: "That is the truth about inheritances. That they have nothing to do with community, the maintenance of property. The power of legacies is all in separation, in the conflict between the older and the younger, the alienation of the living from the dead. What a marvelous fiction, he thinks, that places and things, or even ideas can be transmitted over time, that property can be kept in families, or that families themselves will remain intact."

Exercise 1.4

What would happen if you pretended you were going on a long trip, a trip from which you might never return? What would you decide to take with you? What would you do with things you do <u>not</u> take along? What is the most valuable thing you

own? And what is the most significant thing to you personally? Can you tell clearly where you end the things on your
take-along list begin?

Those who study the dynamics of "total institutions"—prisons and
asylums—report that one of the principal ways to make inmates docile is
to take away everything they own. The result is not only a naked person,
but also a naked personality. Justice Holmes said: "A thing which you
have enjoyed and used as your own for a long time, whether property or
an opinion, takes root in your being and cannot be torn away without your
resenting the act and trying to defend yourself, however you came by it."

Second, property is something I do. One of the first signs of a
beginning of ownership among primitive communistic societies is respect
for primary rights in things that are the fruit of labor. Among the Yamana
of South America, for instance, if I catch a whale, the blubber belongs to
everyone in the village. But I get first pick, and, to some extent, get to
choose who gets second and third pick. In the Semang society, on the
Malay Peninsula, there is no ownership of land or buildings, but every
warrior owns his own poison tree. The Eskimos of Greenland and the
Arctic Siberians recognize almost no exclusive ownership, but if you want
to learn a spell or a hunting song you have to pay the person who knows
it. In each of these instances—and in the case of American
businesspeople—my property is what I do. And this is true beyond
consideration of wealth. We asked a veteran life-insurance underwriter
about his business clients. He said they were always greatly concerned
about what would happen to their businesses when they died. We asked
him if they knew how much their businesses were worth, and he said they
usually did not.

Third, property is something I use. There are three radically different
aspects of property as use: First, property may be a conduit to other
people; it may be a cornerstone for human relationships. Freud noticed
this in his *Psychopathology of Everyday Life.* I am enjoying myself at your
house but have to leave, and when I leave I forget my coat. I have to go
to the office on a Sunday afternoon, and resent it, and find when I get
there that I left my keys at home. My things—coat and keys—are where
I wish I were. A patient of Freud's was having trouble with his wife; she
gave him a book and he misplaced it. Six months later their relationship
improved, and the patient found the book in some obvious place in his
desk.

It has usually been thought that primogeniture, the legal system
under which property is inherited by an eldest son to the exclusion of
everyone else, is medieval and undemocratic. But societies which have
observed primogeniture—including fairly modern societies—are often
prosperous. This comes about because of a communal morality that says
the central family member—father or eldest son—should take care of

everyone else. Property is used to keep the family together at least as much as the family is used to keep the property together. That was the "marvelous fiction" Jeremy Kirshner, in Goodman's novel, scoffed at when he pondered the practices of his own family and of the modern Hasidic community they were part of.

The line between rights in things and rights in persons is functionally obscure. Most legal systems have always recognized rights in persons as a species of property. The levirate—a custom under which a widow is given to her husband's brother—is a cruel instance of that, but it is not really so different from child-ownership, or even wife-ownership, in our own society. Engels saw the connection; he wrote that marriage would disappear as private ownership of property disappeared. The two go together. The Engels dogma caused great theoretical turmoil in the Soviet Union until Stalin rejected it. Closer to home there is the observation of William Wyeth, big-deal, big-firm New York city property lawyer, in Colin Harrison's novel *The Havana Room* (2004): "[A]nyone who has practiced real estate law is soon conveyed into a realm of human affairs where the pressures behind decisions are often enormous, and include death, divorce, illness, stupidity, greed, sexual indiscretion, grief—everything. Whatever is in the human spirit becomes expressed through bricks and mortar, which is also to say there's always a story."

Property is something I use, in a second sense, as a significant personal expression not otherwise available to me. There is a custom among one tribe of Native Americans in Arizona, for example, that everything a dead person owns is destroyed when he dies; survivors are afraid of the dead; they want solid earth between them and all extensions of the dead person—including his property personality. (The theme occurs regularly in Tony Hillerman's Navajo police stories.) The only ownership recognized in many primitive societies is the ownership of things to work with. A quaint example of that is the Hopi garden. A husband may own the garden, and he may do whatever he wishes with his produce as long as he is in the garden. But if he brings the produce into the house—his wife's house, as the Hopi see it—the produce doesn't belong to him any more and only his wife is allowed to give it away.

The idea of ownership begins when self-expression with property requires exclusive control of it; the need for exclusive control has important psychological significance. The anthropologist Rene Millon hit upon the very rude beginnings of land ownership among the Sierra Populaca of Mexico; the people there were just beginning to permit a person to demand exclusive rights in his grove of coffee trees. They had recognized for a long time that a person could own the trees, but only recently had they expanded this idea to the land. The apparent explanation of the extension was that they discovered they could grow more and better coffee that way. Millon does not guess—we wish he had guessed—at the effects of this transition on the social and psychic personality of the coffee grower.

Which suggests a third sense in which property is something I use, and that is as a means of assuming and protecting power. There are many instances in our own history: An example is the use of land grants in the United States and in Spanish America, not only as a means of economic development, but as a means of solidifying power. For another example, the English feudal system, out of which our law of property grew, was above all a system of government. The transmission of status—which is a symbol of power—and the transmission of property are functionally inseparable. Titles and positions of honor illustrate that throughout Western history; and there is more transmission of status in our own culture than we may be ready to admit. One can reflect on that fact as she runs down the roster of names, past and present, in the United States Senate. In societies entirely alien to our own, the transmission of corporate membership—in clan groups, in castes, in the primitive equivalent of the country club—is property used to assume and protect power.

An old-fashioned probate lawyer might understandably decide that political reformers make a mistake when they attack abuses of power by attacking property ownership. And the mistake may lead them far beyond anything they had in mind. There is a kind of revolution which is callow, and unwittingly inhumane, and which fails. Successful revolutions—and the most successful of all revolutions (the American Revolution) was designed and implemented by lawyers—are built on a healthy respect for the way people are. Callow revolutions tend to catastrophe. It could be, as Justice Holmes said, that "the notion that with socialized property we should have ... a piano for everybody" is "an empty humbug." One thing every reformer ought to try for—on pain of failure—is an appreciation for what is most important to the people he proposes to serve. In terms of national policy, an appreciation for the way people are, and for the way people own, might even support a federal tax structure in which businesspeople are taxed just this side of destroying their desire to own more than they have. And death taxes are kept just low enough so that a person does not lose all hope of aggregating status and power and passing them along to children. A primary goal of the American welfare state—supported by taxing policies which take realistic account of the way people are—is that every household should have a house. Principles of modern Christian social teaching say that a person should have enough property to guarantee and safeguard personality; for dignified labor; for sound relationships with those he loves; and for self-expression.

Most people are more concerned with their things and with what it takes to acquire and protect their things than they are with righteous indignation. The comparison is important because self-expression—the "firstness of the first" (amendment)—appears in law school to be a primary, non-negotiable value. But most people worry as much about the

non-vocal dimensions of their personalities. All of us are more involved in
our things than many of us care to admit. Anyone who proposes to be a
reformer should realize that, as Judge Prettyman said, "The right of a
man to warm his slippered feet before his own open fireplace is as great
as his right to gather with his neighbors in the corner pub and cuss the
government."

Exercise 1.5

1.5.1.   One might attempt to experience the feelings of
clients toward property by asking himself a couple of questions:

(i)   What is the *most valuable* thing I own?

(ii)   What among all of the things I own is *most impor-
        tant to me? (If I were running from my burning
        house, what would I take with me?)*

1.5.2.   A group experience for this is an office-interview
exercise with a lawyer, a wills client, and two or more
observer-reporters on the lawyer's effectiveness in the professional world.

The lawyer's job is to decide what the client wants in the
will. Try to get over assets quickly—give rough estimates of
property, insurance, etc. Get to the dispositive provisions—
what the client wants done with the property—as quickly as
possible: Who are his property people (and, maybe, why)?
How does he want them to own his property—outright, in a
trust, for life only—and, maybe, why?

The observer-advisors should gather data on this—just
listen—and not participate until the lawyer and client give
them enough data. One way to make sure the *real* data is
being generated is for the lawyer to remember to explore all
the possibilities. For example: (A) Client says: "I want to give
my property to my wife." What if she dies before he does?
What if she dies when he does? What if she dies a week after
he does? (B) Client says: "Then to my kids." But is he
considering the age of these kids? Who is looking after them?
What if one of them is dead? (C) Consider similar questions
about partners, brothers and sisters, parents, and pet
animals.

When enough data is generated, stop the consultation—
even if lawyer and client are not finished—and hear from the
observer-reporters their opinions on what kind of counselor
the lawyer is. The observer-reporters might sooner or later
want to think about the standards they use to evaluate the
lawyer's performance.

Assuming some useful information is generated by attempting to share, or even think about, these client feelings: What are some of the personal issues raised when you consider the law-office professional world in the wealth-transfer context?

1.5.3.   One likely possibility, familiar to law-office practitioners, is that client feelings of this intensity raise issues of trust and dependency. How does it feel to be *dependent*? How does it feel to *not know* what is being done to you (on a used car lot, say, or in a doctor's office or dentist's chair)? How would it feel to be blindfolded and led by a stranger? How would it feel to fall backwards into the arms of a stranger, a person you wouldn't even *see*? How does it feel to be *depended upon?* Are you parental? Annoyed? Bored? Afraid? (The blindfolded "trust walk" and the falling backwards experiments are easy to try out.)

1.5.4.   Another possibility is that these exercises will raise issues of attention and alertness. What are you (lawyer) feeling when things are happening? What would you feel about the client who:

(i)   doesn't trust her husband and wants a will which will keep him from controlling her property?

(ii)   is choosing for guardian and trustee for her small children a relative who seems to you cruel, unreliable, or dishonest?

(iii)   wants to cut off his wife and children entirely and give all his property to a television evangelist?

Do you understand your own feelings? Do you think you should relate them to your client? Why? (Why not?) Consider some possibilities:

—   You feel moral disapproval of him and anxious over possibly helping him to be immoral.

—   You feel that she is ignoring your advice (rebellion, competition).

—   You can't seem to control her.

—   You feel you should protect him from himself.

1.5.5.   A third set of issues that emerges when considering client feelings in the wills context is issues of *dis*trust and inappropriate trust. Maybe the client distrusts you. Maybe he suspects you may cheat him. Maybe, on the other hand, he trusts you too much. What will you do if the rich old gentleman who is your client suddenly looks up with tears in

his eyes and says, "I want to give everything I have to you"?
Will you draft that will for him?

D.   FEELINGS IN THE FAMILY

1.   SAD STORIES

Consider four sad stories from the literature of "Dear Annie"[3] and Dr. Terry D. Hargrave:

"Dear Annie,

"I wonder what you would say to a son who is constantly demanding that his father make out a will and leave his 10–acre property to him, excluding his sister.

"My husband and I have been married just over a year. He has a grown son and daughter from a previous marriage, both of whom are married with children of their own. I have two grown daughters who are doing very well. None of our children lives anywhere near us.

"My husband is 59 years old and is a very caring person who loves all our children. Several years ago, he generously told his son, 'Johnny,' that he could visit the property any time he wants, and if would like to do some landscaping or whatever, he should feel free to do so. Johnny gestured, rubbing his thumb and finger together, saying, 'Not until I have that piece of paper.'…."

* * *

"Dear Annie,

"My grandmother recently passed away, and my once close-knit clan has been at one another's throats ever since. Her 11 grandchildren have not spoken to each other since the reading of the will.

"Grandma left ten of us a meager inheritance, which was wonderful considering we were not expecting anything at all. Then, as a shock, she left $15,000 to the 11th cousin, 'Sherry.' Grandma justified this decision in the will, stating that Sherry has a severe vision problem and she hoped her gift would make Sherry's life a little easier.

"Well, Annie, Sherry's life may be financially easier, but the rest of us have had little, if anything, to do with her. There is such horrible resentment that we do not care to be around her. Also, our fond memories of Grandma have been tainted by this one severe act of favoritism…."

* * *

3. From, respectively, Kathy Mitchell and Marcy Sugar, "Annie's Mailbox," The South Bend Tribune, August 3, 2005; January 8, 2006; and August 10, 2003. This Section D is new in this fifth edition.

"Dear Annie,

"I always referred to my father's second wife as 'The Geriatric Gold Digger.' Because I suspected she was only interested in his money, I helped my father draw up a new will, leaving the bulk of his estate to his three sons.

"When my father had his fatal heart attack, 'Lulu' and her family did not notify the rest of us for almost 24 hours. During that time she repeatedly attempted to have his life support terminated. At Dad's house, we discovered Lulu had broken into every locked cabinet and container. When she grilled me about secret bank accounts, I said, 'It's all in the will.' She replied, 'He did not have a will.' ... [U]nder California law, she gets everything if there is no will...."

* * *

Dr. Hargrave, a psychologist (see References), tells a story similar to those from people who write to Dear Annie about wills, but in this case the family got together and together sought Dr. Hargrave's help:

"Bob's Story: When I walked into my father's den, I couldn't believe my eyes. His book collection—old books that he had collected since I was a little kid—was gone. When I asked my mother what had happened, she casually told me that my nephew Craig had visited last week with his family and asked for the books. It's bad enough that the kid asked for my father's books, but worse that my mother actually gave them to him....

"I can't remember if my father ever specifically promised the books to me because I never would have asked for them directly. But when I found out my mother had given them to Craig, I felt as if I'd been sucker-punched. Was this my reward for being respectful and discreet? I couldn't help thinking she'll start to give other things away to anyone brash enough to ask for them....

"Elizabeth's Story: I've never been so shocked in my life as when Bob blew up at me over those books. I doubt if the whole lot is worth five dollars. When Donna's boy asked for them, I thought it would be great because I could start getting rid of things. I'm 79 years old, and I have to start planning to move from this big house.

"If I had known that the books were important to Bob, I never would have given them to Craig.... To tell the truth, I don't see why Bob thinks it's his right to tell me what to do. He said things I never thought I would hear from my children....

"I want both of my children to have my things, but I guess I should just wait and let them sort it out after I die so I won't make anyone angry.

"Dr. Hargrave's View: ... Often what people want to fight over has nothing to do with the financial value of the objects....

"When I met with Bob, Donna, and their mother, I realized quickly that the problem wasn't books, but a lack of communication. I saw that this was clearly a loving family, but, as Bob freely acknowledged, they were all pretty reserved. Sometimes just assuming everyone knows how you feel isn't enough....

"... In fact people usually know what is right in their hearts, but sometimes it takes an objective observer to spell it out in plain English....

"In the end, Elizabeth divided the book collection and gave some books to Craig and some to Bob. As for the rest of her possessions, Bob and Donna did not get everything they wanted, but both felt that their mother had been fair...."

2. ENTER THE LAWYERS

These stories bring to mind the aspiration of a wise old Hoosier judge, sitting in on a slightly fractious meeting between some of his judicial colleagues and a collection of law deans. He said within my hearing, "I just try not to make things worse." That was the succinct Hoosier version of what Hippocrates (not a lawyer) prescribed for physicians: "I will use treatment to help the sick, according to my ability and judgment, but I will never use it to injure or wrong them." Do no harm. More of a challenge, as Dear Annie and Dr. Hargrave would say, than we lawyers doing wills for families might at first think. Some—perhaps all three—of the testators in these cases might look down from the Great Beyond and say they wish they hadn't bothered to make wills—that their lawyers made things worse. And in the fourth (first "Dear Annie") case the potential testator might decide not to bother. The testator Dr. Hargrave wrote about might not agree, but that would be because her family had the benefit of the psychologist's timely and effective efforts at healing.

Stephanie Francis Ward wrote about Western lawyers who know all of this in the January 16, 2004, *A.B.A. Journal Report*, under the heading "Who Gets the Rambler? Creative Methods Can Squelch Family Squabbles Over What's Not in the Will":

"A 1950 Nash Rambler, which no longer runs, may not have much monetary value, but that didn't stop one family from fighting over it, says Dennis S. Voorhees, an estate planning lawyer in southern Idaho.

"The dilapidated vehicle, a sheepherder's wagon, a Freemason's ring, and a transoceanic radio from the 1940s were just a few of the items he watched a group of siblings battle over after their parents died without specifying who should get what.

" 'They just assumed that all would go well at their demise,' says Voorhees, of Twin Falls. 'What ensued was a scrap.'

"Lawyers who regularly deal with wills, estates, and family law matters are familiar with such incidents—and undoubtedly have amassed their own collection of war stories. Like Voorhees, they know a simple will with specific instructions, or a family meeting to discuss the distribution of personal items, can avoid significant legal costs and hurt feelings after a loved one dies.

"Most of the time, that is. But sometimes lists are not enough. And Voorhees says he has seen the family meeting solution go south, too, specially when 'Mom promises two or three items to more than one person'....

" 'Symbolically, whoever gets what the others want ends up being the fair-haired child,' Voorhees says. 'It's kind of a symbolic battle to find out who's the mightier.'

"In such situations, it often takes a creative solution to resolve things harmoniously. Voorhees mentions a will executor who created an online auction for family members, where they could bid on specific items. Each person was given a code, and the Web site did not disclose who made which bid. All items purchased were subtracted from the buyer's share of the estate....

"Creating a lottery system, either on or offline, might also work.... Under this approach, the decedent's personal items are grouped by value and family members are given random items from each group."

Ms. Ward quotes David J. Dietrich, will-making lawyer from Billings, Montana, who referred to the list device in the Uniform Probate Code for tangible personal property (and recently picked up by Indiana). (See Chapter 9 herein.) " 'I'm not as confident that the tangible personal property list is as good as it's cracked up to be,' he says, 'because sometimes it is not filled out, or it's not found.' "[4]

Mr. Voorhees took his experience into teaching a community-college course where he talked to those who signed up (potential clients all) about these problems—"how to avoid conflict when distributing personal property." "The course, he says, is intended to help parents find a fair way to distribute personal possessions. He hopes it will help them 'get more in touch with what's preventing them from coming to some good planning.' "

* * *

3. CONSIDERING THE SOLUTIONS

Ms. Ward and the lawyers she talked with Out West surveyed the obvious possibilities:

> — *the family meeting while the will is being made*, a solution endorsed by the eminent "estate planner" Rene Wormser, who said he would not work for a client who would not have such a meeting;[5]

---

4. The list is authorized by statute—see the statutory appendix herein; it is not particularly formal, but under most statutes needs to be signed by the donor, and should be dated. It can be changed without changing the donor's will, which, of course, should mention it.

5. Consider, though, this warning from the January–February 2006 AARP Bulletin, citing the Hartford Financial Services Group, Inc: "Don't expect your kids to bring up end-of-life issues such as financial planning and medical care. Seventy-six percent of parents ages 70 to 79 are very comfortable talking about their estates, compared with just 45 percent of their baby boomer kids."

— *the family meeting afterwards*–a version of which is recommended in our forms in Chapter 9:

> "I give ... to those of my Children who survive me, in shares of substantially equal value, to be divided as they shall agree, or if they fail to agree within five months after my death, as my executor shall determine."

"Trish Nicholson's 'divvying' " essay (see References) describes an extended family meeting that turned out well (probably because all of the siblings were women): "Three sisters in their 40s gathered one summer to empty the house where their late mother had lived since they were children. Tempers flared as the siblings tussled over items that more than one of them could not live without. To quell the bickering, they placed the disputed items on a 'fight shelf,' which grew into a 'fight room' as the weeks wore on.

"In the fall, the sisters returned to divvy up the goods. Drawing straws, they took turns and each selected a few meaningful items. Soon, however, the pickings began to look slim. As one sister considered the merits of an ugly tray, they all burst into laughter, wondering what could have possessed them a few months before to hang onto—and fight over—a room full of rubbish....

(In their book—see References:) "Hetzler and Hulstrand advise taking breaks to collect memories. Browse through old photo albums, dance to 45 rpm records, or watch those old Super 8 movies. Or turn on a tape recorder as family members talk....

" 'Taking time lessens the intensity and stress,' Hulstrand says. 'And it allows for communication to take place'....

" 'When we asked people what they thought was important to tell others,' Hulstrand says, 'they said, "Before you do anything—think." ' "

— *the statutory list*;

— and such exotic variants as the *on-line auction*.

— Our clients have sometimes proposed, on their own, inviting family members in, one at a time, and *letting each person take what she or he wants*. We try to talk them out of this, partly because some system of affixing values would seem to be required, and any such system would ignore the wise insight that these things are not valued, usually, because of how much they will bring on the market; and partly because the client making the suggestion never seems to have a workable system for setting the order in which people should be invited in. It is a solution workable only when used by a mother—and, alas, in this case, there may be no mother there to make it work.

— And most of us have known people—relatives probably—who went around the house putting *tags with names on them* on their things. I (Shaffer) recommended to a client once that she put everything for Betty in the dining room, everything for Sam in the living room, and then make a will—with my help—giving the contents of the living room to Sam and the contents of the dining room to Betty. Then she would not even need to use tags or a list: She could just move the furniture. The problem, of course, is that doing that is a way to stop living. Lawyers who bring clients to such a pass fail to "do no harm." My client did not follow my advice in this respect.

Exercise 1.6

Without ignoring all of this advice, but taking into account all of the cases in this exotic array, and taking into account, too, the fact that Dr. Hargrave's solution for Bob and Elizabeth and Donna was at best a solution for the moment: Elizabeth lives on, and, given what has happened in her family, she comes to see a lawyer (you!) about her will. What do you suggest she do as to tangible personal property, including, no doubt, many of the things that once belonged to her late husband.

---

4. MEDIATION

Finally, there is Alternative Dispute Resolution—not so much the hired-judge or arbitrator models for these situations as the mediator model (which, when you think about it, was the one being followed by Dr. Hargrave). From Ms. Gary's article (see References), which puts a case involving two sisters, daughters of a recently deceased wife and mother ... a dispute between sisters involving the entire estate ... the not uncommon situation in which one sibling has cared for their ailing parent and feels taken advantage of ... under a will that divides the parent's property equally:

"If Alice and Barbara litigate the case, one of them will win and the other will lose. In addition, they will lose their relationship with each other, at a time when they have lost their mother and would otherwise benefit from family connections. They will also face legal bills and the emotional strains of litigation.... Barbara's lawyer [or Alice's] might suggest mediation. Even if Alice thinks that she would win in a lawsuit, she may be willing to mediate to avoid the litigation and because she cannot be sure of the outcome in court. Barbara may be willing to mediate for the same reasons." Or, possibly, they would rather not end up hating one another.

"Assuming Alice and Barbara agree to mediate, they will meet with the mediator either with or without their lawyers present...." Or without lawyer or lawyers, if they have, or one of them has, no lawyer—a useful point to insert here because a dispute over tangible personal property could even end up in a small-claims court, where people go when they have no lawyers; mediation then may come about because the judge orders or suggests it. "During the mediation each sister will have a chance to tell her story *and will listen to her sibling's story* [emphasis added]. Barbara may be able to understand.... Alice may be able to understand.... The daughters may be able to reach an agreement.... [T]hey will have opened channels of communication and may be able to build a better sibling relationship. The result may well be a 'win' for both of them."

Mediation may also be possible at the planning stage, with the will maker and the objects of his bounty—possible, too, on broad allocations of wealth, as well as the division of things. (This would be to bring mediator skills to bear on the late Mr. Wormser's suggestion that the family meet together to plan the patriarch's will. See the Larsen–Thorpe essay.) My (Shaffer's) colleague Michael Jenuwine and I have suggested, for example, family meetings to discuss a matriarch's intention to disinherit an adult child, and (another case) a grandmother's plan to create trusts for grandchildren, skipping her children (parents of the grandchildren) without knowledge of provisions the children were making for grandchildren.

REFERENCES AND BIBLIOGRAPHY

I. Abrahams, Hebrew Ethical Wills (1976)

P. Aries, Western Attitudes Toward Death (1974)

H. Fingarette, Death: Philosophical Soundings (1996)

A. Barnes, L. Frolik, and R. Whitman, Counseling Older Clients (1997)

B. Barros, "Home as a Legal Concept," 46 Santa Clara Law Review 225 (2006)

D. Binder and S. Price, Legal Interviewing and Counseling: A Client–Centered Approach (1977)

S. Cline, Lifting the Taboo: Women, Death, and Dying (1997)

R. Colby, "Estate Planning: The Transfer of Wealth to the Baby Boom Generation," 39 New Hampshire Bar Journal 38 (1998)

L. Cutler and R. Bogan, "Understanding the Four C's of Elder Law Ethics," American Bar Association, GP/Solo Law Trends and News: Family Law, May 2005 (client identification, conflicts of interest, confidentiality, and competency)

J. Diggory and D. Rothman, "Values Destroyed by Death," 63 Journal of Abnormal and Social Psychology 205 (1961)

H. Feifel (ed.), The Meaning of Death (1959) (paperback ed. 1965)

H. Feifel (ed.), New Meanings of Death (1977)

M. Fellows, R. Simon and W. Rau, "Public Attitudes About Property Distribution and Intestate Succession Laws in the United States," 1978 American Bar Foundation Research Journal 319

B. Fogel, "Estate Planning Malpractice: Special Issues in Need of Special Care," American Bar Association, GP/Solo Law Trends and News: Estate Planning, May 2005

S. Gary, "Probate: Mediating Probate Disputes," American Bar Association, GP/Solo Trends and News: Estate Planning, May 2005

J. Goody, Death, Property, and the Ancestors (1962)

C. Harbury and D. Hutchins, "Women, Wealth, and Inheritance," 87 Economics Journal 124 (1977)

T. Hargrave, Ph. D., "Who Gets All the Good Stuff," Modern Maturity Magazine, May–June, 2001, p. 30

L. Hetzler and J. Hulstrand, Moving On: A Practical Guide to Downsizing the Family Home (2004)

W. Hocking, The Meaning of Immortality in Human Experience (1957)

D. Irish, Ethnic Variations in Dying, Death, and Grief (1993)

E. Kubler–Ross, On Death and Dying (1969)

G. Laderman, The Sacred Remains: American Attitudes Toward Death, 1799–1883 (1996)

R. Larsen and C. Thorpe, "Elder Mediation: Optimizing Family Transitions," 7 Marquette Elder's Advisor 293 (2006)

K. Lauchland and M. LeBrun, Legal Interviewing (1996)

R. Lifton, Death in Life (1969)

K. Menninger, Man Against Himself (1938)

T. Nicholson, "Divvying Up the Old Home Place," A.A.R.P. Bulletin, April, 2004, p. 12

F. O'Connor, "Bring in the Whisky Now, Mary," The New Yorker, Aug. 12, 1967, p. 36

E. Porter, An Introduction to Therapeutic Counseling (1950)

J. Price, "The Transmission of Wealth in a Community Property Jurisdiction," 50 Washington Law Review 277 (1975)

C. Rogers, Client–Centered Therapy (1951)

J. Sartre, Existential Psychoanalysis (Barnes tr. 1953)

T. Shaffer, Death, Property, and Lawyers (1970)

T. Shaffer and J. Elkins, Legal Interviewing and Counseling (4th ed. 2004)

T. Shaffer and R. Redmount, Legal Interviewing and Counseling Cases (1980)

E. Shlesinger, "Dealing With the Dying Client," Ninth Annual Institute on Estate Planning, Univ. of Miami, ch. 2 (1975)

E. Shneidman, Death: Current Perspectives (1975)

J. Stillion, Death and the Sexes (1985)

S. Stouffer, Communism, Conformity, and Civil Liberties (1955)

W. Teahan, "Why Don't Our Clients Like Their Wills?" New York State Bar Journal, Nov. 1997, p. 26

S. Ward, "A Question of Class," American Bar Association Journal, July 2004, p. 37

A. Watson, Psychiatry for Lawyers (1968)

A. Watson, The Lawyer in the Interviewing and Counseling Process (1976)

R. West, "Desperately Seeking a Moralist," 29 Harvard Journal of Law and Gender 1 (2006)

Chapter 2

REBUILDING TOGETHER

Strengthen my widow, let her dream on me
thro' tranquil hours less & less.

Abrupt elsewhere her heart, I sharply
hope. I leave her in wise Hands.

— John Berryman (from "Eleven
Addresses to the Lord")

Counseling in wills-trusts practice has two divisions, as different as the stages in life in which two kinds of "estate planning" clients come to see lawyers. The first division is discussed, as to the client's death, in Chapters 1 and 12, and, as to issues such as the client's ability to act for herself, in Chapter 11. The second division, covered in this chapter, involves a surviving client's rebuilding his life after the death of the planner. The second has traditionally been identified as probate law. It is law-office practice in reference to the lonely, universal, human experience of separation and bereavement.

Dr. Colin Murray Parkes' book, *Bereavement,* was built on Parkes' and John Bowlby's work in the broader context of attachment, loss, and major changes in life—what Parkes and Bowlby elsewhere wrote about as "psychosocial transitions." The broader context is of no small importance to lawyers; most of our clients come to our law offices as a result of major transitions—birth, death, or marriage; drastic changes in business; crime, loss, and outrage.

A probate client comes to a law office in mourning. That means two things: First, the property owner has died; what is left is memory and property, and the property—so far as the law is concerned—has a new owner. The probate process is provided or imposed, by the state, to allow the new owner to take over with authority, and with a minimum of fuss. And, second, the person who now comes to the law office, the new owner, may be undertaking a frightening adventure—a second adolescence that is as involuntary and as painful as first adolescence was. The adventure is an intense form of the social task a person has after losing a job or being the victim of violent crime. The realities of it have to do with commitment and the loss of commitment, sorrow, alarm, anger, guilt, and an irrational searching for what is lost and will not come back. It is a sad, scary business, even if it is also an adventure. Professional assistance for such a person, from a lawyer, is possible; it should be hopeful; and it is sometimes not given when it is needed.

A. PROBATE

"Probate" means proof. The reference is to proof of a will (meaning the document) of a dead person as a source of formal evidence for transfer of ownership of property. The state provides a way to look at evidence of the formal act a dead person took, before death, and to certify the effectiveness of that act. If a person died without performing the formal act, the state provides a way to validate that fact and to direct transfer of ownership according to the law. "Probate court" is the agency a state provides for these purposes. Certifying facts in this way, and supervising the functions necessary to transferring ownership, are most of what a probate court does. Probate courts do not routinely involve themselves in litigation over the validity of wills; litigation is a minor part of their business. A probate court is rarely a place for lawsuits.

In normal course, the family of a dead person, or one of the dead person's creditors, has gone to a lawyer who has initiated the process of probate. The lawyer notifies everyone who might have a claim to the dead person's property that she is seeking the approval of the probate court for a formal transfer of ownership to legatees or heirs. The system is not self-executing. If no one from the family, and no one among those who are named in the will, and no creditor seeks probate supervision, the property will probably be transferred informally, and questions of ownership will either not be raised or they will be raised and resolved without the prompt, routine sanction of the state.

Invoking the law of probate, then, results either in a proved (probated) will (*testate* estate), or in a formal undertaking to transfer ownership according to what the legislature has provided for people who die leaving property but no will (an *intestate* estate). The ordinary day-to-day duties of protecting the property during a traditional, conventional, and even stately process of transfer, and of carrying out the burdens of placing the new owners in possession, fall to the *personal representative* of the dead person. If the estate is testate, that person will probably be named in the will and called an *executor;* if the estate is intestate, that person will be chosen by the probate judge, according to statutory priority, and called an *administrator.*

The probate process, in the hands of such a person, who follows statutory procedures and seeks guidance as necessary from the probate court, involves three steps, after (or along with) this initial invocation:

(A)   gathering the property together and making it safe;

(B)   paying the dead person's debts and state and federal death taxes due from the estate and the new property owners; and

(C)   distributing the property to its new owners.

The first set of duties includes everything from kicking trespassers off the farm and locking the doors to the house, to making sure casualty insurance premiums and property taxes are paid, to feeding the cat. It requires that the personal representative have the legal power to function, temporarily, as owner.

The second set of duties involves giving notice to taxing authorities and anyone who might be a creditor. Because the probate process cannot wait until all statutes of limitations run on debts, probate imposes on creditors a special, statutory, shortened limitations period. (E.g., the statute may require that contract claims be presented within six months, even though the statute of limitations on contract claims is otherwise six years and the contract claim at issue was incurred the day the decedent died.) Because death taxes are levied on non-probate property (e.g., joint bank accounts, jointly held real estate, life insurance proceeds), the personal representative is required to evaluate, report, and pay taxes on property she does not control as well as on property she does control.

The third set of duties involves reporting to the probate court that debts and taxes have been paid, proposing who the new owners of probate property should be, and in what proportions, and obtaining from the court an order directing distribution. When all three sets of duties are accomplished, the personal representative reports that fact and is discharged, thence to fade back into the community, as if she were an old soldier, an exhausted juror, or a basketball player after her last college game. Recent reforms in many states simplify this process, and remove the necessity for court supervision of it in many cases, but this three-part description is generally accurate even for the unsupervised administration of decedents' estates.

Fading into the community may be the task of a client who is also becoming a new person. If the dead person was the wife or husband of the client, the client's old life in the community is changed. The legal and social apparatus that comes with being a married person in a social order that is still—however much violence we have done to the practice—built on the family has been removed by death. What replaces the family-centered, somebody's-darlin' set of roles in the community is similar to what replaces the routine of a pimply adolescent after high-school commencement. Tony Earley's short story "The Cryptologist" describes the situation: A recent widow visits the home of another recent widow, and knows both how it is and how it will be before long: "Rose stopped at the foot of Plutina's driveway and stared sadly at her neighbor's house. It was tucked far back up the hollow on a knob that Charlie had deemed too rocky to plant. A single light burned in the living room, and a thick gauze of wood smoke hung immobile above the kitchen chimney in the still, dusky air. Charlie had died two months earlier, and Rose knew from personal experience that Plutina was just now crossing over into what would be the darkest days of her widowhood. The officious stream of Sunday-school classes and bereavement committees bearing casseroles and Jell–O molds would have begun to dry up, if it hadn't already, and the other visitors would have returned to their normal pattern of stopping by only when it suited them, if they came at all."

The probate process is, in the most common case, part of and parallel to the painful business of taking on and developing a new identity—and doing that, typically, late in life. The human side of law-office professional assistance to such a person builds on four counseling principles:

1. Feelings are a vital part of the practice of legal counseling in probate work.

2. Openness in dealing with feelings is the most efficient, effective, and comfort-giving strategy for legal counselors.

3. Lawyers are counselors in bereavement, whether they want to be or not.

4. The grief reaction probate clients bring to lawyers is deep, serious, and dislocating.

B.   FEELINGS ARE VITAL

A widow (to take the female survivor of a marriage as the prototypical, more common case)[1] is within four weeks of the loss of her husband when she first sees a probate lawyer. She is in the midst of deep feelings of *searching* and *finding;* both feelings come and go. "The most characteristic feature of grief is not prolonged depression but acute and episodic 'pangs.' A pang of grief is an episode of severe anxiety and psychological pain. At such a time the lost person is strongly missed and the survivor sobs or cries aloud for him" (Parkes). She (or he) is yearning and protesting, in a pattern of behavior that lies deep in our biological history. Parkes invokes Konrad Lorenz's aggression studies, especially the behavior of a greylag goose that has lost its mate. The situation is characterized by aimless search and calls for help. "The value of such behavior for the survival of both individual and species is obvious, crying and searching both making it more likely that the lost one will be recovered." The cry is also a cry for help—help in searching, help from pain and danger, protection even from oneself. The emotions involved are grief (at loss), fear (at danger, because the protector is gone), and a restlessness that leads to the sort of hyperactivity any experienced probate lawyer can tell you about—unnecessary concern about technical transfer questions, compulsive telephone calls, too much worrying about whether the doors are locked.

Parkes quotes Lindemann's description: "The activity throughout the day of the severely bereaved person shows remarkable changes. There is no retardation of action and speech; quite to the contrary, there is a rush

---

1. The life expectancy of an adult woman remains longer than the life expectancy of an adult man, although the gap is narrowing. Most survivors of marriage are widows.

of speech, especially when talking about the deceased. There is restlessness, inability to sit still, moving about in an aimless fashion, continually searching for something to do. There is, however, at the same time, a painful lack of capacity to initiate and maintain normal patterns of activity."

The experience may also be characterized by a trick of visual memory in which the lost person is "found"; these may go so far as clear, waking hallucinations, and will often include visual images in dreams. The feelings are typically accompanied by a physical sense of dread, loss of appetite, sleeplessness, and a compulsion to return and remain at physical sites where the lost person often was, and where, somehow in the psyche, he might again be found. This resembles what Parkes calls "home valency." The individual who has lost one source of emotional security is likely to remain near or return to other people, or to familiar places.

The searching part of the normal grief reaction tends to become a search for mitigation, for some relief from the pain of loss. Searching may be expressed in strong attachment to things—photographs, furniture, even (some widows report) a bolster or pillow which can be touched or held, as the lost person was. There is also a tendency to "find" the lost person in intensified religious practice or spiritualism. Where guilt is a significant factor, Parkes says, these intense social indicia of grief may last an abnormally and disablingly long time. In virtually all cases these weeks and months of bereavement are deeply, steadily painful.

Exercise 2.1

2.1.1. A mundane law-office question at this point is this: As a general proposition, building on your experience and observation, do you think it is a good thing for the dead person's spouse to be the personal representative? This question comes up in will drafting when the client or clients answer the lawyer's question about who the executor of the will is to be. And it comes up again after the will client dies and the lawyer's new client is the will client's family.

2.1.2. A useful tip for law-office practice here is to notice that there are ways of talking to a client that tell the client *not* to open up, and there are ways that *invite* openness. Anne Lamott's character Mattie Ryder finds such an invitation from her beloved Daniel: "When she told him things she was thinking ... he said it back to her in language that showed he understood what she'd said. He had the time to hear, like a person who believed there was someone alive beneath the rubble of herself, who heard the soft sounds she could still make from the broken parts...." The counseling issue is whether the *lawyer* is open. There are techniques for the practice of openness, as there are techniques for drafting and for cross-examination. In "active listening," for example, the object is to indicate to your client that you have heard what the client said and to invite the client to say more.

Here is a little exercise on active-listening skills: Talk to someone for two or three minutes with the object of getting the other person to open up, to say as much as possible. (This can be a make-believe client, but it need not be; it is not important that you be talking about legal business.) Record your conversation and then score yourself or ask a partner to score you on the quality of your responses (this can be done by three people, observer, commentator, and score-keeper):

— No points for a response that ignores the client's statement by changing the subject or saying something irrelevant to it.

— One point for a response that touches on what the client said but doesn't get to the essence of it; the client can tell the lawyer is listening a little bit but not that the lawyer really heard all of what the client said.

— Two points for a response that restates what the client said, that gets the content of it without adding or subtracting anything. (Two points, in other words, for showing the other person that you are a good mental note taker.)

— Three points for a response that reflects both what the client said and what the client meant—including meanings that come from inflection, tone, gesture, posture, and implication. (Top score for demonstrating understanding, acceptance, sympathy, and maybe even a little bit of empathy, and for accepting correction when the lawyer didn't get it right.)

C. OPENNESS IS THE BEST STRATEGY

Parkes found that widows and widowers *want* to talk about their feelings:

"At the outset I had some misgivings about the entire project," he said. "It was not my wish to intrude upon private grief and I was quite prepared to abandon the study if it seemed that my questions were going to cause unnecessary pain. In fact, discussion of the events leading up to the husband's death and of the widow's reaction to them did cause pain, and it was quite usual for widows to break down and cry at some time during our first interview; but … they did not regard this as a harmful experience. On the contrary, the majority seemed grateful for the opportunity to talk freely about the disturbing problems and feelings that preoccupied them."

When he did not impose time limits, he found that "the first interview usually lasted from two to three hours, not because I had planned it that way but because the widow needed that amount of time if she was to 'talk through' the highly charged experiences that were on her mind. Once she found that I was not going to be embarrassed or upset by her grief she seemed to find the interview therapeutic.... I had no sense of intrusion after the first few minutes of the initial contact."

Bereaved people who are inhibited from free expression of their feelings are more inclined to suffer the worst effects of bereavement— depression, deterioration in health, prolonged disability. The idea that proper behavior for a mourner is control, and avoidance of contact with mounting sorrow, is a stupid idea and a harmful convention. It robs our "civilized" funeral rituals of much of their value. It seems also to excuse the insensitivity of a probate lawyer who lets himself be a bureaucrat instead of a counselor. What is significant for lawyers is the fact that these feelings are not as intense at the time of the funeral ritual (within a week, at most, of death in our culture) as they are when the bereaved person gets involved in "settling the estate": "The peak of pangs of grief ... tends to be reached during the second week of bereavement. The 'bold face' put on for the funeral can then no longer be maintained and there is a need for someone [lawyer?] to take over many of the accustomed roles and responsibilities of the bereaved person, thereby setting him or her free to grieve. The person who is most valued at this time is ... the person who ... quietly gets on with day-to-day ... tasks and makes few demands upon the bereaved.

"Such a person must be prepared to accept without reproach the tendency of the bereaved person to pour out feelings of anguish and anger, some of which may be directed against the helper. In fact it may be necessary for the [lawyer] to indicate to the bereaved that he or she expects such feelings to emerge and that there is no need for them to be 'bottled up.' The [lawyer] should not 'pluck at the heartstrings' of the bereaved person until breakdown occurs any more than he or she would connive with the bereaved in endless attempts to avoid the grief work. Both probing and 'jollying along' are unhelpful. The bereaved person has a painful and difficult task to perform which cannot be avoided and cannot be rushed. True help consists in recognizing this fact and in helping the bereaved person to arrange things in whatever way is necessary to set him or her free for the task of grieving."

Probate lawyers say that not all of these feelings will be conventional mourner's feelings. When the atmosphere the counselor provides encourages free expression, the bereaved person may demonstrate anger and protest, even at the dead person, and strong aggressive feelings at almost anybody. "Help derives," Parkes says, "from the quiet communication of affectionate understanding and this can be conveyed as well by a squeeze of the hand as by speech. Into such a warm silence the bereaved may choose to pour the worries and fears that are preoccupying them. It is not necessarily a bad thing if they become upset, for they may be glad of an opportunity to express their feelings. 'Give sorrow words,' says Malcolm to Macduff. 'The grief that does not speak, knits up the o'erwrought heart and bids it break.'" The evidence indicates that someone outside the family, such as a probate lawyer, may be more helpful than a relative at this time—probably because an outsider is not able so easily to add to the hurt of loss by expressing his own grief, or bringing out feelings of competition that center around the dead person.

What property law does as a result of and parallel to this work of grieving is provide new ownership. Probate lawyers see to that, but the lawyer's work in a broader focus helps provide a new position in the community. Both transitions occur in a period of significant social risk which is also a period of opportunity for growth; all significant relationships are more or less up for reevaluation. "I have my memories as they said I would," a young widow said. "But what it amounts to is so simply stated. The joy of living is gone. Life exists and I exist. I go on. But the joy of living, the joy of sharing ... is gone." The pain of loss can be directed toward oneself (destructively), toward the world (antisocially), or toward other survivors (hatefully). The risks are violence to important relationships, withdrawal, or worse—even the loss of one's ability to function. The opportunity is nothing less than a new—and necessary—social, economic, and personal identity. It is no time for neglect, or for law-office routines that do more harm than good.

Irish short-story writer William Trevor's character Emily, a recent widow, begins to see her new horizon at about the time the Misses Geraghty visit her in the house she and her husband have lived in—not always happily—for 28 years. Emily notices that the light is dim: "[H]e'd been particular about low-wattage electric bulbs.... [S]he wondered what she'd do when another bulb went ... if she would replace it with a stronger one or if low-wattage was part of her now." Then, after the sisters finally leave her, and she is alone again, "She ... pulled the curtains back and the day came in. Hers was the ghost the night had brought, in her own image, as she had once been."

D. LAWYERS ARE, INEVITABLY, COUNSELORS

The best reason for lawyers to see to their counseling skills—in this or any intensely personal client context—is the reason Hillary climbed Mount Everest. The client is there; the need is there. A lawyer who chooses not to be open to feelings harms her clients, diminishes the humane range of her professional usefulness, and declines an opportunity to contribute to the growth and dignity of another person.

The normal period of intensity for the bereaved begins from two to six weeks after the death of the lost person and continues for six months to a year. Many of the indicia of grief (most notably the visual image of the dead person) increase during most of this period. The period of grief occurs after the usual officers of bereavement—undertaker and clergy—have come and gone, and usually after related medical attention has been withdrawn. Probate lawyers are more likely to be around than any of the other professionals who preside over death in our culture. It is during this period, the probate period, that the bereaved person has finally to accept the fact of death. Until the initial several days of numbness pass the client is likely to *deny* death. "I just didn't want ... to talk about it," one of Parkes' widowers said, "because the more they talked the more they'd make me believe she was dead." This period of numbness is chronologically over at about the time the probate lawyer appears; the material realities of survival—need for material support, bank accounts, registration of automobiles, and early probate procedures—contribute to the dawning clarity of the consequences of death.

"An odd byproduct of my loss is that I'm aware of being an embarrassment to everyone I meet—at work, at the club, in the street," C.S. Lewis said. "I see people as they approach me trying to make up their minds whether they'll say something about it or not. I hate it if they do and if they don't. Some funk it altogether.... I like best the well-brought-up young men—almost boys—who walk up to me as if I were a dentist, turn very red, get it over, and then edge away to the bar as quickly as they decently can. Perhaps the bereaved ought to be isolated in special settlements like lepers."

Classical psychology says that we tend to defend ourselves from pain by flight or by fight. One or the other. Counseling is a matter of companionship *through* these defenses—companionship that does not oppose them but, at the same time, provides support in the struggle to overcome dependence on them. Flight, for example: Parkes says, "The widow, whose world has suddenly changed very radically, withdraws from a situation of overwhelming complexity and potential danger. Lacking her accustomed source of reassurance and support, she shuts herself up at home and admits only those members of her family with whom she feels most secure. She avoids stimuli that will remind her of her loss and attempts ... to regain some part of her lost spouse." But, "at the same time, and to an increasing extent as time passes, she begins, little by little, to examine the implications of what has happened and in this way to make familiar and controllable the numerous areas of uncertainty that now exist in her world...." At any given time an individual may respond more to one of these tendencies than to the other, and over time he will often oscillate between them, so that a period of intense pining will alternate with a period of conscious or unconscious avoidance of pining.

Beyond the progress that defenses provide, and provide a pace for, are the realities of a new social identity. These, like defenses, are ways to progress through bereavement constructively. Economic planning—

marshaling of assets, provision for support, payment of debts and taxes, the basic law-office stuff of probate practice—are involved here. Part of the loss of death is a loss of economic security. Most bereaved families undergo a drop in income, often a drastic financial loss. Many widows are forced into the employment market for the first time. And even where means are adequate, most widows and widowers are forced to assume unaccustomed responsibilities of management. What occurs is a new system of territoriality. Survivors have to fashion a new community, and assume responsibility for the functions performed by the dead person. The choice is stark: Unless survivors shoulder new responsibilities the community will disintegrate as its members die. These social realities—in family communities, business communities, and personal associations—are the interpersonal stuff of probate practice. What a probate lawyer is doing is protecting and preserving her client's relationships.

"A major change in life, such as that produced by the death of a spouse, not only alters expectations at the level of the focal action pattern (how many teaspoons to lay on the breakfast table) but also alters the overall plans and roles of which these form a part," Parkes says. "A widow is no longer a wife; she is a widow. Suddenly, and always in some degree unexpectedly, 'we' has become 'I,' 'ours' has become 'mine'; the partnership is dissolved and decisions must be made alone and not by a committee of two.... The newly bereaved widow confronts the same problems as the [high-school graduate]. A new set of expectations and roles faces her and she must learn a new repertoire of problem solutions before she can again feel safe and at ease. Like the adolescent she may feel that too much is being expected of her and she may react with anxiety, insecurity, and irritability.... 'I hate it when people use the word widow,' said one widow. The very word implied an identity she was not willing to assume."

E. BEREAVEMENT FEELINGS RUN DEEP

The two most serious forms of bereavement are prolonged grief and delayed grief. If depression, withdrawal, or serious restriction in activity persists for more than a year, doctors get worried. They also worry when grief does not appear for weeks or months after loss. The medical evidence in such a case is that the bereavement will be harder, longer, deeper, and less likely to resolve itself in normal functioning. There are some situations in which "pathological" grief is particularly likely to appear: loss of young children by young mothers, loss of spouses by young married people, loss of a person on whom the survivor was strongly dependent, or vice versa. The dependency that has been shattered may have been like the case Anne Tyler described in her novel *Celestial Navigation,* and in such a case it is not hard to understand that bereavement will be difficult: "It seemed all I could do was give him things and do him favors, and make him see how much he needed me. The more he depended on me the easier I felt. In fact I depended on his dependency, we were two dominoes leaning against each other." Bereavement, then, is what happens when one domino is taken away.

The "high risk case," Parkes says, might be "a timid … person who had reacted badly to separation in the past and had a previous history of depressive illness.… [S]he would not have prepared herself for his unexpected and untimely death. Cultural and familial tradition would prevent her from expressing the feelings that then threatened to emerge. Other stresses occurring before or after the bereavement—such as loss of income, change of home, and difficulties with children—would increase her burden. Although she may at first appear to be coping well, intense pining would subsequently emerge, together with evidence of pronounced self-reproach and/or anger. These feelings, instead of declining as one might expect, would tend to persist."

Parkes recognizes that a probate lawyer may feel more comfortable when she can arrange for her "pathological" client to talk to a psychological counselor. But that advice may not be taken and, even when it is taken, the law-office work still has to be done. A lawyer, "by accepting, without criticism, the anger, guilt, despair, or anxiety … implicitly reassures [his client] that such feelings, however painful, are not going to overwhelm the [lawyer] or destroy [their] relationship.… Having discovered that it is safe to express feelings the [client] is now free to carry out the grief work … " His pathological grief may be transformed into normal grief and "follows the usual course towards resolution."

F. HELPFUL HINTS

The *first* principle of legal counseling in probate work is to provide *a place and an interpersonal climate* in which feelings can be freely and fully expressed. Parkes's advice for the clergy seems to be transferable: "The role of the visiting clergyman is similar to that of any other friendly person who wishes the bereaved person well and would like to be of help. He too should be prepared to show by his manner acceptance of grief and particularly acceptance of the bitter anger against God and man that is likely to be expressed. He will not help matters by returning the anger, by meeting emotion with dogma or agony with glib assurance. He will help best by listening and, if invited to do so, by trying to collaborate with the bereaved person in an honest attempt to 'get things straight'.… It is tempting to hide behind … 'easy' answers and avoid involvement by too readily prescribing 'magical' solutions to grief. Nobody can provide the one thing the bereaved person seeks—the lost person back again. But an honest acknowledgment of helplessness in this respect may make the visitor more acceptable than a spurious omniscience."

A *second* principle relates to the possible development of *dependence* on a counselor, to what psychiatry usually talks about as "projection," "transference," or "distortion." If a client is searching for the dead person, it is reasonable to suppose that some "displacement" may occur—that the client will "find" the lost person in someone who can bring out feelings in the client that resemble the feelings he had toward the lost person. We believe that this often happens—and are supported in that belief, in at least a general sense, by popular psychology and by the curious line of litigated cases that involve a bereaved widower (or widow) who gives all of his property to his lawyer or physician. (Both professions have been, as they should be, stern with members who take advantage of such situations.)

Openness is probably the best solution to this tendency to overdependence. The Rogerian school of thought (named for the author and psychotherapist Carl Rogers) claims that clients will not develop dependence if their feelings are expressed and accepted without being judged. The Rogerian theory turns on the difference between *accepting* what somebody does and *approving* (or disapproving) of it. Other schools of counseling agree that dependence will become less dangerous if it is kept in the open, and that would seem to involve identifying it when it is present and talking to the client about it.

G.M. Gazda, in the book *Human Relations Development* (1973), points out the challenge in practicing non-judgmental legal counseling: The counselor tries to get as close as possible to a frame of reference she will *never fully understand.* Even with the help of perceptive specialists such as Parkes, a lawyer can never be sure she understands how her client sees things. "It is impossible ... to be the other person," Gazda says. "The best we can do amounts to reasonably correct but approximate understandings," and requires *caution* in making guesses, being "open-minded in appraising others," tentative in forming conclusions. "At best we have a limited understanding of the unique person with whom we are communicating."

Gazda recommends phrases such as these for the times when conversation with the client seems to be going well:

You feel....

From your point of view....

It seems to you....

In your experience....

From where you stand....

As you see it....

You think....

You believe....

What I hear is....

You're....

I'm picking up that you....

You figure....

You mean....

Notice that phrases such as these—rather than lawyers' *questions*—are both (i) ways to show that you hear what the client is saying and (ii) invitations to the client to correct your misunderstandings. They are probably the most efficient way to "get the facts" in a short period of time, because they encourage the client to speak openly, in the client's words, and from the client's frame of reference.

If the conversation is not going so well, if you feel that you are not understanding your client or that your client is not as forthcoming as he might be, Gazda suggests some cautious intrusions into the client's frame of reference:

Could it be that....

I wonder if....

I'm not sure I'm with you, but....

Would you buy this idea:....

Correct me if I'm wrong, but....

Is it possible that....

From where I stand, you're saying....

You appear to be feeling....

It appears you....

Perhaps you are feeling....

I'm not sure I'm with you; do you mean....

It seems that you....

As I heard it, you....

Let me see if I understand; you....

I get the impression that....

I guess that you're....

This second list of suggestions is worth thought and discussion, or, even better, worth *practice:* Try saying these things out loud and notice how any one of them can sound about right or all wrong. The difficulty Gazda proposes to meet here is the appearance of obstacles to communication; the perception, by the lawyer, that obstacles are appearing is the difference between the first list and the second. The two risks you take in tackling the problem of perceived obstacles, with phrases such as those in the second list, are: (i) that you will come across as if you were a parent talking to a child; and (ii) that you will come across as being devious. ("Aren't you really pretty tired, little boy? Don't you really want to go to bed now?") Any of Gazda's corrective phrases can, with the right tone and inflection, say in effect: "I'm having trouble understanding you; I need your help." Or, with the wrong tone and inflection, any one of these phrases can come across as saying either that the client is not performing up to snuff or that the client is suffering from a disability that the lawyer understands and the client doesn't understand.

A *third* principle is that disabling grief is least likely to develop, and the bereavement experience most likely to result in a healthy, new, and self-reliant identity, when the dying person and her likely survivors have prepared for the loss of death. Death may be unavoidable and even unpredictable, but it is foreseeable, notably so for clients who are being cared for by hospice agencies and AIDS ministries. Parkes disapproves of our refusal to talk to dying people about death, and of our false notion that they will feel better if they and everyone around them try to deny that death is at hand: "The wife who has shared her thoughts and plans with her dying husband and with others, who has begun to anticipate what life without him will be like, and who has made adequate preparation for managing practical affairs, is in a far better position to cope with bereavement than one who has pretended that her husband is going to survive until it is too late for her to prepare for anything. When both know that there are others around who will help her through the period of adjustment [the family lawyer, for example], it is easier for them to face the situation and, having faced it, to enjoy what remains of their time together."[2]

Fourth: The goal of counseling in this situation is competence. A time comes, for example, when a young widow says (or thinks) that she does not need to remarry in order to rebuild her life. "I have far more peace of mind and acceptance now than I have had since Dwight's death," one young widow said. "And I can accept his death more philosophically, if that is the word to be used. We must live our lives here on earth. The future is rather nebulous. In my acceptance I am more content. I still have up and down days, but these are to be expected. Life is worth living."

Part of competence is social confidence. "Primitive" cultures, with funeral rituals that often extend for months or even years, show more wisdom than we do about the difference between *physical death* and *social death*. Social death can occur even before physical death, but, for us, it typically occurs after. It occurs after those who were close to the dead person have made the fact of loss real to themselves and have rebuilt their relationships so that they can go on without the dead person. "Primitive" societies institutionalize this reality by delaying the final disposition of the corpse until social adjustments have been given time to develop. We don't do that. The probate process may be the best we have. Our analogue for the final funeral procession may be the probate judge's order discharging the personal representative and closing the dead person's estate.

2. Chapter 12 discusses "end-of-life" planning by clients in their families.

Here is what C.S. Lewis wrote about his life as he "recovered" from bereavement after the death of his wife: "How far have I got? Just as far, I think, as a widower of another sort who would stop, leaning on his spade, and say, in answer to our inquiry, 'Thank you. Mustn't grumble. I do miss her something dreadful but they say these things are sent to try us.' We have come to the same point. He with his spade, and I, who am not now much good at digging, with my own instrument. But of course one must take the phrase 'sent to try us' the right way. God has not been trying an experiment on my faith or love in order to find out their quality. He knew it already. It was I who didn't. In this trial He makes us occupy the dock, the witness box, and the bench all at once. He always knew that my temple was a house of cards. His only way of making me realize the fact was to knock it down.

"Getting over it so soon? But the words are ambiguous. To say the patient is getting over it after an operation for appendicitis is one thing. After he's had his leg off it is quite another. After that operation either the wounded stump heals or the man dies. If it heals, the fierce continuous pain will stop. Presently he'll get back his strength and be able to stump about on his wooden leg. He has got over it. But he will probably have recurrent pains in the stump all his life. And perhaps pretty bad ones. And he will always be a one-legged man. There will hardly be any moment when he forgets it. Bathing, dressing, sitting down and getting up again. Even lying in bed will all be different. His whole way of life will be changed. All sorts of pleasures and activities that he once took for granted will have to be simply written off. Duties too. At present I am learning to get about on crutches. Perhaps I shall presently be given a wooden leg, but I shall never be a biped again."

REFERENCES AND BIBLIOGRAPHY[3]

M. Albom, Tuesdays With Morrie (1997)

W. Berry, The Memory of Old Jack (1974)

J. Bowlby, Attachment (1969)

L. Caine, Widow (1974)

B. Goldsmith, Obsessive Genius: The Inner World of Marie Curie (2005)

J. Goody, Death, Property, and the Ancestors (1962)

J. Hick, Death and Eternal Life (1976)

J. Hinton, Dying (1972)

T. Earley, "The Cryptologist," The New Yorker, January 2, 2006, p. 74

F. Fromm–Reichmann, Principles of Intensive Psychotherapy (1950)

3.   See also the Striker interview in the Appendix and the bibliography for Chapter 1.

V. Koch and J. Rodgers, "The Specter of Death," A.B.A. Journal, Nov. 1998, p. 82

C. Kruse, Jr., "The Elder Law Attorney: Working with Grief," The Elder Law Journal, Spring 1995, p. 99

E. Kübler-Ross, On Death and Dying (1969)

A. Lamott, Blue Shoe (2002)

C.S. Lewis, A Grief Observed (Bantam ed. 1976)

E. Lindemann, "The Symptomatology and Management of Acute Grief," 101 American Journal of Psychiatry 141 (1944)

K. Lorenz, On Aggression (1967)

M. Luecke, "Grief: Helping Clients Through a Loss," Christian Legal Society Quarterly, Winter 1990, p. 11

C.M. Parkes, Bereavement: Studies of Grief in Adult Life (1972)

E. Porter, An Introduction to Therapeutic Counseling (1950)

R. Prince, "Attending to the Emotional Aspects: The Process of Grief," Trusts and Estates, April 1995, p. 82

C. Rogers, Client–Centered Therapy: Its Current Practice, Implications, and Theory (1951)

D. Schaper, Mature Grief: When a Parent Dies (2002)

T. Shaffer, Death, Property, and Lawyers (1970)

T. Shaffer and J. Elkins, Legal Interviewing and Counseling (4th ed. 2004)

E. Shneidman, Deaths of Man (1973) and Voices of Death (1980)

J. Simons and J. Reidy, The Human Art of Counseling (1971)

D. Stannard, Death in America (1974)

W. Trevor, "Sitting With the Dead," in A Bit on the Side (2004)

Chapter 3

WILL INTERVIEW WITH DR. AND MRS. KENNEDY

This interview is conducted, by appointment, in the home of the clients. Dr. Kennedy telephoned Susan Bernstein, at her law office, and asked for an appointment to talk with her about "getting our wills done." Ms. Bernstein, as is her custom, arranged to conduct the interview in the clients' home, rather than in her law office.[1]

1 L: How are you today?

2 M: We are fine. Please sit down.

3 L: Would you like to be referred to as "Doctor and Mrs.," or by your first names?

4 M: Our first names will be fine—Dick and Mary.[2]

5 L: Okay. Well, first I will need to obtain some background information in order to assist you in your estate planning. Estate planning can be difficult because it encompasses discussion about your own death as well as your children's. If you have any questions, let me know. After this meeting, I will prepare a will and we will meet again so that you can review it and make any changes you want to make before it is prepared for your signatures. What I need to do first is to gather some basic information—such as your address, to begin with.

6 M: 265 Tipperary Court, Hoynes City.

7 L: What are your ages?

8 D: Mary is 44; I am 46.

9 L: Has either of you been previously married?

---

1. Even numbers are used for statements by the clients; "D" is Dr. Kennedy (Dick); "M" is Mrs. Kennedy (Mary); odd numbers are statements by Ms. Bernstein, the lawyer. See the footnote in Chapter 9 on the geography of Hoynes and Rollison.

2. It would be naive to suppose that two people who are married to one another and evidently happy are without the stresses and strains that give rise to conflicts of interest, even conflicts that might provoke Rule 1.7 of the Rules of Professional Conduct. It would be equally naive to suppose that such spouses should therefore have separate lawyers. Many of us found comfort in such cases under Rule 2.2, the "intermediary" rule, and took preliminary steps—no later than this point in the interview—to make sure the requirements of Rule 2.2 were met (discussion of the issue, mutual disclosure, and—we think—not talking to either spouse out of the presence of the other spouse). Some lawyers did this in writing with signed acknowledgment from both spouses. Then the American Bar Association withdrew ("deleted") Rule 2.2, a step disapproved of and not followed by many states, including Indiana. See T. Shaffer, "My Client the Situation," *Res Gestae*, October 2005, p. 24.

10 D: No.

11 L: Do you have any siblings, Mary?

12 M: Yes. I have one sister, Jean.

13 L: How old is she?

14 M: Forty-eight.

15 L: And Dick, do you have any brothers or sisters?

16 D: I have three sisters: Roberta, who is 51; Deborah, who is 44; and Jeanne, who is 40.

17 L: Do they have children, Dick? And, if so, what are their ages?

18 D: Yes. Jeanne has five girls and one adopted boy. Roberta has three daughters, ages five, seven, and 13; and Deborah has two boys, ages 22 and 19.

19 L: Mary, does your sister have any children? And what are their names and ages?

20 M: She has one child, Claire, who is 13.

21 L: Are your parents alive? And, if they are, what are their names and ages?

22 D: Both of our fathers and my mother are deceased.

24 M: And my mother is Katherine Hull, who is 78.

25 L: Are you employed?

26 D: Yes. I am a chemist at Rodes Laboratories—

28 M: I am not working outside our home.

29 L: (to Mary): Do you think you might go back to work?

30 M: I don't know. I am an R.N.

31 L: (to Dick): What is your annual salary?

32 D: It is $100,000.

33 L: Have you made a pre-nuptial agreement?

34 D: No.

35 L: Do you have a will?

36 M: Yes, we have.

Exercise 3.1

3.1.1. What word would you use to characterize Ms. Bernstein's approach to Dr. and Mrs. Kennedy? Parental? Filial? Official—like someone in the county clerk's office? Some word of your own? How do the following factors bear on your characterization of Ms. Bernstein's initial interviewing style:

(a) It is this lawyer's custom to conduct initial will interviews in the client's home.

(b) There was no "small talk" at the beginning of this interview.

(c) The permission to use first names was given by the clients, but neither asked for nor given as to the lawyer's first name (statements 3 and 4).

(d) The lawyer provided an agenda not only for the day but also for the rest of the will-making process (statement 5).

(e) The phrase used to describe this lawyer-client activity was not the clients' ("getting our wills done") but the lawyer's ("estate planning").

3.1.2. Ms. Bernstein gathers initial information through questions. How would you characterize her questions?

(a) "Direct-examination" or "open-ended"? A test for the difference will be whether the client provides all of the information asked for and even goes beyond what is asked for. Compare statements 11 through 24, above, with statements 69 through 80, below.

(b) "Cross-examination" or "direct-examination"? The difference is whether the question suggests the answer.

3.1.3. Is there an alternative to asking questions at the beginning of a will interview? (Consider, for example, how you would begin the interview of a client who came to you in a bereavement case in Ch. 2 *supra*; or with evident injury, and distraught, the day after an automobile accident.) What are the advantages and disadvantages of the alternative?

3.1.4. How is Ms. Bernstein doing in terms of building rapport with her clients? Answer this in general and then in reference to statements 25 through 34. Compare those statements with statements 91 through 98, below.

3.1.5. How is Ms. Bernstein doing in terms of getting the information she will need to draft the documents these clients will need? Compare questions and answers:

(a) on the married names of Dick's and Mary's sisters (11–16)?

(b) on the names of Dick's nephews and nieces as compared with the name of Mary's niece (17–20)?

(c) on the spelling of Claire (20)? (Clare? Clair?)

(d) on whether Mary's name is Hull (24)?

(This is nit-picking, of course. Filling in information later, even by a telephone call after the interview, is not difficult: There is no comparison between leaving things out in this sort of interview and leaving things out in an examination in court. But, still, filling in later takes time, and, as Abraham Lincoln said, a lawyer's time is a lawyer's stock in trade.)

37 L: What is your reason for wanting to make a new will?

38 M: New provisions. Lots of things have changed—our life, our savings, his earnings, and the status of our children. They're older and when we made our original will we didn't take into consideration the third son. Our third son is mentally retarded and we are now aware of things, and the law concerning those trusts that need to be considered—because of his condition.

39 L: So you would like this will to revoke that previous will that you made. Is that correct?

40 M: Yes.

41 L: And where is this other will that you have?

42 M: Our attorney has it. In his office.

43 L: And do you have a copy of it?

44 M: Yes.

45 L: And you mention that an attorney wrote it?

46 M: Yes.

47 L: And how many children do you have?

48 M: Four.

49 L: What are their names and ages?

50 M: Scott, 22; Patrick, 19; David, 16; and Thomas, 11.

51 L: And you have custody of all the children?

52 M: Yes.

53 L: And were any of these children born out of wedlock, adopted, or step-children?

54 M: No.

55 L: And are any of your children disabled?

56 M: Yes. David, the 16 year old, is mentally retarded.

57 L: Can you tell me a little bit more about his mental retardation? Whether it is severe? Moderate? Mild?

58 D: He is considered moderately mentally handicapped.

59 L: Has he ever been tested—an IQ test, let's say?

60 D: It's kind of hard to do an IQ test on him.

62 M: He is tested through the schools. Their method of testing here, locally, puts him in that category.

63 L: I see. And can you tell me a little more about David's mental competency. For example, is he capable of communicating and making decisions?

64 M: Yes, yes. He has good verbal communication skills. He reads and does math at a second grade level and he is quite capable of making decisions in all activities of daily living. And is very independent in his daily routine.

65 L: So you would say that he is independent with self care.

66 M: Oh, yes.

67 L: And, could he manage—Let's say, if he were to inherit property, could he manage that by himself?

68 M: No, he could not.

69 L: Would he be capable of working, do you think, in the future?

70 D: Yes, I think that he could. There are many jobs in the community that he could do. Of course, there are many he could not do, because he doesn't understand money very well; he's gullible and he would be easy prey for somebody to take advantage of. I think that he would need some supervision or some structure for checking on him periodically. If he lived in a household or lived in an apartment with somebody else, he could be checked on periodically by somebody. I don't see him being able to live totally on his own. He could manage a household.

71 L: Such as?

72 D: Cooking he could do; cleaning he could do; he couldn't pay the bills, and he would have to have help doing the shopping.

73 L: And, if he were to handle wages, how would he handle those? Could he handle wages that he earned?

74 M: He gets paychecks now for the jobs that he has. He does job training at school and he has had a summer job before. And he has a savings account, so he can deposit money and get money out of the bank, and he keeps some cash on hand for spending money. But he would need help in budgeting of any kind.

75 L: It sounds like he is able to manage a little bit on his own.

76 M: On a very small scale. But he understands the concept of saving

for something—you know, that is in the future, that he has to save money to pay for it.

78 D: And I think that he is still on his learning curve. He hasn't leveled off yet. We feel his need for supervision and continued education for living skills is going to continue into his early twenties. He is not going to be done with learning how to get by in society when he graduates from high school in about three years. One of the problems we have is to try to find some further way of teaching him living skills after he is out of high school. In the State of Hoynes, when you are done with high school, you are done. In other states, they keep you until you are 21, and they continue to work on these kinds of things. Hoynes doesn't do that. So we are going to have to look at some other kind of arrangement—

79 L: So you feel a little bit concerned then about his education after he finishes schooling right now.

80 D: Right. The normal attitude by school people is that, you know—well, you feel like they come to do what they do kind of begrudgingly. You know, they never look at a problem and say, "What's the best way we can handle this?" And, "What's the way we can exercise these people's rights to their fullest?" They've always looked at it with, "What's the minimum we can get by with?" And, "We will only do things that we're really nudged to do." So you know that the school system and the state legislature is not going to come out and say, "Gee, we understand now that we have this big need to take care of people with disabilities and educate them better." I mean, they're only going to do it if somebody threatens a lawsuit or something, because that's just the way the State of Hoynes works. The people in those positions don't come forward with, you know, this kind of positive attitude. So, you know, I think, it's not going to just rain on us. This is the battle that we have chosen not to fight. I mean, you have to choose your battles carefully, and we don't feel we have enough reserves, emotionally or financially, to carry on that battle and try to get more education. So, we're going to have to fall into some kind of fallback position and just try to get by. (Pause.) David doesn't respond well to teaching by us. However, parents tend to—my mother or my mother-in-law might be able to do it, but the kids are always kind of resistant to getting direction from us, from Mary and me. Just a parental kind of thing. Everyone is the same way about their parents. Parents don't get smart until we are about 45.

81 L: Yes, Right. Then you'll start listening. So is he—What level of school is he at right now?

Exercise 3.2

3.2.1.   How would you describe the rapport between lawyer and clients at this point? Did it change between statement 40 and statement 81? If so, was the change for the better? How so? What, in your view, caused the change? On this general topic of rapport and change in rapport, consider:

(a)   who answered the lawyer's question 57 and who made statements 62 through 68;

(b)   the lawyer's response to statement 38 compared to the lawyer's statement 55;

(c)   whether the lawyer might usefully have explained some of her questions before she asked them (e.g., 41, 47, 51, 53, 71).

(d)   the lawyer's use of responses other than questions—including silence (as during client statement 80); consider lawyer statements 65, 75, 79, and 81: Which way of seeking information worked better to build rapport?

3.2.2.   There are times, even in a written transcript such as this, when a reader can sense changes in the tone clients use in speaking. Consider, for example, client statements 68 and 70. Would you have responded as Ms. Bernstein did to these statements? Compare lawyer statements 5, 45, and 53.

3.2.3.   How is Ms. Bernstein doing at the task of gathering information for the documents she proposes to draft? In Exercise 3.2.1(d), just above, we asked you to consider her use of statements other than questions, in terms of building rapport. Please reconsider those statements in terms of gathering information. Do non-questions work as well as questions? Better? Non-questions may work better at building rapport but worse at gathering information. Do you see instances of that in this interview? Is the loss of information serious? Would reduced rapport be worse?

3.2.4.   Notice the various ways this lawyer responds after the client has finished responding; e.g.:

(a)   lawyer questions 57 and 63 (and her follow up to client responses), compared with

(b)   lawyer questions 75 and 79.

What is the difference there? What causes the difference?

3.2.5.   How would you have responded to client statement 80—what would you have said (if anything):

| (a) at the "pause"? |
| (b) at the end? |

82 D: [David] is a freshman in high school. He stayed in middle school for three years, so really as far as his high school eligibility is concerned, he is a sophomore.

83 L: And what grade level is he at—that he has been tested at?

84 D: His verbal and math skills are about second grade level.

85 L: So he's in some special class then?

86 D: Yes. It is a contained, moderate, special education class with some—he is not able to mainstream in any kind of regular classes. I mean, he can't go to a regular geography class. All the words—he couldn't understand what they were saying. And math. However, he does do some other things. Like he was on the cross-country team, and he is able to run four consecutive six-minute miles, which is pretty good speed. The only thing is, he has a hard time when he is on the cross-country course, because he gets distracted. But, you know, he has some abilities that are admirable and others that, you know, are also admirable but not considered a normal function.

87 L: Can you tell me a little more about some other skills that he has. You mentioned some of his athletic abilities—

88 D: He has interpersonal skills that are very good. I mean, everybody that knows David, likes David. I mean, everyone cares about him. He's fairly popular. At Murphy Middle School, where he graduated from, he won the Principal's Award. It was the first time that any mentally handicapped kid won the Principal's Award. Our two older boys have gone on to have scholarships to go to college. David got the Principal's Award, and when he was at the assembly, everybody seemed to be real excited about it. The teachers I know out there said that they think David—he'll do just fine. Everyone likes David. So, I don't know. (Pause.)

89 L: Does he have any other athletic abilities other than the cross country team?

90 M: Well, cross-country skiing, swimming, running—

91 L: Horseback riding?

92 D: —horseback riding, bowling. Every time they have some new activity at the Center for Retarded Citizens, we sign David up, and after a while he comes to be very proficient at it. He has a very strange delivery when he bowls, but he gets strikes as often as the rest of us do. He's the best downhill skier in the family. I mean, David can do a lot of things. He has good rapport with

animals, horses, and does well, and knows how to manage a horse, something I never learned to do.

93 L: Neither have I. I'm not very good with horses. So that's a real skill to have.

94 D: He has an understanding of people who don't feel well, people who are ill. He knows that. My aunt one time was sick and he was there when we were there, and we helped her up to bed and let her take a nap. David lay down with her, held her hand and patted her on the forehead: "You'll feel better. It's okay." David is David. That kind of kid.

95 L: Do you feel in the future he could enter into a contract? Let's say something needs fixing, needs to be repaired, could he hire someone to repair it, or could he buy things?

96 D: No, I don't think—the way he works now, he understands how to read the cost of something. He understands generally what it takes, how many dollars that is. But I think that somebody that is quick and fast could, you know—I think that he would be easy prey for somebody who's unscrupulous.

97 L: You feel then that he might need supervision in that.

98 D: Yes. In a major purchase. He would need to be looked after.

99 L: Does he have any physical impairments?

100 M: Nope. Nothing noticeable. He's probably not as coordinated as a lot of other 16-year-olds, but nothing that hinders his activity in any way.

101 L: And, we talked a little bit about some of his skills. What do you feel are some of his limitations? For example, you have mentioned that he would need supervision, pretty much, in making purchases and in some of his living in general, making some of those decisions. What else?

102 M: He probably won't be able to drive. But he is capable of using public transportation.

103 L: How is his memory?

104 D: Well, for some things he is very good. Every time we lose something around the household, David knows where to find it. And—things like that. But if you ask him—dates: He is very aware of dates, future and past. Oh, yes. Every year, when we get the Christmas decorations out, he knows exactly where everything goes. "We had it there last year." Simple things he remembers; but more comprehensive things he has a difficult time with. Concepts: He doesn't grasp concepts, unless it is something concrete like a date or a phone number or a schedule, he has—he has trouble.

105 L: And, ah—

106 D: He can say, you know, what time it is. He can tell you how he feels. What is your opinion, you know—he can't respond to those questions. Where is this? Where is that? You know. Did you have a good time? No, he won't respond well; he'll think about that; he doesn't know how to respond to that.

107 L: And what about making other kinds of decisions? Like you mention that he is fairly independent with his living. But what about going shopping, to the grocery store, let's say. Would he be able to do that on his own?

108 D: Send him to get his hair cut, he walks down on his own. And he buys some items at the drugstore, the grocery store, the video store. He is very good at the video machines. Things like that. He could go to the grocery store with a small list—print it out so he could read it, and he could find a few items. But if it was a long list of 35 items—I'm not going to say he can't—we've never tested him on that. Five or ten, he might be able to find and pay for, and get out of there. (Pause.)

109 L: And, socially? Is he in any social activities?

110 D: Not at school, but the Center for Retarded Citizens has some things that he does. There are dances and things, and some social activities associated with Special Olympics. He participates in that, in a variety of sports. But that is all.

112 M: There are not a lot of social activities for him and people his age unless it is organized through the Center or Special Olympics. On his own, he does not have a lot of friends he does things with.

113 L: Do you feel there is potential change in his condition at this point?

114 D: No. I don't think there will be any.

116 M: Not great change. We don't think he has finished learning and growing, but there are not going to be any drastic changes.

118 D: There is not going to be some medication that's going to restore—not restore, but help him to develop normal mentality.

119 L: Is he on any medication now?

120 D: No. When he was younger, he was hyperactive and we had some drugs for that, but he hasn't been on anything for a long time.

121 L: So you basically feel that there will not be any major changes, that he will pretty much stay the same, then, let's say, in the next ten years.

122 D: Oh, I think he'll—you know, like I said—yes, I don't see any major changes in his abilities, although I think he'll expand

some of his capabilities. Generally he is not going to—I don't see that there will be some breakthrough, so that David will be able to live by himself, or suddenly have these skills and be able to drive a car, or something. Although we have been out on the lake with some friends and he steers the boat better than most of our sons. You know, I wouldn't want him driving a car coming at me at 70 miles an hour.

123 L: Where is David currently living?

124 D: Here.

126 M: He lives at home and attends public school, high school.

127 L: And do you foresee him wanting to move out of the house in a few years?

128 D: I don't think so. Right now—

130 M: Well, he's aware of his brothers getting older and leaving and I think he might—you know, when you get to a certain age, you go some place. I don't really think he has figured out that—

132 D: He was aware that he was of the age that he should be driving cars, and that he wasn't doing it. He asked about that a little bit, but—

133 L: How did he feel about it? Do you know?

134 M: It comes up every now and then.

136 D: He doesn't dwell on things that are unpleasant. He just goes on and finds something happy to do. He was asking about Patrick going off to school. Scott went off to school: "What's going to happen when I get out of school? Where am I going to go? Is there a school for me? Do I get to go, too?" He was asking about that.

138 M: Plus he does not have a lot—I don't think he knows a lot of people that live independently, you know, people he might socialize with at the dances or Special Olympics, even if they do live independently in a group home or something. He is not aware of that.

139 L: Then, in summary, you know that he is aware of what is happening to his brothers, but do you foresee him having that desire to move out of this house?

140 D: No. There are some kids who become behavioral problems when they are retarded, because they understand what it means to be retarded, and they know that there is something out there that they are not able to achieve, and they are angry about it, and they act up. But David has never been that way. I don't think—if you ask David, "Are you retarded?" he'd say, "I'm not retarded." He doesn't understand. He thinks he is the same as everybody

else, but not being able to do some of the things that the rest of us do doesn't particularly trouble him. You know, "Why should I drive when somebody can take me?" If you were stuck somewhere, it may be different. The way I see it, you are not able to have deep conversations about philosophical things because you kind of get a feel for how he reacts to things.

141 L: Would he be capable of living in a group home, let's say?

142 M: Oh, certainly.

144 D: He would do very well in a group home. But I'm not happy the way most of the group homes are run through agencies. I think that there is too big a turnover in the personnel who look after the group homes, and I don't think the administration of the agency is in close enough contact with day-to-day things. And I'm not happy with how there is some kind of absolution of these homes, supervision may be too—

146 M: There is not enough training of the staff, I don't think. Yes. The staff doesn't know what to do.

148 D: Some of them might have been working in a bakery the week before. "Hey, do you want to try this thing with handicapped folks?" Yea, sure, you know—good—give them a little tour around the house, and that's about it. Introduce them to everybody and say don't let this, and don't let that, and don't let this happen and it's over. There are some excellent people that work in the homes. But for the most part, they don't receive a lot of training. (Pause.) Some day we would like to buy a house with some other families, and we would do it on our own, and then we would not have to go through the agency acting for us, and we wouldn't have to meet these federal standards that—

150 M: There's a lot of state and federal Medicaid requirements, on a day-to-day, hourly-to-hourly basis—

152 D: Just record keeping—

154 M: —record keeping and programming. So if you start it privately you don't have to—

156 D: It is very costly and it's—I can see Medicaid's point, that they want to make sure that these are run properly and that they're not abusing their—or wasting the people's time, wasting their money, but, you know, when it is a parent that is involved, and you are paying for it—you're going to do that anyway. If you expect the government to be the parent for you, then they are going to expect documentation. You know—that's the way it goes. But I think that we should be able to afford to do at least our share in some living arrangement for them.

157 L: So, if you were to create a group home, let's say, how many other kids might live with David?

158 D: We don't expect any more than three more. Four, total. More than that gets kind of confusing, in a lot of group homes. The ones with eight are just a grab-bag. Just too much action.

159 L: It's more like a small institution than a home.

160 D: Yes.

161 L: How do you feel about institutions?

162 D: I think they all should be turned into shopping malls.

164 M: I see that there probably is a need when a person doesn't have a family, but there are a lot of people in institutions who should not be there.

166 D: Most people in institutions would have developed better if they had been in a small living arrangement, in more of a family style—

167 L: Was David recommended for institutionalization?

168 D and M: No.

169 L: And going back to this group home as an option—a possibility—that you might want to start: Would these kids be family, from this community, let's say?

170 D: Friends of ours.

172 M: It would be logical that you would know these people who would do this with you.

173 L: What kind of supervision would exist?

174 M: I think they need someone to live there with them.

176 D: Full time live-in person, or a couple. The best arrangement I know about, in other situations, was when there was a couple. And we've thought of doing that here—just have a group home right here—bring in three or four people.

177 L: Where would you find this supervision?

178 D: Well, it's amazing that there are a lot of people around that do that kind of thing—that are very good at it. Some of them are friends of ours. I mean, I don't think that it would be too difficult.

179 L: Would it be paid help, then?

180 D: Yes. You pay them. They get their room and board, and sometimes that's the reason—it's the pay—and sometimes it's room and board plus.

181 L: And this way you feel that you have more control over it, rather than put him in one of these agency group homes.

182 D: Yes. You know—I mean—I've been on some of the committees there. I have dealt with them, with agency group homes, and I know how the people are handled there. I haven't been happy with them. I am real hesitant to get involved there. There might be some evolution, some change that might make it more secure in the future. It's just not now.

183 L: Can you tell me about some people outside the family that David has developed a relationship with?

Exercise 3.3

3.3.1.   There are two pragmatic reasons for a lawyer in a will interview to attend to client feelings. (Reasons such as compassion and fellow feeling are, we suppose, not "pragmatic" in the usual vulgar sense.) One pragmatic reason has to do with effectiveness and power; we build rapport with our clients so that we can work with and influence them. The other reason has to do with information—with data. In "estate planning," *feelings are facts.* From each of these pragmatic evaluations, how well does Ms. Bernstein attend to the feelings of her clients?

   (a)   Begin by thinking about her statement 183, just above.

   (b)   Consider, in terms of influence and of information, her responses to statements 86, 94, 108, 140, 148 and 150, 168 and 176.

   (c)   Assuming you locate an instance or two when, in your judgment, this lawyer did not attend to feelings well, can you explain why she did not? What was she up to when she was not attending to feelings?

3.3.2.   E.H. Porter, a teacher of counselors, suggests that responses to feeling fall into four categories:

   (a)   They probe—like Dr. Freud talking to his patient on the couch.

   (b)   They judge: "Oh, good for you!" Or: "Why did you do that?"

   (c)   They interpret: "Oh, I see. You were angry, weren't you?"

   (d)   They reflect: "Now, if I understand you, you are saying [this] about [that]."

See if you can find one or two of Ms. Bernstein's responses in each of these categories. Do one or two of the four kinds seem to be more characteristic of her style than the others?

3.3.3. It is common in will interviews to talk to spouses together. Often the three-way conversation will provoke disagreement, and sometimes the disagreement will come out in the law office. (More often it comes out after the couple leave the law office—or, in this case, after the law office leaves the couple.) In many cases the answers to routine lawyer inquiry have come from one spouse; the other spouse is passive. This can become so clearly and pervasively the case that the lawyer should become concerned about the passive client's understanding and agreement. In the Kennedy interview, both clients are active, but there may be subtle evidence here that one spouse has reservations about what the other spouse is saying. It would be unusual if there weren't. Try guessing how Dick and Mary—each of them, separately—feel about (i) the level of planning for David that is necessary, and (ii) the idea that is beginning to show up here, that their wealth be used to establish a group home for David and a very few other mentally retarded adults. Consider statements 22 and 24, 38, 60 and 62, 82 through 98, 104 through 116, 128 and 130, 136 and 138, and 168. Your conclusion is ethically significant (see Rules 1.7 and 2.2 of the Rules of Professional Conduct): Ms. Bernstein's ability to proceed to plan with and act for both clients depends both (i) on the continuing consent of *each* of them and (ii) on the lawyer's continuing judgment that it is possible to work for *both* of them.

184 D: [David has developed relationships with] his teachers. He always has good relationships with all his teachers. He will call them—some of his old teachers—every once in a while. One of them, whom he hasn't seen in four or five years, will get on the phone and call him. They talk for a while. I don't even know about it. A friend will mention it. (Pause.) And Special Olympics people—coaches—he has good relationships there.

185 L: What about anyone in the family? Does he have an especially close relationship?

186 D: His grandmother. My sisters. They are real tight. My sister Roberta—anything she wants, he will do. Anything. I have some nieces that he really loves. One of my nieces lived here with us for a year. She was from Oregon—my oldest sister, Roberta's daughter. Boy, he was—she was just constantly enchanted by David. He was always there. Good buddies.

187 L: And how old was this niece?

188 D: At the time she was twenty-something. No, she was 21.

189 L: So all of these relationships that he has are with people who are generally older than he is?

190 D: Yes, I have some nieces that are around ten, that he gets along with, but they don't have any special relationship with him, where they hang out with him. It's not something where we would get together for just that cause.

191 L: And the grandmother that you mention, does she come here to see David or does he go over there?

192 D: In the summer we will send him for a week or two to spend with his grandmother. Mary's father just recently passed away, so her mother just moved to Hoynes City. She lives in an apartment now; it might be David will go to live in the apartment with her for a week. But she's getting up there, and it gets tiring for her to have somebody around. I don't know if she would want that now. Mary's parents lived in a small town 30 miles or so from here. He went down there. He went down to the hardware store, and he swept. He's a good companion, but sometimes he—he wouldn't help very much in a retail business if he was meeting people. He went down there and hung out and slept and ate like crazy.

193 L: Can you tell me a little bit about the children you have that are older than David? Patrick and Scott. For example, let's start with Patrick—no, Scott, instead.

194 D: Scott's the oldest. Senior at the University of Hoynes. He'll start work on his master's in hospital administration soon. He'll be graduating next year. He's done a lot of work. He used to work at Camp Millstone. Camp Millstone is where he found himself. He was one of those kids who were always looking for some reason to do everything. He had one great experience at Camp Millstone one summer. He just loves that kind of work. He worked very well out there with eight or ten handicapped kids. And that really gave him some direction. He decided he wanted to do something to help care for people like that—he's been extremely good with David. He and David get along very well; he's been a lot of help, as far as that's concerned. Patrick, too, loves working with children, and playing with children, doing things with children. He relates to them very well. He is a freshman in college at Bowling Green. At this time he is in pre-med, because he wants to be a pediatrician. We'll see how that goes.

195 L: Do you feel both sons will stay here or go somewhere else after they graduate?

196 D: Our family has always been close. I think kids usually do what their parents did. We wanted to be near our parents and that's why we came back here rather than go to Oregon, or go the East Coast, or stay in Texas. And from the time I was a young boy, I

always had my grandfather live with me. And we were—our family has always done that. We care for each other, so, I think that the boys probably will settle nearby. But, I don't know that. Certainly their careers might take them somewhere else. I would expect that they will not be in Hoynes City, but within 50 to 100 miles.

197 L: And can you tell me a little bit about Thomas. He's 11 right now? What school is he attending?

198 D: He's at a parochial school—in the sixth grade.

199 L: And—

200 D: He makes real good grades. Kind of a free spirit like the youngest child always is. Family comedian—performer—plays saxophone—plays piano—on the wrestling team, and soccer team. He has a good self image.

202 M: I think he has had a more difficult time with David than the older two because he did not have that advantage—

204 D: Of being bigger.

206 M: —of years, and being larger. He's improved with his patience; but he was very impatient with David for many years. David likes to tease him.

207 L: So there is some competition or jealously, sibling rivalry.

208 M: I don't think you would call it competition or jealousy—

210 D: Just taunting. You know how kids are. You have to live with a certain amount of that—direct it, rather than all this—

212 M: —just teaching Thomas ways that he can, you know, cope with David, or handle him, or get along with him better. When he was very young, he just didn't understand any different. Do you have any older siblings?

213 L: Yes, I am the youngest.

214 D: Boys?

215 L: No. Two older sisters. So I do have some—who is the primary caretaker of David right now?

216 M: We are.

217 L: Both of you are. And who would you want in the event of both of your deaths—who would you want as a guardian to help look after David's personal needs?

218 D: We talked this over with my sister who lives here, and we've made a pact where if something happens to them we get their girls, and if something happens to us, they get our boys.

219 L: And which sister is this?

220 D: Jeanne. My youngest—the 40–year-old.

221 L: And in the event that Jeanne would not become the guardian, for whatever reason, then who else do you think?

222 D: Well, we've always raised the boys to think that the oldest one working would have responsibility for making sure David has a good life and works in the community. Scott and Patrick would work together on that.

223 L: How do you think the boys would feel about taking on a role like that?

224 D: Well, I've asked them about that. It's something we've discussed. They haven't really been against it. I think they feel that that was a given. Of course, we—you know—

226 M: I mean, they are both in their education, still in college, so, you know, it's not really feasible. But as they get older, it's a more realistic thing.

228 D: I talked to Scott about it in some detail over Christmas break.

230 M: Plus, I think either of your older sisters—

232 D: Yes, if it would be necessary that Scott—There's no question about my older sister, but I don't think her sister would necessarily—my sisters are pretty capable, and they would pitch in. So would their girls.

233 L: So, in a will you would want Jeanne first, and then Scott, perhaps, as a second alternative.

234 D: Yes. If somehow they were not able or willing then it would kind of go through my sisters, starting with the oldest.

235 L: How do you feel about the volunteer guardians in the community?

236 D: Yes, I think it's an excellent program and it's really fostered there at the Center. The people were pretty much hand-picked by committees that we were on. And I think it's a real good program for some people, particularly ones who have families that are minimally interactive or absent. And sometimes families live near by, but they ask for volunteer guardians because they are unable to meet the physical and financial requirements. They need help.

237 L: So that would be an alternative or a last resort.

238 D: Yes, Well, I think that we have paid our dues at the Center. If we really fell on hard times somehow, the Center would step in and give us a hand.

240 M: There is just not a need for it.

241 L: Sounds like you have plenty of family to help out. Have you

yourself ever initiated any sort of guardianship proceeding—to appoint yourselves guardians?

242 D: No. But we realize that we might have to do that as soon as David turns 18. We don't know exactly what to do. We will probably do something.

243 L: Have you explored any governmental assistance programs? I know you mentioned Medicaid, I believe, and perhaps you have checked on S.S.I. How do you feel that will fit into your—we're going to be getting more into estate planning at this point—how do you feel that is going to fit in? How do you want it to fit in?

244 M: I don't see it fitting in in the near future, especially as long as he is living at home. I'm not saying that we will never take advantage of it. We couldn't until he is 18 anyway. If he weren't home or—right now I just can't see utilizing it, because it's so—if he went on S.S.I., when he was 18 and still living at home, you would have to account for every piece of clothing that is bought. Every small amount spent on them has to be accounted for, and forms turned in, and I can't see utilizing that right now. But I'm not saying that we never will. When he becomes more independent, lives in a group home or something, then, you know, then maybe we will take advantage of federal funds that are available to him.

245 L: So in the event of your death you would want him to be eligible for basic support maintenance. Your other assets, which I want to go over with you in just a moment—how would you want that to be handled—sort of in a general way? For example: Would you want to help provide for just some of the extras, while the government assistance programs are providing for the basic needs?

246 M: It is my understanding that if they are willed money, or if they have money on their own, they are not even eligible to receive that governmental help, and I would like—I mean, if he is at a point where he needs that assistance from the government, I would want him to have that, and not, you know, not be able to get it because of our will or something.

248 D: If it is something that we could go to—something a designated guardian could have available for his use, without actually becoming his money—

249 L: In that regard, Dick, there is a difference between a guardianship and a trust. Generally, trusts are more flexible and easier to administer. You don't have to go through any probate proceedings, so that would be one way to handle money to go to David without it interfering with the governmental programs—as long as the trustee knows how to handle that money, if he doesn't just

start giving David money and make him become ineligible. A trust could be worked out in such a way that it could help him.

250 M: Yes, that is what we understand.

251 L: And, generally also it shouldn't be a support trust, because support is what the government programs provide. They are for the basic support, and if the trust is a support trust, then it will make him ineligible for the government programs. So it sounds, then, like you want to take advantage of those government programs.

252 D: We don't want to do anything that would make him ineligible. I don't know how to do it, but we don't want to close some door that needs to be left open.

253 L: You've got a home. Do you just have one home at this point? And what is the mortgage on your house?

254 M: Just one home. It is mortgaged—for $35,000.

255 L: And is there any mortgage insurance on that?

256 M: Yes, on the balance. Life insurance on the balance.

257 L: And how is the home held? Joint tenancy?

258 M: In both of our names.

259 L: Okay. And so it is in both of your names. Do you own any automobiles?

260 M: Two.

261 L: And how much are those worth?

262 M: One is $9,000 and one is $12,000.

263 L: Any liens on those?

264 D: No.

265 L: And who owns those cars?

266 M: They are in his name.

267 L: What about furniture and personal property?

268 M: Yes, and our insurance coverage is $65,000 on that. That is about what the furniture and personal property is worth.

269 L: And life insurance. Do you have any policies and how much are those worth?

270 M: We have two policies. Both are whole life—one for $80,000, and one for $60,000. They are on Dick, and I am named as the beneficiary.

271 L: And who owns those policies?

272 M: Dick does.

273 L: And who sees to the premiums? I think you do.

274 M: Yes.

275 L: Do you plan to purchase any additional life insurance at this time?

276 M: No. We have those two policies, and his employer provides $75,000 term insurance. We don't have any plans for additional insurance.

277 L: Do you have any savings accounts, stocks, or other securities?

278 M: We have a savings account in a local bank, in both of our names, for $23,000.

279 L: What bank is that located at?

280 M: Old Hoynes.

281 L: And do you own any stock in a closely held business?

282 M: No. We just have a retirement program through Dick's employment. It's currently worth $250,000. That's the death benefit on it.

283 L: And who is the beneficiary on that?

284 M: I am.

285 L: Do you own any community property?

286 M: No.

287 L: Any assets other than that?

288 M: No.

289 L: Any debts other than a mortgage?

290 M: No.

291 L: I guess in order to prepare your estate plan, now we will get into a little bit more of the specifics of how you would like the property to be disposed upon your death. And, generally, I guess, to have a general sense: What would you like to have happen to your property? What do you want to see happen with the children and David? Sort of a general sense. In other words, do you want all the property to go to the children, or—

292 D: I think, upon the death of one of the spouses, we would want the other spouse to have all of it, then, after that, after the death of both of us, after a certain age, they could have their share of whatever we have.

294 M: I think it would be split up equally among the children—

296 D: Unless it needs more to keep David in a good—

298 M: —or however that is worded in a will. It has to go to a trust fund, or to him. I think they would split it equally, even though there

is quite a bit of difference in age. I think they should all share equally if there is anything to will at the time of our deaths.

299 L: So, if David, let's say, needed more than the other boys—how do you feel about that? Sometimes it is difficult to know.

300 D: If it would take more to establish him somehow, it would be okay. Although, I would not like 90 per cent to go to him and the other kids split ten. I don't think that it would create hard feelings, because they understand that we are not providing him with a college education like we are the others. So we feel that it all works out.

301 L: There are special trusts. There is one called a contingent inter-vivos revocable insurance trust. It is set up during your lifetime, and it is contingent upon your death, and on the children being minors when you are both dead. But with David, obviously, it would not be contingent. What would happen there is that the insurance would go into this trust, then the trustee, depending on what powers he has, would basically give the money to whomever. He would use his discretion—or her discretion—according to who needs the most, or the least, or whatever. And then, after the termination of it, the trust, it goes to whomever you want it to go to.

302 D: Yes, I'm aware of this trust.

303 L: So, it sounds like you would like to have it fairly equally distributed amongst the children unless David needed more.

304 M: Yes. I don't know if that's something we determine right now, or if in writing the will we have to have those proportions set up in the will—

305 L: What would you like the purpose of the trust to be?

306 D: Well, primarily to take care of the children—for their education, and to take care of them.

307 L: Would you want the trust to be divided in equal shares, or would you want it to be a "one pot" trust, where the trustee would distribute the money as he or she saw fit?

308 M: We would like to have equal shares. Are there advantages to having the other kind?

309 L: Yes. The trustee could distribute the money as it was needed by each child. It would be similar to how parents spend the money from time to time on each child. Parents do not split the money equally among the children. They spend it as they see fit.

310 M: Well, maybe we should have the trust set up that way.

311 L: How long would you want the trust to provide for?

312 M: The trust should provide until the youngest child is 25. I guess it would have to provide for David, though, for the rest of his life.

313 L: This is a difficult question. If your children do not survive, who would you want the money in the trust to go to?

314 M: Their children if they have them.

315 L: What about a surviving spouse of a child?

316 M: Yes, if the spouse has children.

317 L: Who do you want as trustee?

318 D: Probably my sister Deborah's husband, Mike.

319 L: And who would you want as successor trustee, in case Deborah's husband could not be trustee?

320 D: I am not sure. Maybe a bank. What about co-trustees?

321 L: You can have co-trustees if you want. The disadvantage is that they would have to make all of their decisions together. Maybe you can think on that and let me know. Who would you want as executor?

322 D: Probably Deborah's husband.

323 L: What about a successor executor?

324 M: We thought about having one of our two oldest sons. We are not sure.

325 L: You can let me know. How do you want Hoynes death taxes, and burial and administrative expenses paid? From the estate, or have the people who inherit from the estate pay proportionately?

326 D: We would want the expenses paid from the estate.

327 L: How would you want debts, such as any mortgages, liens, and so forth, handled? Have the executor pay them?

328 D: Yes.

329 L: Well, I think I have enough information to get me started on a first draft of a will and trust. As I said previously, you will have a chance to review it and make any changes. We can add information you were uncertain about today. If you have any thoughts or questions in the meantime—let me know.

330 M: Okay. Thanks very much.

331 L: Thanks to both of you. See you soon.

332 D: Good bye.

Exercise 3.4

3.4.1.   Suppose you are the lawyer who is now going to sit down and do a first draft of instruments for the Kennedy family. Do you feel you know enough about them and their children to sketch out what they want in terms both (i) of the disposition of their property and (ii) of the management of it for children who need management? Please think about that before you proceed to the next question. Think about where this lawyer was successful, and where not so successful, at finding out what her clients want. You will no doubt notice, when you reach Chapter 10, that further discussion between these clients and with their lawyer resulted in changes to what they indicated here in statements 220, 316, and 318. Might Ms. Bernstein have arrived at these changes in this interview?

3.4.2. The answer to the questions in Exercise 3.4.1 is bound to be: No. I don't know enough. Lawyers who are experienced at this work will tell you that this first interview is only the beginning of what a lawyer will learn about what the clients want. This is an adventure at the end of its first chapter. Even so, there is a job to do here, and we don't have enough information to do it. There are a number of practical ways to proceed. Which of these do you think is best?

(a) telephone calls (or even another visit) (or a visit to the law office by one or both clients) to fill in the gaps;

(b) assumptions and guesses for now; we will draft the instruments in dependence on these, and point them out to the clients when the documents are ready for them to study;

(c) presumptions—something more than assumptions and guesses; we will draft in what we think would be best for them; we will let them tell us what they want changed.

3.4.3. Review the interview for facts you will need to do this work. Consider whether you will need more information about assets; where you will need full names; who else you need to know about. (For example: Do you need to know the name of the lawyer who has their wills?) One way to get a sense of what is needed is to look ahead to Chapter Ten (Forms 4A and 4B) and see what has to go into the documents. However you measure the interview from this mundane perspective, you will probably conclude that there are many details Ms. Bernstein does not have in her notes. Some lawyers guard against inadequate detail in their interviews by using "estate planning checklists" that are available in books on the subject and in looseleaf services. Some use documents that are like those they will be drafting for the present clients. Are there some other devices to take care of this relatively minor problem?

3.4.4.   Now, please, look at this interview more broadly. Apply what might be called two tests of outcome:

(a)   There is a *problem* dimension in law-office work that asks: If this lawyer gave legal advice to these clients, would they follow the advice? (Think about statements 309 and 321 in this regard, but please don't limit your thinking to those points.)

(b)   There is also a *personal* dimension, which asks: If these clients had further and different legal business, would they return to this lawyer with it? (In this case, you might think about them deciding they would like to see about Supplemental Security Income for David when he is 18.)

3.4.5.   Was this interview an efficient use of the lawyer's time? It took slightly less than two hours, and what you have here has not been edited significantly. Should it have been shorter or longer? If so, what lines of discussion would you, as the lawyer, have either cut off or extended? (Consider, for example, statement 215.) Notice that attempts of this sort have two aspects to them: They have a *content* aspect, and they have a *process* aspect. The latter has to do with the lawyer-client relationship, how the people feel about one another.

In Chapter 10, we will pursue the task Ms. Berstein and Dr. and Mrs. Kennedy set for us. We pause here to notice other situations presented by the fact that one member of the family is handicapped and other members are both concerned for his care and are standing by to care for him. We now pause for a moment to consider two other cases and to subtly suggest that lawyers can help.

First case (from the "Dear Annie" column, by Kathy Mitchell and Marcy Sugar, South Bend Tribune, November 15, 2004). "I am married to a wonderful woman, and we have a young son. My wife has a mentally challenged sister, 'Jane,' who recently was diagnosed as being legally blind. Jane lives with my mother-in-law. I've tried to get my wife to convince her mother to get Jane into a program for the visually impaired, but Mom refuses. Neither my wife nor my mother-in-law is willing to take the necessary steps to help Jane become somewhat independent, and this is the problem.

"I want to prepare Jane for a group home or assisted living, but my wife wants Jane to live with us when her mother dies. Annie, I would love to spend my older years with my wife—vacations, long weekends, going to the mall, etc. If Jane lives with us, none of these things will be possible without having to take Jane along everywhere we go. I love my wife, but I don't want a lifetime commitment to Jane...."

Dear Annie: "It's wonderful that your wife is willing to care for Jane, and you do have an obligation to your sister-in-law that is ongoing. However, it is unfair to Jane to keep her so dependent if she is capable of more. In fact, Jane could outlive you and your wife, and then what?

"We suggest you ask Jane's doctor to talk to the family about Jane's capabilities and what's best for her. You need to reassure your wife that you will not neglect her sister, while making it clear that Jane should make the most of her life."

Should Mom also be talking to a lawyer?

* * *

Second Case. Nancy J. Sulok, intrepid investigative reporter for the South Bend Tribune, in her column "Commentary" for March 30, 2003:

"Marcia Anita Robinson, 52, died in November without leaving a will.

"That fact served to exacerbate a nasty family feud involving her surviving siblings and her father. Her 18–year-old son, Eric, is caught in the middle.

"Eric weighed only 2 pounds, 11 ounces when he was born. He has had physical handicaps ever since, including some paralysis on his right side. He also has learning disabilities that require him to be in special education. He will receive a certificate of completion instead of a diploma from Adams High School later this spring.

"Marcia had taken some steps to secure the future for Eric by investing in a 401(k) plan and by taking out life insurance policies on herself. Eric was her beneficiary.

"What she didn't do is draw up a will. That left open the question of who should handle her estate and who should take care of Eric.

"The teen's grandfather, Nathaniel Robinson, has been a key figure in the boy's life. The 81–year-old man helped to raise Eric since he was a baby.

"Nathaniel and his late wife had a total of eight children, but it's not a close family. In fact, various fights over the years have split the family into two factions. Marcia's death made things worse.

"Nathaniel Robinson and Mary Mattai, a sister of Marcia, had been named co-representatives of the estate in January. Mary, who lives in Cleveland, took steps immediately to put Marcia's affairs in order.

"She narrowly avoided foreclosure on Marcia's house by bringing the mortgage payments up to date. She said she used her own money to do that. She also used some of her own money to pay up the insurance on Eric, which was close to being canceled for lack of payment. She changed the locks on Marcia's house and took an inventory of her belongings.

"However, she said she was stymied in some of her efforts to handle the estate because her brothers and sisters took some things from Marcia's house, including insurance papers and other documents and property.

"Mary filed a motion to compel her siblings to turn over the property so she could settle the estate. She said the various insurance and retirement accounts will add up to more than $200,000, which she wants to use to establish a trust to take care of Eric's future needs.

"On the day the hearing was to take place in late February, Mary's brother, Marcus Robinson, filed papers to have Mary removed as co-representative and himself named instead. Family members were in Probate Court … to argue over who should fill that role.

"Eric said he preferred his Aunt Mary because 'I know I can trust her.'

"Two of Mary's sisters, Marguerite Taylor and Myra Carter, and Marcus Robinson argued for Marcus to be the representative.

"The animosity between the two sides was obvious. Taylor, Carter, and Marcus Robinson tried to portray Mary as a conniver who doesn't have Eric's best interests at heart. Marcus admitted he was not close to Eric. He argued Mary has never been close to the boy, either.

"After listening to the conflicting accounts, Probate Judge Peter J. Nemeth said he was impressed by the work Mary had done in January and February on behalf of the estate. It didn't take him long to decide Mary should continue as co-representative of the estate. He ordered Marcus to turn over all of the items he had taken from Marcia's house.

"Still to be resolved is the guardianship of Eric. One of his cousins, Calvin Carter, Jr., has filed a petition to have Eric declared an incapacitated person in need of a guardian, and Calvin wants to be named the guardian.

"Mary is concerned about that because of Calvin's background. Calvin and his brother, Kevin, pleaded guilty to the vicious assault of a man in 1986 at the LaSalle Square shopping center. The victim was left permanently brain-damaged. Calvin was sentenced to 7–1/2 years in prison.

"Judge Nemeth appointed an attorney to represent Eric in the guardianship hearing."

Part Two

TOOLS

Chapter 4

WILLS

A. ALTERNATIVES AND HABITS

The appendix includes a lawyer's interview of a client named Rose Striker. Mrs. Striker is an elderly widow who has no children and very little property. Her principal concern is the disposition of her house after she dies. The "object of her bounty," as the old probate lawyers used to call such people, is a friend named Leslie Stuart. Her likely heirs (the people who would inherit the house if Mrs. Striker died without a will) are nephews and nieces.[1]

Mrs. Striker told her lawyer that she was consulting him because she wanted her will drafted. The discussion between her and her lawyer assumed that the preparation of a will was what Mrs. Striker needed. It was, after all, what she said she wanted. Nonetheless: Should Mrs. Striker's lawyer have discussed alternatives to a will? What would those alternatives have been? Would no action at all have been an alternative? What we're doing here, in other words, is locating the will, as a tool in law-office practice, by noticing first of all what a will is not and what a will does not do. We needed to ask similar questions in reference to Dr. and Mrs. Kennedy (Chapter 3), and, as to what wills do not do, we will need to consider management of property for one or more children who will not be able to manage it for themselves (Chapter 10).

1. PRESENT CONVEYANCE

Mrs. Striker could give her house to Leslie Stuart. She would need to execute a deed in his favor, because you cannot hand over a house as you would a book or a gold watch. The reason her lawyer did not suggest that alternative was, apparently, that Mrs. Striker wanted to keep ownership of the house until she died. She wanted a conveyance of the house that would take effect at her death, and not until then. There seem to be two parts to that intention. The first and most obvious part is a question of necessity: Mrs. Striker needed a place to live.

However, if a place to live were the only consideration, her lawyer might have suggested that she convey the house to Stuart and reserve a

---

1. The interview is also in T. Shaffer and R. Redmount, *Legal Interviewing and Coun-*   *seling Cases* (Matthew Bender 1980).

life estate in herself. She could have done this by provision in the deed. Stuart would then have received, upon delivery of the deed to him, a vested remainder in the house, but he could not have entered into possession until after the life estate was terminated—that is, after the death of Mrs. Striker.

Another and somewhat similar alternative would have been to convey the house, by deed, from Mrs. Striker to Mrs. Striker and Stuart as joint tenants. (Dr. and Mrs. Kennedy own their house that way.) This, too, would have given Stuart an interest in the house. In the case of the vested remainder, his interest would not have been possessory; he would not have become entitled to move onto the property until after the life estate terminated. In the case of the joint tenancy, his interest would have been both present and possessory, but his present, possessory interest would have been limited to an undivided half of the house. The two devices resemble one another, in normal effect, in that they produce complete ownership at the death of the donor—without a will, and without intervention by the probate court. In the case of the vested remainder, all obstacles to Stuart's ownership of the house, in fee simple, would have been removed by Mrs. Striker's death. In the case of the joint tenancy, her death would have removed the obstacles to his fee-simple ownership of the whole house only if he had survived her.

The immediate difference between a vested remainder and a joint tenant's interest is that, under a joint tenancy, part of Stuart's interest would have been possessory. Although Mrs. Striker probably would not have intended that he exercise his right to possession, in legal effect Stuart would have had a present, possessory right to one-half of the house. His right would have been undivided and subject to the possibility that Mrs. Striker might have survived him. But, in most states, he could have eliminated the survivorship contingency by severing the joint tenancy (survivorship interest) to tenancy in common (no survivorship) and then have converted his possessory interest from an undivided interest to a physically discrete, metes-and-bounds interest, by partition.[2]

Mrs. Striker would have given Stuart, in every sense, one half of her house. He could have sold his half, either as an undivided half or, after partition, as a physically separate half. Without partition, in addition to all of these rights, Stuart would have had the right to receive Mrs. Striker's half interest in the house when (if) he survived Mrs. Striker.

Exercise 4.1

4.1.1. Both of these forms of ownership have been recommended to clients of modest "estates" as what were once called poor-men's wills. Both avoid the delays and costs of the

---

2. Case law in some states—notably Michigan—attempts to make some joint tenancies unseverable by treating them as joint life estates followed by remainders.

probate process. Each will probably cost less in lawyer's fees, now, than a will would. Would you have recommended either of these forms of present conveyance to Mrs. Striker? Why not? What are the advantages of a will here, other than the fact that lawyers will make more out of it? (Reasons discussed in this chapter do not exhaust the possibilities; see especially the section on revocable living trusts in Chapter 11 and discussion of the *Farkas* case in Chapter 5.)

4.1.2. Would you recommend that Dr. and Mrs. Kennedy—who have a joint-ownership arrangement in their home when they come to the law office—leave this arrangement as it is? What factors bear on deciding what to recommend to them in this respect?

Note: Your choice of what to say in both of these cases is crucially relevant. One of the awesome lessons from experience-based legal counseling, particularly in "estate planning" practice, is that clients follow their lawyers' advice. That means lawyers bear the responsibility for bad choices. Or does it?

Most lawyers would probably recommend against the conveyance of a present interest in either of these arrangements. Most would choose instead to suggest that Mrs. Striker take advantage of the fact that a will has no effect as a conveyance until the death of the person who executes it. In terms of what Mrs. Striker appears to want, a will not only provides for postponed possession—as a deed with reserved life estate would—but it also makes it possible for the testator to *change her mind*. (The person who makes a will is called a "testator"; an archaic word for the document is "testament"; the intent necessary for making a will is said to be a "testamentary" intent.) In traditional terms, a will is *ambulatory;* it is said not to speak until death. That is not always true; it is probably accurate, though, to say that a will is not effective as a conveyance of property until death—and that means the will is effective only if it is not revoked or changed by the testator in the period of time between execution, when the will is signed by testator and witnesses, and death.

Probably, therefore, Mrs. Striker *does* want a will, and nothing else. And the reasons she wants a will are two: So that she can retain possession and control of her property until she dies; and so that she can change her mind. These reasons apply in the Kennedy case as well, but not in the same way. They want possession and control of their property in both of them or in their survivor. Joint ownership will work for them so long as the cotenants are Dr. and Mrs. Kennedy, and as long as they remain married to one another. (Chapter 10 deals with the matter in some detail.)

2. INTESTACY

Mrs. Striker seemed to know that she would need a will in order to get the house to Leslie Stuart after her death and in a way that would leave her free to change her mind. It would not have been given to Leslie Stuart unless she had taken steps to achieve that result. In this respect, Mrs. Striker was an unusual client. The property of most clients, including unmarried clients, will go to the persons they wish to receive it whether they make wills or not. A childless married couple typically tell their lawyer that they want wills that will give all of their property to the survivor of them. That will often be the result if they do not make wills. A married couple with children typically tell their lawyer that they want their property given to their children, after they are both dead, and that will typically be the result whether they make wills or not. These dispositions will take place because of the form in which the clients' property is held, or because of the provisions of a statute on intestacy (death without will), or both.

If Mrs. Striker's husband had been living, no will would have been necessary to provide for his taking the house at her death, or her taking it at his death. In half to two-thirds of all cases in the United States, the family residence is held by spouses (or "domestic partners") in joint tenancy or in tenancy by the entirety. It passes to the surviving cotenant by operation of law. Where the house is held by one spouse solely, intestacy statutes often provide for distribution of the house to the surviving spouse, and to no one else, if there are no children. (This will not be true of "domestic partnerships"; see Ch. 10 on planning for couples who are not married.) In all likelihood, if Mr. Striker had been alive (his name was Matthew), Mrs. Striker's modest insurance policy would have been payable to Matthew; and whatever insurance there was on the life of Matthew would have been payable to Rose. The couple's greatest asset, retirement income and medical care under the Social Security program, would by Act of Congress have been available to the surviving spouse, without competition from anyone else. (See Ch. 11.)

Dr. and Mrs. Kennedy are typical clients; they want their property—house, insurance and whatever cash there is—to go to their children after the survivor of them is dead. Parents also usually want division among children in equal shares. (The Kennedys may be forced to be atypical in that regard; you may recall that this was an issue in their interview.) And that, too, will probably happen whether they make wills to that effect or not. In only one circumstance—when a spouse survives, and children of the marriage also survive—do typical clients in the United States change the disposition provided in intestacy statutes, which typically give part of the estate to the children.

The most pervasive modern reform of the probate system—the Uniform Probate Code—attempts to retain traditional intestacy features and to move the rules on distribution even closer to what the typical family wants. The comments of the Commissioners on Uniform State Laws, on this part (Article II, Part I) of the Code, represent a commonly-held philosophy on the subject:

The principal features of Part I of the 1990 revision of the Uniform Probate Code are:

1. The entire estate is given to the surviving spouse, if the decedent leaves no surviving issue, or parents, or if the surviving issue are also issue of the surviving spouse and the surviving spouse has no other issue.

2. Inheritance by collateral relatives is limited to grandparents and those descended from grandparents. This simplifies proof of heirship and eliminates will contests by remote relatives.[3]

3. An heir must survive the decedent for five days in order to take under the statute. This is an extension of the reasoning behind the Uniform Simultaneous Death Act and is similar to provisions found in many wills.

4. Adopted children are treated as children of the adopting parents for all inheritance purposes and cease to be children of natural parents; this reflects modern ["substitution"] policy of recent statutes and court decisions.

5. In an era when inter-vivos gifts are frequently made within the family, it is unrealistic to preserve concepts of advancement developed when such gifts were rare. The statute provides that gifts during lifetime are not advancements unless declared or acknowledged in writing.[4]

While the prescribed patterns may strike some as rules of law which may in some cases defeat intent of a decedent, this is true of every statute of this type. In assessing the changes it must therefore be borne in mind that the decedent may always choose a different rule by executing a will.

The current version of the U.P.C. gives a surviving spouse from $100,000 plus one-half to all of the intestate estate and is, generally, far more generous to spouses than older statutes. In the 1990 comments of the commissioners:

---

3. "Heir" means a person who takes under the intestacy statute. Lawyers use "legatee" or "devisee" for persons who take under a will. (A legacy is a testamentary transfer of personal property; a devise is a testamentary transfer of real property.) If a document that purports to be a will is denied probate, the dead person's property will pass by intestacy. This means that each heir—each person who would take property if the dead person died intestate—has an interest in the validity of the will and standing to argue that the will should be denied probate. The U.P.C. significantly reduces the number of potential contestants in most families.

4. Advancements are transfers, during life, that are taken into account in making intestate distributions. The original theory was that an advancement was like dowry for a daughter or setting up a son in business.

Under the pre–1990 Code, the decedent's surviving spouse received the entire estate only if there were neither surviving descendants nor parents.... Empirical studies support the increase in the surviving spouse's share, reflected in the revisions of this section. The studies have shown that testators in smaller estates (which intestate estates overwhelmingly tend to be) tend to devise their entire estates to their surviving spouses, even when the couple has children.

Now: A short diversion into distribution to descendants, a term used in the forms in this book and defined by reference to the U.P.C.: The 1991 revision of Article II, part 1, adopts a pattern of "per-capita at each generation" distribution and rejects the patterns of per stirpes distribution in some case law, and per-capita by representation distribution, followed in a majority of jurisdictions. For example, in per stirpes distribution, the intestate's estate is divided into shares with one share being created for each surviving child and for each deceased child who left descendants who survive the intestate. Each surviving child receives one share and the share of each deceased child passes to that child's descendants. Per-capita by representation distribution, used in the pre–1991 U.P.C., keys to a system which assures that the first and principal division of the estate will be with reference to a generation which includes one or more living members. The intestate's estate is divided into shares starting with the generation that has at least one living member. Each surviving descendant and each deceased descendant who left surviving issue take an equal share. The deceased descendant's living issue then divide that descendant's share among themselves.

In its per-capita at each generation system, the 1991 U.P.C. sought to remedy unequal shares in a generation:

> The system begins like the per-capita by representation system, with the estate being divided into equal shares starting with the first generation that has at least one living member. Each surviving descendant and each deceased who left surviving issue take an equal share. The next step is where the two systems differ. Here, the remaining shares, if any, do not go directly to the surviving issue of the deceased descendant. Instead, the remaining shares are combined and then redistributed among the surviving issue of the deceased descendant(s). Each surviving issue of a deceased descendant takes an equal share.

Exercise 4.2

Nina, a widow, left an estate of $50,000. She also left three children, two sons-in-law, one daughter-in-law, and five grandchildren:

— Nina's daughter Amelia and her husband had three children: Mary, Kay, and Sam.

— Nina's son Harold and his wife had one child: Vicki.

— Nina's daughter Sarah had one child: John.

4.2.1. If Nina is found to have died without a will, and all of these people survive her for five days, and the jurisdiction has adopted the revised Uniform Probate Code, how much does each of these eleven people get?

4.2.2. Same question but assume that Amelia, Harold, and Sarah died before Nina.

4.2.3. Same question as "4.2.2," but assume that, on facts such as these, the jurisdiction follows a rule of "per capita" distribution.

If the survey of statutes and family situations leaves you insufficiently confused, consider *Dahood v. Frankovich*, 746 P.2d 115 (Montana 1987); *In re Estate of Tjaden*, 402 N.W.2d 288 (Nebraska 1987); Estate of Amundson, 621 N.W.2d 882 (South Dakota 2001); and *Boston Safe Deposit and Trust v. Goodwin*, 795 N.E.2d 581 (Massachusetts 2003).

B. LIMITATIONS

There are limits on property that can be given at death, and on the persons to whom it can be given. The history of Anglo–American wills law is, from one point of view, an evolution from the day when only trinkets and cows could be disposed of at death (1100, say); to an intermediate day when almost anything could be disposed of, but only through the use of esoteric legal devices (1400, say); to the present day, when the limits are few but hard to evade. The basic issues in a survey of modern law on the subject are, first, a consideration of the substantive limitations, and second, a consideration of how far the limitations apply to will substitutes such as deeds, inter-vivos trusts, life-insurance arrangements, and joint ownership. Formal requirements for wills are also, in a sense, limitations; those are considered in the next section.

1. LACK OF CAPACITY; UNDUE INFLUENCE; FRAUD

The person making a will (1) must have the mental acuity to do the job; and (2) must be free of pressures that preclude free choice; and (3) the will must not be the product of fraud. Those three categories of limitation, under common law even where statutes do not impose them, are the classic sources of lawsuits seeking to deny probate to wills. (Defective execution—see the next section—can be added as a fourth.) Evidentiary presumptions often determine the facts, though. Thus:

In *Hays v. Harmon*, 809 N.E.2d 460 (Indiana App. 2004), the trial and appellate courts avoided a finding of lack of testamentary capacity (the traditional way to describe mental acuity in this context) by applying a rebuttable evidentiary presumption that the testator was, as the appellate court put it, *competent*. The three aspects of testamentary capacity are that, at the time the will is signed, the testator knows (1) the extent and value of his property; (2) those who are "the natural objects of his bounty"; and (3) "their deserts, with respect to their treatment of and conduct toward him." (Another way to say the third thing is to say the testator had a rational plan with regard to his property and those he wanted to give it to.) The suit was brought by the testator's son, who sought to defeat a will benefitting charities; the application of the presumption resulted in the will being upheld.

As is often the case where *fraud* is the theory used to attack a will, in *Morfin v. Estate of Martinez*, 831 N.E.2d 791 (Ind. App. 2005), the issue was decided by applying a theory of constructive fraud. The offender was the testator's uncle; the relationship between the two was like that between brothers; this closeness, the judges (trial and appellate) said, created a "fiduciary relationship," and all of that raised a presumption that the uncle's spending the money (life insurance proceeds, estate assets) on himself rather than those who benefitted under the will was close enough to (actual) fraud to justify a remedy (constructive trust) that would require the uncle to give the money back.

In *White v. Regions Bank*, 561 S.E.2d 806 (Georgia 2002), a similar confidential-relationship presumption was applied by the trial judge, who instructed the jury: "If you find a confidential relationship existed and … the [testator] was weakened mentally … you may infer that there was undue influence, but you are not required to do so if the gift is satisfactorily explained." The Georgia Supreme Court corrected the trial judge, who should have said "presume," not "infer," but affirmed anyway because the plaintiff did not prove that the person benefitting from the will was in a position to use his influence to benefit himself. (One could infer, therefore, that it is not enough for a beneficiary to reap benefit if it is not shown that the reapee had power to cause the testator to be unduly influenced. The case is discussed in the April, 2002, *Elder Law Advisory*.)

Undue influence cases also tend to raise evidentiary questions under the hearsay rule and the so-called dead-man's statute. *Lasater v. House*, 841 N.E.2d 553 (Ind. 2006), held that what the testator said at the time of the execution of the will is not admissible to show undue influence but is admissible to show lack of testamentary capacity.

2. SPOUSE PROTECTION

The oldest, most durable, and most pervasive system of limitations on testation is rules that save some of a man's property for his wife. These are, now, for the most part, administered without sexual discrimination, but historically they were a system of protection for widows. A few American states retain some vestige of *dower*, under which a wife owns an "inchoate" interest in her husband's real estate. Common-law dower was a right to a life interest in one third of the real estate the husband owned during the marriage. The dower interest was limited, but, within its limitations, could not be defeated by inter-vivos conveyances after marriage. There were, of course, attempts to defeat it by conveyances shortly before marriage. English lawyers invented devices, such as the conveyance before marriage with retained power to appoint, or conveyances in lieu of dower (jointure), to evade the wife's interests. The dower system was paralleled by a system of *curtesy* for widowers, which was subject to somewhat the same system of protections, but which provided a surviving male spouse a life interest in *all* of his wife's real estate. Some American statutes have modified dower to give the spouses an equal interest, to extend dower rights to personal property, and to recognize and broaden legal devices for defeating dower rights. A majority of states have abolished the system altogether and instead give a surviving spouse a right to claim a full-ownership interest in some portion of the dead spouse's real and personal property; that right cannot be defeated by will but is often defeated by conveyances during life.

The Uniform Probate Code's approach to protection of spouses (1) recognizes that modern forms of ownership extend beyond real estate and include such sophisticated and substantial forms of wealth as life insurance and employment benefits, joint ownership, and interests in trusts; (2) enacts sexual equality (even though the comments occasionally lapse into an assumption that the surviving spouse is always a woman); and, most controversially, (3) when determining the amount that a surviving spouse may claim, considers both conveyances made during life *to* the surviving spouse and conveyances made during the life *away from* the surviving spouse. The Commissioners provide a prelude to all of this radicalism in their comments to Part 2 of Article II of the Code:

> The elective share of the surviving spouse was fundamentally revised in 1990 and was reorganized and clarified in 1993. The main purpose of the revisions is to bring elective-share law into line with the contemporary view of marriage as an economic partnership....

> The general effect of implementing the partnership theory in elective-share law is to increase the entitlement of a surviving spouse in a long-term marriage in cases in which the marital assets were disproportionately titled in the decedent's name; and to decrease or even eliminate the entitlement of a surviving spouse in a long-term marriage in cases in which the marital assets were more or less equally titled or disproportionately titled in the surviving spouse's name. A further general effect is to decrease or even eliminate the entitlement of a surviving spouse in a short-term, later in life marriage in which neither spouse contributed much, if anything, to the acquisition of the other's wealth, except that a special supplemental elective share amount is provided in cases in which the

surviving spouse would otherwise be left without sufficient funds for support.

The Code then, adopting basic principles and some language from the Internal Revenue Code, extends spouse protection beyond the probate estate to kinds of inter-vivos transfers (under § 2–205):

(1) a broad, introductory category of property "owned in substance" by the decedent;

(2) property over which the decedent held a power of appointment;

(3) property in which the decedent held a survivorship joint interest;

(4) property in which the decedent's interest was "payable on death" to a donor;

(5) insurance on the decedent's life, and death benefits payable at his death, if the decedent either owned the insurance or benefit or held a power of appointment over the proceeds of either sort of plan;

(6) property in which the decedent held a right, until death, to possession or income; and

(7) "any transfer of property ... made to or for the benefit of a person other than the decedent's surviving spouse" where the property is more than $10,000.

In summary, then, the 1993 U.P.C. "Elective Share" provisions enable a spouse to elect to take a percentage of a deceased spouse's estate, rather than settling for the amount the deceased spouse's will provides. This election overrides the deceased spouse's intent as expressed in his will:

1. The deceased spouse's estate is not simply his probate estate, but also includes the decedent's *nonprobate assets* (such as life insurance and property owned in joint tenancy with the right of survivorship), and his *nonprobate transfers* both to others and to the surviving spouse. The U.P.C. labels this the "Augmented Estate."

2. The surviving spouse can elect to take a percentage, *based upon the length of time the decedent and spouse were married to each other*, of the Augmented Estate.

3. First, though, assets credited against the elective share are net probate assets which have already passed to the surviving spouse by testate or intestate succession and nonprobate transfers which the decedent made to the surviving spouse. This assures that a windfall is not given to the spouse who has already been over-compensated by the way the couple's marital assets have been titled.

The Code then provides that a spouse's share must be reduced by transfers to the spouse during life and by non-probate transfers such as life insurance and joint tenancy assets at death. The Commissioners originally explained the system as having two purposes:

> (1) to prevent the owner of wealth from making arrangements which transmit his property to others by means other than probate deliberately to defeat the right of the surviving spouse to a share, and (2) to prevent the surviving spouse from electing a share of the probate estate when the spouse has received a fair share of the total wealth of the decedent either during the lifetime of the decedent or at death by life insurance, joint tenancy assets and other non-probate arrangements.

"The purpose of combining estates and non probate transfers of both spouses," the Commissioners said in 1993, "is to implement a partnership or marital-sharing theory. Under that theory, there is a fifty/fifty split of the property acquired by *both* spouses. Hence, the redesigned elective share includes the survivor's net assets in the augmented-estate entity."

Most states provide several other categories of protection for surviving spouses; these include

— exemption of certain property, or certain gross amounts of property, from creditors and legatees of the deceased spouse, under homestead or exemption legislation. Many such statutes also provide protection for the family during the life of the property owner.

— family support during the administration of the property owner's estate, the idea being to make temporary provision for family expenses. For the most part, though, a parent's legal duty to support children does not survive death.

— a separate system of widow's (and widower's) allowances, which, in many states, provide larger amounts of money for support than family-support legislation does. In some states the amount and duration of widow's allowances are broadly within the discretion of the judge who supervises probate administration.

These and similar categories of family protection typically enjoy priority over a deceased property owner's creditors and those to whom she leaves property by will or by intestate succession. They do not extend (except for homestead exemptions in some situations) to transfers made during life.

An entirely separate theory of family protection obtains in the eight community-property states (Texas, Louisiana, New Mexico, California, Arizona, Washington, Idaho, and Nevada), and under marital property legislation in several common-law states (e.g., Wisconsin). (However, the system may be different in theory without being different in operation. Our rules differ from state to state, but our habits and conventions, like our television, are national.) Community property theory disposes of questions about a surviving spouse's share of a property-owner's wealth by making the spouses equal owners from the time property is acquired. Traditionally, "community property is all property acquired during marriage by either spouse, other than that acquired by gift, bequest, devise, or descent, or as damages in a personal injury action. Conversely, property owned by either spouse at the time of marriage or inherited or received by gift by either spouse during marriage, or received as damages in a personal injury action, together with the rents, issues and profits therefrom, is separate property."[5] Community-property states provide a system of intestate succession for each spouse's community and separate property, which system is similar to that in common-law states. Modern revisions in community-property systems move toward equality of the sexes, so that, for examples, both spouses or neither of them have authority to "manage" the entire family wealth, and presumptions as to what is community property and what separate property are applied without regard to the sex of the recipient of property. A similar range of issues arises under marital-property statutes in common-law states, and, in both community-property states and marital-property states, clients are free to characterize property as separate, community (marital), or jointly held.

There has been a significant amount of litigation in the reporters on efforts by property owners to defeat the protections provided by law for their spouses. The Uniform Commissioners were probably right when they predicted that the application of their complex system of "augmented estates" would reduce this litigation. The cases involve, as to dower, ancient authority on transfers made just before marriage, and, as to statutory-share substitutes for dower, transfers made during marriage. Typically the cases turn on some concept of "fraud" on the surviving spouse, but "fraud" in this context has not required that the grantor have an evil heart. It has, in fact, not turned on *any* clear concept that will fit all of the cases. There appear to be three schools of thought:

Intent. The "fraud" question is whether the grantee had some purpose other than defeat of his spouse's interest. If a husband set up a trust to provide for the support of his children, he obviously had an intention—a reasonable intention, as some of the cases say—which was other than "fraud" on his wife. Therefore she cannot reach the children's property with her dower or statutory claim.[6]

Reality. The "fraud" question turns on the form of the transfer. If the

---

5. Forster et al., *Tax, Legal, and Practical Problems Arising From the Way in Which Title to Property is Held by Husband and Wife,* in Eighteenth Annual Tax Institute (Univ. of Southern Calif. 1966), at 35, 45–46.

6. In *Estate of Weitzman*, 724 N.E.2d 1120 (Ind. App. 2000), for example, a case-law intent test was applied to determine that assets in a so-called "living trust" (see Chapter 11) were not subject to the elective share of the settlor's widow. Only "when a testator executes a trust in contemplation of his impending death and does so in order to defeat the surviving spouse's statutory share, [will] the trust will be considered testamentary in nature and ... defeat the spouse's share."

transfer is formally effective, it is not fraudulent. A wife's undelivered, unrecorded deed might be, in this sense, fraudulent; her husband can reach the property covered by the deed. A valid transfer to a valid inter-vivos trust is, in form, operative; he cannot reach it. This "test," characteristic of judges who would leave businesspeople a free hand, is obviously hard for the surviving spouse to meet.

Control. This is the easiest test to meet and is in many ways a case-law analogue to broad protective statutes such as the Uniform Probate Code and modern provisions in New York and Pennsylvania. The leading case on the test is *Newman v. Dore*, 275 N.Y. 371, 9 N.E.2d 966, 112 A.L.R. 643 (1937), which involved a death-bed inter-vivos transfer to an otherwise valid trust. Judge Lehman gave as his (difficult to apply) test whether "judged by the substance, not by the form, the testator's conveyance is illusory, intended only as a mask for the effective retention by the settlor of the property which in form he had conveyed."

There is no parallel system of protection for children—not even for minor children. The typical statutory provisions for support of the family apply only during the period of probate administration (typically up to three years; often much less than that). The Anglo–American system has not adopted a forced share for children; and not even the drafters of the U.P.C. suggest change in the custom. Cultural interest in protecting children from disinheritance shows up in case-law under pretermitted-heir statutes and attacks on wills as invalid. In theory, a classical pretermitted-heir statute provides an intestate share (applicable even though there is a will) for descendants who are born after the property owner makes a will, but only if there is no indication that the will disinherited afterborn descendants on purpose. Some statutes apply even to children born before the will was made, "unless it appears that such omission was intentional." (See, for example, Oklahoma Statutes, Tit. 84, §§ 131–132.) Some few statutes include descendants who were living when the will was made, on the theory, apparently, that the will-maker forgot about them.

Attacks on a will, on the ground that its execution did not meet formal requirements, or that the testator lacked testamentary capacity, or was subject to undue influence from others, or was defrauded, do not turn on specific legal provisions for disinherited children. However, most such lawsuits are subject to trial by jury, and folklore has it that there is a jury-made law of forced inheritance for a will-maker's children. Neither the pretermitted-heir theory nor the jury-made law of forced inheritance is a satisfactory substitute for advertent protection of children, though; most attacks under the oblique case-law theories fail.

There are several miscellaneous restrictions on will making—some of which extend, sometimes, to other forms of conveyance which pass property on death—but they are relatively insignificant:

3. GIFTS TO CHARITY, KILLERS, PHILANDERERS, AND ALIENS

Charity. Restrictions on testamentary gifts to charity take two common forms. One is restriction on the amount of the estate which can be given *to* charity and *away from* certain members of the family; the other is a prohibition on will provisions favoring charity when the will is made shortly before death. Both suggest legislative fears of importunate clergy.[7]

Transfers to persons who kill the decedent: The usual assumption is that a killer should not be permitted to improve his position by the killing. U.P.C. § 2–803 provides that a person who "feloniously and intentionally kills the decedent" may not take under the decedent's will, or, if she died without a will, under intestacy provisions. Property that would have passed to the killer passes as if the killer died before the decedent.

Transfers to a philandering spouse. The old Virginia statute is an example: "If a husband or wife wilfully desert or abandon his or her spouse, and such desertion or abandonment continues until the death of the spouse, the party who deserted the deceased spouse shall be barred of all interest in the estate of the other...."

Transfers to a citizen of another country are sometimes restricted; such restrictions are sometimes limited to enemy aliens, or citizens of countries with Communist governments, and all, probably, are unconstitutional (under either the supremacy clause or the due-process clause of the federal constitution).

C. FORMALITIES

Finally, statutes on wills formalities impose formidable limitations on transfers at death by (1) providing that a document will be recognized as a will only when it satisfies formal requirements, and (2) providing that forms of transfer which are like wills in purpose but not in form are invalid.

A document is said to be "testamentary" when its purpose is to do what a will does—that is, to transfer property at the death of its owner, without the creation of any ownership interest in the grantee until the owner's death, and with a retained ability in the donor to change his mind. If a testamentary document satisfies the requirements of the

---

7. A "Good Steward" mailing distributed in 2006 by Catholic Relief Services suggests that both of these are archaic and abolished in most places. The C.R.S. mailing uses old-fashioned catechism style, and asks *inter alia*, "(True/False) There is no limit on what you can give tax-free to charity, either presently or through your estate at death.... (True/False) A residual bequest gives what- ever is 'leftover' in your estate after all other bequests in a will are satisfied." Answers: "TRUE. Apart from the good it can do, charitable giving is one of the best ways to reduce your taxable estate.... TRUE. It ['residual bequest'] can be an excellent way to remember a charity in your will if you have family and friends you want to take care of first."

statute on execution of wills, it possesses formal validity. In that case, "testamentary" means valid. If the document shows the requisite intent but has not been executed with the requisite formality, it is also said to be "testamentary," which means it is invalid.

Wills statutes require certain elements in the *document,* certain *people,* and certain *acts* by the people. The cases say that a testator also needs testamentary intent to make a will. However, intention is demonstrated in the document, in the presence of the prescribed people, and in the acts of the people. It cannot be demonstrated in any other way (since the holder of the intention has, by hypothesis, gone on to Glory). So that, for the most part, as to formalities, it is probably accurate to say that if document, people, and action requirements are met there is not likely to be an inquiry into intention.

The Uniform Probate Code (§ 2–502) simplified these three formal requirements:

Document: "in writing."

People: "testator … and … at least two individuals."

Acts: "signed by the testator or in the testator's name by some other person in the testator's presence and by his direction, and … signed by at least two persons each of whom witnessed either the signing or the testator's acknowledgment of the signature on the will."

The formal documentary requirement is, as a matter of preventive law, expanded to include recitals in the will of the testator's and the witnesses' actions and intentions; these typically consist of:

1. A statement or a title for the document that says "This is my will."

2. A formal recital of execution (signing), before the testator's signature, something like this: "I now sign this will, in the presence of the witnesses whose names will appear below, and request that they witness my signature and attest to the execution of this will, this ___ day of ___, ___, at ___, ___."

3. A recital before the witnesses' signatures that they have done what the statute and preventive law require, something like this: "Rose Striker, in our presence, signed this document. Before she signed it, she declared to us that it was her will and requested that we act as witnesses to its execution. We now, in her presence and in the presence of each other, sign below as witnesses, all on this ___ day...."

Some lawyers add a statement of the witnesses' observations of the testator's capacity and freedom: "We believe her to be of sound mind, possessing testamentary capacity, and not subject to undue influence, fraud, or coercion."[8]

Most wills statutes are more complex than the Uniform Probate Code, and, because people in America move around and own property in more than one state, most lawyers seek to draft wills, and to conduct execution conferences, in such a way as to satisfy *any* American statute. If that is the object, and ordinary safeguards are observed:

The *document* will be continuous (i.e., nothing significant will stop at the bottom of a page); unaltered; securely fastened together; and it will clearly be a will (e.g., it will say "Will of Rose Striker" at the top of its first page). (*Estate of Snell*, 846 N.E.2d 572 [Ohio App. 2005], is a sort of shotgun will-contest case in which, *inter alia*, the contestant raised the objection that the signatures were on their own, unnumbered page.)

The *people* will all be together and watching when each of them signs the document, and none of the witnesses will have an interest in the testator's property (*i.e.,* not heirs or legatees or anyone closely connected with heirs or legatees). And all witnesses will be competent to testify in court.

The attestation clause (for witnesses, above) will always be in the will, since many of the cases raise a virtually irrebuttable presumption of due execution when that clause appears in the will.

The testator will sign at the end of the dispositive parts of the will (some statutes require signatures to be "subscribed" and some require the testator's signature to be at "the foot or end" of the document). The testator will say aloud that the document is her will and, aloud, will ask the witnesses to observe her signature.

Three witnesses will be used (some states still require three) and the lawyer supervising their actions will make certain that they know what they're doing, that they observe the action closely, and that they understand that they may be asked to testify in court as to what they see and do.

Most states require that the witnesses be disinterested and competent. If a witness stands to gain under the will, or to gain if the will is held invalid, she may be disqualified as a witness; or she may be permitted to testify as a witness but not to receive the property the will gives her. Even where disinterested witnesses are not a statutory requirement, ordinary precaution will argue against using someone who

---

8. The addition of these elements of testamentary capacity (with the addition of legal age) may, by statute, make the will "self proved," which means that it makes a prima facie case of valid execution, all by itself, and can be provisionally admitted to probate without an evidentiary hearing. See, for example, the ending formalities in our will forms in Chapter 9 and Chapter 10. These follow the Indiana wills-execution statute, which was litigated extensively in *Estate of Dellinger*, 793 N.E.2d 1041 (Ind. 2003), reversing the Indiana Court of Appeals; the litigation also drove the Indiana General Assembly to amend the will-execution statute.

is vulnerable to impeachment or whose presence may provoke claims of undue influence. An additional and complex set of issues may arise when the witness is also the lawyer who did the legal work on the will, although many lawyers still witness the wills they draft and some analysis approves of the practice, because, as S. Bien put it, "the drafting attorney … is the ideal attesting witness."

There are many cases about what interest is and what is to be done when a witness is interested. The preventive-law principle is to use witnesses who do not have an interest in the client's property, but, particularly in cases where contest is a possibility, are able to talk about the testator's normal personality and to relate whether he was acting normally when he signed the will. This preventive-law principle argues against using family members or persons employed by organizations (charities or banks) who might be interested in the will. It also argues against using casual witnesses—employees in the lawyer's office, or somebody from across the hall. The ideal witness is a neighbor or friend who is likely to continue living in the community and who has known the testator for some time.

All of this formality is advisable for any will execution. The requirements are extensive enough to suggest that lawyers should not leave will execution to clients, but should conduct the ceremony personally and with some attention to its solemn import. The late Professor Barton Leach recommended that the lawyer close his office door before he starts. We sometimes think the solemn language used to describe and embody the process may require candles. One school of thought has it that the purpose of will-execution requirements is to impress on the testator's mind that his action is a serious one. Another school has it that the technical requirements of the ceremony are the law's protection against perjury and fraud after the testator dies and people begin squabbling over his things. Under either theory, the will-execution conference is a quiet sort of judicial hearing. The signed document is a record of the hearing; it will be offered in court after the testator dies.

Some states allow for a kind of will that is less than the formal will described so far in this section. The burdens of life sometimes require a will that is much more. The lesser will is a *holograph*—a will that is not witnessed but is written entirely in the testator's hand and dated and signed by her. (The California statute, California Probate Code § 6111, and U.P.C., § 2–502, require handwriting only of the "material" provisions and do not require dating.) About half the states recognize holographic wills. Some few also recognize oral (*nuncupative*) wills of minor amounts of property or when made in extreme circumstances, such as on a battlefield.

More formality than is normal in the law office may be necessary. An especially stern, *protective* execution may be necessary when the lawyer has reason to suspect that someone will contest the will—that is, when a relative or legatee under a prior will is likely to be disappointed, or when the testator is weakened, distracted, or under pressure. In these situations, the will execution should be overwhelmingly convincing, so that potential will-contest plaintiffs will be discouraged from filing lawsuits. All will executions should be sound enough to survive contest; the object of a *protective* will execution is to *discourage* contest.

The protective will execution conference takes account of the normal grounds of contest: inadequate formality, lack of capacity, undue influence, and fraud. All formal requirements are carefully met and carefully documented. (Some states provide for "self-proving affidavits" after a will execution; under this practice, the witnesses all recite what happened, immediately after it happened, much as they will in court when the will is offered for probate.) A protective conference might involve a court reporter taking down statements of the witnesses, and where frailty or senility may be an issue, statements of medical people attending the client. Some lawyers now videotape the execution and interviews with witnesses and medical personnel.

The usual object of these precautions is to demonstrate that the client has capacity to make a will, is acting freely, and is not being duped. Capacity means that she understands what she owns, who is in her family ("the natural objects of her bounty," as the old cases put it), and what she wants to do. Freedom means that he is not overborne by someone else. These facts, in a protective execution, can be established by a detailed discussion of the will; by having the client go through the will and talk about it on more than one occasion; and by the advice and opinions of medical personnel at and around the time the will is made.

D. REVOCATION

Wills are ambulatory, which means that the author of a will is able to change her mind and make a new will. When she does change her mind, and acts on her change of mind, she revokes the will. This revocation is accomplished in one of three ways:

1. By an act to the document accompanied by intention to revoke (and intention is usually inferred from the act). The statutes enumerate the range of effective acts. The U.P.C. (§ 2–507) is typical in the range of actions: A will is revoked by "burning, tearing, canceling, obliterating, or destroying" it. The meaning of each such word is, of course, a litigated question; most of the cases require some sort of physical violence. Putting the will in a pile of paper for the Boy Scout paper drive might not be violent enough. The U.P.C. is unusual in recognizing the validity of a revoking act to part of the document; most statutes do not permit revocation by act of a *part* of a will.

2.   By a writing. The writing is usually a new will, which says somewhere near its beginning, "I revoke all other wills." The U.P.C. provides (§ 2–507), "A will or any part thereof is revoked ... by executing a subsequent will which revokes the previous will or part expressly or by inconsistency." The latter phrase ("inconsistency") represents the result under case law in states with older statutes. The U.P.C. does not recognize a testamentary document that has no office except to revoke a prior will; many other statutes recognize a testamentary revocation that is not a new will.

3.   By implication. The law on revocation by implication (or, more honestly, legal rules that revoke a person's will whether facts imply revocation or not) is tangled. Classically, a will was revoked by the marriage of a woman or by the marriage and the fathering of a child by a man. Modern cases and statutes have tended to equalize the sexes, usually by providing for revocation by marriage and, often, for revocation of provisions in favor of a spouse in the case of divorce. There are also cases of revocation by presumption—as, for example, when a dead person's will is not found among her effects and was known to have been in her possession before death. In that situation, some courts have held, the will is presumed revoked. (It does not otherwise make a will ineffective that it cannot be found; it is possible to probate an unexecuted copy of a will, or even to probate a will on oral testimony.) The U.P.C. takes the modern view in providing that divorce (or annulment) revokes provisions in favor of a spouse (§ 2–802). The Code does not revoke a will when a testator marries, but provides instead for a pretermitted share for a spouse when their marriage is contracted after the will is made (§ 2–301).

Statutes are not an entirely dependable guide to state law on implied revocation of wills. Some statutes seem to recognize an evolutionary process that would accommodate divorce, or divorce with marital property settlement, as revoking events; but the courts in such states often hold that the statute bars revocation by implication except in the situations enumerated in the statute. Some statutes expressly preclude any form of implied revocation except one of those specified (as in U.P.C. § 2–508), but even so are sometimes construed to permit forms of revocation by implication which the statute does not enumerate.

A will is said to be ambulatory. This word is said to mean that a will has no effect until the testator dies without doing anything about the will. Revocation is one circumstance, though, in which that generalization is not dependable. Suppose, for example, that a testator made Will A in 1975, giving his farm to his wife. Then he became disaffected with his wife and, in 1985, made a will giving the farm to his son and revoking the 1975 will. Finally, in 1990, he revoked the 1985 will, by tearing it up.

Many statutes provide that a will, once revoked, cannot be *revived*. To adopt that doctrine in the farm example—to hold, that is, that the testator died intestate—gives *some* effect to the revoked 1985 will. It gives it the effect of revoking the 1975 will. Giving no effect to the 1985 will, on the other hand, appears to "revive" the 1975 will. The courts, as you might suppose, have taken both positions; the dominant doctrine now is probably that the 1985 will is given the limited effect of revoking the 1975 will. There are, as a matter of fact, three possible ways to resolve this case; each way has a rationalization to accompany the result:

One school of thought would hold that the tearing did not revoke the 1985 will, which remains in effect, on the theory that the intention to revoke was conditional, and subject to a condition (revival of the 1975 will) which was not met. This is an instance of what is sometimes called the doctrine of dependent relative revocation. It depends on evidence of the testator's intention in 1990.

A *second school* of thought would hold that the 1985 will revoked the 1975 will and that the tearing revoked the 1985 will; the testator died intestate.

A *third school* of thought would hold that the removal by tearing of the 1985 will left it with no effect at all, which means that the 1975 will was never revoked. It could not have been permanently revoked by the execution of an ambulatory will; revocation could occur, by means of the 1985 will, only if the testator had died with the 1985 will in effect.

Under the first doctrine, the second will is probated. Under the second doctrine, neither will is probated. Under the third doctrine the first will is probated. Most courts appear to recognize the first doctrine in proper cases and otherwise follow the second doctrine. Statutes that speak strongly against revival of wills encourage this result.

E.   INCORPORATION AND INDEPENDENT SIGNIFICANCE

If a testator says in his will "I give ten dollars to each of several members of my family, according to a list, which I will make and keep with this will," he seems to seek to make a part of his will a document (the list) which was not executed with testamentary formalities. The list was not even, for all that appears, in existence when the will was made. Some courts have taken the position that such an "extraneous" document can never be part of the will. The reference to the list, in the view of these courts, is entirely ineffective; the relatives get nothing. Others—most of the United States—have taken the position that the list can be part of the will, but only if it is (i) in existence when the will is made, is (ii) clearly identified in the will, and is (iii) there identified *as existing* at the time the will is executed. This latter doctrine is called the doctrine of *incorporation by reference*.

If a testator says in her will, "I give ten dollars to each of the members of my family whose name is recorded in the family Bible kept by my Uncle Ned," she does not, arguably, allude to a list of legatees, although the names of the relatives are in a document: She alludes to a *fact.* The relatives are relatives and their names are in the Bible, or not, according to standards of validation which have nothing to do with the testator's will. What the testator has done, or so a defender of the will might put it, is to refer to a *fact of independent significance;* this is arguably an issue which need not be decided according to the jurisdiction's treatment of incorporation by reference.

The defender might point out that legacies of the contents of a safety deposit box, or of a house, or even of a cookie jar, are valid. He might note that gifts to the members of a club, or to all of the veterans whose names appear on the walls of the courthouse, are valid, even though members and names may be added or dropped after the will is made but before the testator dies. The advocate's effort will be directed to placing the list of relatives within the *fact* doctrine, which is widely accepted by the courts and which—particularly in the matter of changes made after the execution of the will—is more flexible than incorporation by reference. The fact doctrine is probably invoked most often, and most routinely, in cases involving reference to the will of another person, or "pour over" transfers to trusts set up by the testator, or by someone else, during life. (We put it to work in Chapter 10.) The American Law Institute, applying the fact doctrine, has taken the position that such devices do not offend the wills statute, and many states have adopted specific statutes (such as the Uniform Testamentary Additions to Trusts Act; see the Statutory Appendix) to the same effect. U.P.C. § 2–513 cuts through these case-law traditions with a concession to human weakness—in some cases. It establishes the testamentary effectiveness of a list of "items of tangible personal property" in existence at the testator's death, provided the list is signed by the testator and that it describe the items "with reasonable certainty." It does not apply to money. (See the Statutory Appendix.) Indiana added such a provision in 2005: Indiana Code § 29–1–6–6(m). The U.P.C. and Indiana provisions and the Wisconsin Probate Code, § 853.32(2), may include money, depending on how the word "tangible" is construed.

Exercise 4.3

Our client Mr. Knox, a retired widower, has three collections to which he devotes most of his time—all valuable and all precious to him and his two adult children, Angus and Patricia.

Mr. Knox changes his will two or three times a year, always and only as to specific legacies of his collections of stamps, coins, and autographs. Sometimes he gives stamps and autographs to his daughter, coins to Angus, sometimes coins and stamps to Angus and autographs to Patricia. (Etc., etc.)

Can you review ways for Mr. Knox to avoid the expense of a new will every few months? See the "Family Feelings" discussion in Chapter 1.

F. JOINT OWNERSHIP AND WILLS STATUTES

Much of Dr. and Mrs. Kennedy's property is not subject to the will of the first to die or to the probate system. Most of an average married couple's wealth is in joint ownership, life insurance, and benefits under employee retirement plans or under the Social Security system. One of the principal concerns of an "estate planner" is to help a client pull all of her wealth under a single, simple, low-cost plan of disposition—in the Kennedys' case, a plan for the care of their children.

While lawyers think of new probate devices, and work on reform legislation and judicial doctrines to accommodate them, non-lawyers show a steady preference for non-probate transfer. The most common examples are survivorship forms of ownership. Expert advisors tend to tell people not to put their real property into joint tenancy or tenancy by the entirety; judges and legal scholars, almost without exception, wring their hands and shake their heads over joint bank accounts. But surveys indicate that purchasers of residential and family agricultural real estate use joint ownership (that is, survivorship forms of ownership) more often than not, and that most liquid family wealth in the country is held in joint-and-survivor bank accounts or in securities that are held in joint tenancy. The public does not listen very well to its legal advisors. Legal advisors tend as a result to become advocates for the validation of devices they disapprove of. In any event, courts tend to uphold will substitutes and to overlook or explain away the fact that will substitutes often do not satisfy the classic doctrines on what is "testamentary" and what is not.

Joint bank accounts, perhaps because they do not have the common-law history that joint ownership of real estate has, have produced the most problems. The ownership of the donee of a joint bank account is inherently ambiguous. If the intention of the depositor is important, the only document typically involved—a signature card—does nothing to resolve the ambiguity. The account might have been a matter of convenience, in which the donor, an aged grandparent for example, contemplated that the donee, a youthful, helpful, and sprightly grandchild for example, would act as an agent. It might have been a gift, so that the grandparent could avoid ravages of the probate process on a small transfer of funds to his favorite grandchild. In that case, the deposit might have been a present gift, or it might have been a will substitute, in which the gift was not of the amount put in the account, but of whatever amount remained there at the death of the donor. And, finally, it might have contemplated a partnership over the funds—as marital accounts no doubt often do—in which the intended gift is of one half the amount deposited and both parties contemplate that it will all be spent before either of them dies.

Judicial decisions on joint bank accounts—and, to a lesser extent, on jointly-owned securities—are all over the doctrinal map. Some of them are simply pragmatic, the judges saying in effect that since people use such things for donative purposes, as will substitutes, such things must be permitted. The wills statutes, which appear to disapprove of transfers to take effect at death that are not instituted with testamentary formalities, are held not to be an obstacle to this concession to human weakness. Some courts hold that the accounts represent a present gift (*i.e.,* present at the time of deposit), but then are hard put to specify how large the present gift is. If, for example, the present gift is of half the deposit, and the donee cotenant promptly withdraws all of the deposit, can the donor get half of it back?

Many of the cases resolve the situation presented by the facts (a quarrel, after the donor dies, between the donor's executor and the donee cotenant, for example) without consideration of doctrinal difficulties (a specification of the interests created at the time of deposit, for example). Some courts stretch the meaning of statutes designed to protect bankers who pay the deposited amounts to donee cotenants, and hold that the banking act validates the joint account as a will substitute. Some courts have developed strong presumptions of present gift and, then, gradually, held that almost no amount of evidence will be enough to overcome the presumption. Some courts have attempted to treat joint accounts as third-party-beneficiary contracts between the donors and the banks. The U.P.C. (Art. VI, Part 2) specifies rights during life, and rights of creditors and dependents, according to the source of the contribution to the account, and otherwise follows the cases which erect a rebuttable presumption of gift—so that the account is recognized as a will substitute but not as a form of inter-vivos gift transfer. The U.P.C. also protects financial institutions which pay out of the account during life, or after death, according to the form of the account.

Some states (New York, for example) have for some time recognized a similar device, usually called a "Totten Trust," under which a donor depositor sets up a bank account which is in form a trust ("Donor, as trustee for Donee") but is not accompanied by any document or oral transaction that establishes trust terms. The New York courts, in a doctrine similar to that used by other courts when they have recognized joint bank accounts as will substitutes, have held that these trust accounts are not really trusts but operate, as exceptions to the wills statute, to pass property at death. See *In re Totten*, 179 N.Y. 112, 71 N.E. 748 (1904).

In *Estate of Shea*, 848 N.E.2d 185 (Ill. App. 2006), the late Mr. Shea's executor argued with Mr. Shea's neighbor over two joint-tenancy bank accounts, a checking account of $1,000 and a savings account of $30,000. The Appellate Court of Illinois (O'Malley, J.) covered the doctrinal map:

"[W]hen a sole owner of a bank account adds an apparent joint tenant to the account, the law presumes that the original owner intends a gift.... The relevant statute provides that '[w]hen a deposit in any bank or trust company * * * [is] made in the names of 2 or more persons payable to them when the account is opened or thereafter, the deposit or any part thereof * * * may be paid to any one of those persons.' 765 ILCS 1005/2(a) (West 2002). The presumption of a gift arises because [quoting precedent] 'an instrument creating a joint account under the statutes presumably speaks the whole truth.' ... A party challenging the presumption can overcome it only by clear and convincing evidence....

"Illinois authority treats evidence establishing that a joint account was used as a convenience account as overcoming the presumption of a gift.... A convenience account is an account that is nominally a joint account, but is intended to allow the nominal joint tenant to make transactions only as specified by, and on behalf of, the account's creator....

"The typical purpose of such an account is to allow the nominal joint tenant to pay the owner's bills while the true owner is unable to do so. These cases reasonably assume that a person does not intend to give away the funds in the very account he or she relies on to pay bills....

"To expand on this, if the gift of an account is to take effect only on the creator's death, its ownership is different from that for which a joint account agreement provides—the function of a joint account agreement is to *immediately* share ownership. If the owner of an account intends to make a present transfer of a future interest in the account, e.g., the remainder of the account upon the owner's death, that is also something for which an ordinary joint account agreement does not provide...."

A footnote at this point says that the court did not find in Illinois law "any clear recognition of future interests in ordinary tangible or intangible personal property," except when the property is held in trust. "[S]uch an interest." the court said, "is an oddity."

"... We point out that any evidence that decedent intended respondent to own the accounts, but only at decedent's death, helps petitioner meet the first burden, but may weigh against him in meeting the second burden. Such evidence would tend to show that the two had not agreed to a simple joint tenancy, but might weigh for respondent's ultimate entitlement to the accounts." The court, affirming the trial judge, waded bravely though all of these presumptions, on what appears to have been a thin testimonial record, and found for the estate.

A few states (and U.P.C. § 6–203) permit bank accounts that are "payable on death" to the survivor, and an Act of Congress permits certain federal savings bonds to be held in that form. "P.O.D." ownership is not likely to be permitted in the absence of statute; where it is recognized it operates in much the same way as a joint bank account which is treated as a will substitute. The U.P.C. (in Art. VI, Part 2) sets up rules on "P.O.D." accounts that are similar to those it sets up on joint bank accounts.

G.   CHANGE

Suppose a testator says in his simple will: "My prize cow Rose to my children; $10,000 to my brother Henry; and the rest of my estate to my Wife." The testator, having settled on this disposition, feels relief; and the lawyer who drafts the words feels like an artisan. The trouble is that her words are obsolete a minute after she writes her name under them. Rose is, by then, older, may be pregnant, and may be dead; the testator's $10,000 may have been doubled or may have been lost; the "rest of my estate" which the testator had in mind may have dwindled to nothing or have tripled. Change begins to work on a will even before it becomes a will, and often the change is significant. Time aggravates the problem—time and the fact that clients rarely revise their wills as often as lawyers say they should. Advocates and courts have devised concepts and doctrines for dealing with change. The "estate planner's" challenge is to *avoid* the concepts and the doctrines, the advocates and the courts, and to adopt a healthy realism about the client's resolve to review his will.

The changes which are likely can be dealt with under four headings—changes in *people* and changes in *things;* changes that are *individual* (in people or things); and changes that are *collective* (in people or things). One might make a chart to express the four changes, and then insert in the chart some of the concepts and doctrines that drafters should avoid:

	individual	collective
property	ademption —by extinction —by satisfaction exoneration accession	abatement shrinkage
people	lapse	class gifts

1. ADEMPTION

If Rose, the cow, dies, the testator's wife will assert that the legacy of Rose to the children has been *adeemed by extinction*. A gift is adeemed by extinction if the legacy is specific and the property is not in the estate at the time of the testator's death. This means that Rose is simply not there any more and nothing should be given to the children. That doctrine will succeed if the prevailing cases in the jurisdiction recognize the gift of Rose as being specific (of a specific thing), rather than general (of a share of wealth). In all likelihood, this case will be resolved by the children getting nothing.

If the testator retires and decides to give Rose to the children before he dies, the wife will argue that the legacy has been *adeemed by satisfaction* (a doctrine that is similar and is sometimes confused with the doctrine of advancements in intestate succession). The children might argue that they are still entitled to another cow, but, under prevailing doctrines, they will probably argue without success. The case might also be resolved under the doctrine of ademption by extinction, since the estate no longer contains Rose.

2. EXONERATION

If the testator comes on evil days and has to borrow money, for which he uses Rose as collateral, and if he then dies leaving a lien on the cow, the children will argue that the general estate (the testator's money) should be used to pay off the loan. *Exoneration* is the legal doctrine they will use. The wife will argue that the cow passes *cum onere*. Under prevailing doctrine, the wife will prevail if the jurisdiction presumes against exoneration (which word means the discharge out of the general estate of debts secured by a legacy), and will not prevail if the jurisdiction presumes the other way. Circumstances—such as a purchase money mortgage on Rose, the proceeds from which did not benefit the general estate—might alter the case; in the purchase-money situation, exoneration might not be presumed. The common law presumed in favor of exoneration on legacies (devises) of real property, and many states still follow that doctrine. Exoneration of legacies of personal property, such as Rose, whose ancestors contributed the word "chattel" to the language, usually is said to turn on intention.

In *Estate of Mayfield*, an unpublished opinion of the Michigan Court of Appeals (2000 WL 31188765), the will devised the testator's house to the person who had taken care of him for years, and the will directed (as our forms do) that the executor pay "all my just debts." The house carried a mortgage; the legatee and executor disagreed on whether "all my just debts" included paying off the mortgage; the trial judge held it did not, and the Court of Appeals, saying the matter presented a "latent ambiguity," affirmed, relying on a Michigan statute that provides that "a specific devise ... passes subject to any mortgage or other security interest existing on the date of death, without right of exoneration, regardless of a general directive to pay debts." The argument there was whether the statutory exception, wills that provide "a clear indication of a contrary intent," applied. Both the Michigan court and the Supreme Court of Tennessee, in *Estate of Vincent*, 98 S.W.3d 146 (2003), held that an "all my just debts" clause is not such a clear indication (in view no doubt of the common law on exoneration.) The lesson for us office lawyers is that the will needs to provide expressly for what is to be done with mortgages (and with liens on personal property), as our forms do. (See Chapter 9.)

3. ACCESSION

Suppose Rose has a calf. Do the children get the calf? If the legacy of Rose is classified as specific, and the calf is born after the will is made, they probably do. The doctrine of *accession* says the legatee of a specific legacy is entitled to property that has been produced by the legacy. The rules are less clear on accession than they are on ademption and exoneration. (See U.P.C. § 2–605.) If the calf is born after the death of the testator, but before Rose is, as the probate lawyers say, "distributed" to the children, they are entitled to the calf only if the legacy is classified as specific. (See Form 2, Chapter 9, for examples of specific legacies.) General legacies do not carry accession until the day for distribution arrives.

Exercise 4.4

Suppose Mrs. Kennedy wants a minor, special provision in her will, giving her shares of common stock in General Motors to her niece, Bridget Donovan. This stock was an inheritance from Mrs. Kennedy's grandmother (who is Miss Donovan's great-grandmother); it is at present 1,000 shares. Draft that very minor part of Mrs. Kennedy's will, and then test your knowledge, from other sources, of such things as stock splits and stock dividends.

---

4. ABATEMENT

One way abatement becomes an issue is when the general estate (residuary estate) is insufficient to pay debts of the decedent and taxes on the transfers that occur because of his death. The controversy arises—as do all of these change controversies—because the testator's property no longer has a single owner; it has as many owners as there are children, plus two more, the widow and Henry. If the testator lacks enough money at death to both settle his accounts and satisfy all the legacies in his will, which, among all of the testamentary bequests, must bear those costs? Every state has a statute listing the order of abatement. Most of the statutes would use up any property not disposed of by the will first (here there is none); then the widow's "residuary" estate; then cash legacies, such as the $10,000 to Henry; and, finally, Rose, who is a specific legacy to the children.

5. SHRINKAGE

The estate's shrinkage to cover debts and costs, as well as shrinkage that will occur in the testator's property before he dies, often results in a diminution of the residuary estate—the portion of the testator's property which is, here, being given to his principal legatee, his wife. Clients who make wills like this one usually anticipate that most of their property will be given to their residuary legatees. But the law does not follow this anticipation. The law looks first to the residuary legatee when shrinkage occurs. In this case, the children might get their cow, and Henry his $10,000, and the widow get nothing at all.

6. LAPSE

Lapse occurs when the people the testator has in mind are not around when he dies. Henry, for example, may die before the testator dies; in that situation, what is to happen to the $10,000? In the absence of an applicable lapse statute in the jurisdiction (see U.P.C. § 2–603), Henry's family will not be able to claim the money; it will "lapse into the residue," and Henry's sister-in-law will get it. Many jurisdictions have lapse statutes, which are really anti-lapse statutes. A lapse statute saves the deceased beneficiary's legacy and allows it to pass to relatives of the beneficiary, usually the beneficiary's lineal descendants.

If the jurisdiction has a lapse statute, there will, typically, be two questions on the applicability of the statute: (1) Is Henry's relationship with the testator close enough to trigger operation of the statute? (2) Is the relationship between Henry and those who claim his $10,000 close enough to satisfy that statutory requirement? Under most lapse statutes, assuming Henry's son seeks to claim his $10,000, both answers will be yes. Both the relationship between Henry and Henry's son and the relationship between the testator and Henry satisfy the statute.

The gift of the cow to the children presents an historically tangled issue with respect to lapse. Suppose the testator has three children when he makes the will, and that one of them dies leaving a child, before the death of the testator. That would seem, in one view, to present a lapse situation which the statute would cover. However, the common law of class gifts (of which more below) did not treat this as a lapse situation. It reasoned that the use of a group word, by definition, connotes an indefinite number of people. The focus on a group required that the word be applied not as of the time of the will (which would create a lapse), but at the death of the testator, which would not create a lapse. In the example involving Rose, the dead child would not be a member of the group. Some modern lapse statutes reverse this doctrine, and apply the statute to class gifts, but most do not, which leaves the issue for the courts, which have, of course, decided it both ways. (At common law, a gift to someone who died before the will was executed did not lapse into the residue, but passed as intestate property; it was called a void legacy; many modern statutes eliminate the distinction between void and lapsed legacies.)

7.   CLASS GIFTS

The principal collective change in the people contemplated by the testator is this same issue of gifts to a class. Class gifts are often unavoidable in drafting wills for transfers to the next generation, and are sometimes unavoidable in making gifts to collateral relatives. In those situations, a testator's obligations, or her beneficence, runs to individuals because of their membership in groups—her children, her cousins, or her nieces and nephews. Her lawyer therefore uses a general word to describe the legatees; but many lawyers have failed to ask necessary drafting questions—change-oriented questions—about what the group words are to mean. For examples:

Is it necessary to use class gifts at all? If the testator in the Rose example had two children, or in the case of a gift to parents, the answer would seem to be no; "half to my son John, and half to my daughter Mary, or all to the survivor of them, if they or either of them survives me," is, believe it or not, easier for the law to cope with than a gift to "my children," even when there are only two children.

Who are to be the members of the class? In the case of "children," for example, some courts, in an obvious effort to avoid common-law rules on construction of lapse statutes, have held that the word designates indefinite lineal descendants; that is, it includes grandchildren. In almost all cases, "children" is ambiguous as to adopted children and, often, as to illegitimate children. Words such as "issue" or "descendants," left undefined, present even more ambiguity.

When is the class to be determined? In a gift to a spouse for life, and then to children, which is common in modern trust drafting, it is often not clear when the group word ("children") is to be applied. Suppose a child does not survive the testator. Suppose she survives the testator but not the spouse. In cases such as a life estate in someone who is not related to the persons entitled to the remainder, or where the group word (*i.e.,* "issue" or "descendants") is not generationally limited, it is necessary to consider class members born after the death of the life tenant. The cases are numerous and confusing.

In what shares is the gift to be divided? A gift to "descendants," or "issue," or using another word that is construed to connote indefinite succession, is often unclear as to whether a member of the class is to take a share equal to all other shares, or a share of the share his parent would have taken. This is the per-stirpes-or-per-capita problem. We discussed it earlier in this chapter in reference to U.P.C. provisions on inheritance by descendants.

When are the shares to be distributed? Even if it is stated, or decided, when class membership is to be determined, it is often unclear whether distribution is to be postponed beyond that time—as in a gift "to my descendants when they are 21"—and, if distribution is to be postponed, whether a condition of survival, a divesting condition, is imposed.

Exercise 4.5

In the last exercise you were asked to draft a minor part of Mrs. Kennedy's will, giving a sort of modern capitalist heirloom to a niece. You ask Mrs. Kennedy, hoping to get this minor part of the job out of the way quickly, "Who do you want to get the stock if Miss Donovan dies before you do?" She says, "Oh, I hadn't thought of that. She is only 23. Well—her children, I guess." Please review your draft to make sure it includes provision for Mrs. Kennedy's answer.

When the class-gift word is one that implies allusion to the statute on intestate succession—a word such as "heirs" or "next of kin"—a number of additional questions arise. For examples:

Did the testator intend to invoke the statute on intestate succession? Not everybody knows that "heirs" and "next of kin" are statutory words.

If so, which statute did she intend to invoke? In some states, there are separate statutes for real and personal property. Many testators own property in different states, with different schemes of intestate distribution. The statute as it exists when the will is drafted may be changed before the will becomes effective, and then changed again before the class gift is available for distribution.

Are any exclusions intended? In part, this is a question of whether the child or descendant (or even spouse) of a class member is to take that member's share.

When is the statute to be applied? This is similar to the question of class-gift determination when a non-statutory word is used, but it tends to have special meaning when a statutory word is used, since history and judges are accustomed to determining heirs and next of kin at the moment of the ancestor's death, and at no other time.

* * *

All of these questions about changes in the family and in property are answered in good drafting, along with lots of other questions which do not occur because of the passage of time but occur because of the complexities of ownership. For examples: Does the gift of Rose carry with it insurance premiums paid on insurance covering Rose? Does the gift carry insurance payments if Rose is delivered to the legatee with a calf *en ventre sa mere*, or in a barren or an injured condition, or worse? To ask them is usually to answer them, and to draft for them is, for the most part, a matter of saying what the drafter understands the testator to mean.

H. CADAVERS

Folklore and Agatha Christie stories have the family drive or walk back from the cemetery where they buried the patriarch, gather in the living room (parlor), servants standing to the rear, and invite the family lawyer, seated holding 14–inch paper, to read the patriarch's will. It will be in such stories, as it is in modern family life, unfortunate when the will is found to order that the patriarch's remains be cremated and dispersed over the pond—given that the people with the shovels have already finished covering his unburned remains with topsoil. In other words, then and now, wills are poor places for instructions on funeral and burial. (The cadaver is not part of the estate anyway; it belongs to the next of kin and disposal of it may be subject to statutes on such things as "disposition" and organ donation.)

Many clients, before or after legal advice, work out these arrangements (and payment for them) with undertakers and cemeteries while they are able to see to them on their own; in such a case the arrangements should trump instructions in the will or other instructions the family may come up with after the arranger dies. The modern cases seem to involve quarrels in the family, when the decedent has not made arrangements, and an uncomfortable number of them seem to involve cremation:

"Dear Annie,

"Two years ago, my husband passed away very suddenly at the age of 38. While he was in the hospital, his family verbally attacked me regarding where he should be buried. They thought he should be with them, in his hometown, 2,500 miles away from me and our three children.

"I decided to have him cremated and planned to give his parents some of his ashes. Later, however, I thought it would be too confusing for our children, having Daddy in two different states, so ultimately, I kept his ashes with us. I figured I would reconsider sharing his ashes when the children are older.

"My husband's family was so upset, they left before the funeral service without saying goodbye....

"I feel so sad for our children. They not only lost their father, but his whole family, too. They abandoned us when we really needed their support....

"How can I forgive and forget?"

* * *

The trial judge in *Estate of K.A.*, 807 N.E.2d 748 (Ind. App. 2004), divided the ashes of a deceased child between the child's divorced parents, and was upheld, the appellate court noting statutory direction placing "ownership" of the child's body in the child's parents (as next-of-kin), which statute did not say what to do when the parents were divorced and fighting in court over the child's body. It may not be clear, legally, who trumps whom where the decedent has made arrangements for himself or given oral instructions. The child in *K.A.* left oral instructions asking that his ashes be scattered in three directions. Some states—e.g., Washington (Rev. Code of Washington, § 68.50.160 [2006])—have by statute authorized people to direct the disposition of their remains. The Gordon, Thomas firm in Seattle and Tacoma uses a form, under this statute, under which the client indicates a choice between "cremated" and "interred," and protects both the undertaker and crematorium from liability for carrying out instructions.[9]

Payment of the undertaker, the cemetery, and (where applicable) the crematorium is, under the forms used here, both directed by will and required by statute. What the will does is allocate the burden among survivors (legatees). Clients will often tell their lawyers that they have thought of this expense and provided for it with life insurance. (One thinks of the immigrant-community stories in which the life-insurance salesman, can in hand, goes from door to door collecting a quarter a week for "burial insurance.") In such a case, the lawyer needs to make certain that the beneficiary of the life insurance has an obligation to use the insurance money for that purpose; and the client's instructions in that regard should, perhaps, give some idea of what client/insured has in mind (solid gold casket?), along with directions on what is to be done with what, if anything, is left over. In our opinion, a letter from the client/insured to the beneficiary of the life insurance, containing these directions, dated and signed by the client/insured, establishes an express trust. (See Chapter 5.)

I. ETHICAL WILLS

Ethical wills are sometimes mentioned in publications for lawyers and in popular publications such as the bulletin of the American Association of Retired Persons. The idea, a revival of sorts, is (as Friedman and Weinstein put it) that "too many people fail to even consider, much less plan for, the transfer of wisdom, insight, experience, and similarly related intangibles.... The transfer of these intangibles may provide families and friends with a continuity and sense of purpose that traditional wills do not." They mention the will in which Jacob blessed his sons, in the Book of Genesis, and references in the Gospel of John. The tradition, they say, is for such ethical wills to be rendered orally; but the modern style is to do them in writing, or on disks "with all the

---

9. With thanks to my—Shaffer's—daughter-in-law, Sandra Rovai, of the Tacoma Bar.

accompanying bells and whistles (video clips, photography, sound bites, music, etc.)." They say it is permissible to include biographical (autobiographical) information, and recommendations of books and movies. The traditional contents include as well "a statement of values and examples," lessons, hopes, advice, and "expressions of love, gratitude, appreciation, and forgiveness."

In an essay in the A.A.R.P. bulletin, K. Cheney says, "More and more people are recognizing the value of bequeathing loved ones the most precious memories and lessons of a lifetime. 'President Bill Clinton ... recently advised a crowd of booksellers in Chicago, "I really think that anyone who's fortunate enough to live to be 50 years old should take some time, even if it's just a couple of weekends, to sit down and write the story of your life, even if it's only 20 pages, and even if it's only for your children and grandchildren." ' " Ms. Cheney says a "mini-industry is springing up around the modern practice. Professional writers will assist you in penning an ethical will." One can, she says, buy a leather album to bind it in, "with silk lining and acid-free paper.... There are even therapists who specialize in helping you work through any emotional issues involved...."

She quotes Kenneth Wheeler, a lawyer in Winter Park, Florida, who has incorporated the idea into his wills practice. And she recommends recent books on the subject by Dr. Barry Baines and Rabbi Jack Riemer. The formal requirements seem to be minimal (assuming, of course, that the ethical will is not allowed to confuse people, including lawyers and judges, over which is the will and which is the ethical will). But "for the document to have any meaning, what you write has to square with how you live," so that, for example, the experience of writing the document may point to something more than the Great Beyond: Ms. Cheney quotes an artist "who lives half the year in Minneapolis and the other half in La Jolla. After urging her children to pursue their dreams in her ethical will, Sandy Swirnoff realized that she needed to go after her own dream as well. Last May, the mother of two and grandmother of one took a trip to Japan to pursue her interest in textiles and art...."

REFERENCES AND BIBLIOGRAPHY

Standard treatises on wills, trusts, and future interests are, in our opinion, interchangeable. The reader can use whichever of them is available and up to date. Research on Social Security benefits is a special case and one that is usually served by a visit to the local offices of the Social Security Administration. All of the Administration's regulations should be in the Federal Register and the Code of Federal Regulations, but we would not wish the task of searching through those sources on anyone who was kind enough to buy this book. Some other sources:

T. Andersen, "Dellinger: Once Is Enough," Res Gestae, December 2003, p. 24

M. Beckerman, "Points to Ponder for that 'Simple Will,' " 44 Practical Lawyer 43 (1998)

R. Berger, "The When, Where, and 'What's Mine' of Community Property," Trusts and Estates, August 1996, p. 24

S. Bien, "The Connecticut Attorney as Draftsperson and Attesting Witness to a Will: Connecticut Cases and New York Considerations," 5 Connecticut Probate Law Journal 331 (1991)

C. Caldwell, "Comment: Should 'e-wills' be wills: Will advances in technology be recognized for will execution?" 63 University of Pittsburgh Law Review 467 (2002)

P. Champine, "Expertise and Instinct in the Assessment of Testamentary Capacity," 51 Villanova Law Review 25 (2006)

K. Cheney, "Family Matters: Gift of a Lifetime: Increasingly popular, ethical wills are a way to bequeath your values along with your valuables," A.A.R.P. Magazine, September–October, 2004, p. 33

M. Clark, "Keep Your Hands Off My (Dead) Body: A Critique of the Ways in Which the State Disrupts the Personhood Interests of the Deceased and His or Her Kin in Disposing of the Dead and Assigning Identity in Death," 58 Rutgers Law Review 45 (2005)

D. Esmont, "Revocable Living Trusts—Traps and Pratfalls," Res Gestae, April 1993, p. 458

J. Fleming, "Changing Functions of Succession Laws," 26 American Journal of Comparative Law 233 (1978)

J. Friedlin, "Planning: After Writing a Will, You Still Have i's to Dot," The New York Times, January 2, 2005, p. 7

S. Friedman and A. Weinstein, "Reintroducing the Ethical Will: Expanding the Lawyer's Toolbox," American Bar Association, GP/Solo, August 2005

K. Greene, "Pass It On," The Wall Street Journal, March 25, 2002

E. Halbach (ed.), Death, Taxes, and Family Property (1977)

H. Hartog, "Someday All This Will Be Yours: Inheritance, Adoption, and Obligation in Capitalist America," 79 Indiana Law Journal 345 (2004)

K. Higgins, "Essay: Passing It On: The Inheritance, Ownership and Use of Summer Houses," 5 Marquette Elder's Advisor 85 (2003)

S. Jones, "The Demise of Mortmain in the United States," 12 Mississippi College Law Review 407 (1992)

K. Knaplund, "Postmortem Conception and a Father's Last Will," 46 Arizona Law Review 91 (2004)

L. Marsh, Wills, Trusts, and Estates: Practical Applications of the Law (1998)

D. Marson, J. Huthwaite, and K. Hebert, "Testamentary Capacity and Undue Influence in the Elderly: A Jurisprudent Therapy Perspective," 28 Law and Psychology Review 71 (2004)

V. Mikesell, "The Magic Circle: Inclusion of Adopted Children in Testamentary Class Gifts," 31 South Texas Law Review 223 (1990)

A. Newman, "Incorporating the Partnership Theory of Marriage Into Elective–Share Law: The Approximation System of the Uniform Probate Code and the Deferred–Community–Property Alternative," 49 Emory Law Journal 487 (2000)

M. Randolph, 8 Ways to Avoid Probate (2004)

T. Shaffer and R. Redmount, Legal Interviewing and Counseling Cases (1980)

T. Shaffer, Confidential Relationship, Undue Influence, and the Psychology of Transference, 45 Notre Dame Lawyer 197 (1970)

T. Shaffer, Death, Property, and Lawyers (1970)

W. Stoebuck and D. Whitman, The Law of Property (3d ed. 2000)

R. Volkmer, "The Complicated World of the Electing Spouse," 33 Creighton Law Review 121 (1999)

M. Weatherford, "An Ethical Outlook on Attorneys Preparing Wills and Trusts," 23 Journal of the Legal Profession 391 (1999)

Chapter 5

TRUSTS

A. ESTABLISHING TRUSTS

1. KOZIELL

Richard Koziell had a job at the A & P supermarket. One of the fringe benefits of the job was a life-insurance policy which, when he first took the job, he made payable to his wife Katharine. Some time during the last two years of his life, he came in to the store, went to his supervisor, Mr. Paladino, and told Mr. Paladino that he wanted to change the beneficiary designation on the insurance policy from Katharine Koziell to Richard's sister, Jessie Barry. In a lawsuit after Richard's death, Mr. Paladino testified that the conversation that day went like this:

> A: … I talked with Mr. Koziell and he said he didn't want his wife to have the insurance. His sister would take care of his boys in the event of his death.… Just how it was to be gone about, I do not know. All I was told was that in the event of his death, his sister would take care of his two boys.… He did not want his wife to have the money. He wanted to give it to his sister so she, in turn, could take care of the boys.… There was no plan as to how the money was to be given to the boys, but his sister was to take care of the boys is what he told me. That was the reason for the change of beneficiary.
>
> Q: What did he say?
>
> A: That his sister would take care of his two boys by giving them whatever they needed from the insurance.… He did not want his wife to have the insurance money. He wanted his sister to have it. She would take care of his boys.…
>
> Q: His words that he used, in substance?
>
> A: My sister will take care of the boys.

Richard died almost two years later, leaving Katharine, his wife; two minor sons, David and Richard, Jr.; and his sister, Jessie Barry. In a lawsuit over the insurance proceeds, Katharine testified that Jessie told her, at the hospital and again at the funeral, that the proceeds of the life-insurance policy, which Jessie received promptly after Richard's death, belonged to the boys and that she, Jessie, wanted none of the money. But, as it turned out, Jessie did want the money. She got it. Katharine and the boys sued her for it.

The theory of the suit was that the insurance funds were held in a trust—an express, inter-vivos trust, to describe it technically. The trial judge thought that the evidence was not strong enough to establish a trust, even accepting all of Katharine's testimony as to what Jessie said at the hospital and funeral, and Mr. Paladino's testimony as to the change of beneficiary. "There was no testimony whatever," the judge said,

> that Mrs. Barry had entered into any *agreement* of any kind with Mr. Koziell in his lifetime as to the use of the proceeds of his insurance for the benefit of his wife or sons. There was no testimony that Mr. Koziell had stated that his sister would hold the insurance *proceeds in trust* for his children. In fact, Mr. Paladino, who may be considered a disinterested witness, testified that he tried to talk Mr. Koziell out of making the change of beneficiary as it was done, and tried to have him provide for a *trust* for his sons, but without success. There was no proof of any *statement or admission* by Mrs. Barry during the lifetime of Mr. Koziell that she was to *receive* the proceeds of his insurance *for* his wife or children. (Emphasis added.)

The judge appeared to believe that a trust would have required an agreement, or acknowledgment by Mrs. Barry that she understood herself to be a trustee, or the use of the word "trust" by Mr. Koziell, or some combination of these.

Mrs. Koziell and her sons took an appeal from this decision, and prevailed. The appellate court sent the case back for the judge's decision on the credibility of the witnesses—notably as to the statements at the hospital and funeral, which Jessie denied having made—and held that Mr. Paladino's testimony, if taken to be true, was sufficient to establish a trust. "There are many cases dealing with parol trusts of *personalty* in which it has been held that no communication of intention to establish a trust need be made to the trustee.... We [have] also held that a trust can be created without notice to or acceptance by the trustee." (*In re Koziell's Trust*, 412 Pa. 348, 194 A.2d 230, 1963.)

A trust is not like a will. For one thing, a trust is not a document; it is a relationship among three persons—a grantor of property; a grantee who is not entitled to use his property for himself, but must use it for others; and a person who is entitled to the benefit of property to which he does not hold legal title.

For another thing, a trust does not require much formality in its creation; it is not an agreement; it does not even require communication. In *Koziell* neither of the other two parties, the trustee or the beneficiaries, knew about the trust. Such communication as there was was significant only as evidence; Richard's words could have been spoken to anyone, or even spoken to no one, provided there was later some evidence of them. The trust turned on what he intended to do, without regard to form or ritual or the indicia of solemnity that the wills statutes contemplate. And the intention need only have been an intention to impose a duty on Jessie. Richard need not have thought the word "trust." It is not significant that he thought, "This is *not* a trust."

The appellate court noted that this trust was a trust of personal property; that is significant because most states have as part of their statutes of frauds a requirement that trusts of real estate be in writing. But, in most states, a trust of money or any other kind of personal property need not be in writing. A few states have extended the writing requirement to trusts of personal property, but only a few. What seems to be required is that there be property; that it be effectively transferred from the settlor (the person who establishes the trust) to the trustee; that the evidence demonstrate some purpose for the trust; and either that the transferor intend to impose duties—fiduciary duties—on the transferee or that the transferee intend to accept fiduciary duties. Given those requisites, the law will enforce the duties. The property can be transferred by physical delivery, assignment, deed, or will. A promise to transfer property is not enough to establish a trust, unless the promise is for consideration; but once property is transferred, the duty is imposed on gratuitous transfers as well as for-consideration transfers. Trusts do not turn on consideration or bargain. They are a moral charge the law enforces on the grantee of property—a moral charge, particularly, in that the grantee is forbidden to use the property exclusively for her own benefit.

A trust is, in that it has legal effect, like a marriage or a corporation. Except as to legal effect, it is more like a friendship than like either a marriage or a corporation. A trust is, like a friendship, private and interpersonal; no act of the state is involved in its creation. The trust (originally called a "use") had its origin as a device for evading the English rule against wills of real estate; the grantor ("testator," in effect) would transfer to another "for the use of" himself for life and then to a third person ("devisee," in effect). The transfer was treated as an inter-vivos conveyance to the trustee; if the trustee, who held legal title, performed his duty, the evasive device worked as a modern will would work. The use first came to be a legal device when courts of equity began enforcing the trustee's duties. And, since it was in equity that the duties became enforceable, the trust has always had a moralistic cast to it; it has always created a fiduciary duty between trustee and beneficiaries. Professor Scott quoted an 18th Century chancery barrister who said, "The parents of the use were fraud and fear, and the Court of Conscience was its nurse."

It might be said that a trust cannot be a trust unless it involves property, a trustee, a beneficiary, trustee duties, and a purpose. But each of those requirements must be tested against the inherent flexibility and history of the device. To treat them as checklist requirements exaggerates the law. Property is required, but courts have held, as *Koziell* implied, that the thinnest sort of property interest—a fully revocable designation as beneficiary of life insurance on the life of a living person, for example—is enough.

Trust creation requires that the trust have a beneficiary but courts have struggled for centuries to place under trust law gifts for the upkeep of graves, construction of statues, care of dogs, and for charitable objects. Equity has always been willing to supply a trustee, if the grantee of trust property dies or refuses to act. It cannot be said, even in a strict sense, that any particular trustee is necessary. And, although a trust has to have a purpose in order to be a trust (otherwise equity's involvement is frivolous), courts often infer purpose. The Statute of Uses (1535), common law in the U.S., requires that the trustee have duties to perform, but very slight duties will satisfy the requirement; a couple of states have passed legislation or developed case law which overrules the Statute of Uses, in this respect, as to trusts of real estate. It can be said, too, that a trust must have a legal and moral object—for how else can equity be expected to enforce the object?—but modern courts have tended, when faced with a trust that involves illegality or immorality (as, for example, is the case when the beneficiary is required to change his religion or to get a divorce), to remove the illegality and otherwise let the trust take effect.

Most trusts that are created with the help of lawyers are in the form of agreements—a fact that probably misled the trial judge in *Koziell*—but a trust is not an agreement. Trusts can be created by the declaration of the settlor, usually made when she transfers the trust property; or by the declaration of the trustee. The latter form of trust creation was an alternative theory for the creation of the trust in *Koziell,* and probably explains why the appellate court sent the case back to find out if Mrs. Koziell was telling the truth when she said that Mrs. Barry had declared or acknowledged the trust at the hospital and at Richard's funeral.

A transfer of property seems to be a fundamental requirement in trust law. Courts have been fairly stubborn in refusing trust status to a claim when there has been a transfer that is legally insufficient—a habit which probably traces to the historical fact that equity would not decree a conveyance of property. But the forms of valid property transfer are now almost infinite; they include such things as designation of beneficiaries in contracts and assignment of choses in action.

2. NON–ESTATE PLANNING

One of the modern uses of trusts is the care of minor children whose parents die prematurely. This "non-estate planning" usually involves clients who have little property and who consult a lawyer because they are concerned about airplane accidents, fast automobiles, and the orphanhood of their children. The property they propose to have used for child care is usually and principally the proceeds of life insurance (which young clients can buy cheaply) and death benefits under retirement programs. Lawyers serving such clients usually suggest the trust device as a way to manage property for children in a flexible and inexpensive way, and as a way to gather together disparate assets and focus them on a single purpose. The trust can be set up in the clients' wills (Form 3, Chapter 10) or in unfunded, contingent, revocable, inter-vivos, life insurance trusts (Form 4A, Chapter 10):

Unfunded in that ownership of the insurance policy is not transferred to the trustee; the trustee is only made beneficiary of it; the insured person continues to pay insurance premiums.

Contingent in that the trust will come into effect only if both parents die while at least one of the children is a minor or is disabled. If one spouse survives the other, the insurance will be payable, outright, to that spouse. If all of the children are adults, and none of them is disabled, when the second parent dies, the trust will not be needed and whatever transfers there are will be outright to the children.

Revocable in that the clients can change their minds and amend or revoke the trust if they want to. (In some states a trust is not revocable unless the words creating it say so.)

Inter vivos in that it is, in this prototype, a document separate from the will. It is often in form an agreement. The device can be set up in a will, too; when it is an inter-vivos trust, the will is usually a simple document which "pours" probate property into the trust—that is, transfers it to the trustee (Form 4B, Chapter 10). The "pour over" transfer, by will, to a trustee, is sustained under the doctrine of incorporation by reference, or the doctrine of independent legal significance, or under a modern statute such as the Uniform Testamentary Additions to Trusts Act (see the Statutory Appendix).

A life insurance trust in that life insurance proceeds and insurance-like, retirement-plan benefits are usually its principal asset. The trust does draw in other kinds of property, though—probate property through a "pour over" will; and jointly-held property through the will of the surviving cotenant. It draws in life-insurance benefits and retirement-plan death benefits through beneficiary designations on the contracts. The only significant assets which cannot now be drawn into the arrangement are survivor benefits under the Social Security system, which are paid to a "representative payee" and are not subject to the planning choices of the person insured under the program.

3. BENEFICIARIES

Trusts have to have beneficiaries so that there will be someone available to enforce the trustee's duties. The courts have, with fair consistency, held that transfers to vague groups of people fail to meet this requirement. Examples are trusts to benefit "my friends" or "my relatives." The two greatest exceptions to the beneficiary requirement are the charitable trust and the so-called "honorary" trust. As the result of a stormy history on both sides of the Atlantic, trusts for charitable purposes are enforced by the government; the typical official in an American state is the attorney general, although some states now have administrative agencies that are charged with that duty.

An "honorary" trust is a trust for a non-charitable object (1) which is not capricious or otherwise against public policy, (2) which can be performed without violation of the rule against perpetuities, and (3) for which the property transferred is in an appropriate amount. One classic example is probably a "trust" to care for an animal. The modern American rule is that such "trusts" can be enforced indirectly; if the "trustee" is willing to perform the stated purpose, she will be allowed to do so. If she will not perform the stated purpose, the property returns to the settlor or his estate. Some scholars analyze such "trusts" as, in effect, powers of appointment. The donee of the property has a power to perform the stated purpose, but no duty to do so. If she fails to perform the purpose, or appropriates the money or property to herself, she will be forced to give it back. She will not be forced to perform the "trust" purpose, nor will a successor "trustee," because none will be appointed to take her place; the honorary trust is not a trust. The doctrine has been used in cases involving the care of graves, construction of monuments, and even the saying of masses for the repose of a deceased settlor's soul. (The English courts did not regard trusts for masses as charitable; American courts would probably sustain such a trust as charitable rather than as an honorary trust.) If the value of an honorary trust is more than is needed for the purpose, the excess is returned to the settlor or his estate. About half the states now have specific statutory trusts for the care of animals. (See Part "D" of this chapter, *infra*.)

Exercise 5.1

5.1.1.   Suppose Dr. and Mrs. Kennedy have (by way of simplified review of Chapter 3):

(a) life insurance on Mrs. Kennedy's life;

(b) life insurance on Dr. Kennedy's life;

(c) their home, held as tenants by the entirety;

(d) securities and funds in joint-tenancy accounts;

(e) automobiles owned by Dr. Kennedy; and

(f) furniture and jewelry owned by Mrs. Kennedy;

Suppose they establish a revocable, contingent, inter-vivos trust for the care of their children. Suppose, further, that they both die as the result of a traffic accident, although Dr. Kennedy survives Mrs. Kennedy. Please explain how each of these assets is to find its way into the trust (assuming one or more of their children is a minor at Dr. Kennedy's death).

5.1.2. What happens to ownership of each of these assets at the death of Mrs. Kennedy if Dr. Kennedy survives her?

5.1.3. What would have happened to the ownership of each of these assets at the death of Dr. Kennedy if Mrs. Kennedy had survived him?

5.1.4. What happens to the ownership of each of these assets after the deaths of both parents if at that time David has died and all of the other children are adults?

B. TRUSTS AND THE WILLS STATUTE

A document may be characterized as "testamentary" so that it can be given effect as a will. Or it may be characterized as "testamentary" so that it can be found not to satisfy the formality required by the wills statute and then declared ineffective. Trusts that are challenged under the wills statute are usually in the second category and usually involve documents that have not been witnessed or labeled in such a way as to be regarded as wills. If such an attack is successful, the result is that the attempted transfer in trust fails and the trust property is either probate property or belongs beneficially to the purported trustee. The latter result was the trial-court judgment in *Koziell*. The "testamentary attack" is an attack on *validity under statutes on wills*. Consider two cases:

1. FARKAS

Dr. Albert B. Farkas, a Chicago veterinarian, died at the age of 67, intestate. His administrators found in his safe deposit box four mutual-fund stock certificates and four trust instruments. Each of the stock certificates was registered to "Albert B. Farkas, as trustee for Richard J. Williams." The trust instruments were brief, lawyer-drafted documents, each labeled "Declaration of Trust." Each of them stated that the mutual-fund shares were held by Dr. Farkas in trust; each said that Dr. Farkas as trustee was to give himself as a trust beneficiary the dividends from the shares. Each said that Dr. Farkas as settlor retained power to vote the shares, to trade them, and to deal with them as owner. Then, each declaration said, "Upon my death the title to any stock subject hereto and the right to any subsequent payments or distributions shall be vested absolutely in the beneficiary," that is, Mr. Williams. *Both* Dr. Farkas *and* Mr. Williams were beneficiaries. Dr. Farkas was settlor and trustee as well as beneficiary. Each declaration stated that the trust was revoked if Mr. Williams failed to survive Dr. Farkas. Dr. Farkas reserved the right to change each beneficiary and to revoke or amend each trust. Each document provided that the sale of any of the stock was to be considered a revocation of the trust as to that stock.

Dr. Farkas's administrator, concerned primarily, no doubt, about the interests of intestate heirs, decided that the arrangement appeared to be "testamentary"; since none of the declarations of trust was in form or formality a will, that would mean that they failed to create trusts and that Mr. Williams would not get the mutual-fund shares, which would be probate property if the trust failed. The administrator filed a petition for instructions in the probate court. The probate judge found that the trusts were testamentary. The Illinois Appellate Court affirmed. The Supreme Court of Illinois reversed.

The Supreme Court saw two issues—(1) whether the trust created any ownership in Mr. Williams at the time Dr. Farkas declared it; if Mr. Williams had become an owner during Dr. Farkas's life, the transaction was not testamentary, since a testamentary transfer is one that transfers ownership at the death of the transferor; and (2) whether Dr. Farkas retained so much control over the trust assets as to make his disposition of them, for all practical purposes, a testamentary disposition. The source of concern on both issues was the wills statute.

The court held that Dr. Farkas had, at the moment he declared each trust, given up valuable rights of ownership. The court reasoned that those ownership rights had, at that moment, to end up somewhere. It held that they ended up in Mr. Williams. At the moment of declaration, the court said, Dr. Farkas gave up his right to deal with the stock as an absolute owner could deal with it. He had then to obey both the terms of the trust declaration *and* all of the rules and traditions developed over the centuries on the duties of trustees:

"The disposition is not testamentary and the intended trust is valid, even though the interest of the beneficiary is contingent upon the existence of a certain state of facts at the time of the settlor's death." The court invoked a comment to Section 56 of the Restatement of Trusts, which sustained an inter-vivos trust when an owner of property declared that he held it in trust for another. The court's test here is often said to be whether the beneficiary of the trust acquires a "present interest" in trust assets; that would distinguish the trust from a will; *Farkas* is widely cited as authority for that test.

On the control issue, the court reasoned that trust law (*i.e.,* law upholding trusts despite the wills statute) has long held that a trust may be subject to revocation and amendment, and that Dr. Farkas' reserved powers of control would have been, for the most part, implicit in old-fashioned powers to revoke and amend:

It seems that many of those powers which from time to time have been viewed as "additional powers" are already, in a sense, virtually contained within the overriding power of revocation or the power to amend the trust. Consider, for example, the following: (1) the power to consume the principal; (2) the power to sell or mortgage the trust property and appropriate the proceeds; (3) the power to appoint or remove trustees; (4) the power to supervise and direct investments; and (5) the power to otherwise direct and supervise the trustee in the administration of the trust. Actually, any of the above powers could readily be assumed by a settlor with the reserved power of revocation through the simple expedient of revoking the trust, and then, as an absolute owner of the subject matter, doing with the property as he chooses. Even though no actual termination of the trust is effectuated, however, it could hardly be questioned but that the mere existence of this power in the settlor is sufficient to enable his influence to be felt in a practical way in the administration of the trust.

The court added a couple of parting observations. One was an insistence that its view of Dr. Farkas' duties as a trustee was not fanciful:

> Consider what would happen if, without having revoked the trust, Farkas as trustee had given the stock away without receiving any consideration therefor, had pledged the stock improperly for his own personal debt and allowed it to be lost by foreclosure, or had exchanged the stock for another security or other worthless property in such manner as to constitute gross impropriety and gross negligence. In such instances, it would seem in accordance with the terms of these instruments that Williams would have had an enforceable claim against Farkas' estate for whatever damage had been suffered. Contrast this with the rights of a legatee or devisee under the will. The testator could waste the property or do anything with it he wished during his lifetime without incurring any liability to those designated by the will.

The court's second afterthought was a reflection on the policy of the wills statute. The court was not startled by what it had done, it said, because Dr. Farkas went through at least as much trouble, and gave himself as much opportunity for sober reflection, as would have been the case if he had executed a will instead of a trust:

> Historically, the purpose behind the enactment of the statute on wills was the prevention of fraud. The requirement as to witnesses was deemed necessary because a will is ordinarily an expression of the secret wish of the testator, signed out of the presence of all concerned. The possibility of forgery and fraud are ever present in such situations. Here, Farkas executed four separate applications for [the] stock ... in which he directed that the stock be issued in his name as trustee for Williams, and he executed four separate declarations of trust in which he declared he was holding said stock in trust for Williams. The stock certificates in question were issued in his name as trustee for Williams. He thus manifested his intention in a solemn and formal manner.

(*Farkas v. Williams*, 5 Ill.2d 417, 125 N.E.2d 600, 1955.)

Would the *Farkas* rationale apply to a savings-account trust, in which the settlor merely deposits funds in an account denominated "S, in trust for B," but as to which there are no other terms of trust? Arguably, it would not. The savings-account or "Totten" trust does not involve any evidence of a statement of trust duties. The only evidence involved, in the classic example, is a bank signature card which contains printed language, or refers to a statute protecting the bank when it pays the deposited amount to B, after the death of S. The New York courts have worked out the validation of these bank accounts as exceptions to the wills statute—as concessions to human weakness—rather than as in compliance with the statute. The New York rationale—which was picked up by the Restatement of Trusts (§ 58)—avoids discussion of "present interest" or retained control in the settlor; it assumes that the beneficiary receives no present interest, and that the settlor retains as much control as he would have over assets mentioned in his will. The "Totten Trust" under New York doctrine is not a trust; it is a will substitute. The Illinois courts have tended to sustain savings-account trusts under a *Farkas* rationale, though, rather than under the New York rationale, and have left several issues (e.g., can a savings-account trust be revoked by a will?) in doctrinal confusion, if not in doubt.

Exercise 5.2

Fiona Samson, a prosperous corporate manager, died last month leaving a probate estate of $2 million and a will which gives "half of my probate estate to my husband Bernard" and the remaining half to the Museum of Art. Bernard Samson survived Fiona Samson. (If you are a reader of Len Deighton's spy stories, you already know that Bernie is a survivor. We have been required for purposes of legal education to hasten the death of Fiona; there are those who would say she had it coming.)

Fiona Samson also left an inter-vivos trust arrangement. All of the trust property is shares in public companies; the designation on the stock certificates and the language of the trust document are identical (except for names) to the ones Dr. Farkas used. Shares designated as trust property were, at her death, worth $1 million. The income beneficiary, until Mrs. Samson's death, was Mrs. Samson herself; the beneficiary after her death (who was to receive the trust balance outright) was a friend named Bret Rensselaer. Mrs. Samson was trustee.

5.2.1. Assume the highest court in the controlling jurisdiction considered the issue in *Farkas v. Williams,* in a similar case, and ruled the other way: Such a trust is "testamentary" and, unless the document which purports to create it is executed with the formalities required by the Wills Act, the trust is not valid. The Fiona Samson trust was not executed with those statutory formalities and is therefore invalid.

(a) What does Mr. Rensselaer get?

(b) What does Mr. Samson get?

(c) What does the Art Museum get?

5.2.2. Assume *Farkas v. Williams* controls and answer the same three questions.

5.2.3. Assume *Farkas v. Williams* controls and that, under the U.P.C. or similar statutes on claims by surviving spouses, or under case law, Mr. Samson has a claim as surviving spouse (see Chapter 4). In other words, the Fiona Samson trust is vulnerable to Mr. Samson's claim, even though it is a valid trust. He is entitled to "augment" the Fiona Samson probate estate for purposes of his statutory election, which, assume, is one half of the assets that are subject to the election, less other (here, probate) assets that pass to him at his wife's death.

(a) What does Mr. Samson get?

(b) What does the Art Museum get?

(c) What does Mr. Rensselaer get?

2. PAVY

The *Koziell* and *Farkas* cases indicate a relatively relaxed attitude in the courts toward the formalities of trust creation. That is, by and large, the judicial trend; but those two cases may leave the wrong impression: It is still the case that evidence showing a clear intention to do something reasonable may not be enough to overcome the technical requirements of "estate planning" law. Lawyers who work in this field have long known that to be the case with creation of future interests which might violate the rule against perpetuities (the subject of Chapter 7) or with failure to comply with the formal requirements of the tax laws. It has long been true of statutory requirements for will execution, although many modern statutes (such as the U.P.C.) and some cases (such as *Totten*) relax those requirements. Lawyers do not often find such technicality in trust law, but sometimes lawyers and their clients get rude surprises. The Pavy family in Indiana ran into a sad example:

John Pavy, an Indianapolis businessman, decided to change the beneficiary on a $50,000 life-insurance policy from his wife, who was seriously ill, to a trust for his children. The new beneficiary was the People's Bank; Mr. Pavy's letter to the insurance company said that the insurance proceeds were "to be held in trust." He wrote this letter to the insurance company, directing this change—which was all the formality required for the insurance contract—and then, three days later, made a will. The will directed that all of Mr. Pavy's property be paid to the People's Bank and held by the Bank in a trust for Mr. Pavy's wife and children. The Bank was also named executor of Mr. Pavy's estate. Six days after he made the will, John Pavy took his own life; the police found a suicide note in which Mr. Pavy said that a Mr. Johnson, at the Bank, "will have control of all the property and insurance money for the family."

Mr. Pavy left debts of more than $51,000; the value of the property in his probate estate did not total $1,000. The Bank, as executor, asked the probate judge for instructions; the judge ruled that the insurance funds were held in an inter-vivos trust by the Bank. That meant that Pavy's creditors could not reach the $50,000, since proceeds of life insurance payable to a named beneficiary are not subject to creditors.

The creditors were disappointed; they took an appeal. The Indiana Appellate Court reversed the probate judge, holding that the insurance proceeds were part of Pavy's estate, and therefore subject to his creditors. Insurance proceeds are vulnerable to creditors when they are paid to the estate of the insured; that form of payment gives them the same status as other probate assets. The court also held that Mr. Pavy's attempt to create an inter-vivos trust was ineffective, under the rules for establishing trusts. Under those trust rules, the court said, it was not possible to construe together the suicide note, the beneficiary letter to the insurance company, and the will. If the trust provisions in the will were left out of consideration, as the court held they had to be, the note and the letter did not contain enough information to establish a trust: "The purpose of the trust, the subject matter or property impressed with the trust, the objects or the beneficiaries thereof, and the manner in which the trust is to be performed, all ... must be declared if the trust is to be upheld."

The court was being excessively formal, of course. To be consistent it had also to be excessively formal about what happened if there was no trust of the insurance proceeds. The excessive formality chosen was the remedial device called a "resulting trust"—an equitable remedy for returning legal title to property to the settlor or his estate when its owner has attempted, and failed, to place it under trust management. The court completed the theory under which creditors won by allusion to the probate code:

> A resulting trust arose by reason of the decedent's change of the beneficiary from his wife to the bank, as trustee, and the decedent's attempt to create an express inter vivos trust therefore failed. The equitable interest in the insurance policy funds lodged or reverted to the decedent payee since he was living at the time. Upon his death, however, it became a part of his residuary estate ... "chargeable with the expenses of administering the estate, the payment of other claims

and allowances to the widow and family...."

(*Pavy v. Peoples Bank*, 135 Ind.App. 647, 195 N.E.2d 862 (1964).)

Exercise 5.3

If Mr. Pavy had sought your advice on his trust arrangement what would you have advised him to do?

C. SPENDTHRIFT TRUSTS

The common law would not permit a disabling restraint on alienation. One could not, in transferring property to X, effectively add, "but he may not sell it." The limitation was inconsistent with the idea of ownership in X. But American courts, beginning in the late 19th Century, have permitted disabling restraints on the interests of trust beneficiaries. The prevalent example is the "spendthrift" trust, in which property is transferred to a trustee, for the payment of income or principal or both to a beneficiary (A), the settlor of which adds, "but A's attempts to alienate or assign his interest shall not be effective and the beneficiary's interest shall not be available to his creditors." The American rationale has been that the property belonged to the settlor, who was free to do what he wanted with it. The English courts have rejected the idea, and a couple of American courts have followed the English position. These courts reason that the property no longer belongs to the settlor, who is, in the typical case, dead when the issue arises, but belongs to the beneficiary, and no one should be allowed to own something that she cannot assign and that is not available for the payment of her debts.

There are a number of exceptions to the prevailing American rule. For example, although general creditors cannot reach trust interests, the interests usually can be reached for the support of the beneficiary's spouse and children; the state may be able to reach trust interests for reimbursement of welfare benefits provided to the beneficiary or for payment of taxes; and one who provides necessaries for the beneficiary can reach his trust interest. The alienability of a beneficiary's interest is also restricted in *support* trusts and *discretionary* trusts. A support trust does not say that trust interests are inalienable, but has somewhat the same effect by providing that a beneficiary's interest is not a specific share of property but is an interest in being supported. ("To T for the support of X, and then to Y.") That sort of trust has the effect of a spendthrift trust as to any creditor who has not provided support and as to assignments which are not assignments for support. If the trust leaves the determination of what is support to the judgment of the trustee, even creditors or assignees who provide support may be barred from satisfaction of their claims against trust assets, on the theory that the definition of "support" turns on the trustee's discretion.

The American Law Institute took the position that the exceptions on spendthrift-trust creditors extend also to support-trust creditors, so that spouses, children, providers of necessaries, etc., can reach support trust interests. However, a second variant on the spendthrift idea has not been considered to be vulnerable to these special classes of creditors. This is a *discretionary trust* interest, where the beneficiary is not given anything specific—not even anything as specific as "support"—but is only given what the trustee wants to give him ("to T in trust, income and principal to X, as the trustee, in her discretion, determines, remainder to Y"). Even the English courts have upheld the discretionary trust as a device for immunizing trust assets from assignees and creditors of a beneficiary. The reasoning is that a beneficiary of a discretionary trust has no interest to assign or to be levied upon.

Attempts to alienate principal (the interest of Y in the above examples) pose special complexities. For one thing, even in the absence of a restraint on alienation, the principal interests cannot be reached in possession while an income interest in another beneficiary is outstanding. To allow Y, in the support-trust example, above, to alienate the trust property would deprive X of his support interest. That problem is usually resolved by permitting alienation of a remainder interest as such, so that it cannot become possessory in the assignee or creditor until the intermediate interest is satisfied. Another alternative is to put a lien on the trust property, in favor of the remainderman's assignee or creditor, which lien can be foreclosed only after the intermediate interest is discharged. If there is a spendthrift clause applicable to the remainder, most courts in the United States will enforce it, subject to the exceptions noted as to special classes of creditors. But most judges are reluctant to infer a restraint on principal from the imposition of a restraint on preceding income, support, or discretionary interests.

The history of this subject in the courts parallels in an unusual way the personal decision clients have to make about it. The considerations that appeal to clients in deciding how much post-mortem pushing around they want a lawyer to draft for them resemble the considerations that appeal to judges in deciding how much pushing around to allow. The issue is usually put in terms of who *owns* the property. We see three wholly different approaches to the problem, on both levels:

The owner of the property is the settlor. This dogma supports the majority American rule permitting spendthrift trusts; it turns on a *laissez faire* view of property ownership, and it offers a measure of immortality to the propertied. Chapter 1 suggests that the view of middle America is that the acquisition of property, and the motivations and human efforts that go into it, are morally good. Many Americans probably no longer feel that acquisitiveness is of the unqualified value the Puritans thought it was, but even they may feel that property acquisition serves socially useful ends (1) because it can be manipulated to carry out social policy indirectly (tax incentives, for example), and (2) because it can be taxed to finance the welfare state and to accomplish distribution of wealth. The economy of what some (sterner and less pragmatic) believers in private property might call "creeping socialism" therefore makes acquisition socially useful.

A social policy that encourages acquisition takes account of the death of the property owner. One of the motives for property acquisition is that the owner can achieve immortality through his property. Anglo–American law, at least since the Battle of Bosworth Field, has encouraged owners to plan for death through property, subject to loose and highly malleable chronological (generational) limits such as the rule against perpetuities and statutes limiting trust accumulations (see Chapter 7). The principal device for effecting this policy—and the point has a peculiarly American ring to it—is the promise of ownership rights (that is, limited control of property) to people when they are dead. This promise of limited control encourages acquisition and therefore serves both the manipulative objects and the economic objects of a "free enterprise" economy. Decedents were encouraged, for example, to acquire, to give to charity, and to plan for the devolution at death of their property. The results have been stimulation of the economy, funding of useful, nongovernmental, philanthropic ventures, and the financing of governmental ventures. That is why dead people own, and it defines the range of their ownership, which range arguably includes the power to direct spendthrift clauses that stick. Of course, the encouragement of acquisition as a social policy has not advanced social concern as much as it might have, and there are those who would blame it for the failure of the United States to respond more generously to its poor.

The owner of the property is the beneficiary. This is the modern English view and the view of a small minority of American jurisdictions which do not allow disabling restraints on the alienation of equitable interests. Given the minority dogma, *laissez faire* ownership again controls, and the decision-maker reasons that a person (beneficiary) cannot own property which is immune from her creditors, her spouse and children, and the demands of government. This policy tends not to encourage citizens to be acquisitive.

The owner of the property is the beneficiary, but only in terms of his obligations. This is the developing American rationale for spendthrift trusts. It permits restraints on alienation which are seen to have socially deleterious purposes. It implies that the encouragement of acquisition is not a sufficiently useful social purpose in itself. In a sense it rejects the indirect economic avenue to paying for the welfare state. Its dogma is paternal; however, the human objects of its paternalism are not society's children but only the children of the propertied. The paternal answer on spendthrift clauses is evident in modern legislation in several states where, despite a spendthrift clause, the beneficiary's creditors and other claimants can reach amounts of trust income over stated dollar amounts, or amounts needed for priority claims, or amounts not needed to support the beneficiary, or amounts not needed to carry out a defined purpose of the spendthrift trust, and in modern decisions (in most jurisdictions) which permit public authorities, certain classes of creditors, and spouses and children to reach spendthrift trust income (and even principal). These decisions, and, to some extent, these statutes, increase the power (and, one might almost say, the ownership) of the *trustee*, which is a sort of paternalism. It is not clear to us whether this policy seeks validation in the pragmatic goals of acquisition, private philanthropy, and the financing of the welfare state; it is certainly unclear whether the policy will serve any of these ends.

Exercise 5.4

You are in a law firm that uses standardized forms for the usual kinds of "estate planning" trusts—the inter vivos, revocable, contingent, life-insurance trust, for example. As you are working for two young parents one day you notice that your firm's standard form for this sort of trusts contains the following:

No interest of any beneficiary of the trust shall be subject or liable in any manner to or for the beneficiary's anticipation, assignment, sale, pledge, debt, contract, engagement or liability or sequestration under any legal, equitable or other process. The trustee is empowered and directed to disregard and defeat any such anticipation, assignment, sale, pledge or other act or attempt in contravention of this provision by (a) accumulation of income to the extent permitted by law, (b) direct payment for the benefit of the beneficiary, or (c) payments of all or any part of the beneficiary's share of income or principal to his or her spouse or children, all as the trustee, in her discretion, may determine.

5.4.1.   You ask one of the other lawyers in the firm why they make such a provision standard, and this colleague says, "Oh, it never hurts to play it safe. Clients never ask about it anyway." Comment, please.

5.4.2.   Whatever the value of your colleague's opinion on the clause and on whether it should be standard or not, her opinion on whether clients ask about it proves, in the case you are working on, to be wrong. You send a draft of a trust to the clients and ask them to come in and talk about it. They come and the young father puts his finger on this very clause and says, "Can you tell me why that's in there?" Proceed.

The complex American law on spendthrift trusts has implied or provided that a property owner cannot set up a spendthrift trust for himself—a self-settled spendthrift trust, in one descriptive phrase, or, in a modern focus, an *asset protection trust*, "impervious to claims by the settlor's own creditors," in Professor Hirsch's phrase. However, eight states now permit such trusts and place them under a trustee-ownership rationale. Professor Hirsch suggests that the development is explained by the fact that "states are vying for trust business," and discusses the Delaware statute as an example.

D. TRUSTS FOR PETS

Our client is an elderly widow without children or grandchildren. She rents her home, has five thousand dollars in a savings account, lives on retirement Social Security, and devotes much of her time to three cats. She brings her lawyer a newspaper clipping that reports that 500,000 pets are killed each year because their owners have died. She tells her lawyer that she wants her cats to live on and she wants to leave her savings to her cats so that they will live on. Her lawyer, being a compassionate and understanding sort, does not tell her that she cannot leave property to cats (no one to give a receipt to the executor). And he doesn't yet ask, but he will, eventually, who will care for the cats.

The situation seems to call for a trust; 27 states have statutes permitting and limiting trusts for pets, and the Uniform Probate Code now has a section on the subject. So, maybe, what the client wants done can be done (within limits) in a trust, or, if not, something that will probably be called a trust even if it isn't. (Some clients want their pets destroyed; there is ancient authority disapproving of that solution, which is, in any case, distasteful.) The time-honored common-law device, as we pointed out above, is what is called an "honorary trust." It is honorary because it is not really a trust: It is a gift of property to a (human) person, given with a take-it-or-leave-it condition and a gift to another (human) person if the condition is not accepted or met. (By some analyses it is a power of appointment with a condition and gift in default.) If the gift is accepted and the condition is met ("take care of the cats"), the gift is effective; there is doubtless some legal duty in the donee or legatee (or appointee) to take care of the cats. The problem may be who will enforce the duty, since cats lack standing—hence the gift over: The (human) person who will get the property will claim it if the condition is not met. If, some way or other, the failure to take care of the cats is laid in front of a judge, the remedy will probably not be enforcement of a duty, but forfeiture of the gift for failure to meet the condition.

Indirection or statute seems to be the way to carry out this client's wishes, since, at least since the Statute of Uses, equity has insisted that a trust has to have somebody who can enforce it, and cats aren't good enough. (Charitable trusts have been enforceable since the Statute of

Charitable Uses, 1603, through a governmental official, classically the attorney general. A trust to take care of animals in general is probably a charitable trust under modern law, and therefore need not meet the enforcement requirement; but these dispensations are probably not available to protect a trust for three specific cats.)

Honorary trusts are, by the way, subject to the rule against perpetuities, so that one way to call one of them into question is to say that cats cannot be lives in being; "To T in trust to care for my cats until they have all died" won't work, absent either a statute permitting it or a savings clause keyed to designated human lives in being. If one is going to carry out this client's wishes, then, it will be with a "trust" that follows the requirements under one of the new "pet trust" statutes or is a common-law "honorary" trust with a perpetuities clause keyed to designated human lives and is in an amount that does not exceed what is needed for the purpose. (Maryann Mott, writing in the New York Times for May 22, 2005, suggested that the trust appoint both a trustee and a "caregiver"— probably a pet-care business that can be supervised by the trustee. The A.A.R.P. Magazine for July and August 2004 reported the findings and advice of Ms. Peggy Hoyt, a lawyer in Florida, from her recent book "All My Children Wear Fur Coats": Even states that do not have statutes permitting and limiting trusts for pets may still "honor" them [her word]. Ms. Hoyt recommends a phone call "for a free 'estate-planning kit' to the Humane Society of the United States, 202–452–1100.)"

Here are excerpts from the new Indiana statute on trusts for pets (Indiana Code Sec. 30–4–2–18, adopted in 2005):

> A trust may be created to provide for the care of an animal alive during the settlor's lifetime.
>
> A trust authorized by this section terminates ... on the death of the animal ... [or] on the death of the last surviving animal [and] may be enforced by ... a person appointed in the terms of the trust [or] a person appointed by the court.... A person having an interest in the welfare of an animal for whose care the trust is established may request the court to ... appoint a person to enforce the trust; or ... [to] remove a person appointed to enforce the trust....
>
> Property of a trust authorized by this section may be applied only to the trust's intended use, except to the extent the court determines that the value of the trust property exceeds the amount required for the trust's intended use.... Except as provided in the terms of the trust, property not required for the trust's intended use must be distributed to ... the settlor, if the settlor is living [or] the settlor's successors in interest, if the settlor is deceased.

E. TRUSTEE'S POWERS

Executors and guardians hold offices that have a certain inherent quality. Most of their essential powers come from the task given them by the law; an executor (or administrator), whose duty it is to collect a dead person's property, pay the claims against it, and distribute it to the dead person's family, has the powers that accompany his duties. These are largely inherent powers.

Trustees, on the other hand, have no powers that spring automatically from their office, because there is nothing inherent in the trustee's office. Trusts may exist for *any* lawful purpose; every trust is defined and confined by its stated purpose. This is a corollary of the statute which gave birth to the modern trust—the Statute of Uses of 1535—and of the fact that it executed (abolished) trusts that had no purpose. A trust, to exist at all, must have purposes, and those purposes define both the duties of the trustee and her administrative powers. The source of the trustee's power is the peculiar relationship involved, rather than the idea of trust itself; that means that all trustee powers are either *express* or *implied;* there are no inherent trust powers.

Trustee powers come from the verbal exchange that creates the trust relationship—either because that verbal exchange (a trust instrument, for example) grants powers or because the exchange, or the duties it creates, or the powers it gives, imply powers. For instance, a trustee commissioned to operate a business probably has the implied power to borrow money for current operating expenses; the express power to invest, for another instance, implies the power to employ a stock broker; and the duty to support a minor beneficiary implies the power to invade corpus if current income won't pay for the minor's support.

These examples can easily be drawn too far. The law of administrative powers was forged in another time, when, as Professor Fratcher once put it, "the principal purpose of the [trust] was to keep the ancestral land in the family and to preserve it in the condition in which it had been received from the settlor's ancestors." The manifestation of this history is the modern judge who reads the precedents and decides he must be stingy about implying trustee powers. Modern law on implied trustee powers suggests a contradiction: "From one side of his mouth the chancellor admonishes the trustee to manage the trust property as a prudent man would manage his own; from the other side he warns him and all who deal with him that the law in its wisdom will not permit prudent management according to twentieth century standards." The contradiction turns up such specific things as a trustee of a business enterprise whose powers are too limited to permit effective conduct of the business (by, for example, hiring agents to carry out business functions). The trustee may even find a cold shoulder from the court when she repairs to the law for judicial augmentation of her inadequate express and implied powers.

Case law is lagging, something lawyers have known for about half a century. The past five decades have seen a significant amount of interest in catching up, but fifty years is only a moment in the law of property. Some of the interest has been evident in the professional literature on draftsmanship, which recommends exhaustive lists of express fiduciary powers in wills and trust instruments. Some of the interest has tacitly admitted that lawyers are hopeless—or that their secretaries' time has finite limits—and has resorted instead to the legislature to protect clients from inadequate trust-power drafting. The statutory movement has been the concern of the Commissioners on Uniform State Laws and of most of the professional and professorial groups who have worked on powers legislation.

Pressure for statutes on trust administration is also the product of the remarkable growth, since World War II, of professional trust administration, and, even more recently, the interest in using revocable intervivos trusts as will substitutes (see Chapter 11). Corporate trustees now control trillions of dollars; they are prominent, influential, and sophisticated. The Bar has not developed as rapidly; instruments under which professional fiduciaries must act, and lawyers must draft, have not been good enough. Progress in the skills of draftsmanship has not kept pace with progress in the skills of administration.

In England, agitation for a statutory solution on trust powers started sooner and culminated in a comprehensive statute (The Trustee Act) three-quarters of a century ago. Possibly progress came sooner in England because, traditionally, lawyers who litigate there are not the lawyers who draft instruments; litigators and planners are in separate professions. It was less awkward for trial lawyers to raise the question of bad drafting in England than it is for any lawyer to raise it here. When the movement for comprehensive powers statutes started in this country, statutory law on the subject tended to be archaic and directed to a very few, very narrow trustee problems—statutory procedures for the sale of real property in trust, for example, or procedures (largely ignored) for the judicial approval of claim settlement. No single-purpose statute is related to any other, and the statutes are sometimes mutually contradictory.

The National Conference of Commissioners on Uniform State Laws, in 1964, adopted and recommended the Uniform Trustees' Powers Act (U.T.P.A.), which was adopted in seventeen states and influenced enacted and proposed statutes in several others. (See the Statutory Appendix.) In 2000, the Commissioners withdrew the U.T.P.A. and substituted a new, broader Uniform Trust Code (U.T.C.), which has not been widely followed yet but has clearly influenced bit-by-bit amendments.

The U.T.P.A. made three radical changes in the case law of administrative powers. First, it takes a pervasive approach to express powers themselves and grants a wide array of the powers most good lawyers have been putting in their instruments. These powers are applicable to all trusts, unless the instrument expressly denies them. Second, the Act goes beyond express powers in an innovative use of the "prudent man" standard (familiar in the law of trust investment); powers not specified in the statute are present if the act in question is one "a prudent man would perform for the purposes of the trust." (We prefer "prudent person," of course; but the law, in 1964, had not caught up with our preferences.) Third, the Act furnished extraordinary protection for third persons who deal with the trustee:

> With respect to a third person dealing with a trustee or assisting a trustee in the conduct of a transaction, the existence of trust powers and their proper exercise by the trustee may be assumed without inquiry. The third person is not bound to inquire whether the trustee has power to act or is properly exercising the power; and a third person, without actual knowledge that the trustee is exceeding his powers or improperly exercising them, is fully protected in dealing with the trustee as if the trustee possessed and properly exercised the powers he purports to exercise. A third person is not bound to assure the proper application of trust assets paid or delivered to the trustee.

The imposed-powers approach probably will prove most popular with professional trustees, because it offers protection which an inept drafter is not likely to frustrate. The theory seems to be that he will not negate imposed statutory powers because he will not know about the statute.

There are other ways, of some modern popularity, in which the statutory problem might be approached: One alternative is to provide well-drafted and exhaustive powers for incorporation by reference into instruments. Statutes that provide powers for incorporation have been enacted in half a dozen states. The incorporation-by-reference statute is valuable mainly in saving paper and secretaries' time; it is of no value at all to the drafter who does not know it exists, or who knows about it but neglects to refer to it. The trustee has only the statutory powers which the drafter incorporates for him. Even more troublesome is the fact that these statutes have often tended to be *too* exhaustive, so that a drafter who incorporates them indiscriminately creates more problems for his trustee than he solves, especially if the trust happens to be attractive to the Internal Revenue Service. Professor Herman L. Trautman, of Vanderbilt, noted of a Tennessee statute adopted in the early 1960s that it was not the product of professional deliberation; it was "privately sponsored," he said, and teemed with tax difficulties. (Trautman, 17 Vanderbilt Law Review 1027, 1031–33, 1964.) Some proposals attempt to capture the best of both worlds, apparently without the dangers that worried Professor Trautman in Tennessee. They use an imposed-powers format for most powers and an incorporation-by-reference format for a few powers thought to be undesirable for *some* trusts.

A more telling comment on the incorporation-by-reference statute is that it is not necessary to bother the legislature with it. Any local—or state—bar association could provide the same list for incorporation, with the same legal effect, by recording in a public office the best set of trust powers in use in the community. They could even be engraved on stone and mounted on the courthouse lawn. The rules governing incorporation by reference don't require an act of the legislature; they are satisfied if the incorporated document (or stone tablet) is in accessible existence when the draftsman refers to it, and when it is needed by the fiduciary.

Another alternative, used in a couple of states, gives judges power to augment by decree inadequate fiduciary powers. Professor Fratcher notes of that alternative that the courts are slow and expensive, and subject to jurisdictional doubts; the statute is probably not necessary because, even without it, "a trustee is not ordinarily liable for failure to use care and prudence in deciding to enter into a transaction specifically approved by the court."

A fourth alternative is to adopt a vague, general source of powers and leave it to the courts to decide how much reform it contains. That has not been done by *itself,* but Professor Fratcher did prevail on the Uniform Commissioners to add a general provision to the 1964 Act:

> [A] trustee has the power to perform, without court authorization, every act which a prudent man would perform for the purposes of the trust....[1]

It is probably just as well that no state has considered this sort of statute as sufficient; the "prudent man" concept has a good deal of history on the narrow issue of trust investment, but almost none on other aspects of administration. Lawyers would not rely on such a general provision; instruments would be as long as they are now; and litigation would produce no certain answers short of the courts of last resort.

The U.T.P.A. model is probably the most likely source for efficient express-power creation by statute. To say that it is efficient is not, however, to recommend it. There are lawyers who find it too broad, too liberal with respect to trustee control, and even dangerously protective of third persons to the detriment of trust beneficiaries. (See Hallgring, "The Uniform Trustees Powers Act and the Basic Principles of Fiduciary Responsibility," 41 University of Washington Law Review 801, 1964.) Even so, the Act is the best approach to statutory powers, if not the best vehicle for them. Incorporation-by-reference statutes, by contrast, provide too limited a cure; the judicial-power statute is not much help; and the broad, "prudent-man" proposal seems to be too vague to cure anything.

A bar-association or legislative drafting committee might use the 1964 Act's approach to enumerating (and composing) statutory powers, but might decide to avoid the curious "prudent man" standard adopted

---

1. Compare the introduction to 2005 amendments to the Indiana Statute, Indiana Code § 30–4–4–3(a) [2005]: "... a trustee has the power to perform without court authorization ... every act necessary or appropriate for the purposes of the trust...."

there[2] and to delete or narrow the protection given third persons at the expense of the beneficiaries; this would, in effect, merely broaden existing law in most states. It would seem advisable to us to make the new powers statute cover other fiduciaries, especially personal representatives and attorneys-in-fact, and to consider the English provision of 1925 which recognizes the power of a court to relieve a trustee from liability for breaches of trust in good faith. Several powers statutes are closer to the statute we are suggesting than the 1964 Uniform Act is, but the result is a similar *imposition* of powers (subject to contrary provisions in the instrument) rather than *incorporation* of them.

Many existing modern powers statutes (1) do not apply to fiduciaries other than trustees, (2) contain fairly conservative language for the protection of third persons, (3) do not contain either Professor Fratcher's "prudent man" clause, or a provision on judicial relief from breach, and (4) are, unlike the Uniform Act, expressly and exclusively prospective in operation.

Drafting. For purposes of draftsmanship, here are some summary suggestions on fiduciary powers:

If the state has no modern powers statute—and this is the situation in about half of the states today—the lawyer should draft her own adequate set of trustee powers, using for her guide form lists such as the U.T.P.A., and as her ultimate sanction a cautious awareness of the Internal Revenue Code, the specific circumstances of her client, and her own experience with fiduciary administration.

If the state has an imposition-of-powers statute such as the 1964 Uniform Act, the drafter should review it and decide (1) whether the express statutory powers are adequate; and (2) whether they are excessive. If the Uniform Act is enacted, for example, lawyers will probably conclude it has insufficient power for dealing with a sole-proprietorship business, or a going-concern farm, and will draft special powers for those special assets. They may decide that such things as the Act's power to sub-divide real estate, or to ignore the duty to hold property in the name of the trust, are not necessary in a given situation; it may be advisable to strike these express powers from some trust relationships.

If the state has an incorporation-by-reference statute, it is probably useful and economical to use it. But it is almost certainly perilous to use it without critical analysis and the elimination of some of the language typically included in these statutes.

---

2. Compare Sections 12 and 13 of the Uniform Transfers to Minors Act (Statutory Appendix) for a similar approach to the broad statement of fiduciary-powers but, unlike the U.T.P.A., one that stands alone. The key reference in that statute appears to be "authority that unmarried adult owners have over their own property," limited, as in the U.T.P.A., by fiduciary capacity, but without the reference to prudence.

Exercise 5.5

Suppose you are drafting a proposed testamentary life-insurance trust for Dr. and Mrs. Kennedy and have come to the article on trustee powers.

5.5.1.   Assume your jurisdiction has adopted an imposed powers statute (e.g., U.T.P.A., in the Statutory Appendix). Please draft provisions in reference to that statute.

5.5.2.   Assume your jurisdiction has adopted the imposed-powers statute as an incorporation-by-reference statute; draft in reference to that imaginary incorporation-by-reference statute.

5.5.3.   Assume your law firm's form provides the executor powers in Form 1, Chapter 9. Instruct your secretary on adapting that form to your draft of the Kennedy Trust.

In earlier editions, we included the U.T.P.A. in our Statutory Appendix, and we continue the practice in this fifth edition, even though the Commissioners have replaced it and substituted the Uniform Trust Code, because the U.T.P.A. is more likely than the U.T.C. to be included or reflected in statutes that are in effect, not merely proposed. In practice, and in the trust forms we propose, the lawyer who is invoking an imposed powers statute will be looking at a statute that is in effect (not a proposed uniform statute) and will add to and reduce those powers according to the needs of her clients. We believe the U.T.P.A. is a more realistic suggestion of what will be in front of the lawyer in that situation.

F.   THE TRUSTEE'S OFFICE

1.   GENERAL IDEA

A trustee holds a fiduciary office; this is a role and an idea that do not yield entirely to categorical definition. If categories are used to describe the fiduciary anyway, it is useful to talk about the duties of loyalty and competence, a trustee's personal responsibility for the administration of the trust (her duty not to delegate), and her role as a representative of the settlor. But those categories do not explain the fiduciary idea itself, and no number of categorical ideas can explain it. For that, one needs more fundamental sources:

"Dear Ann Landers:

"From now on my motto is: Be a stinker. Let someone else be 'Miss Nice Guy.' Here's what happened:

"A gal in our office was being married. We were all invited to the wedding. There are 38 employees here. We decided to buy one important gift instead of 38 insignificant ones. I volunteered to collect the money and select the gift. It was quite a job, considering I had to drive 100 miles to get exactly what I wanted.

"Well, the gift was too large to lug, so I had it mailed to her. Unfortunately, I did not insure it.

"The gift was lost in transit. Now everyone is furious with me. They think I ought to replace it out of my own pocket. I don't have $380 to throw around. Do you feel I should bow to the pressure or should I ignore the insults and refuse to handle office collections in the future?—Abused.

"Dear Ab: I doubt that you'll be asked to handle anything in the future. A person who would send a $380 gift in the mail, uninsured (and other people's money yet!), is extremely irresponsible.

"Yes, I believe you owe it to them to replace the gift."

Ann Landers gives modern cultural context to the fiduciary idea. She, like a judge in the court of equity, pronounces both liability and moral outrage. Liability and moralism go together in the law on fiduciaries.

One who proposes to study fiduciaries in the law has also, as Justice Holmes would have insisted, to look at the historical dimensions of fiduciary responsibility in the law of trusts; an exploration of the development of American rules on trust investment does that. One can see there the old picture of a trustee as a certain kind of person—an upright, circumspect, cautious Boston businessman. One can see a picture, too, of the typical trust asset in that economy, and in the Southern economy, where wealth was land. (From those pictures of trust assets came the idea of the trust as a corpus, a thing, that needs to be preserved. The idea of the trust as a thing is under considerable pressure in modern trust law, where distinctions between wealth and what wealth produces seem often to be artificial.)

Fiduciaries include agents, coadventurers, attorneys-in-fact under powers of attorney, and personal representatives in probate estates, as well as trustees. The word is used here in reference to trustees. The law of fiduciaries in probate administration is, of course, similar in many respects; but it is also narrower, because the personal representative has a well-defined, inherent set of duties—collect the assets of the estate, pay charges on them, and distribute the remainder. A trustee's duties are defined by the purposes of the trust in the light of fiduciary principles, and therefore vary more widely and require more frequent consideration of general principles.

Fiduciaries are always, in one way or another, supervised. Sometimes trustee supervision is imposed in a routine way; more often it is provided when a beneficiary seeks supervision from a judge. Supervision of trustees has been one of the principal categories of jurisdiction in the courts of equity since the chancellor first began enforcing trusts in the late Middle Ages. The fiduciary office, maybe because it is rooted in equity, tends to aspire beyond itself. "Not for him," Judge Cardozo said, "the morals of the marketplace." It always retains a certain local character—hence the value of Professor Friedman's analysis of Boston trusts, New York trusts, and Southern trusts. And, from an "estate planner's" point of view, there is often a choice of whether to invoke for one's client the full array of fiduciary supervision, as, for example, in a trust, or to use some more limited form of property management—a guardianship, for example, a power of attorney, or a custodianship under the Transfers to Minors Act. (See the Statutory Appendix.) Considerations of availability, level of supervision, cost, flexibility, and ease of administration, and the indirect costs of fiduciary management, bear on the choice a lawyer recommends when property needs to be subjected to management by a fiduciary.

2. LOYALTY

The fiduciary idea implies that a trustee think only of the beneficiary, that she not use her fiduciary power as a means of profit or advancement for herself. There is occasionally a case where a fiduciary appears to have used her power for her own benefit, or for her friends. The issue in such a case is whether the court has accurately read the facts. There is not much argument about the propriety of a court's using all of its power to punish wrongdoers. Still, few loyalty cases are clear cut. The most interesting ones involve the fiduciary's gaining profit for himself but also obtaining maximum benefit for his beneficiaries; or a conflict in fiduciary duties; or conflicts which the settlor—not the trustee—created. A 1948 opinion of the Surrogate in New York County is an interesting example of some of the principal doctrines on the duty of loyalty, doctrines which apply in all of these categories of loyalty cases:

Mr. James left $30 million, a fifth of it to his relatives and four-fifths to a foundation for charitable purposes. A single group of business associates, friends, and lawyers acted as executors of his will and trustees of the foundation. Several of them were directors of corporate businesses in which the estate held stock. Their error, as it turned out, was that they assumed they could decide among themselves how to resolve the inevitable conflicts among the foundation, relatives who had been given some $6 million, and the business enterprises in which they and Mr. James had been associated.

Two serious issues came up which involved the investors, charities, and James relatives who looked to this group of fiduciaries for management. One issue involved the valuation of estate assets; the other involved allocation of the burden of death taxes. The corporate, estate, and trust fiduciaries had a meeting on these issues and decided how to resolve them. Their agreement was arguably fair; members of the James family, for example, suffered disadvantage in valuation and allocation, but gained the advantage of prompt distribution of estate assets, in cash. Some of the control-group members—those who were acting, among other offices, as executors—agreed to the arrangement, on behalf of the estate (i.e., on behalf of the relatives); but they took the additional step of writing to each of the members of the family to seek individual approval (ratification) of the agreement. In a letter to each relative, the executors gave a sketchy explanation of the arrangement, stated that, in the opinion of the executors, the arrangement was to the advantage of the family, and gave it as their legal opinion that the tax allocation was the one mandated by the will and by the law of New York. Neither the will nor the law of New York were clear on these points of law. Three-fifths of the relatives then filed what were styled as "releases," agreeing to the arrangement. Later, and after learning more, relatives filed a petition in the Surrogate's Court, to set aside the "releases" and to prevail upon the Surrogate to review the entire arrangement. Their petition was granted.

The Surrogate noted first that, when fiduciary duties are in conflict with the *individual interests of a fiduciary*, which they were here, the appropriate judge of the propriety of what the fiduciary does is the court: "The courts of this State have consistently invoked the rule that agreements between a fiduciary and a beneficiary are looked upon with suspicion and where the fiduciary makes a bargain with or receives a benefit from the other, the transaction is scrutinized with the most extreme vigilance and will not be upheld unless the beneficiary has been given full knowledge of his rights and of all of the material facts and circumstances."

Second, the court said, *agreements to fiduciary action* are not valid—not even as to adult beneficiaries—when the beneficiary has not been given full information and honest advice (quoting a precedent case):

> To establish a ratification by a *cestui que trust* [beneficiary], the fact must not only be clearly proved, but it must be shown that the ratification was made with a full knowledge of all the material particulars and circumstances, and also in a case like the present that the *cestui que trust* was fully apprised of the effect of the acts ratified, and of his or her legal rights in the matter. Confirmation and ratification imply to legal minds knowledge of a defect in the act to be confirmed, and of the right to reject or ratify it. The *cestui que trust* must therefore not only have been acquainted with the facts, but apprised of the law, on how these facts would be dealt with by a court of equity. All that is implied in the act of ratification, when set up in equity by a trustee against his *cestui que trust, must be proved, and will not be assumed.* The maxim "ignorantia legis excusat neminem," cannot be invoked in such a case. The *cestui que trust* must be shown to have been apprised of his legal rights.

Third, where *a fiduciary serves two masters*—where there is a conflict of fiduciary duty, as there was here among the foundation, the corporations, and the family—the fiduciary is safe only if he lays the matter before a judge:

> Even when there is merely the usual relationship between a fiduciary and the beneficiaries, the fiduciary is under a duty of absolute loyalty to *all* beneficiaries and of fairness and impartiality to *all*. If in dealing with the respective beneficiaries their interests are so conflicting that the fiduciary cannot deal fairly with respect to them, he cannot properly act without applying to the court for instructions. … Where an executor or a trustee acts merely as a bystander while two beneficiaries attempt to adjust as between themselves matters which are in dispute and the fiduciary joins them in an agreement merely to carry out the terms of the settlement, the fiduciary may not be called upon to aid or advise either disputant. But where he affirmatively undertakes to deal with one beneficiary for the benefit and profit of another he cannot be unmindful of his duty of loyalty to all beneficiaries and of his duty to effectuate the terms of his trust. Both beneficiaries are entitled to expect impartiality and even handed justice from the fiduciary.

Finally, where there is *a possibility that a trustee will profit* himself if he acts one way, and not profit himself if he acts another way, the fiduciary is probably safe only if he rules against himself (paraphrasing Scott's treatise on trusts):

> A trustee occupies a position in which the courts have fixed a very high and very strict standard for his conduct whenever his personal interest comes or may come into conflict with his duty to the beneficiaries. As long as he is not acting in his own interest the standard fixed for his behavior is only that of a reasonable degree of care and skill and caution. When, however, the trustee acts in his own interest in connection with the performance of his duties as trustee, the standard of behavior becomes more rigorous. In such a case his interest must yield to that of the beneficiaries. Where he deals directly with the beneficiaries, the transaction may stand, but only if the trustee makes full disclosure and takes no advantage of his position and the transaction is in all respects fair and reasonable.

(*In re James' Estate*, 86 N.Y.S.2d 78, 1948).

Exercise 5.6

The interview in Chapter 3 indicates that Dr. and Mrs. Kennedy are thinking primarily of Dr. Kennedy's sisters and their husbands as fiduciaries for their children. As it turns out (see Chapter 10), the choices are somewhat other than indicated in Chapter 3; no doubt that is the product of continuing discussions among the Kennedys and their lawyer, and between themselves. The decision is a delicate one, and there are indications in the interview that the clients were not then entirely in agreement on it. In any event, they are no doubt relieved to have the matter settled, *but:* For all their care, they have probably not thought of the various fiduciary offices involved as separate from one another, as the surrogate in *James* thought of them. These "roles" are now performed by the clients themselves, but death will separate and define them into at least five different jobs:

(a) *executor.* Since the Kennedys apparently want their property transferred to the survivor of them, at the death of the first to die, the executor that is of concern with regard to provision for the children is the executor appointed under the will of the survivor. Assume that will be Dr. Kennedy's executor. In Form 4B, Chapter 10, he appoints his sister Deborah to be executor, and a bank if Deborah refuses or cannot take the job.

(b) *guardian.* Minor children and, perhaps, David, the Kennedys' handicapped son, even if he is of age, will require guardians to act for them and to manage whatever property they own outside the trust. Dr. Kennedy's will (Form 4B, Chapter 10) nominates his sister Roberta to be guardian, and their trust (Form 4B, Chapter 10) names Roberta to be trustee. One of the duties of the guardian will be to approve accountings made to the children (the beneficiaries of the trust) by the trustee and to initiate action for breach of trust, against the trustee, if that is necessary. How does the *James* court indicate a person in Aunt Roberta's position is supposed to handle both jobs? (Our experience and observation—lest you think you are being set up—is that it is not unusual for clients such as the Kennedys to make the same person trustee and guardian.)

(c) *trustee.* Aunt Roberta, as trustee, will receive assets from Aunt Deborah, as executor, from the estate of the surviving parent, and she may receive life-insurance and retirement-plan funds directly from insurers and plan administrators.

(d) *parent.*	Aunt Roberta and her husband have three daughters, ages five, seven, and 13. They may have more children, and they will have grandchildren some day.
(e) *surrogate parent.*	If the Kennedy children were to be orphaned this afternoon, Aunt Roberta and her husband would find they had a family of nine—four sons and three daughters, ranging in age from 22 down to five, and one of their sons would be handicapped. The possibilities for having grandchildren have been more than doubled.
(f) *representative parent.*	One way or another, one or more of the Kennedy children may be eligible for disability or survivor benefits on the Social Security account of one of his parents or under the federal Supplemental Security Income program. In some cases the benefits will be paid to his parent; in others to the child; and in still others to a representative payee appointed by the Social Security Administration (usually on the payee's application to the local S.S.A. office). The representative payee is a fiduciary governed only under loosely enforced federal regulations.

Dr. and Mrs. Kennedy no doubt trust Aunt Roberta and her husband not to take for themselves what has been provided for the Kennedy children. That is not an issue. What is an issue—and one the clients may not appreciate—is possible conflicts in fiduciary duties: Roberta, for example, would have five of these six fiduciary offices, as things stand, and she could have all six (and that doesn't count being an aunt); the defendants in *James* had three.

5.6.1. What advice do you feel it necessary to give Dr. and Mrs. Kennedy about conflicts in fiduciary duties? Notice, please, that there are two phases to this professional agenda: (i) What do you imagine as possible difficulty? And (ii) What do you feel you have to mention to your clients?

5.6.2. What devices would accommodate what our clients want and at the same time protect against the breaches that were at issue in *James?*

3. PERSONAL RESPONSIBILITY

The general and ancient rule was that a trustee was not allowed to delegate his duties; that rule developed before the days when competence in the world had been divided up among experts, by experts. The more accurate modern statement is probably that a trustee is not permitted to delegate functions he can reasonably be expected to perform himself. A bank trust department probably cannot delegate the selection of investments, for example, or the preparation of tax returns.

If a trustee delegates improperly, the delegation itself is a breach of trust, and breaches of trust lead to surcharges for losses, removal from office, and sometimes even more punitive sanctions. If, for example, a trustee slavishly follows the recommendation of a beneficiary on investments, he has breached the trust and is accountable for any losses incurred as a result of the investment policy, whether or not the investments, in themselves, would have been proper if the trustee had chosen them himself.

When a trustee does delegate, she has a duty to choose her agents with care. "Care" in most trust-administration contexts means that she choose with information and with the caution befitting one who is handling the property of another. It also means that she proceed with skill; minimum levels of skill imposed on a trustee vary with who the trustee is. Every trustee is subject to a certain, minimum "prudent-person" level of skill; those who possess more skill (experts in banks, for example) are held to the level of skill they possess. And those who advertise expertise are held to the level of skill reasonably implied by their advertising.

Having made a proper delegation, and having chosen an agent with appropriate skill, a trustee remains, broadly, responsible for what the agent does. There are, of course, limits. One limit is a sort of "scope of employment" consideration. A trustee who carefully chooses, informs, and supervises an electrician to re-wire a house owned by a trust may not be responsible for the "expert mistakes" made by the electrician in carrying out his assignment. A theory of surcharge that turns on a trustee's failure to supervise an agent properly, or to choose him carefully, cautiously, and with skill, will likely be more successful than a theory that attempts to fasten responsibility on a trustee for every act of the trustee's agent.

An interesting modern example of the delegation principle is investment by trustees in shares of mutual-fund companies. The characteristic case is one in which a trustee has purchased shares in an investment company (or investment trust) and has lost money on them. The beneficiaries attempt to recover losses from the trustee, not only on the theory that the investment was a bad choice under investment rules, but also on the theory that the investment was an improper delegation, since officers of the investment company choose the securities the investment company holds and that the trust, in effect, buys when it buys investment-company shares. For the most part, courts and legislatures that have considered the question have held the delegation proper, on the general theory that an investment company buying securities is not unlike Standard Oil buying oil wells or General Electric buying a book-publishing enterprise. The investment company is treated, generally, as an entity, rather than as a conduit. Some of the opinions and commentaries have suggested that the investment-company shares are a proper investment for a lay person who is asked to be a trustee, but not for a professional trust company which, theoretically, has as much expertise at choosing securities as an investment company does.

4.   THE REPRESENTATIVE OF THE SETTLOR

Professor Scott, searching for a general principle to govern exercises of trustee discretion, said that a trustee should act in the state of mind which the settlor contemplated when he set up the trust. That general principle points to a human fact about trustees and to a source of tension in the development of trust-administration law. The human fact is that a trustee is usually seen as a surrogate for the settlor; professional trustees usually sell their services to settlors by an implied or explicit promise that they will represent the settlor after he has turned his possessions over to them. The idea was illustrated, years ago, by the advertisement in *Trusts and Estates* magazine in which a dapper playboy says to a bank trust officer, "But Daddy would have wanted me to have a Rolls Royce."

The source of tension is the oldest and most general question in trust law: Who owns the trust assets? In one view (illustrated by the dominant American rule on spendthrift clauses) the settlor, who is, typically, long dead, owns the trust property and the trustee acts to vindicate her ownership interests; this is the view cherished and exploited by professional trustees. In another, and, in some contexts, inevitable view, the beneficiary owns the trust property. If there is no spendthrift clause in the trust instrument, the beneficiary can assign his interests and his creditors can execute on them. When the trustee misbehaves, it is the beneficiary who is plaintiff in calling him to book, and it is the beneficiary's property interest that is then being vindicated.

In a third view, sometimes illustrated by the position professional trustees and courts take on administration questions, the trustee owns the trust property. Trustees do, of course, hold legal title to the trust property; but that is a legal fiction adhered to early in trust law in order to resolve questions of ownership adjudicated in the law courts. The modern cases that treat trustees as owners go beyond legal fiction; they almost suggest that a trustee has the power to be capricious. A focus for this tension, and for discussion about it, is the routine trustee power to compromise claims advanced against or on behalf of the trust:

It was not at all clear at common law that trustees had power to compromise claims; the early cases required a trustee to list claims against third persons at their full value and to account for them fully when the trust was terminated; she was not allowed to collect less than the amount "due" or to pay any amount which was disputable but not resolved by the courts. That was, of course, a wasteful rule, and alert drafters soon began to give trustees express power to compromise—something like this: "My trustee shall have the power to pay, compromise, adjust, settle, compound, renew, or abandon claims held by her and claims asserted against her, on whatever terms she deems advisable, without prior court authority." Modern statutes on fiduciary powers (such as the Uniform Trustees Powers Act) typically impose the power on any trust that does not expressly deny it; modern incorporation-by-reference statutes contain a power to compromise that draftsmen can incorporate without writing it out.

If, through one of these means, a trustee has power to compromise, what ability does a beneficiary have to complain about or enjoin a compromise the beneficiary does not favor? It might be interesting to look at that question, for a moment, as an example of the tension created by a trustee's duty to be a surrogate for the settlor: A trustee has a duty to act "in that state of mind in which it was contemplated by the settlor that he should act." The formula has been invoked often enough in courts of last resort that it can now be considered more than simply a scholarly conclusion. It is one of Professor Scott's monumental contributions to the law of trusts. And it obtains whether the instrument vests discretion in limited terms or in absolute terms.

But, any discussion of the discretion afforded fiduciaries should make a preliminary distinction between *dispositive discretion* and *administrative discretion,* between discretion to allocate distributions among beneficiaries and discretion in managing trust property. When discussion centers on *dispositive discretion,* there is no doubt that courts review the use of fiduciary judgment, and that they do it, of course, at the behest of beneficiaries. This is a necessary corollary of the adoption of the American trust-termination rule: Trusts on this side of the Atlantic are not subject to termination at the behest of adult beneficiaries; they may not be terminated as long as a "material purpose" of the trust remains to be accomplished. Beneficiaries in the United States have therefore lost the most potent leverage British beneficiaries have over the conduct of the trustee—the threat to terminate the trust. Trusts in this country are in a much more immediate sense subject to the dead hand of the settlor. (It is, usually, dead.)

The cases in which the Scott formula has been invoked, and in which fiduciaries have been forced to act against their own discretionary decisions, are *dispositive discretion* cases. They involve things like invasion of principal and discretionary allocation of income. They do not involve decisions on investment, or decisions on sales or mortgages of trust property, or decisions on whether or not to compromise claims. The state-of-mind principle, in other words, tends to be ignored or only invoked theoretically when the discussion is one involving *administrative discretion;* it is irrelevant in a discussion of fiduciary discretion in compromising claims, which is clearly a matter, not of dispositive, but of administrative discretion. The state-of-mind rubric has been given little bearing in these cases. The following case on power to compromise illustrates these points:

Helen D. Geffen left her entire estate in trust for her daughter, Melinda. Melinda was life beneficiary and remainderperson; no one else had any possibility of sharing in Helen's estate, except through Melinda. The executor of Helen's estate, a bank, entered into litigation with Melinda's father over an income-tax contribution claim which, the executor said, might have involved the recovery for the estate of as much as $521,800. Melinda and her father agreed to settle this litigation for $12,500, but the executor refused to honor their agreement. Melinda then brought a petition in surrogate's court to compel the compromise; the executor moved to dismiss, which motion the surrogate granted.

The reason Melinda petitioned, the surrogate noted, was non-economic; it arose from the "normal and affectionate relationship" she had with her father. The litigation between him and the estate had "placed a strain upon this relationship" and Melinda concluded that the family advantages of accepting her father's offer of compromise were greater than the purely economic advantages, if any, of continuing it. Not only that, but Melinda offered to release the executor from any liability it might incur for accepting the compromise. The surrogate obviously sympathized with Melinda, but found, on good authority, that his power to control the conduct of fiduciaries "does not permit the Surrogate to substitute his judgment and discretion for that of the fiduciary." It was, he said, a "well established rule" in New York that "the court may not interfere with the exercise of judgment and discretion on the part of a fiduciary."

The surrogate made it clear, however, that he dismissed the petition only because of the certain fate of his ruling on appeal. "This decision is based upon the lack of authority to grant such relief and is not to be construed as in any way approving of the action of the executor." He added that his ruling was "without prejudice to the right of the beneficiary to hold the fiduciary accountable for its acts and transactions and to object to any loss or expense that might result to this estate by reason of the litigation." He finished his written opinion with a lecture to the executor on its duty to ignore the possibility of greater fees for itself in continuing the litigation.

Melinda's theory was that the property in the trust "belongs" to the beneficiaries; it is their property. This has been elementary to the trust for five centuries, and, indeed, the whole concept depends upon its being elementary. Therefore the trustee cannot deal with the property as if it were his own. The beneficiaries arguably should have some voice in what is done with it. The rubric protecting beneficiaries in this country is abuse-of-discretion and the forum in which the rubric has been invoked is equity. Judges, that is, have a right to overrule fiduciary discretion when it is abused.

The Geffen case suggests, however, that a surrogate's only power over compromises is consequent to petitions by the fiduciaries; it does not include consideration, in that proceeding, of whatever objections are raised by beneficiaries. The beneficiary's only other recourse is a petition for surcharge which will, typically, arise long after the compromise is concluded, or the opportunity to compromise lost, and in which her only relief is economic—the sort of relief that Melinda Geffen was willing to surrender in favor of family harmony. (*Matter of Estate of Geffen*, 25 Misc.2d 734, 202 N.Y.S.2d 599, 1960.)

Exercise 5.7

Dr. Charles H. Dressing established an inter-vivos revocable trust for his daughter 40 years ago; it provided generally for her support after his death and for distribution to grandchildren 21 years after her death. The trust instrument provided:

> The Trustee shall ... manage, care for and protect said fund in accordance with its best judgment and discretion, invest and reinvest the same in real estate mortgages, municipal bonds or any other forms of income-bearing property (but not real estate nor corporate stock).

The trustee is a large bank. Dr. Dressing died 30 years ago and the trust became irrevocable; at that time the trust corpus was worth $957,000. Ten years ago the trust corpus was worth $968,000. Throughout this period it was invested in municipal bonds, which paid income of about five per cent, most of it free from federal income taxes.

Dr. Dressing's daughter and a guardian ad litem for owners of the remainder brought a petition last year for instructions to the trustee to deviate from the above restriction and to invest in "other forms of income-bearing property." The trustee's custom in other trusts of this size and type is to invest between 60 and 70 per cent of the corpus in common stocks of its selection.

The beneficiaries point to these factors: 1) The value of common stocks in the last 20 years increased by about 8.5 per cent a year, or 409 per cent total. 2) The Consumer Price Index indicates that the value of the Dressing trust corpus now is, in "real dollars," only 27 per cent greater than what it was ten years ago, while the corpus would have grown by 76 per cent if invested in common stocks during the same period—a difference of about $612,000.

The trustees, who oppose the petition, point to the well-documented principle of law that a trustee's duties are fundamentally 1) to carry out the intention of the settlor, and, to the extent consistent with his intention, 2) preserve the trust corpus and produce a reasonable yield from it for the life beneficiary. The trustees argue that both purposes are being carried out and that well established principles of trust law forbid interference with the intention of the settlor by the beneficiaries.

5.7.1 How should the Dressing trust petition be decided and on what fiduciary principles?

5.7.2 Suppose you are counsel for the trustee of the Dressing Trust. An officer of the bank, disgusted at the difficulties the trustee is having with the family, says to you: "Look, why don't we just get a waiver from everybody and then do what they want to do? The daughter is of age and knows what she is doing. The minors and unborn or unascertained beneficiaries are represented in court by a guardian ad litem who has been arguing on the daughter's side on this investment business. Let's get their agreement, all in writing, good and tight, and then reinvest the way they want to reinvest." Is there anything the matter with that? If not, how would you advise going about the waiver process?

5.7.3 The case that this problem is based on was decided in 1960 (*In re Trusteeship under Agreement with Mayo*, 105 N.W.2d 900 [Minn. 1960]), and at the time, the financial data was even more convincingly in the beneficiaries' favor. Due to high inflation rates, the trust was actually losing significant value in real dollars—as much as 50 per cent over the previous ten year period. Meanwhile, the value of common stocks had grown over 200 per cent over the previous twenty years. If you would have decided against the beneficiaries, would this more persuasive data change your decision? Why or why not?

REFERENCES AND BIBLIOGRAPHY

L. Blocher, "Trustworthy," Los Angeles Lawyer, December 1997, p. 24

G. Bogert, Trusts (6th ed. 1991)

C. Cave, "Trusts: Monkeying Around With Our Pets' Futures: Why Oklahoma Should Adopt a Pet–Trust Statute," 55 Oklahoma Law Review 627 (2002)

R. Danforth, "Rethinking the Law of Creditors' Rights in Trusts," 53 Hastings Law Journal 287 (2002)

J. Dobris, "Changes in the Role and the Form of the Trust at the New Millennium," 62 Albany Law Review 543 (1998)

C. Fox, "Are Spendthrift Trusts Vulnerable to a Beneficiary's Tort Creditors?" Trusts and Estates, February 1998, p. 57

N. Fratcher, "Trustees' Powers Legislation," 37 N.Y.U. Law Review 627 (1962)

A. Friedman, "The Dynastic Trust," 73 Yale Law Journal 547 (1964)

E.C. Halbach, "Significant Trends in the Trust Law of the United States," 32 Vanderbilt Journal of Transnational Law 531 (1999)

P. Haskell, Preface to Wills, Trusts, and Administration (2nd. ed. 1994)

A.J. Hirsch, "Fear Not the Asset Protection Trust," 27 Cardozo Law Review 2685 (2006)

A.J. Hirsch, "Trusts for Purposes: Policy, Ambiguity and Anomaly in the Uniform Laws," 26 Florida State University Law Review 913 (1999)

J. Langbein, "Questioning the Trust Law Duty of Loyalty: Safe Interest or Best Interest?" 114 Yale Law Journal 919 (2005)

K.P. Marcus, "Totten Trusts: Pragmatic Pre–Death Planning or Post–Mortem Plunder?" 69 Temple Law Review 861 (1996)

K. Millard, "The Trustee's Duty to Inform and Report Under the Uniform Trust Code," 40 Real Property, Probate and Trust Journal 373 (2005)

V. Moschella and G. Twohig, "Understanding Living Trusts," The Wisconsin Lawyer, March 1992, p. 22

M. Mott, "And to My Dog, I leave a $10,000 Trust Fund," The New York Times, May 22, 2005, p. BU–6

A. Newman, "The Rights of Creditors of Beneficiaries Under the Uniform Trust Code: An Examination of the Compromise," 69 Tennessee Law Review 771 (2002)

A. Newman, "The Intention of the Settlor Under the Uniform Trust Code: Whose Property Is It Anyway?" 38 Akron Law Review 649 (2005)

A. Newman, "Spendthrift and Discretionary Trusts: Alive and Well Under the Uniform Trust Code," 40 Real Property, Probate and Trusts Journal 567 (2005)

C.E. Rounds and E.P. Hayes, A Trustee's Handbook (1998 ed.)

A. Scott, The Law of Trusts (1987)

T. Shaffer, "Fiduciary Powers to Compromise Claims," 41 New York University Law Review 528 (1966)

R. Silverman, "Trust Laws Get a Makeover," The Wall Street Journal, January 29, 2004, p. D–1

C. Walker, "The Uniform Trust Code," Res Gestae, January 2001, p. 19

Chapter 6

DEATH TAXES

(We are indebted to our colleague Professor Michael S. Kirsch of the Notre Dame Law Faculty for valuable suggestions and revisions in this chapter and in cases presented in the Appendix.)

Clients such as those we have been talking about, and clients such as those presented in the Appendix, sometimes ask about the effect of death taxes on their "estates." They rarely need to worry: Significant amounts of death taxes, federal or state, probably will not be required from any of their families. For the better off among them, exposure to death taxes, if any, can probably be removed with relatively simple tax planning.

For wealthy clients, the situation as to federal estate and gift taxes is remarkably confusing as we write in 2006 (and as to state inheritance taxes increasingly unimportant; nearly half the states have repealed their inheritance taxes.) The federal estate tax remains a tax on the estate of the donor; it is supplemented by a federal gift tax on gratuitous transfers the donor makes before she dies. The common sort of state death tax is a tax on the *donee*, payable by the estate of the donor. State law has also commonly imposed a state estate tax to soak up funds an estate is allowed to credit against the federal estate tax for amounts paid in state death taxes. Some states have repealed their inheritance taxes but not their estate taxes. Some have repealed both.

Families who receive wealth under two million dollars are unlikely to pay any federal death taxes. Some of them may pay inheritance taxes in some states, but amounts imposed by state governments are usually so small that lawyers do not attempt to plan for them. Lawyers for families with both spouses living, whose wealth is under four million dollars, can usually avoid federal death taxes (imposed under what is now called the Uniform Transfer Tax) with planning that is simpler and easier than, say, the contingent trusts for minor children we talk about in Chapter 5 and Chapter 10 or the Medicaid planning we talk about in Chapter 10 and Chapter 11.

Neither surviving spouse in the families we discuss in Chapter 10 will be required to pay federal transfer tax, nor will Mrs. Eustace (Chapter 9) nor Mr. or Mrs. Villalobos (Chapter 11). When these surviving spouses die, their families, or trustees for their children, will receive their property free of federal tax, and with only minor amounts of state inheritance tax (if any), in some states. In all of these cases the amount at issue for federal-tax purposes will be covered, at each death, by a "unified credit" covering two million dollars in assets. (This credit, in its modern version, is the vestige of a long-standing federal policy to avoid imposing death taxes on the middle class. Professor Kirsch: "The increase in 2001 might be viewed as an attempt to also avoid imposing the tax on many wealthy families.")

Of course, after the unified-credit amount is passed, the unified transfer tax can be significant, and it takes planning to avoid or reduce its bite. In estates of more than two million dollars, for example, the marginal transfer-tax rate is forty-six per cent. The tax on a four million dollar net taxable estate is more than $900,000, all of which can be avoided by a married couple whose lawyer is paying attention to tax considerations.

(Professor Kirsch: "In mentioning the changes [i.e., higher estate unified credit and lower marginal rates] brought about by the 2001 tax act, you might also want to mention that the 2001 tax act, as currently in effect, envisions a one-year repeal of the estate tax (but not the gift tax) in 2010. As of January 1, 2011, the estate tax springs back to life [with the lower unified credit and higher marginal rates contemplated by pre–2001 law]. Everyone expects Congress to do something to fix this mess—in particular, the moral hazard of having a one-year window where those 'fortunate' enough to die during 2010 will have no estate tax liability. However, no one knows precisely what form the 'fix' will take [most likely a permanent very high estate tax unified credit].

("The 2001 tax act also repeals the credit for state death taxes, replacing it with a mere deduction. This makes state 'estate' taxes more important than under prior law [under prior law they weren't as important because in most cases they merely resulted in a dollar-for-dollar reduction in federal estate taxes by reason of the credit].")

Assume such a lawyer. And assume, for example, that Dr. and Mrs. Kennedy have *two million dollars* at the time Dr. Kennedy dies, survived by Mrs. Kennedy. Assume further that they own this property so that one half of it (one million dollars) is owned by each of them. Each of them has a will that gives her or his half to the children, or to a trustee for the children, rather than to the other spouse. There is no federal death tax due at either death; both estates are covered by a unified credit that exempts two million dollars (this as of 2006—more as of 2009[1]).

Usually in such planning, though, wills that leave half the family property to children, rather than the surviving spouse, are not what clients want. They want it all to go to the surviving spouse, and to the children only after the second death. The planning objective—in those few cases where death-tax planning is relevant—is to have the property go *for tax purposes* as if it were half-and-half, but to have it go in beneficial effect as if it were all paid to the surviving spouse, and to the children after the second death.

---

1. As we write, in 2006, the amount is $2 million. It moves up to $3.5 million in 2009. We speak here as of 2006.

Dr. Kennedy's will (Chapter 10) provides that all of his probate estate go to Mrs. Kennedy, and, anyway, most of their wealth is held in such a way that ownership will pass to her outside of the probate process and of Dr. Kennedy's will (but, as we will see, not outside of the taxing process). If the surviving spouse is a citizen, the federal taxing statute provides a one-hundred-per-cent marital deduction for at-death transfers between spouses (Internal Revenue Code Sec. 2056); state inheritance-tax systems usually provide a marital deduction that, coupled with an exemption or credit for middle-class estates, will cancel state death taxes.

But when Mrs. Kennedy dies (without having remarried), and her property passes to a trustee or to adult children (as we discuss in Chapter 3 and Chapter 10), and maybe if one of the Kennedys wins the lottery, there may be enough wealth to bring the transfer into the tax collector's sights: The federal system (as of 2006) will remove two million dollars from consideration by way of the unified credit; this tax is a tax only on the relatively wealthy.

If Mrs. Kennedy dies with *four million dollars,* the likely federal transfer tax at that point could exceed $900,000. This result occurs, from a planner's point of view, because, when Dr. Kennedy died, the family did not take advantage of the unified credit in *his* estate. (It did not need to do so to avoid tax at that time, since everything went to Mrs. Kennedy, and the marital deduction for transfers to her is one hundred per cent.)

If the transfers at Dr. Kennedy's death had been carried out in such a way that his estate took advantage of the two-million-dollar unified credit, and if the transfers at Mrs. Kennedy's death could be carried out so that only half the family's remaining property were taxed in her estate, the family would have avoided $900,000 in federal death taxes. This would be the result of planning that, for tax purposes, divides the family property into two parts, one part (but not the other) considered, for tax purposes, at each death. The federal statute provides several ways to do that and at the same time provides, for all practical purposes, that Mrs. Kennedy have it all.

If this family held its property in a pure, hypothetical community-property regime, each spouse would have owned, at death, half of the family property. If each spouse had provided that her or his community property go to the other for life, remainder at the second death to the next generation, taxes would have been avoided. At Dr. Kennedy's death, his community property (two million dollars) would be covered by the unified credit. A life interest in it would not have qualified for the marital deduction, but his estate does not need the marital deduction on his community property to escape tax. The unified credit covers his community property. At Mrs. Kennedy's death, the community property she received for life at Dr. Kennedy's death is not taxable: Her life interest disappeared at her death. Her own community property (assuming no significant increase in value) is covered by the unified credit applicable to her estate.

The simple way to do this elsewhere, assuming the Kennedys live in a common-law state, and that all of their property is legally held by Dr. Kennedy, would be to leave half outright to Mrs. Kennedy and half to her for life, remainder to the children. This sort of arrangement, though, is not acceptable to most clients. At least if the estate-planning texts and form books are to be believed, most clients with wealth of this magnitude want trust management of *both* halves. (You can imagine why this might be if you contemplate the complexity of a life estate in a mutual-fund portfolio, two automobiles, and an array of fishing equipment.) So—to begin with—we talk about a trust. Then what we need is a trust arrangement that is treated, for tax purposes, as if half the family property went to the surviving spouse for life, then to the children, and half went to the surviving spouse "in fee." What planners do, in very broad outline, is to put the entire family property in a life-estate arrangement for the surviving spouse, qualify only half of it for the marital deduction, and restrict the other half enough that it is not taxable at the second death. The marital half is not taxed at the first death, but is taxed at the second; the other half is taxed at the first death but not at the second. Each half is covered by the unified credit, which is taken advantage of at each death.

In one version of this plan, the trustee of the non-marital half is directed to pay all income to Mrs. Kennedy, with power in her to reach principal, which power is limited enough that it does not pull the property into her taxable estate (cf. Sec. 2041). The other half, the "in fee" portion, is put into one of the several forms of trust that, in effect, make Mrs. Kennedy the "fee" owner of that half, with trust provisions that control both its disposition during her life and its disposition after her death. (Time was when this arrangement assumed male control of the family wealth, even long after the male's death.)

These "marital trust" arrangements all turn on particular, specific, relatively complex provisions in the Internal Revenue Code. Remembering that the object is to get the marital deduction for this trust, at the first death, and to have the marital deduction property taxed at the second death and there covered by the unified credit:

One such form would give Mrs. Kennedy all income from half, with an array of restrictions on access by anyone else, and would be agreed to, by Mrs. Kennedy, at Dr. Kennedy's death. This is the so-called QTIP trust ("qualified terminal interest trust," under Internal Revenue Code Sec. 2056[b][7]). Another version gives her all of the income during her life and makes the remainder subject to her general power of appointment (Sec. 2056[b][5], Sec. 2041). In any of these arrangements, this half of the trust is deducted at Dr. Kennedy's death, as a qualifying marital-deduction transfer. The other half is, for tax purposes, a life-estate arrangement that is taxable at Dr. Kennedy's death (not qualified for the marital deduction) but is covered at that time by his unified credit. That half is not taxed at Mrs. Kennedy's death.

The way any of these planning devices avoids tax, on four million dollars in family wealth, is to take advantage of both unified credits. If the arrangement at the first death is not adequate, it may be possible to re-arrange it through the use of disclaimers by the surviving spouse (Sec. 2518).

* * *

If the family wealth is greater than four million dollars, there are a number of devices to attack the 46-per-cent exposure that comes after four million dollars. Suppose, for example, that a couple has, in their late middle age, five million dollars, three adult children, two children-in-law, and four grandchildren (nine family members in addition to themselves), and suppose they are willing to transfer some of this wealth to the next generation while they are both living, in order to reduce the death-tax bite.

What those clients need to do is to give away a million dollars. The federal transfer-tax system, however, is a "unified" system. That is, it reaches gratuitous transfers during life as well as transfers after death: You cannot (in theory) avoid the tax by giving property away during life. In its modern, "unified" form this tax reaches all transfers during a person's life. (Professor Kirsch notes that "the gift and estate unified credits are no longer perfectly unified: Only $1 million can now be passed tax-free as a gift, while $2 million can pass tax-free at death.") The unified credit is applied, as needed, for gift transfers up to $1 million per lifetime. After the first $1 million of lifetime gifts, a donor begins paying "gift tax" at rates ranging from 41 to 46 per cent. When the unified credit is needed after death, all that remains available is the part of it that was not used during life. And the rate structure is applied in the same whole-life manner.

Well—not quite. And the not-quite is one of five principal death-tax-saving tactics for clients not adequately covered by the unified credit and the marital deduction. There is, in the "gift tax" part of the federal unified tax system, an "exclusion" for each inter-vivos gift, each year—the annual per-donee exclusion. And there is, in that system, the ability available to spouses to file joint gift-tax returns, without regard to which spouse owned the gift asset. (That is, a gift of $24,000 from one of these clients to her youngest son can be treated as if it were from both spouses, half from each of them.) The exclusion in 2006 was $12,000 per donee, per donor. (It is indexed for inflation and may be higher in other years.) That means each spouse can each give $12,000 to each of their nine descendants, each year, free of gift tax and free of any effect on their testamentary planning—a total of $216,000 per year. It would take about five years of giving (assuming steady values) to soak up and avoid transfer tax on that exposed million dollars.

(The annual per donee provisions, Sec. 2503 and regulations thereunder, are, of course, complex. They are subject to a "present interest" requirement that makes transfers into trusts, or for minors, tricky but possible. There are a number of more or less standard ways to do this, the easiest of which, for minor grandchildren, would be transfers under the Uniform Transfers to Minors Act. [See the Statutory Appendix.] Gift transfers for the donee's medical expenses and for tuition are exempt in addition to the annual-per-donee exclusion—and without limit, if they are paid directly to the provider or school [Sec. 2503(e)]).

The *second* (as we think of it) principal way to cut down death-tax exposure is to make *significant transfers to charity*, which are deductible whether given during life or at death. These need not be outright; the code permits some highly specific trust arrangements under which a donor can retain part of the transfer for life, and get gift-tax and income-tax deductions, at present, for the remainder given to charity. One of these, for example, will qualify the remainder for deductions even when a fixed annual amount is payable to the donor (or to some other person) (Sec. 2055). Charitable institutions, such as mission societies and universities, are, for some reason, happy to provide expert assistance to potential donors and their lawyers in devising these charitable-remainder gift arrangements.[2]

The *third* (as we think of it) principal way to cut down death-tax exposure is to *give away appreciation* to property before it occurs. Life insurance proceeds are, for example, included in property taxable at death—whether payable to a named beneficiary or to the estate. What makes them taxable is that the decedent held, at her death, "incidents of

2. We think that lawyers pay too little attention to charitable giving by their clients—and this aside from tax considerations. Our friend Jane Farrell, of the Hot Springs, South Dakota, Bar, numbers among her clients the Red Cloud Indian School. She writes with an example of a human aspect of charitable dispositions that, we fear, is too much neglected by "estate planning" lawyers: "One of the questions I always have in my mind when I am looking at the probate notices that come from across the country is what triggered that individual to leave something to Red Cloud. Recently, Red Cloud received a $1 million bequest. I wrote the attorney and asked if he knew why, and the response received was that the woman involved had begun a correspondence with one of the priests at Red Cloud many years ago. I

would estimate that most of the bequests we get are from individuals who have no immediate family members (spouse and children). I find this true in my own practice as well, that oftentimes people feel good about naming a charity in their estate plan, but the charity is an alternate beneficiary and comes into the picture only if everyone in their family is deceased. They feel good, but the reality is the charity will never see anything. The figure that approximately $11 to $18 trillion will be passed from one generation to the next in the next 20 years is somewhat staggering. The experts say that the wealth is going from a generation used to giving to charities to a generation that is not. There are over 900,000 recognized charities under the I.R.S. at the current time.... "

ownership" under the life-insurance policies (e.g., the ability to borrow on the accumulated value of the insurance, or to change beneficiaries) (Sec. 2042). If the insured person transfers these "incidents" during life she makes a taxable gift but the value of the gift is the value of the insurance at that time—when the insured person is living. This will often be a fraction of the "face value" of the insurance: $30,000, say, on a transfer of $100,000 in life insurance. The other $70,000 accumulates after the transfer and belongs to the donee of the gift. (Professor Kirsch points out that this works only if the insured person survives at least three years after the gift is made—this under Sec. 2035.)

As we write, for another example, virtually all business investment in the past decade has appreciated dramatically. A ten thousand dollar gift of mutual fund securities, made to an adult child in 1990, may be, as we write, worth one hundred thousand dollars. If your reasoning processes regard payments to the federal government as a species of disaster, you will rejoice at the fact that ninety thousand dollars has passed to the next generation free of transfer tax. There are dramatic and complex examples of this strategy involving family-owned businesses, some of which have grown into giant corporate enterprises controlled by succeeding generations of wealthy families. These plans achieve this sort of savings through incorporation, recapitalization and reorganization, allied trusts, and various "estate freezes." One set of learned authors, surveying this sort of thing in the 1970s (before many dramatic examples had even come to be), referred to the federal transfer-tax system as a "voluntary" tax. That is, anyone can avoid it who wants to. (Professor Kirsch: "It was easier to do estate freezes in the 1970s. It's a bit trickier now." *Sic transit gloria mundi.*)

Fourth, somewhat allied to the policies that have overlooked transfers of appreciation are a series of code *provisions that favor farms and small businesses*. This form of family wealth is often characterized by high frozen value. A modest family farm, modestly supporting a family at, say, income of $100,000 a year, may be worth six million dollars. When the record-title owner of the farm dies, the family is burdened with transfer-tax bills it cannot pay without selling the farm. The relief provided includes such things as special provisions for valuation (see Sec. 2032A) and for installment payment of tax (Sec. 6166). (Empirical reports that have followed the creation of these statutory palliatives indicate that they are only marginally successful at keeping farms and small businesses family owned.) The agricultural columnist Alan Guebert wrote, after describing the politics of federal tax reform in summer 2006, "[The] years-long battle to eliminate the 'death tax'—and, to hear them talk, save every 'family farm' from IRS destruction—was as phony as the phrase 'federal budget.'" South Bend Tribune, July 8, 2006.

Fifth: One way to reduce transfer tax that was widely talked about (probably not widely used), and that was theoretically put under control during the administration of President John F. Kennedy, is the *generation-skipping transfer*. Suppose twenty million dollars in family wealth and a family such as the one we have been discussing. Suppose our clients, before they die, have managed to transfer four million of that at death, without significant tax payment, and sixteen million of it by transferring appreciation to their children before the appreciation has occurred.

Looking ahead a generation, even after all possible planning for transfers at the deaths of the oldest generation, there will remain perhaps six million dollars owned by each of the three adult children and their spouses—six million that will be appreciating, because the rich always get richer. So perhaps we are really talking about much larger transfers from the second to the third generation and even larger transfer tax exposure.

When the clients we are discussing made transfers to younger members of their family, they might have considered making them not to children but to grandchildren. (In fact, if they made maximum use of the annual per donee exclusion they did some of that.) Anything that, at the deaths of the grandparents, is owned by grandchildren, rather than by children, has escaped transfer tax at the deaths of children. That is the skipping of generations, which is what the taxing intellectuals proposed in the 1960s to reach with a separate death tax, called the Generation Skipping Transfer Tax (Secs. 2601ff). When a transfer is made to the second younger generation, it is taxed, under this additional tax, as if it had been made by the first younger generation. The tax is remarkably complex; it is riddled with exceptions; and it is subject to an exemption of two million dollars per taxpayer (in 2006). A married couple can make generation-skipping transfers of four million dollars without invoking this separate tax. (Of course, whether their family incurs "unified transfer" tax is another and unrelated question.)

Both of these transfer taxes have, from a policy point of view, been remarkably unsuccessful. They have not produced significant revenue; often they have not raised enough money to cover the cost of administering them. The overall expense of them—adding fees paid to lawyers, accountants, and insurance professionals—far exceeds the benefit they bring to the cost of government. They have not succeeded in reducing concentrations of family wealth, either, particularly not when compared with income taxes. Many states have repealed their death taxes. Abolition of the federal transfer tax has become a perennial issue in congressional debate. (Professor Kirsch reminds us: "As a result of 2001 legislation, the federal estate tax [but not the gift tax] is scheduled to expire *for one year*—in 2010—then to spring back to life in 2011, when it will take back the form it had in 2001.")

* * *

Our focus so far in this chapter has been on planning, as distinguished from legal provisions that have to be followed by those responsible for paying transfer taxes. It may be useful to notice several provisions that provide background for planning. Using the federal provisions (state inheritance-tax provisions are similar):

The "gross estate," or annual "gross gifts," is a place to start. The statutory concept here does not resemble what "transfer" would mean in any other context. It is, over nearly a century of development, the stopping place in a ping-pong game, a history in which Congress proposed to reach beyond what lawyers thought of as transfers at death; Congress's attempt was met by clever lawyers (worthy successors to the British lawyers who evaded the rule in Shelley's Case and the rule against perpetuities). To consider the stopping place more descriptively, and in reference to the "estate tax" part of the unified transfer tax, "gross estate" includes:

— property the decedent transferred with a reserved life estate or the power to direct disposition to other people (Sec. 2036);

— property the decedent transferred but in which he retained a partial reversion (Sec. 2037);

— property the decedent transferred but in which she retained the power to revoke or direct benefits (Sec. 2038);

— some survivor annuities (Sec. 2039);

— joint and survivor property, to the extent the family cannot prove that someone other than the decedent contributed to ownership (Sec. 2040);

— property over which the decedent held a general power of appointment (which power is particularly defined for tax purposes) (Sec. 2041);

— proceeds of life-insurance policies when the decedent held, at her death, "incidents of ownership" under the insurance contracts (Sec. 2042);

— (Professor Kirsch: "Property transferred within three years of death if it would have been included under sections 2036, 2037, 2038, or 2042 [Sec. 2035]. This mainly applies to life-insurance policy transfers.");

— and, generally, any property in which the decedent had an interest, at the value of the interest (Sec. 2033). (Note that the amount includible here is often less than the amount includible under provisions reaching transfers with retained interests or powers, which reach the full value of the transfer, valued at the decedent's date of death.)

* * *

The unified transfer tax allows for several commonsense *deductions*, in addition to the marital and charitable deductions we have discussed. The costs of administration, debts, etc., are deductible (Sec. 2053) as are state death taxes (see below) (Sec. 2058). Losses incurred by the decedent's estate during administration are deductible (Sec. 2054: "storms, shipwrecks, other casualties ... theft").

The value of the gross estate is generally calculated at date-of-death values, although there is a provision for valuing assets as of a year later, a remnant of the Great Depression, when property values plummeted (Sec. 2032). (Professor Kirsch: "This also helped when the internet stock bubble burst a few years ago.") And there are the provisions we have discussed providing special valuation for farms and other small businesses.

Once the "gross estate" calculation is made, and the deductions are taken, a tentative figure for the tax can be calculated, using statutory rate tables (Sec. 2001). Against that figure, there are a number of *credits* available. The most potent of these is the unified credit, which will reach the tax equivalent of two million dollars in assets in 2006. There are also credits for death taxes paid to foreign governments (Sec. 2014). (Professor Kirsch: "State death taxes are now only deductible, rather than a credit as a result of the 2001 legislation. See Sec. 2058. This makes state death taxes more of a concern than they used to be.") And there is a credit for taxes paid in previous estates on the same property (Sec. 2013). This last has a descending benefit, so, in estates taxed within two years of one another, the tax paid on the first estate can be credited against the tax payable by the second estate, up to eighty per cent—sixty per cent if the gap is four years, down to twenty per cent when the gap is nine or ten years. (There is a great deal of credit language in Secs. 2010 through 2015, and provision for a couple of credits we do not mention here.)

* * *

"Tax planners" generally agree that the federal income tax is a far graver source of concern for middle-class and wealthy clients than is the unified transfer tax. The income tax is the federal government's principal source of revenue and is probably the principal device for forcing property distribution out of the accumulations of the wealthy.

Income-tax concern shows up brightly in the context we have been talking about in this chapter with regard to retirement plans, pension and profit-sharing plans, "401(k)" plans, "Keogh" plans, and "traditional" Individual Retirement Accounts (not the so-called "Roth" accounts)—all devices under the federal income tax for setting aside money today, before taxes, that will be subject to income tax when it is paid out. These pay-out impositions occur regardless of who gets the payment. ("Roth" accounts do not postpone income taxes, but appreciation that accrues later gets favorable income-tax treatment.) Otherwise, for the most part, the property a client leaves at death is not income taxable (accumulations of securities and life insurance proceeds are both dramatic examples). In fact, accumulated gain ("capital gain") is still, despite occasional efforts by the federal tax intellectuals, escaped by death. The share of stock Grandpa paid a dollar for and held for fifty years, worth a thousand dollars when he died, would have incurred federal capital gains tax on the gain ($999) if Grandpa had sold it during his life. When he gives it to his favorite granddaughter in his will, the basis on which capital gain is thereafter computed is the value at Grandpa's death. Nobody pays income tax on the $999 gain. But retirement plan benefits are an exception to that principle (if it is a principle). If Grandpa made his I.R.A. payable, at his death, to his granddaughter, payments to her are as income-taxable as if she had earned them working at the drug store.

There are, of course, many other income tax dimensions to planning for the well-to-do. We mention this one in order to make a sort of footnote point about the importance of income tax planning, and also because retirement plan benefits are now much more significant for middle-class clients (such as the Kennedys and the Jaramillos) than they were forty years ago.

REFERENCES AND BIBLIOGRAPHY

D. Darlin, "With a Little Planning, Your House Can Stay in the Family," The New York Times, January 21, 2006 (Business Section)

C. Davenport, "Estate Tax Repeal: Myths and Misunderstandings," America, September 23, 2000, p. 15

S. Jack, "A History of the Wisconsin Inheritance Tax," 88 Marquette Law Review 947 (2005)

D. Johnston, "Encounter: The Loophole Artist," The New York Times Magazine, December 21, 2003, p. 18

J. Jedrzejewski, "The Growth and Tax Relief Reconciliation Act of 2001 and Its Effect on Estate Planning," 6 Marquette Elder's Advisor 301 (2005)

C. Timberg, "The Estate Tax Lives On," The Washington Post National Weekly Edition, April 1–7, 2002, p. 30

S. Waldeck, "An Appeal to Charity: Using Philanthropy to Revitalize the Estate Tax," 24 Virginia Tax Review 667 (2005)

Chapter 7

THE RULE AGAINST PERPETUITIES

A. PROBLEM

Your client, Francis Gresham, is a prosperous farmer. One aspect of your work for him involves a 360–acre tract of wooded hills which adjoins his working farm. He has a contract involving that tract with the Scourge of the Earth Mining Corporation. The contract calls for Scourge to strip-mine the tract for coal and then to return the land to its original contour, spread topsoil on it, and re-seed it in grass and trees. Scourge has been working the tract for a couple of years and is taking substantial quantities of coal out of its open-pit mine on the tract.

Under the terms of the contract, Francis is paid ten per cent of the wholesale value of the coal that is mined. He has no duties to maintain the land; Scourge pays all taxes, including real-property taxes, and pays all mining expenses. Francis has nothing to do but collect the proceeds of the mining operation. These have totaled more than $100,000 in each of the last two years.

Francis wants the payments from Scourge to go to his church after he dies. His church is the First Presbyterian Church of Howell Hollow, which is a congregational church and a not-for-profit corporation that owns the church's property. As a separate feature of his planning for his death, Francis wants his interest in this tract devoted to his son Mike and Mike's family. Francis's wife Grace is alive and well. Mike is married to Griselda Grantly Gresham; they have three minor children, all sons. Francis and Grace have four other adult children, all of whom are married and three of whom have children of their own. Francis wants to give the mining tract to Mike because Mike is the only son who is not interested in farming and that tract is not likely to be good farm land, even after it is restored.

If Mike dies before the mining is completed, Francis wants the tract to go to Mike's wife Griselda, and, when she dies, to their children. If all of Mike's and Griselda's children are dead—you actually talked this long—Francis wants the tract to go to their grandchildren.

Two facts are fairly clear: (1) Francis does not know when the mining will be completed. He feels that, when the coal supply declines, Scourge will quit mining vigorously and may not return to the mine for years. If Scourge were to continue to mine vigorously, Francis guesses, the coal would probably be gone within ten years. If they postpone vigorous mining at any point, the tract may not be ready for restoration for a long

161

time, and there is nothing in the contract that sets a deadline for Scourge. (It says that Scourge's duty to restore becomes timely "when the said tract is no longer practicable for the mining of coal.")

(2) Francis does not like trusts. You have talked him into one testamentary trust, for a portion of his estate, but, on this tract, he sees no need whatever for a trust. You have decided that you should try to work out a plan for him, if you possibly can, that will create legal rather than equitable interests.

Exercise 7.1

Suggest a plan for Francis, under alternative assumptions: (1) Assume that your work is governed by the common law of future interests. (2) Then assume that your jurisdiction has adopted the following statute:

Upon the expiration of the period allowed by the common law rule against perpetuities as measured by actual rather than possible events any interest in members of a class the membership of which is then subject to increase shall be void.

B.   A BRIEF TOUR OF THE RULE AGAINST PERPETUITIES

"Estate planning" operates under two general systems of limitation in addition to the rules on institution and administration of wills and trusts. One of these systems is ancient and is usually studied in law school as part of the course in property. It is the common-law rule against remoteness in the vesting of ownership, the rule against perpetuities. The other system is taxation. This chapter is about perpetuities.

The rule against perpetuities renders invalid a contingent future interest which may not vest or fail within lives in being and 21 years. It was adopted and developed in 17th century England in order to place limits on ownership devices that take property—especially real property—out of the marketplace. The ultimate social purposes of the rule appear to have been—and to be—(1) restriction on the sort of private power which is gained through the accumulation of property, and (2) encouragement of transactions upon which the government is able to fasten death taxes.

The rule does not reach all, or even most, of the devices lawyers invent for rendering property inalienable. It is a narrow rule, now loosely applied and widely revised by judicial and statutory reform. It is far less important than teachers of property lead law students to believe, but it can be, nonetheless, a significant limitation on dynastic forms of planning. A practitioner in our field has to know a little about it.

A contingent future interest is invalid if it will not vest, if at all, within lives in being and 21 years. These words have a technical meaning in perpetuities law: A *future interest* is the result of an Anglo–American property owner's ability to spread ownership on the plane of time, to create ownership in an owner who cannot demand possession or use of the property. It is possible, in fact, to create ownership in someone who does not even exist, as in the disposition "to S for life and then to the children of S." The children of S (some or all of whom do not exist and may never exist) have an ownership interest, an interest which the law will enforce, but they have nothing that can now be possessed. "Children of S" is not even a defined group of people so long as S is alive; there is no child of S who can demand possession of the property. The rule against perpetuities applies only to future interests; it does not apply to interests that can be possessed. The life interest of S is not subject to the rule. After S dies, the interest of his children becomes possessory; it is subject to the rule now but after S dies it will be no longer subject to the rule.

The rule applies only to *contingent* future interests. If the grantor in the example above says "to S for life and then to T," the remainder is not contingent but vested; the rule does not apply to it. If he says "to S for life and then to the descendants of T," the descendants of T do not have a vested remainder, until T dies; after T's death, but before S dies, the remainder may[1] become vested (not possessory, but vested); the rule does not apply to interests which are vested, whether or not they are possessory. If the grantor says "to S for life, then to the children of T, but if any child of T becomes a Unitarian, his share to the children of X," the interests of children of T may become vested subject to a divesting condition; the rule would not apply to those interests. However, the interests of the children of X are contingent; they are shifting executory interests, which cannot be vested until they are possessed. The rule applies to them and, since a child of T may change faith after the end of a life in being and 21 years, they are invalid. If you do not understand why that is, review the example, with particular reference to the concepts "future interest," "vested," and "contingent."

"Vesting" is an artificial concept, as the last example indicates. The children of T have a vested interest which they will lose if they become Unitarians. The children of X, whose ownership turns on exactly the same events, have only a contingent interest. Neither interest is vested in possession; both are future interests. Much of the flexibility of the rule against perpetuities turns on what judges do with the distinctions (a) between vested future interests and contingent future interests, and (b), more mysteriously, between contingent interests and interests vested subject to a divesting condition. These are distinctions law students should remember from their first course in property. Judges can do

---

1. Or may not. See Part "7," Chapter 4, *supra*. A person's descendants—if she has children—may be born after her death. A judicial construction that this class closed at the death of T would save the gift. See Part 2, *infra*.

wonders by way of saving or invalidating property interests by seeming to manipulate the vesting concept *before* they apply the rule against perpetuities.

Exercise 7.2

Assume you are able to conclude that the property interest Francis Gresham gave to S.E.M. Corporation is a leasehold (term of years). S.E.M. Corporation has a present possessory interest. Francis has a future interest.

7.2.1.   Is Francis's interest subject to the rule against perpetuities?

7.2.2.   If Francis's interest is given to Mike in Francis's will, will Mike's interest be subject to the rule against perpetuities?

7.2.3.   If Francis's will says "to Mike, but if the mining is not completed when Mike dies, to Griselda when the mining is completed," is Griselda's interest subject to the rule against perpetuities?

The rule against perpetuities is not a rule against making property inalienable; it is only a rule against remoteness of vesting. If the grantor says "to the children of T, so long as they do not become Unitarians," there is no remoteness of vesting; all interests are vested. The children's interest is vested subject to a divesting condition; the left-over interest has not been given away and remains vested in the grantor. But the property is as inalienable as it was when the disposition gave the left-overs to the children of X. Perpetuities law does not worry about the inalienability; it only worries about remoteness of vesting. Within its narrow range, though, the rule applies to all kinds of property—real and personal, legal and equitable, remainders and executory interests, business interests and family wealth transactions, powers of appointment, class gifts, and mining leasehold interests.

The rule proved for some reason to be significant in the formative era of American property law; it became a barrier and a bastion. It was thought to protect the stability and order of property ownership from experimentation and reform. Ageing lawyers are familiar with the rigorous view of the rule taken by Professor John Chipman Gray, a 19th century Harvard Law School worthy, and familiar as well with the humor and outrage expressed about it in the 1930s, in the famous first "Nutshell" article by Gray's successor, Professor Barton Leach. It was Leach who described from real cases humorous examples of ridiculous rigor. He provoked a generation of reform legislation and, to a lesser extent, skepticism about the rule among the judiciary. Here are some of Leach's examples:

— "to S for life, then to S's widow for life, then to the lineal descendants of S." The remainder fails because the widow of S is not identified. The person to whom S is married when the transfer is made may die, and S may marry someone who was not born at the time of the transfer. This person might be an *unborn widow* and so cannot be used as a life in being to measure the time period under the rule. The interest of S is vested from the beginning and is therefore valid. The interest of the widow of S, even if she *is* unborn, will vest or fail at the end of a life in being (S's) and is therefore valid. But the interest in lineal descendants is void.

— "Blackacre to S when the gravel pit is exhausted." Although there is only two years' worth of gravel in the gravel pit, digging it out may take more than lives in being and 21 years. The gift to S fails. This is the *magic gravel pit*. The principle has been most troublesome in cases where the disposition is "To S when my estate is settled."

— "To my nieces and nephews for life and then to my descendants." The grantor's parents are living and aged 79 and 77. They have had two children, the grantor and the grantor's sister; but, the common law said, they may have more children, and those children may then have children, so that not everyone who meets the description "nieces and nephews" would be a life in being. It is presumed that anyone can have children, and it is the rule that no member of a class may be used as a measuring life unless every other member is also a life in being. This is in part the case of the *fertile octogenarian*.

— "My estate to T in trust, to pay the income to Q for life and thereafter to pay the principal to those of Q's grandchildren who are living at my death, or born within five years thereafter, and who attain the age of 21." Q is a 65–year-old widow, but, the law says, she may marry again and have another child, and that child may have children of his own, and all of this may happen within five years, so that the children of Q—under principles announced in the unborn widow case—cannot be used as lives in being. This is the case of the *precocious toddler.*

— Left to the reader's imagination is a final case, suggested to Professor Leach by a eugenicist who thought that (male) astronauts should donate to sperm banks, so that their physical and mental characteristics would not be lost to the nation's gene pool. (As we write in 2006 there is a parallel discussion in the press, about fashion models and beautiful actresses.) This is the case of the *fertile decedent*.

1. DRAFTING

An occasional client has dispositions in mind which could violate the rule. They are not absurdities, but are genuinely dynastic. They call for pushing to the limits of the rule. A case in the Court of Appeals of North Carolina (*North Carolina National Bank v. Norris*, 21 N.C.App. 178, 203 S.E.2d 657, 1974) is an example. The disposition there—drafted for the will of a client named Montague—was "to my Wife, W, for life, then to my children, A, B, and C, for life, then to my grandchildren for life, and then to my great grandchildren." At the time of the will, Montague had only one grandchild, Thomas, and no more grandchildren were ever born. The draftsman avoided problems with unborn widows, fertile octogenarians, and precocious toddlers by naming names, so that wife and all three children were lives in being. But the draftsman did not interview enough, or draft well enough, to repeat that precaution in the next generation, which meant that no one in the grandchild's generation could be used as a life in being—even though there was only one grandchild, Thomas, and he was living at the time Montague's will became effective. The rule does not operate on facts as they occur *after* the testator's death, but on facts as they might occur, or, rather, *might have occurred* after that time: Mr. Montague's will said "grandchildren" and he left three living children. At the time of the litigation it was clear that the only grandchild was Thomas, but, looking at the family on the day Mr. Montague died, there might have been additional grandchildren. The final remainder in great-grandchildren therefore failed. It would not have failed if the instrument had said "then to my grandchild Thomas for life" or "then for life to those of my grandchildren who are living at my death." Careful drafting could even have added 21 years to this dynastic disposition without risking invalidity: "… then to those of my great-grandchildren who are living 21 years after the death of the last to die of those of my grandchildren who are living at my death."

Exercise 7.3

Please apply this planning device to the gift of the mining tract to take effect when the mining is concluded, in Francis Gresham's will.

Another way to draft for dynastic safety is to grant a power to a fiduciary to reform the instrument if it proves invalid under the rule against perpetuities; several states now provide statutes which give this power to judges. (See the Statutory Appendix.) A grantor can give the same power to a private fiduciary, in a clause (adapted from the Vermont statute) something like this: "An interest which would violate the rule against perpetuities shall be reformed by my trustee, within the limits of that rule, to approximate most closely my intention." In the case of Montague's will, the trustee could have reformed the life interest in grandchildren to confine it to Thomas, which would have made no difference at all, and thus have saved the remainder interest in great-grandchildren.

A third form of drafting, one that is common and advisable in instruments that do not create dynastic dispositions but which could run into trouble under one of the historic absurdities in the rule, limits interests to those allowed under the rule. Here is an example: "All interests created in this will shall vest no later than twenty-one years after the death of the last to die of me, my husband Sam, and those of my lineal descendants who are living at my death. Upon the expiration of this period all income interests shall terminate and principal shall be distributed to the persons entitled to receive income."

2. JUDICIAL REFORM

Judges have been more liberal about perpetuities—usually by way of construing interests before applying the rule to them—than Professor Leach's scholarship implied. (See Part C of Chapter 8, *infra*.) There are few perpetuities cases in the reports since about 1930, and, of those, few find interests invalid. By this crude empirical measure, perpetuities is a less serious problem than failures to follow statutory formalities for will execution, or defects in trust conveyancing, and certainly less serious than mistakes about tax law. Judges commonly avoid problems with perpetuities by construing interests away from the rule. Consider the example used above, in a will, "to the children of T, but if any of them becomes a Unitarian, his interest to the children of X." The courts early held the shifting executory interest in X's children invalid, but they also held that the grantor's object could have been achieved in two conveyances: (1) "to the children of T, so long as none of them becomes a Unitarian." (2) "All of my remaining interest to the children of X." The reasoning was that the left-over after the first conveyance was a vested interest, a reversion in the grantor, and that its vested character was retained when it was conveyed separately. That sort of result is sophistry, of course, but it is not offensive to a judge unless she finds moral quality in the rule against perpetuities. It is a delightful bit of evasion for those who find the rule too restrictive. It is less interesting as stating a rule (the *two bites* rule, Professor Leach called it) than as stating a relatively modern judicial attitude.

Exercise 7.4

Please apply this "two bites" rule to Mr. Gresham's will, specifically to the creation of a shifting executory interest in favor of Griselda Gresham.

Another way for judges to avoid problems with the rule is to hold that courts have an inherent equitable power to reform interests so that they do not violate the rule. A couple of American courts have held that judges have this power, usually on loose analogy to *cy pres,* the equitable power to reform charitable trusts.[2] (See the Statutory Appendix.)

---

2. *Cy pres* is Law French for "as close as possible." When a gift is made for a charitable purpose that cannot be achieved, eq- uity will reform the trust so that the object can be carried out some other way.

A third judicial alternative is to reject formal applications of the rule; for example, there is nothing to prevent a modern court from rejecting the presumption that any woman can bear a child; from applying common sense to gravel pits; from presuming that a testator who says "my son's widow" means the person to whom his son is married, either when the testator makes his will or when the testator dies; or, more commonly, from construing "to the children of S when they are 25" as an interest vested subject to divestment, rather than as a contingent interest.

The last example is probably the most common sort of judicial reform, and may justify a few additional words of explanation. If the grantor says "to A for life and then to the children of A when the youngest is 25," the rule, classically applied, invalidates the gift, since any given child of A could reach 25, or fail to reach 25, at a time which is beyond lives in being and 21 years. But that reasoning depends on regarding the interest of each child of A as a contingent interest. Some cases support that construction, but there are also cases which construe as vested a gift "to the children of A, to be distributed when the youngest of them is 25," which probably means the same thing, perpetuities aside. The task of a judge bent on avoiding the rule is to apply the rule in the second line of cases, and to hold that the interests of children of A are vested subject to the divesting condition that a child survive until the youngest of his siblings dies or reaches 25. This is a practical, everyday sort of example. Clients often want to postpone distribution of trust principal to grandchildren until they reach an age regarded by them as mature, and until their youngest grandchild has grown up and been educated.[3]

Exercise 7.5

Here is a set of problems culled from the rich literature of perpetuities in Section 3.20 of Stoebuck and Whitman, *The Law of Property* (3d ed. 2000).

7.5.1. In each case: Is the future interest valid or invalid?

(a)   To A so long as the property is used for church purposes, then to B.

(b)   To A, but if the property should ever cease to be used for church purposes, then to B.

(c)   To A for life, remainder to the first son of A whenever born who becomes a clergyman.

(d)   To A for life, remainder to the first son of A to reach the age of 25.

(e)   To A for life, remainder to the children of A for life,

---

3. This resolution does not address the validity of the "gift over" in case a child dies before the age of 25. (We could have made an exercise out of that!)

and upon the death of the last surviving child of A, to such of A's grandchildren as may be then living.

(f) To A for life, remainder to such of A's lineal descendants as are alive on January 1, 2021 [the testator died January 1, 1999].

(g) To A for life, remainder to such of the grandchildren of A as reach the age of 21 years.

7.5.2. In each case where the future interest is void, redraft it so that it is not void.

3. LEGISLATION

Professor Leach provoked a number of scholars to draft reform legislation; half the states have adopted some of it. There are four broad categories, ranging from drastic to trivial—(1) "wait and see" reform; (2) *cy pres*; (3) specific; and (4) miscellaneous. (See the Statutory Appendix.)

The "wait and see" statutes mandate courts to regard "actual events" rather than the "might have been" factual perspective upon which the common-law rule depends. The actual-events statute would eliminate almost all of Leach's absurd cases, since octogenarians and five-year-olds will not in fact have children, gravel pits will soon be exhausted, and youngest children will attain 25 within 21 years of the end of all lives in being. What judges will do under the statutes, apparently, is to dismiss actions that assert invalidity so long as defending litigants can show that the actual-events period has not elapsed. This possibility has raised professorial questions about what lives can be selected for measuring an actual-events period. Some commentators feel that "wait and see" reform destroys the rule against perpetuities because litigation based on the rule will virtually never succeed. The defender will always be able to find someone who was alive at the effective date of the instrument and who died fewer than 21 years before the lawsuit. The late Professor Lewis Simes, commenting on these statutes, entitled his essay "Is the Rule Against Perpetuities Doomed?"

Exercise 7.6

Assume Francis Gresham leaves the S.E.M. tract "to Mike, but if the mining is not completed when Mike dies to the descendants of Mike and Griselda when the mining is completed." Suppose the statute quoted under assumption "(2)," at the beginning of this chapter, is in effect. Who are the lives in being?

Some statutes attempt to specify which lives can be used as lives in being; these statutes sometimes define lives in being by classes of relatives or donees. They sometimes turn on terms that have to be judicially defined. The phrase, "causal relationship," is an example of the latter sort of reform. Arguments over measuring lives under "wait and see" legislation belong, so far, under the heading of bookish quarrels by law professors. It is fairly clear that, for most perpetuities challenges, Professor Simes' gloom was justified; the legislation will turn plaintiffs away and will eliminate the rule as a limitation on all but the reckless.

Cy pres statutes give jurisdiction to the courts to reform dispositions that violate the rule. They do not modify the rule; they modify the sanction for violation. They are in three forms: (1) A broad form: "No interest ... is ... void ... to the extent that it can be reformed or construed ... to give effect to the general intent of the creator.... This section shall be liberally construed ... to validate such interest...." (2) A second form combines "wait and see" and *cy pres,* so that interests which offend the rule, even after a "wait and see" time period is applied, can be reformed. (3) A few states limit the *cy pres* remedy to specific situations, such as the reduction of age limitations (so that "to the children of A when the youngest is twenty-five" can be reformed to read "when the youngest is twenty-one").

A few statutes are directed to *specific* situations, usually to the absurd constructions Professor Leach is famous for criticizing. A statute may, for instance, overrule the unborn-widow construction by providing that a disposition measured by the life of a widow is deemed to be measured by a life in being, whether it is or not. Some statutes overrule the magic-gravel-pit result. Statutes in some states establish presumptions on human fertility.

Finally, there are, in the miscellaneous category, several statutes that set up novel experiments. Two of the most interesting are statutes that establish gross periods longer than twenty-one years. At common law, a disposition was valid if limited for a gross period of twenty-one years or less ("to the children of A twenty-one years after my death"). Under the new statutes, the time can be much longer. One statute, for instance, says: "No interest ... which must vest, if at all, not later than 60 years after the creation of the interest" violates the rule. A proposed statute promulgated by the Commissioners on Uniform State Laws recommended a 90–year gross period.

More common miscellaneous examples are statutes exempting from the rule employment fringe-benefit trusts, trusts for the maintenance of cemeteries, or dispositions over to charity. (At common law, charitable trusts are exempt from the rule if the interest vests in some charity within the common-law period or shifts, beyond the period, from charity to charity. "To the Baptist Church in 25 years" is, therefore, void, but "to the Baptist Church so long as it uses the property for purposes of worship, and then to the Methodist Church" is all right.)

4.   ACCUMULATIONS

The common-law rule against perpetuities applies only to remoteness of vesting. The fact that an interest is tied up does not render it void, if ownership is to vest in time. This makes it possible to set up accumulations of trust income for three generations or more, a circumstance that has sometimes caused concern. In a celebrated case in England at the beginning of the 19th century, a patriarch named Thellusson provided that his wealth be held in trust, and income from it accumulated, for final payment to his great-grandchildren. (That would not have violated the rule against perpetuities if the period of accumulation were defined as "21 years after the death of the last to die of all of my lineal descendants who are living on the date of my death," or, if the client lacked numerous descendants, "those of the descendants of Her Late Majesty Queen Victoria who are living at my death.") The United Kingdom then passed special legislation limiting the period during which trust income could be accumulated. A number of American states have similar statutes (sometimes called "Thellusson Acts"), but the British legislation is generally not regarded as part of American common law. This bit of arcane trust-accumulation law is behind limits in trust documents that permit a trustee to accumulate income only "to the extent permitted by law."

5.   POWERS OF APPOINTMENT

Treatises on "estate planning" and large-estate form books spend a good deal of space discussing powers of appointment. It should be noted even here that the common-law rule against perpetuities applies to powers. It applies to the creation of a power, so that "to S for life, then to the widow of S for life, then as my eldest descendant living at the death of the widow of S may appoint" is void, because the vesting of the power itself is too remote.

The principal difficulty with perpetuities in powers cases has been appointment of the power property. In historical theory, the exercise of a power of appointment is regarded as an act of agency. Consider "to S for life, then to the widow of S for life, then as the widow of S by will appoints." When the widow of S appoints, in theory she is acting for the donor of the power. In this example, the power itself is void because the appointment may not be made in time (unborn widow). If the disposition is "To S for life, then as Mary, the wife of S, may appoint," that defect is cured. But what if Mary then appoints "to my eldest son for life and then to his children"? That disposition appears to be void because the time period must relate all the way back to the creation of the power, and the eldest son of Mary may not be born within the life of the donor of the power.

If the rule were applied to powers in those terms, many such dispositions would be void. It is not so applied, and most exercises of powers of appointment are saved under one of two exceptions. The first exception is that, if the power is general and presently exercisable (that is, a power in the donee to appoint to anyone, including himself, which may be exercised by deed or by will), the power property is treated as if it belonged to the donee (Mary), and the perpetuities period begins on the date of the exercise of the power. The second exception is a limited "wait and see" doctrine. The facts considered are facts as of the date of exercise, rather than facts as of the date of creation. The example above was "as the wife of S, Mary, may appoint" with an appointment "to my eldest son for life and then to his children." If the eldest son was born after the death of the donor of the power of appointment, the exercise will be void, since it may vest property in the appointees beyond lives in being and twenty-one years. However, the eldest son may, as it turns out, be someone who was living when the donor died. In that case, actual facts will be consulted, rather than what might have been at the creation of the power, and the appointment will be upheld.

REFERENCES AND BIBLIOGRAPHY

D. Becker, "Tailoring Perpetuities Provisions to Avoid Problems," Probate and Property, March–April 1995, p. 10

R. Law, W. Graves, and S. Sponsler, "The Rule Against Perpetuities: An Update," 15 Tax Management Financial Planning Journal 311 (1999)

B. Leach: Professor Leach's work can be traced through a generation of issues of the Harvard Law Review or read in the compilation Future Interests and Estate Planning (Harvard Law Review Ass'n, 2d ed. 1965) and "Perpetuities in the Atomic Age: The Sperm Bank and the Fertile Decedent," 48 American Bar Ass'n Journal 942 (1962)

C. Moynihan and S. Kurtz, Introduction to Real Property (3rd ed. 2002)

Chapter 8

LANGUAGE

A. AN INDICTMENT

"I honestly worry about lawyers," E.B. White said. "They never write plain English themselves, and when you give them a bit of plain English to read, they say 'Don't worry, it doesn't mean anything.' They're hopeless...." The lawyers we know are not hopeless (and neither are we hopeless), but our paper product would be reduced and sharpened by a factor ranging up to half if we gave as much attention to communication as we give to the probate code. The late Mr. White might well have asked us: What would happen if you went through everything you write and removed the illegitimate adjective "said," or reduced by eighty per cent your use of "whereas" and "thereof"?

Legalese in testamentary drafting must be a puzzlement to the average liberally-educated client. (Mr. White was well above average and was a chicken farmer besides.) Does a valid testamentary document need always to be entitled "Last Will and Testament of John" instead of "Will of John"? And must John "make, publish and declare" his will and "give, devise and bequeath" things? Does the what's-left after specific and general bequests in a will inevitably have to be dealt with as "rest, residue, and remainder"?

The General told the Second Lieutenant in "Beetle Bailey": "Just because you can write so nobody understands it doesn't mean you're a lawyer," but it might. A form book we enjoyed, published several years ago, featured a dispositive sentence in one of its trust instruments that consumed 34 printed lines and contained 383 words. In practice the sentence threatened to become even longer because additional contingencies had to be considered, and additional names inserted. (The form left room for only two.) A trust power in the same book contained 161 words and was not a complete sentence.

Sometimes the issue is length; sometimes it is putting phrases in a bad place. An example of the latter: U.S.A. Today reported that second baseman Ryne Sandburg of the Chicago Cubs "missed his second game in a row after playing 74 consecutive contests with a bad case of the flu Monday. 'He's very, very sick,' manager Jim Frey said." The New Yorker picked that up to fill out a column and added the comment: "And tired." Another example: The newspaper in Madison, Indiana, said: "Jefferson County Sheriff Wayne Hamilton this morning discussed the problems of lodging in the jail unconscious people suspected of being drunk with the county commissioners." Baseball managers, police officers, and lawyers would usually be better off, as would the people they manage and arrest and put in jail, with shorter sentences; but sometimes the trouble is not so much length as it is putting words in the wrong place.[1]

Many forms for will drafting turn out to be essays on three levels of law-office rhetoric: (1) Lawyers' English English, (2) Lawyers' Legal English, and (3) English. The distinctive features are: (1) Lawyers' English English is a puzzle-like arrangement of words that are, or were at sometime since Doomsday Book, used by the English-speaking peoples.[2] (2) Lawyers' Legal English is equally complex and also mixes in words known only to lawyers, or, as is often the case, used only, but not known, by lawyers. (3) English is English, when used by Mr. Tutt as much as when used by Keats, Shelley, or Ellen Goodman.

One hard-cover form book suggests a letter from a parent to a child, occasioned by the parent's decision to give the child securities and real property. The letter says, "I have decided to start you on the right road by making the following gifts...." That's English. Two pages later the authors recommend a form for a "deed" to accompany the gift. "KNOW ALL MEN BY THESE PRESENTS," they said:

> ... That (blank), the undersigned, residing at (blank), County of (blank), State of (blank), and sole owner of all right, title, and interest in and to the following described property, DO HEREBY irrevocably and absolutely give, assign, and transfer to (blank), residing at (blank), County of (blank), State of (blank), all of my right, title and interest in and to said property, namely....

In the letter, when the child wants to acknowledge receiving gifts, the child signs under the words "accepted and receipt acknowledged. (Date)." But when this is done officially, it has to say, "The undersigned does hereby accept the aforesaid gift subject to the terms and conditions above set forth and does hereby acknowledge the receipt of the above described property this (blank) day of (blank), (blank). L.S."[3] That's Lawyers' Legal

---

1. For example: James J. Kilpatrick, in his newspaper column "The Writer's Art" (South Bend Tribune, February 22, 2004), noticed, in a police report from Bloomington: "A 61–year-old man reportedly hit an Indiana University police officer who was directing traffic in the leg with the front quarter of his car and in the chest with the driver's side mirror."

2. Willard C. Butcher, chairman of the board of the Chase Manhattan Bank, said, "Banks are being legally estopped from competing." Mr. Butcher had to say estop rather than stop because of his choice of the adverb "legally"; estop is a legal verb. For example, if you give your money to your barber in order to keep your creditors from getting at it, we lawyers warn that you may have estopped yourself from getting the money back after the creditors desist; the idea is, as we lawyers, who know about such things, say, that your hands are not clean. The verb is almost always used in the passive voice: One is estopped; one does not often estop somebody else and one does not estop intransitively either. In theory, you can estop yourself, but we rarely say so.

3. For *locus sigili,* "the place of the seal." Do you have the hot red wax ready? If not, do you know what to tell your client to do with the "L.S."?

English (L.S.), as is another form, some four pages later, which says "NOW, THEREFORE, the Donor does hereby irrevocably and absolutely give, assign, and transfer to the Donee an interest in the net income which the Donor now is, or may hereafter be, entitled to receive during his lifetime."

Lawyers' English English is recommended to a client for a second letter of gift occurring later in the book. The client has forwarded to a foundation "all of my right, title, and interest in and to the following" (securities and a painting), noting that "said shares and painting are hereby given to you for your corporate purposes, irrevocably and absolutely." No one but a displaced person from Thomas More's Utopia, where there are no lawyers, would have any doubt about the identity of the ghost who wrote that letter.[4]

The three levels of language are always identifiable, but not always or easily put in categories in terms of the task at hand. A letter in the same form book, from a testator to his fiduciaries, is in English: "I have today executed a will in which I have named the first of you as a co-executor and co-trustee with my wife and the City Trust Company. I have named the second of you as successor to the first." It is not clear to us why English can be used in addressing fiduciaries, but Lawyers' English English has to be used in addressing a charitable donee. It probably has to do with the English Mortmain Acts and the virtual rejection in the British Isles of the doctrine of papal infallibility.

The vitality of Lawyers' English English, when one considers the eventual decline of Law French, is not easy to understand. Dispositive instruments, to a greater extent than business contracts and corporate forms, retain a level of legalese that betrays a black-magic theory of interpersonal relations in the law office—an inarticulate fear that everything the relatively undereducated 19th century lawyer used had cabalistic significance; although a modern person is incapable of understanding it, it is vital to a document's success. Law, according to this theory, is witch-doctoring with a pencil, and drafting is half exposition and half ritual.

When Professor Gottlieb suggested years ago in the *American Bar Association Journal* that law students should be subjected to English courses, two lawyers wrote to the editor. One of them wondered if a command of English in young lawyers would not be a disadvantage. "Chances are that they will be employed by lawyers whose years of practice have taught them that a lawyer's letter should read like this," he said: " 'Enclosed herewith please find copy of Answer in the above-captioned case, the original of which has been duly filed of record.' Woe

4. Part of the goal in Lawyer's English English is to be obscure, as in this exchange: Somebody put this question to Dave Barry, in his role as "Mister Language Person": "I am often confused about the difference between 'accept' and 'except.' Is there a way to tell them apart?" Mr. L.P. answered, "Not at this time."

betide the junior associate who would suggest the slightest revision of such models of legal writing." The other letter writer, a former bar examiner, thought that sentences in bar-examination answers, while often poor, "were no worse than many of the published judicial opinions that are said to make up the body of the law."

Judge George Rossman, of the Oregon Supreme Court, saw linguistic dangers from behind and in front. He warned lawyers away from fashionable phrases which many of us "seemingly cannot resist." "Such a word," he said, "is 'gobbledygook.'" The judge was equally negative about lawyers' perennial fondness for "and/or." It is not the duty of a draftsman to display her familiarity with the new, he said. Her duties are to ascertain her clients' purposes and to express them with such clarity that they cannot be misunderstood. He quoted Galen, "The chief virtue that language can have is clearness, and nothing detracts from it so much as the use of unfamiliar words." Judge Rossman also worried about old words: He noted the "marked affinity" lawyers have for "the word 'said.' They may deceive themselves into a belief that they have done a good job of draftsmanship when they notice that they have sprinkled about the paper a goodly number of 'saids.' The time has come when, in the interest of good draftsmanship, use of that word should be discontinued."

No lawyer's job is so small that craftsmanship in the use of language is unjustified. At the most immediate and appealing level, that is so because we have human lives and fortunes in our hands. Judge Rossman added a different, sort of "what if" motive: "The lawyer who is asked by a client to prepare a deed or a contract in a transaction that involves only a modest sum may not feel that the course of history will turn upon the outcome of his efforts. But the transaction out of which *Marbury v. Madison* emerged was even more modest than that—the appointment of a justice of the peace. The important detail is for all lawyers to feel that everything they do is important. Each should by all means be determined to prepare the paper he drafts so well that it will not make its way into *Words and Phrases Judicially Defined.*"

The United States Tax Court once decided (or, as we lawyers say, held) that a lawyer who tries to learn the English language is not acquiring a skill that is necessary to his profession. Steven J. McAuliffe there lost his claim for a deduction for the cost of taking English courses at Georgetown University. He argued that the study of poetry, Victorian literature, and writing were important to his being a lawyer. Not so, said the Tax Court: "We are unwilling to declare that the study of English literature ... bears the sort of proximate relationship to the improvement of an appellate attorney's legal skills to justify the deduction," wrote Judge Howard A. Dawson, Jr. Too bad. If Judge Dawson had taken the courses he might not say things like "proximate relationship"; he would say what he means. And if lawyers and others who are paid for using words could get a tax deduction, maybe they would learn not to say things like "give, devise, and bequeath," thereby to corrupt bureaucrats and journalists–as in this letter: "In lieu of a possible postal strike, your monthly benefit check is being mailed early." Or this report (from the Boston Globe): "During the meeting ... [the President] will try to 'widen the areas of agreement,' the official said, in order to 'contribute to the renewal of obstacles.' "[5] There are, on the other hand, some signs of hope. A taxi driver in San Francisco was asked if lawyers who come to conventions there are good tippers. "Oh," he said, "they tip just like real people."

A client's will is only part of the apparatus we lawyers typically assemble and (some of us) call "estate planning." But it is, as Jean Anouilh said the knight-errant's horse was, the most important and the most sensitive part of the enterprise. It may be, despite all of these injunctions against legal redundancy, that a good will (especially a good "simple" will) tends to turn out longer than a poor one. Brevity is not necessarily a virtue in will drafting, and none of us who inveighs against legalisms means to imply that it is. "Frequently," Dean Casner said, "property dispositions cannot be made short and simple without inviting litigation and trouble. Real simplicity has always come through completeness of statement." What we inveigh against here is waste and confusion and black magic and obscurity. The hackneyed phrase in will drafting is as ugly as it is anywhere else, and as dysfunctional and therefore deserving of the great Fowler's condemnation:

"The purpose with which these phrases are introduced is for the most part that of giving a fillip to a passage that might be humdrum without them. They do serve this purpose with some readers—the less discerning—though with the other kind they more effectually disserve it. But their true use when they come into the writer's mind is as danger-signals; he should take warning that when they suggest themselves it is because what he is writing is bad stuff, or it would not need such help. Let him see to the substance of his cake instead of decorating it with sugarplums."

Fowler's conclusion may account for most legalese. Another theory is that the use of legalese can be traced to habit, and to the vague feeling that clients cannot appreciate something they understand. But client understanding is the most conclusive argument *for* using English instead of Lawyers' Legal English and Lawyers' English English. Many of our documents in the property settlement practice have offices far beyond disposition. They are charters for human conduct, which must or should be used routinely by lay fiduciaries, beneficiaries, and parties to

---

5. Graduate education might help eliminate a common confusion between two words used by lawyers that sound alike but aren't: Principal is not principle; in fact some few principals are unprincipled and most so-called principles are far from principal. A bank in South Bend advertised the virtues of "reinvestment of principle and interest," as if character can be bought at a bank.

contracts. "Your task," Joseph Trachtman said to lawyers in this field, "is to write the dispositive and administrative provisions in such a way that the … trustees will do best what *they* are capable of doing well."

B.   A SYSTEM

Drafting often suffers from an absence of philosophy and a lack of system. We have attempted to suggest some—pardon the word—philosophical considerations in Chapter One. Now, for system, we invoke one of the most impressive of drafters, the late Kurt F. Pantzer of the Indianapolis Bar, a thorough and famous systematizer. Mr. Pantzer's system is eminently useful. It is a rarity in the legal profession because it demonstrates thought about drafting, and general application of that thought. We refer to and quote here from an unpublished set of notes, "Guides for Draftsmanship," used by Mr. Pantzer for a series of lectures at the Indiana University School of Law.

Mr. Pantzer's system is divided into what he called the "five legal techniques." These are legal planning, negotiation, drafting, trial court advocacy, and appellate law. On these five techniques he imposed what he called the "seven sanctions." This system of sanctions avoids a weakness in the Langdell case system used in most law schools (and a weakness that can creep into other methods if instructor and student are not careful to emphasize planning, rather than litigation): "[T]he modern law firm gauges its success by its ability to avoid litigation and at the same time insure the legality of the transactions in which its clients are engaged."[6]

1.   THE SEVEN SANCTIONS

"A well-drafted instrument should speak with a sanction," Mr. Pantzer said. "It should generate a mandate of its own, which compels its performance or observance, and which derives from its order, language, and visual appeal, its factual and legal and equitable 'rightness,' and its common sense."

(a) *The Factual Sanction.* A document must show first of all "sufficient conversance with the facts." This sanction, in will-drafting, requires thorough client interviews, examination of title documents and other evidences of ownership, and enough time for the drafter to develop a feeling for her client's attitudes and family situation. The lawyer who interviewed Dr. and Mrs. Kennedy (Chapter 3) was observing and deepening the *factual sanction* when she conducted that interview in the clients' home rather than in her law office, because, in "estate planning," feelings *are* facts, and home is where the heart is.

---

6.   An awkward sentence, because Mr. Pantzer avoided ending it with a preposition: "transactions its clients are engaged in." E.B. White and H.W. Fowler both disdained the rule against ending a sentence with a preposition, and Mr. White invented a sentence ending in five prepositions: "What did you bring that book I don't want to be read to out of up for?"

(b) *The Legal Sanction.* A document must reflect an understanding of the substantive law that governs it. In will drafting,[7] this is a difficult sanction to observe, but if a drafter lacks a grasp of the substantive law of wills and future interests, and the property-law consequences of what he is doing, no amount of graceful English will save him. Yet we are surprised at how many apparently well-thought-out wills contain invalid incorporations by reference or violations of the canons of good class-gift drafting.

Mr. Pantzer divided this legal sanction, first, according to its positive aspect, which includes "all the legal concepts which are involved in the situation covered by the document." For instance, "a well-drawn will expresses whether and when an interest vests and whether and under what circumstances a legacy will lapse." The other aspect is the negative aspect, which is "the exclusion of illegal concepts." The rule against perpetuities (Chapter 7) is an example.

(c) *The Equitable Sanction.* This sanction requires essential fairness and is immediately applicable to bilateral agreements. But it fits will drafting too. One of the property-settlement lawyer's most solemn obligations is to advise her client against being cruel to the objects of his bounty. There are many reasons for attention to the equitable sanction. The most important is moral: For all of our jokes about the witty riposte that is saved until the speaker is beyond retaliation, vindictive will provisions cut more deeply than almost any other form of property-related cruelty; we suppose that is because they usually involve feelings within a family as much as they involve property, and none of us is ever free from the pain and the pleasure of those feelings. And they are final, beyond the likelihood of reconciliation this side of Heaven. There are other reasons, too: A disappointed relative is a potential contest suit, for one thing; a review of appellate opinions in will contest and will construction cases can lead to the conclusion that a will that is vindictive has a heightened chance of being attacked and a lowered chance of surviving attack. Another argument for observing the equitable sanction in will drafting is concern for the equanimity of one's client: The benefit a client gets from making his will is mostly that he gets to feel better afterwards. (He won't take his property with him; *he* won't pay taxes on it; he probably won't even get to be present when the mistreated relative hears the bad news.) It is poor service to leave the client with a will that makes him feel *worse.*

(d) *The Organizational Sanction.* "This sanction," Mr. Pantzer said, "deals with the architecture of the document and whether [it] is adapted

---

7. We deleted the hyphen between "will" and "drafting" as we fixed up our draft for the fourth edition of this book. We follow for the moment the eminent wordsmith William Safire: "Hyphens should be used mainly when not using them causes confusion." Your author for the fifth edition thus had moments of stress with his faithful advisor Nancy J. Shaffer over a hyphen or nothing at all in "health care." What's the answer? See D. Barry, note 4 *supra.*

to its mission. To draw an analogy from that sister profession, some documents are planned as if the front door of the home led, not into the reception hall, but into the dining room." A fairly conventional order is followed in most wills, which you can identify by studying Chapter 4 and the documents included in Chapter 3, Chapter 9, and Chapter 10. The order is unconsciously dramatic, as if the family still gathered in the drawing room after the funeral and heard the lawyer read the will. Of course if that were true, considering the way most wills are drafted, all but the acutely avaricious would be asleep before the residuary clause.

Mr. Pantzer classified the organization of drafting he examined into eight overlapping categories. "Estate planning" documents fall into more than one of these.

(i)   Primitive: "the style of the document has just grown like Topsy."

(ii)   Unilateral: "like an insurance policy, or a warranty deed." (One of two parties is doing all the talking. A will is organized unilaterally.)

(iii) Partisan: organized "according to the parties involved," and stating their respective duties in order. (A will might be organized according to the beneficiaries, but that would be unconventional. An example here is a lease.)

(iv)   Dynamic: "first things first." (This, too, would be an unconventional way to organize wills, which usually place the best in the middle. Some contracts are organized dynamically.)

(v)   Chronological: "organized like a drama, according to the chronology of the covenants or facts." (Wills probably fall into this classification most commonly. Typically, the testator disposes of debts and taxes, then specific bequests, then residuary bequests, then trusts, then powers.)

(vi)   Mandatory: Some documents must be drafted under court rules or statutes, and their organization should follow the prescribed model. (Will drafting often includes this kind of document; insurance planning may occasion the use of prescribed forms, and tax planning and administration certainly do. In many states, durable powers of attorney, living wills, and creation of health-care agencies are done with statutory forms, and some statutes offer statutory will forms.)

Exercise 8.1

Consider for example how a drafter will have to describe the creation of a life estate in order to characterize a transfer to a surviving spouse as "qualified terminable interest property," so that the estate of the drafter's client will receive the federal estate-tax marital deduction, under Sec. 2056(b)(7)(B) of the Internal Revenue Code. A 19th century drafter, not burdened by statutory mandatory drafting, would have said: "To W for life." Please draft what a modern drafter has to say under the statutory provision:

For purposes of this paragraph—

(i) *In general.*—The term "qualified terminable interest property" means property—

(I) which passes from the decedent, [and]

(II) in which the surviving spouse has a qualifying income interest for life....

(ii) *Qualifying income interest for life.*—The surviving spouse has a qualifying income interest for life if—

(I) the surviving spouse is entitled to all the income from the property, payable annually or at more frequent intervals, or has a usufruct interest for life in the property, and

(II) no person has a power to appoint any part of the property to any person other than the surviving spouse.[8]

(vii) Functional: "Organized according to the functions to be performed, rather than their place in time or importance, or the parties who are to perform them." (Since a will is a blueprint for the personal representative, it often could follow this system, and often does, although the tendency is to put specific directions to the personal representative toward the end of the will, and to pay very little attention to them in the drafting stage.)

(viii) Ancillary: "[The] organization [is] incomplete because [the] document is ancillary to another document." (The pour-over will is an example of this, although a good drafter should prepare such a will so that it stands by itself. A codicil is a better example.)

(e) *The Orthological Sanction.* "The Bible uses the term aptly in the phrase, 'How forcible are the right words.' The principal objective of a

---

8. We belabor you with this tedious example for an additional and hidden purpose: so that you can notice how the Internal Revenue Code uses a tabular drafting style in order to make merely difficult what would otherwise be incomprehensible. Notice here that all of this quoted material from the Code is in two sentences. Try writing those sentences out in ordinary prose, after eliminating the dashes and all of the parenthetical Roman numerals. The point we piggyback here is one that belongs more properly under Mr. Pantzer's "visual sanction," below. You may want to compare your drafting here, or the government's, with that in the forms in Chapter 9 and Chapter 10.

document should be to make it understandable." Is the guiding principle exhibited in will cases keyed to that objective? Or is the principal objective exhibited in the history of this part of the law a vague notion that will-drafting is a form of magic—that the instrument certainly will fail if the testator says "I give" instead of "I give, devise and bequeath in fee simple absolute," just as the cave door would not open until Ali Baba said "open sesame"?

"Modern law has made great strides in its attempt to shake the shackles of the abominable legalese with which so many of the statutes, judicial decisions, textbooks, documents and pleadings of the past are encrusted.... [But] the average form book which is available to the practitioner is neither arranged, organized nor drafted according to any particular set of principles." Will form books sometimes contain documents that have been litigated and upheld by the courts. A fabled Hoosier lawyer once said he was the best will drafter in the state, and could prove it: Three of his wills had been upheld in the Supreme Court. Consider in that connection this observation by Professor Barton Leach: "Success is achieved only if no litigation develops out of the instrument. You have failed if the instrument has to be litigated, even though the litigation sustains your plan."

Mr. Pantzer: "A great deal has been said and written about the use of language in the practice of law.... However, writers have generally confined themselves to generalities and have failed to give specific examples. Practically anyone ought, in the first instance, to agree there is no reason why the principles of English composition as they are supposed to be taught in high school and college should not apply to legal draftsmanship as it is studied in a law school. The grammar and syntax of legal expression ought to be the same as the grammar and syntax of literary expression. So far as the elements of style are concerned— simplicity, clarity and grace—they are as fit to adorn a legal document as a novel." Of course, the contagion often works in reverse. How many lawyers write letters almost as full of "heretofore" and "aforesaid" as their wills are? Imagine what their novels would be like.

Mr. Pantzer then spoke of five kinds of orthology:

    (a)   Grammatical: "The elements of style as applied to a legal document would generally result in the following preferences":

        (i)   layman's English "rather than the English of the legal pedant";[9]

        (ii)   short sentences;

---

9. Judge Joe Kargis, of Houston, once had to help a prosecutor communicate with a witness. "Does Mr. Brown frequent that general locale with regularity?" the prosecutor asked. "What?" said the witness. Judge Kargis leaned over and rephrased the question: "Does Jerry hang around the pool hall?"

(iii)   too little punctuation rather than too much;

(iv)   complete statements rather than abbreviations;

(v)   use of the article;

(vi)   single words, rather than multiple-word, redundant phrases;

(vii)   English rather than Latin.[10]

(b)   Primitive: "When one considers a 'primitive' work, there is never any question as to which came first, the egg or the bird—it is perfectly clear that there never was an egg. The language of the document cries out that the draftsman is illiterate in English, and encourages the conclusion that he is probably illiterate in law as well."

(c)   Legalistic: That is, characterized by Lawyers' English.

(d)   Mandatory: For example, a marital-deduction clause drawn in reference to Sec. 2056 of the Internal Revenue Code. (The exercise just above asks for one piece of one kind of such a clause.)

(e)   Ancillary: For example, a pour-over will.

(f) *The Visual Sanction.* "[T]he visual sanction concerns itself with the appearance to the eye. The size and quality of the paper, the side where the pages are bound, the style of type, the spacing, etc., are all mechanical aids, chiefly of the visual sort, toward reading and quickly understanding the document."

(g) *The Pragmatic Sanction.* "Does the document deserve and obtain practical use and acceptance by those for whom it is written? Does it work? Whether a legal document 'works' ideally depends on many considerations and people. It is submitted however that much as the 'acceptance of the market place' is pragmatically to be desired,[11] it is responsible for most of the dents and bulges in documentary 'boiler plate.' "

10.   Bona fide is Latin for "in good faith." A classified ad in the South Bend Tribune sought "realtors with bonified customers."

11.   Mr. Pantzer, who learned Latin in school, labored a bit here to avoid what he apparently thought would be splitting an infinitive. Mensa, an organization that seeks to certify the superior intelligence of its members, complained in its newsletter about split infinitives. The rule here is like the rule on dangling prepositions: There is no rule, and thinking there is messes up a lot of writing. Fowler divided people into five categories on the question, the most blessed being those who neither know nor care what a split infinitive is. People who worry about splitting tend, he said, to "the tame acceptance of the misinterpreted opinion of others." Their fixation traces to the fact that you cannot split a Latin infinitive. Remember "amare," which means "to love"? In Latin you cannot say "to dearly love" and therefore, the non-splitters say, you shouldn't do it in English. Sometimes non-splitters get as fussy as Mr. Pantzer was. They unsplit verbs that aren't infinitives; their phrases could have been written by an academic committee. Fowler's examples: "really to be understood," "generally to be accepted"; and "this is a very serious matter, which clearly ought further to be inquired into." Fowler quotes a critic who praised "the sincerity which enables an author to move powerfully the heart." Non-splitters

Mr. Pantzer developed this theme at some length. Is it really "the Pragmatic Sanction" that has created bad draftsmanship, or is the culprit an almost instinctive, usually unfounded fear in unresourceful lawyers that a readable, explicit piece of drafting will be unacceptable to clients and condemned by colleagues at the bar and on the bench? The question is not what will work, but whether the document possesses the legal magic that gives security at the price of understanding. Compare the success in fostering understanding and observance which the Uniform Sales Act (now part of the Uniform Commercial Code) had with the litigation fostered by the Robinson-Patman Act, which was being construed by federal judges for half a century after Congress passed it. Is the difference between clarity and utility there, or is the utility of the Sales Act a result of its clarity?

2.   EXAMPLES

Mr. Pantzer did not leave his subject without many specific examples of what he considered good and bad usage. These are merely examples. You can probably think of dozens more. Some of these are taken from Mr. Pantzer's original thought; some he borrowed from Professor Reed Dickerson's booklet on drafting military regulations; and some are favorites of ours:

(a)   *Tense*: "Use the present tense, [and] except for using the word 'shall' in requirements or prohibitions, avoid the future tense."

(b)   *Mood*: "The words 'shall' and 'shall not' normally imply [that] someone must act or refrain from acting. Drafters frequently use these words merely to declare a legal result.... In declaratory provisions ... it is preferable ... to use the indicative, rather than the imperative, mood." (Not "if she shall survive me," but "if she survives me.") Examples:

— "The term 'person' means," rather than "the term 'person' shall mean."

— "The equipment remains," rather than "the equipment shall remain."

— "No person is entitled," rather than "no person shall be entitled."

(c)   *Forbidden Words*: These are the hackneyed expressions that make legal documents hard to read. Examples:

tend to make things worse, as in the little puzzler Fowler uses to close his article on the split: "After ... the author's opinion has perhaps been allowed to appear with indecent plainness, readers may like to settle the following question for themselves. 'The greatest difficulty about assessing the economic achievements of the Soviet Union is that its spokesmen try absurdly to exaggerate them; in consequence the visitor may tend badly to underrate them.' "

above, as an adjective	same (as a substitute for "it," "he," "she," "him," "her," etc.)
aforesaid	to wit
aforementioned	whatsoever
and/or (say "A or B, or both")	whensoever
provided that (try "if")	wheresoever
said (as a substitute for "the," "that," or "those")	hereinabove
	hereinafter

If you cannot provide 40 more within the next five minutes, you have not been paying much attention to your professional colleagues.

(d) *Preferred Expressions*: Unless there are special reasons to the contrary:

Say	**Don't say**
shall or may	"it is directed" or "it is the duty" or "is authorized" or "is entitled" or "it shall be lawful"
if or because	"in case" or "in the event that" or "for the reason that"
to and before	"in order to" and "prior to"
after or when	"subsequent to" or "at that time"
a year	per annum
law	provision of law
require	necessitate
use	utilize
Will of John	Last Will and Testament of John
Warranty Deed from Jones to Smith	Warranty Deed Executed By and Between Jones and Smith

Say	**Don't say**
I, John Smith, domiciled and residing in Indianapolis, Indiana, make this will	In the name of God, Amen. I, John Smith, a resident of and domiciled in Indianapolis, County of Marion, State of Indiana, being of sound and disposing mind and memory, do hereby enumerate the following Articles of Testamentary

This list is also painfully exemplar. It should not take very long for you to add a few favorites.

(e) *Circumlocutions*: Groups of two, three or four words that mean the same thing are the commonest sort of legal hocus pocus. The personal injury complaint which charges that the plaintiff was "rendered sick sore and disabled" is much more colorful, after all, than the one that says he was injured, and much easier than finding out, and saying, what his injuries were. James J. Kilpatrick, who writes the column "The Writer's Art," assembled an array of favorites without reading any wills: "free gift," "past history," "very unique," and "exact same size" (South Bend Tribune, May 30, 2004). Archaic will drafting is full of them:

any and all	desire and require
authorize and empower	means and includes
by and with	none whatever
each and all	promise, agree and covenant
each and every	make and execute
final and conclusive	due and legal
from and after	give, devise and bequeath
full force and effect	make, publish and declare
full and complete	seized or possessed
null and void	nominate and appoint
order and direct	signed, sealed, published and
over and above	declared
sole and exclusive	rest, residue, and remainder
type and kind	used and applied
authorize and direct	

Exercise 8.2

Here is one part of the will of Margaret Tyne, late of Illinois, as quoted by the Illinois Appellate Court in *City Bank v. Morrissey*, 454 N.E.2d 1195 (1983):

I GIVE, DEVISE, and BEQUEATH all the rest, residue and remainder of my property now owned by me or hereafter acquired, whether the same be real, personal, or mixed, or wherever situated, one-third part thereof to my son Thomas Tyne, one-third part thereof to my daughter Frances Tyne, and the remaining one-third, I GIVE, DEVISE, and BEQUEATH to my daughter Margaret Henry, in trust for the following uses and purposes to wit:

To lease, manage, control, sell, or operate all real estate; to collect the income from all property of any kind of nature whatsoever; to pay all taxes and assessments levied thereon; to sell and invest the proceeds in other real estate or appropriate securities; to become a party to the agreements for operating all real estate which may be of the nature of an undivided interest with the co-owners; to bring all suits and actions necessary to preserve and protect said property; to distribute the net income to my son, William Tyne, at least quarterly or more often as my trustee shall deem best, and to retain such part thereof as may be necessary to preserve and protect said estate.

Said trustee shall have the right to encroach on principal and expend the same for the purpose of the welfare, health, and maintenance of the said William Tyne and I further DIRECT that the income from said trust and the principal thereof shall be payable to the persons entitled thereto only upon their own individual receipt and shall not be subject to assignment, transfer, or any legal process of any kind or nature. I further DIRECT that upon the death of the beneficiary, William Tyne, that all the assets of the trust be converted into cash or distributed in kind to the heirs at law of the said William Tyne who survive him.

Please assume that this is a draft and that you are to mark it up for retyping, observing as well as you can Mr. Pantzer's seven sanctions. It may be useful to stand back from this for a few minutes and think of what Mrs. Tyne wanted. You may have questions about it that this quotation will not answer (in which case, please, assume you asked her and have her answers).

Winston Churchill said, "Short words are best, and old words are best of all." The Economist, enlarging on those admonitions (October 9, 2004): "Tough as boots or soft as silk, sharp as steel or blunt as toast, there are old, short words to fit each need. You want to make love, have a chat, ask the way, thank your stars, curse your luck or swear, scold and rail? Just pluck an old, short word at will. If you doubt that you will find the one you seek, look at what can be done with not much: 'To be or not to be?' 'And

God said, Let there be light; and there was light,' 'We are such stuff as dreams are made on,' 'The year's at the spring/And day's at the morn … /The lark's on the wing;/The snail's on the thorn.' It can be done, you see. If you but try, you can write well, and say what you want to say, with short words."   ·

Consider, by contrast, the somewhat more subtle advice from the great Fowler on what he called the noun-adjective: "The noun-adjective, useful in its proper place, is now running riot and corrupting the language in two ways. It is throwing serviceable adjectives onto the scrap heap; why, for instance, should we speak of *enemy attack*, a *luxury hotel*, a *novelty number*, an *England eleven*, when we have adjectives *hostile, luxurious, novel*, and *English*? And what is worse, it is making us forget that to link two words together with *of* may be both clearer and more graceful than to put the second before the first as an attribute; to forget for instance that, though *nursery school* is a legitimate use of the noun-adjective, *nursery school provision* is an ugly and obscure way of saying *provision of nursery schools*; that if *a large vehicle fleet* were translated into either *a large fleet of vehicles* or *a fleet of large vehicles* an ambiguity would be removed, and that a girl who *could not allay her guilt feelings* would probably find her *guilty feelings* or her *feelings of guilt* no less persistent. It is significant that we have dropped the old phrase *state of the world*; today it must always be the *world situation*."

C. INTERPRETATION

The process judges use to interpret language in wills deserves some further discussion, if only because the rules of construction have a stubborn integrity. They become rigid because they are so magnificently algebraic and complete. "Accept the premises even for a moment," Professor Schuyler said of them, "and the illusion of certainty is very apt to seize you." But the rules themselves obviously range from insight to sophistry.

The processes of decision should involve genuine interpretation of a testator's disposition. They should involve as little rigidity as minimum consistency demands. They should avoid the rigidity of *stare decisis* because in this sort of case–as in no other–no two cases are alike. Judges should find a way to get as close as they can to intention, and by that we mean as close as they can to what the testator probably would have done had his mind focused on the facts that occasioned the lawsuit.

Genuine interpretation recognizes first of all that language is always limited because words, especially written words, are inherently deficient. This limitation may arise from the use of imprecise words–for instance, the late Dean Joseph O'Meara's example of the sign that read "Please don't walk on the ceiling." The ceiling was glass and the sign was directed to the people on the top side of it.

The limitation may arise because words generally (or formerly) considered precise have been used unskillfully—for example the use of "heirs" in drafting. (Hint: Review the exercise from the *Tyne* case, just above.) It may arise where the word used is inadequate, as the use of "issue" is when it is not defined in the instrument. But even where the words used are precise, they must be matched to circumstances. Words are only ciphers. A testator who gives property to "my son" invites the use of extrinsic facts, and so does the testator who says "my son John X. Jones": Consider "my house in South Bend" or "my cousins ... friends ... relations."

Interpretation genuinely addressed involves taking the words out of themselves; it involves process. There seem to be three processes at work in the appellate opinions. One is a process of verbal interpretation. One is a process of interpretation by precedent. And one is a process of interpretation by inference.

1. *Verbal Interpretation.* Verbal interpretation involves consideration of contexts and relationships. It may be possible to analyze the use of references in terms of two steps: (a) the choice of a context or relationship, and (b) an identification within the context or relationship.

A context is necessary before words can operate; "my son" in the example above is an instance. This may be very broad: The testator says "all my cash to John"; does this include his collection of Spanish doubloons? If the prevalent idiomatic meaning of "cash" is used, obviously not. Or the context may be broad but confined to a more or less esoteric group. Our colleague Professor Robert Blakey once wrote a prisoner who sought his help, telling the prisoner that he might have a "colorable" claim to post-conviction relief. The prisoner checked the definition of "colorable" in a standard dictionary and found that the word means "specious." He wrote an irate reply; Professor Blakey answered the reply by explaining that, to lawyers, the word means "having apparent merit."

The reference may, finally, be so narrow that it is virtually individual: In *Kovar v. Kortan*, 209 N.E.2d 762 (Oh. Prob.1965), the court held that "to my nephew Edward" was not a disposition that fell under the Ohio lapse statute, which requires that the legatee be a relative, where the facts showed that Edward was regarded by the testator as a nephew, but was not his nephew in fact. Or is "in fact" accurate? Does it beg the question? Doesn't the "fact" depend on the relationship the court chooses to consult?

The identification within a relationship is the second part of verbal interpretation—the search for an object, after a relationship has been determined within which the search must take place. Professor Schuyler gives the example, "to A for life, remainder to the children of A and if none survive to A's sisters." All of A's children and all of A's sisters are dead when A dies. One result might be intestacy. Another might be the determination of the membership of the class "A's sisters," and consequent vesting, at the death of the testator. Will verbal interpretation resolve the conflict? It might. The relevant relationship is the testator within A's family. Given that perspective, it is more likely that A's sisters will die before their nieces and nephews will. And it is therefore likely that the object of the testamentary phrase "if none survive" is the fact that the testator's property is intended to pass *through* A's sisters to a select group of collateral takers, rather than pass under the laws of intestacy to all of the collateral takers. To put that conclusion in the familiar judicial rubric, the testator "intended" that the class "A's sisters" be determined at the testator's death and that remainders vest in them at that time.

Exercise 8.3

Please draft the disposition to A, A's children, A's sisters, and others, as suggested in this interpretation of the Schuyler example.

And consider:

(1) *Kelly v. Estate of Johnson*, 788 N.E.2d 933 (Ind. App. 2003), where the will disposed of "remaining living room furniture" and the family got into a fight over knickknacks and things hanging on the walls. The court considered what is sold in furniture stores.

(2) *Estate of East*, 785 N.E. 2d 597 (Ind. App. 2003): The real property at issue was 40 acres; mother's will devised the "residence house" that occupied part of that property, and the family fight was over how much land went with the house. The principal legal issue was whether there was enough ambiguity in the will to justify resort to "extrinsic evidence" on what mother meant; part of that issue involved resort to "common and ordinary sense"—e.g., how much land does a home owner need in order to enjoy the home?

A simpler example is the reference to "my nephew" in *Kovar v. Kortan*. The court decided that, because the statutory term "relative" was involved, the relationship within which interpretation had to be made was the community, and that the community did not regard Edward as the testator's "relative," even though the testator regarded Edward as his nephew. If the court had used the relationship between the testator and Edward—as it might, for instance, in a case involving a class gift to nephews—Edward would have been the testator's nephew. A similar example, where the community relationship was preferred over the personal, was a gift to "next of kin" in *Central Carolina Bank v. Bass*, 265 N.C. 218, 143 S.E.2d 689 (1965); the question was whether a girl the testator thought to be his granddaughter, to whom he referred as "granddaughter" elsewhere in the will, was within the class "next of kin."

The court, construing a will, held not, on weaker grounds than those involved in construing the statute in *Kovar*.

2. *Interpretation by Precedent.* The two-step process of interpretation by verbal reference may betray its own deficiencies. It has either failed to solve or been ignored in most cases. Courts prefer to use rules of construction, which are the stuff of "interpretation by precedent." Rules of construction are definitions of words developed from cases with similar factual situations. They add a new element to the definition of words because they add new sets of facts and new contexts and relationships. The process of definition then involves multiple relationships added to the relationship out of which the present case arises. They differ from statutes in that statutes *impose* a definitional relationship;[12] cases add new ones because cases have their own facts; statutes do not.

When a case defines words such as "children" and "heirs," the process appears simple and deductive because the precedents are so numerous that they generalize into a settled definition. Precedents are consulted as if they provide a sort of dictionary. But it is a dictionary subject to factual distinction and to the erosion of *stare decisis;* it is a less permanent edition than it is treated as being. Cases that define "heirs" so that the rule in Shelley's Case[13] is not applicable are examples of the elements that assault the dictionary of precedent.

In another way, rules of construction are rules of policy. The genesis of the rule in Shelley's Case and the doctrine of worthier title[14]—the prevention of feudal tax evasion—indicate that those rules are as much rules of policy as the pre–1976 Internal Revenue Code on "gifts in contemplation of death." The rule that the word "heirs" as a word of purchase must be construed at the death of the ancestor is perhaps a less emphatic example.

Professor Simes viewed some rules of construction not as vehicles of policy but as gap fillers. Rules are, he said, like the laws of intestacy; they are to be used when a testator is silent by way of ambiguity, just as intestate succession is to be used when he is silent by way of silence. The "rule of convenience" in class gifts to "children" seems to be an example of that. If this view of rules of construction as either vehicles of policy or as gap fillers is sound, the rules are—or should be—subject to changes dictated by economic and social *facts,* as well as by changes in social *values.* But rules affecting the disposition of property are not readily

12. For example, Sec. 2–107 of the Uniform Probate Code: "Relatives of the half blood inherit the same share they would inherit if they were of the whole blood."

13. Black's Law Dictionary (7th ed. 1999): "[I]f ... a freehold estate is given to a person and a remainder is given to the person's heirs, the remainder belongs to the named person and not the heirs...." To A for life and then to the heirs of A gives it all to A.

14. Id.: "... favors a grantor's intent by construing a grant as a reversion in the grantor instead of as a remainder in the grantor's heirs."

subject to either influence. The doctrine of worthier title is evidence enough that policy-oriented rules manage to survive changes in fact and changes in values. That doctrine, to stay with Simes, is today either a rule of policy based on feudal premises or a gap filler where there is no gap.

We doubt, by the way, that Professor Simes intended exclusive categories. Certainly some rules of construction tend to combine a positive policy limitation and a gap-filling function. Consider, for examples, the familiar maxims on preserving alienability, keeping property within a testator's blood lines, favoring natural objects of bounty, and avoiding intestacy.

3. *Interpretation by Inference.* The interpretative process that turns on precedent amounts to manufacturing intention. The process of verbal interpretation might involve manufacture in some cases—especially when a court refuses to use the context or relationship within which the testator spoke. But the third process, the process of interpretation by inference, is more sincere; it involves a *search* for intention; it does not *manufacture* intention. (The outline requires that distinction, even if the decisions themselves will not support it.)

Professor Schuyler gave this example: "to my son A and if he dies, title shall shift to Memorial Hospital." A legatee or creditor of A wants to know whether A had a fee. Precedent, especially because in modern law words of inheritance are not necessary, might argue that a fee was "intended." Verbal interpretation, especially if the relationship is in the testator's world and not in the world of lawyers, might indicate, however, a life estate in A with a remainder in the hospital.

The process of interpretation by inference comes neither from the case reports nor from the dictionary. It comes from the *facts*. It finds, say, that the testator was a supporter of Memorial Hospital fund drives and that A is a spendthrift. Interpretation is now possible based on the inference that the testator thought in terms of A's support—a life estate—with the ultimate fee in the hospital. Or perhaps the facts indicate that the testator preferred the hospital to intestate or residuary takers other than A—which might lead to the inference that the gift to the hospital was substitutional and that, because A survived the testator, he takes a fee.

Exercise 8.4

Please redraft the Schuyler example involving Memorial Hospital.

Another example is *Spathariotis v. Estate of Spathas*, 398 P.2d 39 (Colo.1964), noted in 42 Denver Law Center Journal 52 (1966), in which the testator gave "to my wife for life and, if my wife should predecease me, to my nephew." The testator's wife did not predecease him. It was clear that he gave her only a life estate, and the question was what to do with the remainder. The court found an implied remainder in the nephew. Its process was one of inferring that, because the gift to the nephew was to be substitutional if the testator's wife died before he died, it was also substitutional in preference to intestacy where his wife survived him. The court did not say anything about the rule favoring constructions that avoid intestacy; the Colorado judges preferred to rest their judgment on factual inference, since this was available, as the court put it, "within the four corners of the will."

Exercise 8.5

Please redraft the clause from *Estate of Spathas* to reach the result the court reached without the expense of trial-court and appellate litigation.

Interpretation by inference is of course limited by the rules of evidence, which force us back to rules of construction, and to a great extent rules of construction from precedent are corollary to exclusionary rules of evidence–which suggests that the only reason we have to look at precedent is because the rules of evidence won't let us look at the facts. That is especially obvious where the rules of construction impose a policy; it was obvious in the classical application of the rule in Shelley's Case—if "heirs" was used, inquiry into whether the testator meant to limit or to define purchasers was not possible. The difference between Professor Schuyler's *Memorial Hospital* example and the Colorado case is in the source of the inferred-upon facts; the rules of evidence may make Professor Schuyler's case much harder to solve because his source involves parol evidence. The difference between interpreting with precedent and interpreting with inference is that in the precedent process you *assume* fact B from fact A, and in the inferential process you *infer* fact B from fact A. Both processes refer more or less to human experience, but we think the inferential process is closer to it.

The judicial interpreter thus has an apparent three-way choice: (1) She can define her word by reference to a context or relationship, finding her word within that context or relationship, the process we defined as verbal interpretation. (2) She can define her word by a process of comparing the word before her with words used in instruments in prior cases, a process of definition by resort to precedent. (3) She can make inferences from facts, including facts in addition to those apparent in the instrument, and aside from those reported in precedent cases.

But the choice is only apparent. There is a process supervising the process, a hierarchy of methods. Courts reach one process only after the others fail. The hierarchy appears to have four levels—the three we have discussed, in the order we have used, and a fourth process, which we haven't discussed, if all three fail. Professor Schuyler gives four examples of the supervisory process; they correspond fairly well to what we have been trying to identify:

The first example is cases where the courts say that the intention is "clear" from the circumstances. Decisions that define a class designation to include members the testator probably thought dead (but who are not dead) are examples. It almost appears that the courts need no interpretive process until you reflect that the courts are giving content to words, and choosing relationships in which to do so—because they have to. A verbal interpretive process is at work in these cases, although no inference-making appears to be. (In fact the courts seem to refuse to make the inferences one might have made from the fact that the testator thought one of the class members to be dead.) It may be, too, that precedent is at work in a "clear intention" case. That may be so even though the court says not, even though it involves the common maxim— uncommonly put by the jurist who said that every wills case must stand firmly on its own bottom.

The second of Professor Schuyler's examples is a case where the court expressly invokes precedent, saying, as it does so, that the use of precedent is necessary because the intention is not "clear":

"to A for life and then to the children of B"; precedent may dictate class determination at the death of A;

"to A for life and then to the heirs of B"; precedent may dictate class determination at the death of B.

Precedent will "solve" both of these interpretive problems. And note that precedent here has solidified into a fairly certain set of rules; the day could conceivably come when these rules would even be relied upon in advance, as the meaning of "to A and his heirs" came to have a reliable meaning. Precedent has then become a sort of dictionary of terms and the rules of construction have become guidelines in the practice of preventive law. It all works well when (if) the drafter knows what she's doing.

Exercise 8.6

Please pretend for a moment that you are a judicial clerk in an appellate court, charged with drafting opinions in the two cases involving those last two dispositions. Please draft a sentence or two for each opinion explaining why precedent dictates the result:

8.6.1. "To A for life and then to the children of B." Membership in the class "children of B" is determined at the death of A.

8.6.2. "To A for life and then to the heirs of B." Membership in the class "heirs of B" is determined at the death of B.

Professor Schuyler's next example is a case where intention may be inferred with reasonable probability from the circumstances. This sort of case assumes that a process of verbal interpretation has failed and a process of interpretation through precedent tried and found wanting, or forsworn, or postponed. It obviously can make a difference which of the three processes is used first. Professor Schuyler appeared to believe that standard judicial practice is to use precedent before using inferences. Not all of the cases will bear him out.

Professor Schuyler put a fourth class of cases in which none of these three processes is of any help. The adopted-child case might be an example: "to my son Charles for life and then to his children alive at my death or born between my death and the death of Charles." Charles adopts a son, Henry, after the testator's death. Verbal interpretation is of no help. Even if the world of the testator is before the court, it cannot be said that he had an opinion one way or the other as to whether Henry was one of Charles's children—or whether Henry's adoption is equivalent to birth. Verbal interpretation is of course used in these cases, but not convincingly.

Interpretation by precedent is of no help here either, because the precedents on grandfathers and adopted children are all over the place, often not consistent with one another even within the same jurisdiction. Interpretation by inference is not helpful because there are no facts upon which inferences can be built. The obvious answer is that this fourth class of cases has to be decided in reference to what John Dewey called the "logic of consequences." The framework within which such cases are decided will then define terms for future cases which use interpretation by precedent; the judge has to act responsibly, as the existentialists would put it. Professional concern over the judge's abilities in that direction may explain a sort of trembling movement to deal with particular interpretive problems with statutes. Statutes requiring inclusion of adopted children, in the sort of case Professor Schuyler put, are an example.

REFERENCES AND BIBLIOGRAPHY

A. Casner, "Class Gifts to Others Than 'Heirs' or 'Next of Kin'—Increase in the Class Membership," 51 Harvard Law Review 254 (1937); "Construction of Gifts to 'Heirs' and the Like," 53 Harvard Law Review 207 (1939); "Class Gifts—Effect of Failure of Class Member to Survive the Testator," 60 Harvard Law Review 751 (1947)

S. Fetters, "The Determination of Maximum Membership in Class Gifts in Relation to Adopted Children," 21 Syracuse Law Review 1 (1969)

H. Fowler, Modern English Usage (2d ed. by E. Gowers, 1965)

E. Halbach, "Stare Decisis and Rules of Construction in Wills and Trusts," 52 California Law Review 921 (1964)

J. Henderson, "Mistake and Fraud in Wills," 47 Boston University Law Review 303, 461 (1967)

S. Jarboe, "Interpreting a Testator's Intent from the Language of Her Will: A Descriptive Linguistics Approach," 80 Washington University Law Quarterly 1365 (2002)

J. Kimble, Lifting the Fog of Legalese: Essays on Plain Language (2006)

P. Macalister, "Eliminating Legalese: New Body to Clear the Fog from Legal Documents," Law Society Journal (Australia), February 1992, p. 77

S. Palyga, "Is It Safer to Use Legalese or Plain English? What the Judges Say," Clarity, May 1999, p. 46

M. Ray, "How to Use Legalese," The Wisconsin Lawyer, July 1999, p. 34

D. Schuyler, "The Art of Interpretation in Future Interests Cases," 17 Vanderbilt Law Review 1407 (1964)

T. Shaffer, Death, Property, and Lawyers (1970)

T. Shaffer, Footnotes for Friends: A Backyard Wordwatcher's Dictionary (1987)

W. Strunk, Jr., and E.B. White, The Elements of Style (2d ed. 1972)

Part Three

DOCUMENTS

Chapter 9

JUSTIFIED SIMPLICITY

A. OVERTURES

The overture[1] has three purposes:

— It identifies the testator and the document;

— It identifies the testator's family; and

— It treats of the manner of payment of debts, taxes, and expenses.

The overture—and the rest of the will—are a matter of language, a very special kind of communication which has historical magnitude ("historical" because wills speak from one generation to another). It is also the prelude to a system of disposition—human disposition, physical disposition almost, because the property a person owns is almost as much a part of his life as his right leg or his brain. Overtures in wills are, therefore, important enough to be written with studied clarity and with appropriate respect for human beings. Most overtures are not written clearly, and no more than one in a thousand shows any humanity at all.

Wills are hard to read. Overtures are often harder to read than the rest of wills, and are thought to be either meaningless or unimportant. They are therefore often left unread. Sound legal advice should overcome the erroneous impression that overtures are unimportant. Good English should overcome the impression that they are unreadable: Most overtures could not be harder to read if the lawyers who draw them made a deliberate effort to be unreadable. If E.B. White were put to the proof of his statement that lawyers never write plain English, the beginnings of wills would be his best evidence, and the laypersons—widows, children, guardians, executors, and trustees—who have to deal with testamentary gibberish would be his best witnesses.

If you find that point exaggerated, reflect for three seconds on:

---

1. "Overture" here is a metaphor. The metaphor is symphonic rather than romantic. Overtures in wills are like what Rossini did to William Tell, rather than what Marian the Librarian did to the man (the Music Man) who had no friends in River City, Iowa. Marian's overtures were brazen and had a gilt-edged guarantee. Will overtures ought to be more brazen than they are perhaps, but even so wills are, as we say, ambulatory, which means they are not guaranteed.

197

LAST WILL AND TESTAMENT OF MARGARET MCCARTHY

In the name of God, Amen. I, Margaret McCarthy, being of sound and disposing mind and memory, hereby make, publish, and declare this document as and for my Last Will and Testament, and hereby revoke all wills and codicils by me at any time heretofore made.

1.   IDENTIFICATION OF TESTATOR

The first thing to do in drafting an overture is a cleaning job. Remove the residue of the centuries from drafting habits that are probably otherwise adequate. There is no reason to say "last will and testament of Margaret McCarthy"; there hasn't been any reason to say that since the 18th century. "Will of Margaret McCarthy" will do, just as "I give" is better than "I give, devise, and bequeath."

Compare most will forms on this point with what you can do in five minutes of effort toward clarity and brevity; you may find (as we have found) that you can come up with 20 clear words to begin a will that are as thorough as the traditional 60 or 70. It is important, though, not to go too far: Domicile is necessary to establish the location of domiciliary probate and to provide evidence in the event that more than one state seeks domiciliary inheritance taxes in the estate. Residence helps establish venue for probate. The community of the testator is identified by these two facts. The document is identified when she tells the reader what it is, and that it is the only will she wants to have. There is little to be said in defense of obscuring those important facts with ancient, redundant verbal garbage.

There is no point in adding the testator's self-serving declaration that she is of sound mind; all paranoids and most schizophrenics and psychopathic personalities think they are of sound mind. As a matter of fact, soundness of mind doesn't mean anything; what must be demonstrated in a contest over *testamentary capacity* is awareness of family, property, and settlement. An unsound mind may be able to cope with those things. In any case, the core of the will either manifests those points or deserves to lose.

If the client wishes to make her will demonstrate her faith, her lawyer should of course oblige and assist her. We suspect Mrs. McCarthy's will exhibited her *lawyer's* piety when it dedicated itself to the Lord, and that is a bit of a trespass surely. There is no point in "publishing" the will at the beginning; the witnesses will not be likely to see the publication there. It should be at the end of the will. In any case, "I ... declare that this is my will" *is* a publication. The common, separate revocation of codicils is probably not necessary either, since "wills" includes them and, anyway, the common rule is that revocation of a will revokes any codicil amending it.

Exercise 9.1

9.1.1.　Please demonstrate your understanding of this theory of streamlined drafting of the title and opening paragraph in Margaret McCarthy's will by re-drafting the paragraph that is quoted above.

9.1.2.　The first exercise coerced your agreement with the theory of streamlined overtures. Suppose the coercion is removed: How will you draft the beginning of Mrs. McCarthy's will? Please answer with a drafted paragraph and then explain *your* theory.

2.　IDENTIFICATION OF FAMILY

The second part of the overture—one that many lawyers leave out entirely—identifies the testator's family. For example:

> I am married to Henry Jones ("my Husband"). We have two children, Mary and Carl, both of whom are minors; they and any other children born to or adopted by my Husband and me are referred to here as "my Children."

We have seen wills that put names of people in capital letters: "I am married to HENRY JONES...." We are not sure where that habit comes from, but it implies that things not in all-capitals are not important, which at least exaggerates the case. It is also hard to read; journalists began teaching us a generation ago that capitals get in the way; most of us lawyers could learn a lot from the wire-service style books.

The identification part of the overture serves a number of important offices:

— It tells the executor about family names and relationships (and will often have to be longer than this sample).

— It permits the later use of the defined terms, so that references to the testator's spouse can be "my Husband" rather than "my husband Henry Jones," and collective references can be made to "my Children."

— Identification and definitions in the overture establish the first requisite of testamentary capacity—that the testator knew her family.

— Descriptions clarify disinheritance. If, for instance, the testator fails to provide for any or all of her children, her definition of "my Children" will demonstrate that she did so intentionally. Otherwise, many pretermitted heir statutes provide the "forgotten" child an opportunity to claim his intestate share. In many states, the fictional pretermission argument is open to children who are not mentioned in the will; and, in almost all states, the argument is open to children born after the will is made. A definition of "Children" that includes present children by name and afterborn children by class designation should counter that argument in any state. One needs also to recall that we Americans have a devious kind of forced inheritance for children, applied by judges, or by juries who are told they can't do it, in contest cases and adjudications of probate claims. One system of forced inheritance turns on will contests asserting (i) lack of testamentary capacity, (ii) undue influence, (iii) fraud, or (iv) failure to follow testamentary formalities (any of these or a combination of them). Another method an unmentioned and therefore disinherited child might invoke is a claim to be paid for, say, the years of care she gave her vindictive mother.

— It defines terms that tend to be ambiguous; here, for instance, it clarifies the meaning of "Children" and specifically includes within that term afterborn and adopted children.

Exercise 9.2

This consideration of how to describe a testator's children does not deal with the issue of illegitimate children. This exercise asks you to draft for that, but, first, a couple of background points:

(i) Statutory or constitutional law in virtually all jurisdictions requires that illegitimate children not be discriminated against in the law of intestate distribution, but that law does not reach wills: A testator can disinherit her or his illegitimate children if she or he wants to—as much as she or he can disinherit *any* children.

(ii) If a will is clear, an illegitimate child is included or not according to what the will says. The issue in will construction turns on poorly drafted wills.

9.2.1. Please draft the paragraph, quoted above from the will for Mrs. Jones, so that it includes her illegitimate children.

9.2.2. Please draft the same paragraph so that it disinherits her illegitimate children.

9.2.3. Suppose the will draft is for Henry Jones, Mrs. Jones's husband. And suppose when this subject comes up Mr. Jones asks you for advice on the definition of children. Please advise him.

This part of the overture should also include definitions of such regularly litigated terms as "descendants," "heirs," and "issue," if the will uses them. Here is an example:

> "Descendants" means the lineal descendants of the person referred to who are in being at the time they must be ascertained in order to give effect to the reference to them. Persons who take as Descendants take by right of representation, in accordance with per stirpes, rather than per capita distribution. The term Descendants shall include adopted descendants [only if they are legally adopted when they are under the age of fourteen years].[2]

This is class gift drafting of a critical, complex, and ordinary sort. It is critical and ordinary because most families have descendants or heirs or issue. We conclude that it is complex because *most lawyers* get it wrong. The reasons bad class-gift drafting of this ordinary sort does not end up in court *all the time* are that executors don't need to use these words in order to distribute property, or, if they need to use the badly drafted language, the family gets together and figures out its own distribution.

Consider, first, the guideline questions for sound class-gift drafting.[3] Then consider the question of adopted descendants. The paragraph that is drafted above includes adopted descendants (i.e., usually, grandchildren and great-grandchildren of the testator) only when they are adopted as children. (In many states, a person can adopt an adult.) Fourteen is not magic, but it has some feudal antecedents, and in some states a potential adoptee or ward of that age may get to make his wishes known. The non-arbitrary features of the last sentence clarify the status of adopted descendants—a subject which takes up much too much room in the appellate reports—and reduces the possibility of inheritance-motivated adoptions. It is the issue of off-stage, inheritance-motivated adoptions that causes us to suggest disinheritance of adopted adults who are adopted *not* by the testator but by someone who proposes to reach the testator's property through adoption of someone the testator does not know.

Another issue which arises here was considered in the classic case of *Maud v. Catherwood*, 67 Cal. App.2d 636, 155 P.2d 111 (1945), where some $15 million in California real estate rested on which generation was the beginning generation for this sort of per-stirpes distribution clause. If a grandchild is in the beginning generation and he has seven living brothers, sisters, and cousins, he will take an eighth. However, if he has

---

2. The definitions of "Descendants" in the two wills that appear toward the end of this chapter abandon "per stirpes … per capita" in favor of "by representation" as defined through the 1993 amendments to the Uniform Probate Code. The alternative appears clearer. It invokes a remarkably lengthy, if not arcane, explanation in the comments of the Uniform Commissioners.

3. In quick summary, those are:

– Who are the members of the class?

– When is membership to be determined?

– What are the conditions, if any, on a member's taking at that time?

– In what shares do they take?

one brother, no parents, and two deceased uncles on the propertied side of the family, he may argue that the per-stirpes distribution should start in his dead parents' generation. In one interpretation he will take one eighth; in the other he will take half of a third (one sixth). If the amount at issue is $15 million, the argument is worth $625,000. The preventive-law cure is to define "by representation," perhaps as § 2–106 of the U.P.C. does (modified for will or trust purposes):

> If ... a decedent's intestate estate or part thereof passes "by representation" to the decedent's descendants, the estate or part thereof is divided into as many equal shares as there are (i) surviving descendants in the generation nearest to the decedent which contains one or more surviving descendants and (ii) deceased descendants in the same generation who left surviving descendants, if any. Each surviving descendant in the nearest generation is allocated one share. The remaining shares, if any, are combined and then divided in the same manner among the surviving descendants of the deceased descendants as if the surviving descendants who were allocated a share and their surviving descendants had predeceased the decedent.

Many lawyers will not use this further definition and might cite five reasons for the choice: (1) It is a very complex provision. (2) It is not necessary in most cases because the situation will not present the issue; few families offer the dynasticism and fecundity found in Judge Hastings' family (who were at law in *Maud* v. *Catherwood*). (3) *Maud* v. *Catherwood* involved a reference, in a trust, to the California intestacy statute. It was the statute that was ambiguous. The resolution of the ambiguity involved policy issues not present when one considers the language of the will or trust itself. (4) The recent cases seem to resolve the question the same way the U.P.C. resolves it. (5) There should be a more efficient way to draft the clarification.

Exercise 9.3

Please draft a definition of "issue" that will serve the purposes served by the definition of "decendants" that is quoted above.

---

3. PAYMENT OF DEBTS, EXPENSES, TAXES

The third movement in the overture directs the payment of debts, administrative expenses, and taxes. The important thing about this third movement is that the payment of these charges is not a matter of whether; it is a matter of how. Legal debts, for instance, will have to be paid whether there is a direction to pay them or not; as a matter of fact, directions to pay debts, without explaining whether legal enforcibility is to be considered, tend to be ambiguous with respect to debts barred by limitations, "moral obligations," charitable subscriptions, and debts secured by property given in the will. Expenses of administration, last illness, funeral, and burial will have to be paid whether the will directs their payment or not. This same conclusion is obviously true of state and federal death taxes and unpaid income, gift, and property taxes.

The main office of this part of the overture turns on the fact that property which is now owned by one owner will often become owned by several, and the problem that fact presents to an executor who has bills to pay and the duty to divide what is left after the bills are paid. The several persons who might have to bear the burden of these charges fall into three general classes:

— Those who take property outside the will, the transfer of which is taxed.

— Those who take under the will by way of general, specific, or demonstrative legacy.

— Those who take under the will's residuary clause.

If a will directs that all debts, expenses, and taxes be borne by the residue of the estate, as many will forms do, the residuary legatees will bear everything, a result that may disinherit residuary legatees. That result is serious in virtually all wills that follow modern will forms, including wills following the forms in this book, because modern will drafting almost always calls for the principal disposition to be made in the residuary clause.

Death taxes provide dramatic examples of this. The facts reviewed in Chapter 6 show how death taxes may take more than half of a wealthy estate given to children, and as much as 70 per cent of a wealthy estate given to a friend; state death taxes may become significant (e.g., take as much as ten per cent of an estate) in estates as small as $50,000. The government can become a client's principal legatee; that fact requires careful attention to how distribution of what is left is made in the family, because the government not only leaves a reduced estate in the wake of its exactions; it also, often, leaves a family quarrel. (Remember the protracted difficulties arising from apportionment of tax burdens in the *James* case that we discussed in Chapter 5.)

Consider, for example, a client who owns a farm worth $1 million in joint tenancy with his sister and a personal estate of another $1 million. His will gives his collection of nineteenth-century Bibles to the church and the residue of his estate to his wife. The will form his lawyer used directs that all debts, expenses, and taxes be paid out of the residue of the probate estate, and Henry, his lawyer's secretary, copied that language, as the lawyer instructed Henry to do. The jointly held farm is death taxable under Sec. 2040 of the Internal Revenue Code and under the state inheritance-tax scheme as well. The residuary legacy to our client's wife is not subject to either tax; both the policy of the tax law(s) and our client's intent call for his wife to take $1 million tax free. The Bibles are not taxed because they are given to charity.

Death taxes on the transfer of the farm to our client's sister come to $400,000 and expenses and debts to as much as another $100,000. Our client's will provides that all of these exactions be borne by his wife. When all is said and done, she will get half of what he intended for her and his sister will get twice what he intended (or would have intended if his lawyer had talked to him about the impact of death taxes).

Another example is payment of life-insurance proceeds outside the probate estate, especially business-related life insurance, which is often carried, in large amounts, for the benefit of surviving business associates. Such insurance proceeds are subject to federal (and, often, state) death taxes. (See Sec. 2042 of the Internal Revenue Code.) A clause in a will that directs the executor to pay, from the probate estate, all death taxes, will allow the insurance proceeds to pass tax free to business associates and put significant, unanticipated tax burdens on members of the family.

A third example is property subject to a power of appointment: Imagine a decedent who had $500,000 in estate-taxable property she knew about and $1 million subject to a general power of appointment she had forgotten about. The power-of-appointment property is includible in her taxable estate (Sec. 2041, Internal Revenue Code), even though she exercised no control over it and did not exercise the power in her will. Death taxes on the power-of-appointment property, if they have to be paid from the probate estate, may wipe out about half of what the legatees would otherwise get. Whether that happens will depend on the tax-payment clause in the decedent's will.

So, the first canon of sound drafting of tax-payment clauses is to *take into account the possibility of death-taxable non-probate property.*

The second canon is to *take into account the will's distribution scheme.* Many wills make their principal dispositions in the residuary clause—"$500 each to the grandchildren, $1,000 to the faithful upstairs maid, and the rest ($2 million) to my son." If the tax clause allocates tax burdens according to the traditional rules of abatement, the death taxes will all be borne by the son, which, given these proportions, seems about right. But if the $2 million were given to the son as a general legacy, and the residue were given to the upstairs maid, the maid's having to bear *all* death taxes would seem disproportionate. The gift to her would be wiped out.

The third canon is to *take into account federal and state law on apportionment.* There is a good deal of law on the subject: In the insurance and power-of-appointment examples, federal law (I.R.C. §§ 2206 and 2207), but for the tax-payment clause, would require that the life-insurance beneficiaries and takers of power-of-appointment property contribute proportionately to the payment of federal estate taxes. (In the examples we use, since transfers to the surviving spouse are tax-free, this means that the business associates and those who take the power property will bear all death taxes.) State law, judicial and statutory, varies widely but will probably require similar contribution from takers of joint-tenancy property, from those who receive employment-related benefits, and from beneficiaries of inter-vivos trusts. (See, e.g., U.P.C. Sec. 3–916.)

But most tax-apportionment law prevails only if the will of the decedent does not direct otherwise. Most of it is inapplicable if the will directs the executor to pay all taxes from a specified segment of the estate.

With those three canons in mind, lawyers commonly take one of two approaches to giving direction to an executor on death-tax payment: (i) Pay *no* taxes from probate property that apportionment law does not require you to pay; or (ii) pay *all* taxes from probate property, regardless of apportionment law, except for the categories most likely to be subtle or significant or both. The forms we suggest follow one or the other of these approaches. An example of the first (follow apportionment law):

> … all taxes payable by reason of my death shall be equitably apportioned among those persons receiving my property, either under the terms of this will or outside of it. My executor shall be entitled to collect from the recipients of property passing outside this will the portion of the taxes allocable to it.

An example of the second:

> I direct my executor to pay … all taxes payable by reason of my death. My executor shall not require my wife, as to any property, nor any beneficiary, as to property passing under the terms of this will, to reimburse my estate for taxes paid under this subparagraph.

The principal difference between the two is that the second puts the tax burden on the residue and takes that allocation into account: (i) with regard to the surviving spouse, as to all distributions, (ii) with regard to other legatees under the will only as to distributions under the will. Those who take non-probate transfers, other than the wife, will be subject to apportionment law (which implies, of course, that the drafter knows what apportionment law provides and is satisfied with it). The difference as to the surviving spouse, under either of our clauses, will, in most cases, be unimportant, since transfers to a surviving spouse usually are not taxed.

Another version of this provision, which covers transfers to the surviving spouse of probate *and* non-probate property, is in Form 3, Chapter 10. The somewhat simpler provision here assumes that the surviving spouse is residuary legatee. If the will makes specific or general legacies beyond a nominal level, the will should, in most cases, provide that each legatee bear his proportionate share of these charges, and that legacies abate ratably to pay them. This relieves the residuary legatee, who is normally the principal legatee.

Many lawyers include in their directions on expenses and taxes special provision for the payment of mortgages and other encumbrances on property that is given specifically. This avoids the jungle of esoteric distinctions that accompanies the law of exoneration. Every will should cover the subject by either directing or forbidding payment of mortgages on specifically given property. It may be more orderly to do that in connection with the words of gift, in which case exoneration does not enter into the overture. (See the non-residuary legacy part of this chapter.)

4.   DIRECTIONS AS TO REMAINS

Some wills contain elaborate directions on burial, monuments, and even disposition of the body or parts of it to medical science. The last sort of direction seems to have grown in recent years and has been encouraged by criticism of the practices of undertakers and by statutes that permit testamentary disposition of the body. The argument against putting directions about remains in a will is that it is probably the worst place for them. Most families, when stricken by the death of a close relative, will abstain from reading the will until after the funeral. This is the result of grief, appearances, decency, or ritual.

If the will directs delivery of the testator's body, unembalmed, to a medical school, the fact that the testator has recently been buried in the conventional, well-embalmed manner may prove embarrassing, and may even stimulate unseemly argument in the family. Similar problems can be imagined in connection with directions to cremate, to bury in Arlington Cemetery, to inter in a mausoleum, or to remove organs for transplant. Any directions made as to the testator's remains should be given outside the will as well as, or in lieu of, provisions in the will. Special forms are provided by the medical groups interested in human tissue. Organizations of retired citizens, hospice services, hospitals, and religious congregations now have booklets and forms for planning and stating such things and notifying pastors, the family, the undertaker, and medical personnel. (See the section on cadavers in Chapter 4.)

The traditional order for wills is that legacies begin after the directions on payment of charges. At that point the overture ends. The disposition of property is the main performance. The virtue of a good overture is not so much that the family is alert to the main performance—awakened and soothed by the clarity and order with which they have been prepared for their testator's efforts to realize immortality through his property. That is a dramatic dividend perhaps—one that exists more in English mystery stories than in modern law practice. The real virtue of a good overture is that it makes the main performance clearer, more straightforward, and much less vulnerable to family fights and to being redrafted by judges and juries.

B. NON–RESIDUARY LEGACIES

Consider three of the commonest of legacies, the traditional problems they present to clients and fiduciaries, and the drafting required to make them effective:

1. I give all of my tangible personal property not otherwise given in this article to those of my children who survive me.

2. I give my automobile to my uncle, Henry Hearty.

3. I give five thousand dollars to the First Baptist Church.

The first two of these are usually considered specific legacies; the third is a general cash legacy. All three are common in so-called simple wills, especially wills of relatively impecunious, older clients. In economic terms they are typically a minor part of the will. The reason for care in drafting them is to keep them minor, to save them from problems of construction that exaggerate their importance, and to show a decent respect for the feelings of clients who regard these legacies as important.

Non-residuary legacies do not appear difficult to draft. In the first, many lawyers define "tangible personal property," which is probably not necessary. "Children," on the other hand, should probably be defined, so that adopted and illegitimate children are clearly included or excluded, and the normal canons of good class-gift drafting are honored.

If the testator is likely to own more than one automobile, the second legacy may need to be more detailed. The third legacy should be more detailed as to the location of the church and its corporate status ("First Baptist Church of South Bend, Indiana, an Indiana corporation"). If the religious congregation is not incorporated, we prefer to create equitable duties in an accessible person—"to whomever is, at my death, rabbi of Temple Beth El, of South Bend, Indiana, to be used for the general purposes of that congregation." The best policy on significant legacies is to talk to someone affiliated with the charitable legatee about its corporate status and existing trust funds.

Most of the problems non-residuary legacies present occur because of circumstances not apparent when the will is drafted. They are corollaries of the fact that wills are ambulatory; our clients are speaking today but their words will be heard, and imposed on facts, years in the future. Six situations exemplify many of the problems. The first is the unexpected disappearance of the client's wealth. The next four are expressed in the dusty common-law concepts of lapse, ademption, satisfaction, and exoneration. The last is the specific legacy of tangible personalty to a class. We discussed these situations in doctrinal terms in Chapter 4.

1. DISAPPEARANCE

A person's generosity is in some sort of practical proportion to her wealth. The client who made the three bequests we are talking about may have had $50,000 when she executed her will—with, perhaps, a residuary legacy fairly estimated at a net $45,000 to a handicapped child. If that client comes on evil days and dies with only a $5,000 gross estate, she probably would want her handicapped child to have all of it, and other children, Uncle Henry, and the church to have nothing. But the ravages of estate shrinkage would fall first on the residuary legatee–the handicapped child. As long as debts, taxes and expenses leave enough to pay the specific and general legacies, the residuary legatee—who is this client's principal legatee—will be the only legatee to suffer. A will should protect against shrinkage as much as it protects against intestacy or excessive taxation or incompetent fiduciaries.

There are three ways to protect residuary legatees:

(a) *Proportional Legacies*. The church—and any general cash legatee—can be made to bear shrinkage by legacies drafted in percentages or fractions instead of in dollars. The will can (assuming a probable net estate of $48,000) say "I give the First Baptist Church three per cent of my net estate," rather than "I give two thousand dollars…. " If the client then dies with a net estate of $5,000, the Church will bear its share of shrinkage and receive $150 instead of $2,000; and the handicapped child will get most of the rest of the estate.

(b) *General Limitation*. All non-residuary legacies can be drafted to shift property to the residue in case of unexpected shrinkage. The will can say, for instance, that non-residuary legacies are to be paid only if the net estate exceeds a minimum figure—in our example perhaps $30,000. If the net estate is below that, all property is to be given as part of the residuary legacy. This device will cover both specific and general legacies.

(c) *Both*. Both approaches can be combined, to cover both specific and general cash legacies, with somewhat greater flexibility than is available with either device by itself.

Exercise 9.4

Please draft the legacy to the First Baptist Church in such a way that it will accomplish both purposes.

Such a limitation can be broadened so that all non-residuary cash legacies are subject to the limitation. In that case the limitation can be separately drafted as to each legacy, or applied generally as to all non-residuary cash legacies. This combination is especially useful where the will makes several small cash legacies to relatives, charities, servants, and friends. For example:

> If my residuary estate is less than thirty thousand dollars, all of the legacies in this article are cancelled. If my residuary estate is more than thirty thousand dollars but less than fifty thousand

dollars, the legacies in this article are to abate proportionately so that they do not total more than two per cent of my residuary estate.

2. LAPSE

Consider the legacy of the automobile to Uncle Henry. What will happen if Uncle Henry dies before the testator dies but after the will is executed? The result in most states will be lapse. Assuming the Lord still don't 'low no Model T cars up there, Uncle Henry won't need it. Claimants of Uncle Henry's share under the typical anti-lapse statute won't get it either because Uncle Henry is not a child, descendant or issue of the testator.[4] It will lapse into the residue. That may be what the testator wants. If the residuary beneficiary has no need for an automobile, though, the testator may want someone else to have it, in which case the will should cover the point. Even if the testator wants a lapse, confusion will be prevented if the will says "to my uncle, Henry Hearty, if he survives me … and if he does not survive me I give … as part of the Residuary Estate."

3. ADEMPTION

Lapse was a matter of no-Henry. Ademption is a matter of no-car. To raise the question is usually to answer it. If the testator has no car at his death, what if anything does he want Henry to have? The will should say. If it does not say, the dispute will turn on whether the bequest is specific—in which case it is adeemed by extinction and Henry gets nothing—or general, in which case the executor will have to get a car for Henry. (A legacy of "1,000 shares of General Motors stock" is perhaps a more plausible general legacy than the legacy of a car.) The question suggests trouble that an extra sentence in the will can avoid.

An allied problem is raised by liability and casualty insurance on specifically-bequeathed personal property. This has two aspects, both of them minor and both troublesome enough to justify will language to keep them minor: (1) Suppose our testator pays his semi-annual automobile insurance premium just before his death. That paid-up insurance may be worth $500 or more. In most states Henry will not get it, though, and the executor will have to go to the expense of claiming a premium refund. Most clients, if asked about the problem, would probably want Henry to have the insurance, but he won't get it unless the will says so.

(2) Suppose our testator dies in an automobile collision which also smashes up his (now Henry's) car, and that the testator's collision

---

4. If the claimant were a lineal descendant of Uncle Henry, he could get the car under the Uniform Probate Code, which is relatively generous. Sec. 2–603(b)(1):

If a devisee fails to survive the testator and is a grandparent, a descendant of a grandparent, or a stepchild of … the testator … if the devise is not in the form of a class gift and the deceased devisee leaves surviving descendants, a substitute gift is created in the devisee's surviving descendants. They take by representation the property to which the devisee would have been entitled had the devisee survived the testator.

Notice that Aunt Agatha, Henry's wife, could not claim the car under this statute.

insurance will cover damage to (or the loss of) the automobile. Does Henry get the insurance proceeds? There is some doubt on the legal result; it has been argued that Henry gets the smashed-up car but not the insurance proceeds, unless the company elects to take the smashed-up car and pay its value, in which case he gets the insurance proceeds. Drafting to include automobile insurance may raise a subtle difficulty. A broadly-drawn clause—e.g., "any proceeds of insurance carried on the automobile"—might be construed to include proceeds of limited life insurance carried as travel insurance or as a rider on the automobile policy, and might suggest a claim of testamentary change of beneficiary of that insurance, or a claim on the insurance fund if it is paid to the estate.

Exercise 9.5

Please draft to solve the lapse and automobile-insurance problems in such a way that:

a. Aunt Agatha will get the car if Uncle Henry does not survive our client, and

b. Whoever gets the car will get the paid-up insurance, or proceeds of casualty (but not life) insurance in case the testator has not collected them.

---

4. SATISFACTION

Ademption is one kind of no-car problem. Satisfaction is another kind of no-car problem that arises when Henry already has the car because the testator gave it to him after the will was executed. If the bequest was specific, Henry does not get another car; the bequest has, in the dusty common-law phrase, been adeemed by satisfaction. If the bequest is general, Henry may be entitled to another car. The will can solve that problem, too. Here is a clause proposed by one of our students:

Real or personal property conveyed by me during my lifetime shall not be considered advancements. No adjustment of my estate shall be made on the basis of inter-vivos gifts.

A professor's quibble with using the word "advancement" is that the law of advancements is confined to intestate estates. These are gifts in satisfaction of legacies, but the improper use of "advancement" in this way is so general now as probably to have become proper. A more reasonable observation is that the client has to be put on guard about this provision in his will, so that he knows he has to change it in case he decides to give the church its money for the missions, while he's alive, lest the pastor use it, after he dies, to finance guitar playing in the liturgy.

5. EXONERATION

Exoneration is one of the most esoteric branches of the law of property (although future interests would prevail in the minds and memories of most lawyers). The issue of exoneration arises when a testator gives property specifically which bears encumbrances at the time of his death. In our example, for instance, what does Uncle Henry get if the car our client gives him bears a chattel mortgage securing a $1,000 note?

One way to answer the question would be to say that if the client created the debt, the residuary estate must pay it off, and Uncle Henry takes clear of the encumbrance. That might be the result in states which have not abolished the doctrine of exoneration.[5] However, that result is not inevitable where it can be shown that the debt did not benefit the residuary estate—if, for example, the chattel mortgage secures a purchase-money arrangement.

The distinctions are esoteric and the will should take advantage of the one rule of law on exoneration that is certain and probably universal—a clear expression of intention can dispose of this question. All encumbrances should be clearly paid off or retained in the client's will. This is a clause we have seen widely used in the case of residential real estate, which is probably a more bothersome situation than the automobile:

> The residential real estate given in this article is, at the time this will is written, subject to a mortgage. If this real estate passes to my Husband under the provisions of this article, my executor shall satisfy the mortgage debt, or not do so, as my Husband elects. If this real estate passes to ... it shall pass subject to all encumbrances.

The above clause can be tailored to fit jointly-held residential real estate also. A somewhat different version appears in Chapter 10.

Exercise 9.6

Why would the widower here decide not to have the mortgage debt paid?

---

6.   CHILDREN AND TANGIBLE PERSONALTY

The first of the examples of non-residuary legacies—"all of my tangible personal property not otherwise given in this article to those of my children who survive me"—raises special problems because it is a class gift, to a class of persons that may include minors, consisting of property that does not readily lend itself to fractional division.

Class-gift drafting requires—to repeat our reference to the classic scholarship of the late Professor A. James Casner—(A) clarity as to

---

5. The U.P.C. abolishes the doctrine of exoneration and adopts a statutory presumption against construing debt-payment directions to require that the executor pay secured debts on specific legacies; Sec. 2–607: "A specific devise passes subject to any mortgage interest existing at the date of death, without right of exoneration, regardless of a general directive in the will to pay debts."

persons who are within the meaning of the term; (B) clarity as to the time of determination of membership; (C) clarity as to the time of distribution, and (D) clarity as to the share each member takes. If the term "children" is defined as to adopted and illegitimate children, the other requirements seem satisfied by this clause, suggested by one of our students:

> I give all my jewelry, books, pictures, clothing, and articles of household or personal use or adornment, household furnishings and effects, not otherwise disposed of in this article, to my Wife if she survives me. If my Wife does not survive me, I give this personal property in equal shares to those of my Children who survive me, to be divided among them as they shall agree; if they fail to reach agreement within sixty days after my death, this personal property shall be divided among my Children as my executor determines, in shares of substantially equal value.

We would add to that a special direction as to minor children; here is a useful version used in the Will and Trust Forms once recommended by the Continental Illinois National Bank and Trust Company:

> If any child of mine is a minor at the time of such division my executor may distribute his share to him or for his use to his guardian or to any person with whom he is residing, without further responsibility, and the distributee's receipt shall be a sufficient discharge to my executor.

Power to divide and distribute in the executor, along with the special protection on distribution to minors, are peculiar aspects of this kind of class-gift drafting that Professor Casner's generalizations did not reach.

The use of this paragraph assumes, of course, that tangible personal property is to be kept out of trust arrangements contained in the will, which are normally funded with a residuary legacy. (See Chapter 10.) Professional trustees find storage, insurance, and sale of furniture, jewelry, clothing, and household goods so awkward and uneconomical as to justify this outright disposition of these items, even at the price of losing their value to the trust. There may also be an income-tax advantage in making these shares part of the specific-legacy section in the will. We usually agree with specific legacies of them, except where the will provides for or funds a trust for the support of minor, orphaned children. In that situation, and especially where the fund available to the trustee is small, we think it is best to charge the trustee with the burden of realizing every available dime for the children. We believe the trustee then should be given all property—even tangible personalty.

7. CHARITABLE GIFTS

The most common problems in charitable-gift drafting are ambiguity and enforcement. Ambiguity involves two problems: (1) whether the recipient is an entity that can take the bequest and receipt for it (an unincorporated religious congregation may not be), and (2) whether the legatee is described clearly enough; there are scores of cases involving gifts to old folks' homes, churches, and schools that can be taken by an outside interpreter (*i.e.,* judge) to refer to more than one institution. We try to solve both problems by obtaining the accurate name for the institution, from the institution itself usually. A subtle aspect of this is whether the designation benefits the activity the client has in mind. A gift to a Roman Catholic parish, for example, should be made to the diocese, which is the corporate unit involved; if the client wants to benefit the parish only, however, it should be made in a trust or with an "equitable charge" that will limit the use of the gift to what the client wants. Similar problems arise with strings-attached legacies to educational institutions; we have found it a good use of time to talk to the educational institution before drafting, to determine whether there are existing funds or trusts to which our client's legacy can be added.

The enforcement problem is more technical and also more depressing. Who enforces the client's purposes after the transfer of funds is made? The classical (and probably majority-rule) answer is that the attorney general of the state enforces charitable trusts, which translated usually means that no one does. We have considered drafting gifts to confer standing to sue to enforce on a relative, friend, or corporate entity, so that the trust creates a modern American species of visitor (the officer who traditionally sees to it that charitable corporations in England perform their intended function).

Exercise 9.7

Please draft a legacy of one-half of the Residuary Estate of Margaret McCarthy (a term that you may assume the will elsewhere defines) for the Christian Action Commission of St. Patrick's Roman Catholic Church, Lexington, Virginia. The commission is a small committee of parishioners, appointed by the pastor, who see to the needs of the poor in the community. The parish is not incorporated; title to all of its property is in the Bishop of the Diocese of Richmond. Please make it as certain as possible that this gift will be used only for (i) the care of the poor, (ii) in Lexington and thereabouts, (iii) under the direction of this commission; and (iv) that there is standing in someone who is likely to want to enforce the restriction, in case the Bishop decides it is needed to pay for fixing the roof of the cathedral in Richmond. Be careful in all of this that the charitable purpose of the gift is clear; it will otherwise fail under the rule requiring an ascertainable trust beneficiary, or under the rule against perpetuities, or under both.

A special problem in some states is the mortmain restriction, which either (a) restricts the share of the estate which can be given to charity in a will or (b) makes it impossible to make testamentary gifts to a charity in a will executed less than a stated period before death (a month in some states, up to a year in others), or (c) both. In most states these quaint old statutes can be evaded by inter-vivos transfers, trusts, and even deathbed transfers.

8. JOINT AND MUTUAL WILLS

There are a surprising number of cases in the reports that involve joint and mutual wills, and an even larger number where the wills were not joint and not clearly mutual, but a claim is made that the will involved became, in effect, irrevocable. A joint will is a single document for two testators. It has some sentimental appeal for lovers or close relatives, but is a cumbersome document; when one partner dies, the survivor's will becomes public, if it is probated. An even more imposing disadvantage for the survivor is that the joint will may contain or imply a promise not to revoke. This deprives the survivor's will of its ambulatory character. A joint will with such a contract not to revoke is often called a joint and mutual will. Mutual wills are parallel wills (H gives to W and W to H and each, if survivor, in equal shares to the children) which may or may not contain or imply or refer to a contract not to revoke. Restrictions on revocation are troublesome; the advertent use of them is almost always unwise. The unintended use of them—in, for example, parallel wills for spouses which may imply a contract not to revoke—is an evil to be prevented. This can be done in a clause that says no contract has been made on the subject of revocation.

C. JUSTIFIED SIMPLICITY

Overtures and non-residuary legacies are routine in so-called "simple wills." They are sometimes handled poorly, because the entire will in a "simple will" case is sometimes handled poorly. Lawyers would do a better job for their small-estates clients if they thought about what they were doing, and about the people they were doing it for, and if they *and their clients* saw the job as counseling and not as black magic. What follows are two pieces of simple-will drafting. Most of the drafting choices used are explained in this chapter. Some of them (especially the fiduciary-powers article) are developed more fully, and explained at tiresome length in later chapters involving more complex wills.

The first will, for Elizabeth Eustace, is a *very* "simple will." It does not, for example, contain directions for the payments of debts and taxes; those will be paid whether or not the will directs them to be. This very simple will does not divide legacies into residuary and non-residuary legacies; Mrs. Eustace is dispensing of her property in one lump. She is not married; there is no need to worry about the claims of a spouse or such recondite matters as joint and mutual will issues. The (merely) simple will for her—Form 2—provides alternatives for making specific and cash legacies.

Our client, Elizabeth Eustace, is 63 years old. We interviewed her and gathered this information about her: Mrs. Eustace was married to Florian Eustace, a prominent attorney in town. They were divorced in 1992. The couple have two children, an adult son, Florian, Jr., and an adult daughter, Josephine. Mrs. Eustace has three grandchildren, one of whom, Luke, is starting veterinary medicine school this fall. Mrs. Eustace has never worked outside the home. Her income comes from savings account interest, Social Security, and provisional relief payments (the modern version of alimony) from her ex-husband.

Elizabeth Eustace's property:

1.　A house and lot at 12 Elm Street, Marion City, on which there is no mortgage. The home is owned by Mrs. Eustace in fee simple (as a result of the divorce decree). The home is valued at $170,000.

2.　A savings account in the Rollison Federal Savings and Loan Association, totaling $15,000, paying five percent interest per annum, paid annually.

3.　A two-year-old Ford Taurus sedan.

4.　Household furniture, jewelry, and personal property.

FORM 1.　THE VERY SIMPLE WILL

WILL OF ELIZABETH EUSTACE

I, Elizabeth Eustace, residing and domiciled in Marion City, Rollison County, Hoynes,[6] declare that this is my will and revoke all other wills.

I.　IDENTIFICATIONS AND DEFINITIONS

Comment.　**The first object here is to demonstrate that the client knows who her family is. The names of people identified for this purpose need not be defined terms.**

The second object is to define terms, so that full names need not be repeated later in the will. The key to making this work is to capitalize these defined terms, both here and wherever they are used in the will. Three common mistakes demonstrate insufficient craftsmanship in this regard.

---

6. The county and state here are fictional. We indulge in this book a bit of Notre Dame nostalgia and name our fictional state for the founding dean of the Notre Dame Law School (Col. William Hoynes), and our fictional county for the late Professor William Dewey Rollison, who taught the wills and trusts courses at the law school for several decades. Your elder author was one of Professor Rollison's many students.

One is to define terms and then not use them in the will. The second is to define terms and then repeat the entire definition, later in the will, when all that is necessary is to capitalize and repeat the defined term. The third is to use the defined term, later in the will, without capitalizing it and thereby fail to signal the reader that the word has been defined.

A.   I am not married. I was at one time married to Florian Eustace, but we were divorced in 1992 and I intentionally make no provision for him in this will. We had two children, a son, Florian Eustace, Jr. ("my Son"), and a daughter, Josephine Eustace ("my Daughter"), both of whom are adults at the time this will is written. "My Children" includes these two children and any other children born to or adopted by me.

Comment.   **When a spouse or children are not provided for, it is perhaps a good idea to say they are not. The recognition of the relationship helps establish capacity. The statement that they are not provided for negates a claim of pretermission (unintentionally overlooking or not providing for the person). It is, however, not a good idea to spell out the reasons. That might provoke a battle. There is also such a thing as libel in a will.**

Many lawyers would define "Children" here to include only "lawful" children. That is defensible in the will of a man, since spurious claims of parentage are possible and may be hard to disprove. The use of the adjective assumes, of course, that the drafter is fairly certain there aren't any children who are not "lawful" and is as confident as professional caution allows that there won't be any. "Lawful" is not so defensible in the case of a woman.

Note the use of "lawful" in the definition of Descendants, just below, and consider whether to use the limitation as to a class that includes both women and men. Note, too, the way adoption is handled here and in I–B–1, just below.

B.   The following definitions obtain in any use of the terms in this will:

1.   "Descendants" means the immediate and remote lineal descendants of the person referred to who are in being at the time they must be ascertained in order to give effect to the reference to them, whether they are born before or after my death or the death of any other person. The

persons who take under this will as Descendants take by right of representation as that term is defined in the 1990 Uniform Probate Code, as amended through 1993. The term Descendants shall include adopted descendants only if they are legally adopted when they are under the age of fourteen years.

Comment. **This is a complex definition, one that contemplates a lot of appellate literature and a couple of stabs at definition in the Uniform Probate Code. The object here is to include people who are not yet ascertained (or even born), and to set up distribution *per stirpes*, beginning below the generation referred to. E.g.: In this will, each group of Descendants of each of the two Children will divide the share their parents would have taken.**

This definition should avoid the appalling hassle one finds in recent cases on adopted relatives. It avoids the less common but more appalling hassle over children born out of wedlock—by including them. The age limitation eliminates any doubt as to adopted adult heirs. The use of "fourteen" is, of course, arbitrary and debatable. The fact that it is fairly common probably derives from feudal guardianship in socage, which was not applicable to wards fourteen years or older.

2. "Survive" is to be construed to mean that the person referred to must survive the event referred to by thirty days. If the person referred to dies within thirty days of the event, the reference shall be construed as if she or he had failed to survive.

Comment. **The traditional object here is to avoid issues over order of death, which might occur if the testatrix and one of her children were to die at the same time. (In *Estate of Parisi*, 765 N.E.2d 123 [Ill. App. 2002], father's will benefitted daughter; both father and daughter died the same day; the trial judge refused to apply the Simultaneous Death Act; the appellate court reversed. The case illustrates the family fights and litigation this routine will provision seeks to prevent.) More commonly, the object is to avoid repeated probate administrations of the same assets. E.g., if a child who takes under this will dies within thirty days of the client's death, we do not want the assets involved to be administered in our client's estate and then administered all over again in the** child's estate. **Many lawyers would make the period longer than thirty days. Sixty would certainly be defensible.**

II.   APPOINTMENT OF EXECUTOR

A.   I appoint my Daughter executor of this will. If my Daughter is unable or unwilling to serve as executor, I appoint my Son.

B.   I request that neither bond nor securities be required of any fiduciary appointed under this Article.

Comment.   There may be good reason not to waive bond. The issue is whether to put the estate to the expense of obtaining sureties on the bond from an insurance company—at significant cost. But bonds provide good protection where protection is for any reason necessary.

III.   MY ESTATE

A.   "My Estate" is all of my property, real, personal, or mixed, including property as to which I have an option to purchase or a reversionary interest, and property over which I have a power of appointment.

Comment.   See the discussion of using—and here referring to—a list, separate from the will, to dispose of tangible personal property: Form 2, *infra*, comment to Art. IV, para. "E."

B.   I give my Estate to those of my Children who survive me, if they or any of them survive me, in equal shares if more than one of them survive me, and all of my Estate to the survivor of them if only one of them survives me.

C.   If none of my Children survives me, I give my Estate to my Descendants.

Comment.   Note that this provision leaves out children-in-law and collateral relatives. It is important that the client understand whom she is leaving out and who will get what and how much.

D.   My executor shall have the following powers, which are not intended to be exclusive, and shall also pertain to administrators who succeed my executor:

1.   to take possession of property, keep it safely, and segregate it from other property;

2.   to sell, exchange, lease, rent, mortgage, pledge, give options upon, and partition real and personal property, at private or

public sale, on whatever terms she finds advisable, without notice or order of court;

3. to render liquid my estate, in whole or in part, and to hold cash or readily marketable securities of little or no yield for such period as she finds advisable;

4. to borrow in the name of my estate, upon whatever terms she finds advisable, for the purpose of preserving property held by her;

5. to pay, compromise, or abandon claims held by her, and claims asserted against her, on whatever terms she finds advisable, without court authority;

6. to distribute in cash or in kind, in divided or undivided interests, even though distributive shares may as a result be composed differently;

7. to employ attorneys, accountants, and other professional assistants;

8. to enter into transactions with other fiduciaries, including executors or trustees of estates and trusts in which the beneficiaries have an interest and including herself as fiduciary for other estates and trusts;

9. to pay herself reasonable compensation for her services.

Comment. **The reason to be concerned about powers is to save money for the estate. Many executor actions have to be approved by the probate court *unless* the will says they don't have to be. Court approval is often a good thing to get, but it is expensive; getting it dissipates the estate.**

E.   The executor shall have the power to apply income and principal payable to any beneficiary who is under legal disability or who is, in the opinion of the executor, incapable of managing his or her affairs. In carrying out this power, the executor may distribute income or principal directly to the beneficiary, to the guardian or parent of the beneficiary, to a bank account in trust, to a custodianship or trust for the beneficiary, or to a person with whom the beneficiary resides. The receipt of the beneficiary, guardian, parent, bank, custodian, trustee, or person shall discharge the executor from responsibility for the proper expenditure of income or principal. The executor may also accumulate income and withhold distributions of principal, in carrying out this power, to the extent permitted by law, until the beneficiary's legal disability is removed or until the beneficiary dies or, in the opinion of the executor, becomes capable of managing his or her affairs, at which time all amounts payable to the beneficiary shall be paid to the beneficiary or to the beneficiary's estate.

Comment. **A minor or incompetent person cannot give the executor a receipt for distributions to him or her. If something like this is not in the will, the prudent executor will require the appointment of a guardian, who is able to give the estate a receipt. (In this will a distribution to a grandchild would be an example.) Guardianship is an expensive and inflexible process in this context. The inclusion of custodial transfer as an option contemplates the Transfers to Minors Act (Statutory Appendix).**

I, ELIZABETH EUSTACE, sign my name to this instrument this 1st day of February, 2___, and being first duly sworn, declare to the undersigned authority all of the following:

1. I execute this instrument as my will.

2. I sign this will willingly.

3. I execute this will as my free and voluntary act.

4. I am 18 years of age or older, of sound mind and under no constraint or undue influence.

_____

Elizabeth Eustace

WE, THE WITNESSES, being first duly sworn, sign our names to this instrument and declare all of the following:

The testator executes this instrument as her will.

The testator signs it willingly.

Each of us, in the conscious presence of the testator, signs this will as a witness.

To the best of our knowledge, the testator is 18 years of age or older, of sound mind and under no constraint or undue influence.

_____ residing at_____

_____ residing at_____

Comment. **We want this will to be self-proving. If a will is self-proved, the lawyer who takes it in for probate does not have to take in the witnesses. Of course, if there is litigation over the will, witnesses will need to come in; but in routine probate administration having to round up the witnesses and take them to the courthouse is inconvenient. Self-proving will not prevent pro-**

bate litigation, but it will prevent a probate hearing when no one is complaining about the will.

One way to make the will self-proved is to append an affidavit in which the client and his witnesses swear to having done what they did when they signed the will. That additional document is confusing. There are cases in which the client has signed the affidavit *rather than* the will, and which hold that the will is therefore unsigned and ineffective. In *Estate of Dellinger*, 793 N.E.2d 1041 (Ind. 2003), a case that went through three judicial levels and both houses of the legislature (never mind the governor), the issue came down to whether testator and witnesses all had to sign *twice.* In some states, under modern revisions of the will-execution statute, a better way to make the will self-proved is to use an attestation clause that contains all of the elements the act prescribes. This form, for example, makes the will self-proved under the Indiana statute *without* the self-proving statement.

This attestation clause accomplishes the self-proving objective, under the U.P.C. § 2–504, and under statutes such as Wis. Code § 853.04. Both of these statutes, however, require notarization following the testator and witnesses' signatures–this in order to make the will self-proved. It would be valid, of course, without notarization.

Witnesses must be competent (e.g., not underage) and disinterested–i.e., not people who take or could take under the will, and not people who would take if the client had no will.

There is dicta in some cases saying that, when the lawyer who drafted the will is a witness to the will, the attorney-client privilege for communications between the will-maker and his lawyer is lost. For that reason, except in emergency situations, it is best to have witnesses who have no interest under the will, and who are not working in the lawyer's office.

FORM 2. THE SIMPLE WILL

WILL OF ELIZABETH EUSTACE

(Articles I and II as in Form 1)

III. PAYMENT OF EXPENSES AND TAXES

I direct my executor to pay the following before any division or distribution under the following articles:

1.   all of the expenses of my last illness, funeral and burial and of the administration of my estate;

2.   all taxes payable by reason of my death. My executor shall not require any beneficiary, as to property passing under the terms of this will, to reimburse my estate for taxes paid under this sub-paragraph.

> **Comment.** **Debts and taxes and expenses have to be paid whether the will says so or not. These sub-paragraphs put the burden of such claims on those who will receive the residuary estate otherwise. The sub-paragraphs are also symbolic: Our client probably wants to go on to Glory knowing that her accounts are square. Sub-paragraph "1" is a modest expense-payment clause. We are not suggesting other debt-payment language, so that nothing in this will will affect (i) debts barred by the statute of limitations, (ii) unenforceable debts (compare directions to pay "just debts"), or (iii) "exoneration" of debt secured by property given in the will. These categories of issues often provoke litigation. We think they should either be left to the law (e.g., statutory treatment of exoneration) or dealt with advertently, not in a general debt-payment clause.**

3.   any mortgage debts on residential real estate passing to any of the beneficiaries under this will, or not to do so, as the devisee thereof may elect.

> **Comment.** **The question this sub-paragraph addresses is whether mortgage debts on real estate have to be paid at the client's death, out of property other than the mortgaged real estate. (The mortgage itself may require payment, or it may not.) It is often best not to pay off the mortgage debt (e.g., it may bear an attractive interest rate; there may be a mortgage exemption applicable to state real property taxes). If the mortgage debt is paid out of property other than the mortgaged property,**

one legatee may lose to the gain of another. The election emphasizes this point. If the mortgaged real property is given specifically to A, and the residuary legatee is B, and A has this power to elect, A may elect what is in A's best interest, not considering what the client would have wanted. The point is that the client should think carefully and choose who will have the power to elect. We assume Mrs. Eustace has considered that her daughter's election to have the mortgage paid out of the residue will result in her son's bearing half of a debt on property he will not own.

IV. NON–RESIDUARY LEGACIES

Comment. These paragraphs are for specific legacies. These will "abate" last–i.e., they will have to be used to pay debts, expenses, and taxes only when the residuary estate is all used up. When the client has a lot of these, and they represent most of his wealth, provision should be made for the order in which they abate, as compared with one another. We use a couple of terms here on the assumption that they have been defined in the overture. Many states now authorize separate lists disposing of items of tangible personal property. (See the Uniform Probate Code provision in the Statutory Appendix.) The advantage of the device is that the client can make new lists as she changes her mind, without having to make a new will. The statute on lists may have formal requirements of its own–e.g., signature and date. If a list is used, the statute (as in Indiana) may require that it be mentioned here.

A. I give to my Daughter, if she survives me, the piano that was given to me by my mother.

B. I give to my Daughter–In–Law, if she survives me, my white with gold trim Lenox China dinnerware.

C. I give to my Grandson Luke one thousand dollars ($1,000), if he survives me.

D. I give my farm in Montrose County, Colorado, to my Daughter, if she survives me.

E. I give all of my other personal effects and household goods and the like not otherwise effectively disposed of, such as jewelry, clothing, furniture, furnishings, silver, books, and pictures, together with unused premiums on policies of casualty insurance thereon which are unpaid at my death, and any proceeds of policies of casualty insurance thereon which are unpaid at my death, to those of my Children who survive me, in shares of substantially equal value, to be divided as they shall agree, or if they shall fail to agree within five months after my death, as my executor shall determine.

> **Comment.** **The last part of paragraph "E" should simplify distribution of personal property that is (usually) of small value but may have sentimental or symbolic significance. It is important, though, that somebody have the last word. The most bitter of family quarrels build up around what is to happen to Mama's pickle crock.**
>
> **U.P.C. Sec. 2–513 (1993 Text): "[A] will may refer to a written statement or list to dispose of items of tangible personal property not otherwise specifically disposed of by the will, other than money. To be admissible under this section as evidence of the intended disposition, the writing must be signed by the testator and must describe the items and the devisees with reasonable certainty. The writing may be referred to as one to be in existence at the time of the testator's death; it may be prepared before or after the execution of the will; it may be altered by the testator after its preparation; and it may be a writing that has no significance apart from its effect on the dispositions made by the will."**
>
> **This "list statute" seems to *require* that the will mention the list. (Indiana's version makes the requirement explicit.) The drafting suggestion (for the will) made in the U.P.C. Comment takes that step into account:**
>
> **"I might leave a written statement or list disposition of items of tangible personal property. If I do and if my written statement or list is found and is identified as such by my Personal Representative no later than 30 days after the probate of this will, then my written statement or list is to be given effect to the extent authorized by law and to take precedence over any contrary devise or devises of the same item or items of property in this will."**

F.   Real or tangible or intangible personal property conveyed by me during my lifetime shall not be considered advancements. No adjustment of my estate shall be made on the basis of such inter-vivos gifts.

Comment. **Specific legacies are canceled if the executor cannot find the property among the assets of the dead person. Sometimes the asset is found in the possession of one of the legatees, though, and sometimes, then, the other legatees say he has been paid his share of the residuary estate, or part of it. This provision is particularly important if the will makes cash legacies (e.g., "one thousand dollars to Sam").**

V.   RESIDUARY ESTATE

A.   "My Residuary Estate" is all of my property, real and personal, after the payment of debts and taxes under Article III, above, and after the gifts made in Article IV, above, including property as to which effective disposition is not otherwise made in this will, property as to which I have an option to purchase or a reversionary interest, and property over which I have a power of appointment.

B.   I direct my executor to divide my Residuary Estate into equal shares and to distribute those shares:

1.   one share to each of my Children who survives me;

2.   one share to the surviving spouse of each of my Children who fails to survive me but who leaves a spouse who survives me; and

3.   one share to the Descendants of each of my Children who neither survives me nor leaves a spouse who survives me.

Comment. **Clients may wish to provide further residuary distributions, beyond the immediate family, in case they outlive all the above devisees. For an example of this see the Jaramillo will, Form 4A, Chapter 10. This is perhaps an opportunity to suggest a substitutionary gift to the client's church or synagogue.**

It is assumed in this "not-quite-so-simple-will" that the definitions of Children and Descendants are the same as those in Form 1 and that the family is more numerous.

C.   I give to my executor, and to her successor in office, and I incorporate by reference herein, the fiduciary powers granted trustees in the Uniform Trustees' Powers Act, as that act provides on the date of execution of this will.

Comment. **Because an executor's statutory powers are limited, it may be a good idea to give an executor a set of statutory trustee's powers. If you use the statute on *trustee's* powers, you have to incorporate it by reference, as here. (See the Statutory Appendix.)**

D.   (See para. III–E in Form 1.)

(Testimonium and attestation clauses as in Form 1.)

Chapter 10

NON–ESTATE PLANNING

A. INTRODUCTION

We proceed now with planning for the Kennedy family (Chapter 3). Parents hope to insure that even after their deaths the children will continue to receive love and physical care. Parents also want their "estate plans" to make optimum use of the financial resources they leave to their children. Opportunities for and needs of disabled children require special knowledge and attention. One reason for this is that a disabled child may remain dependent on parents, siblings, or the state for a lifetime; there is, in other words, a planning difference between *dependent* children and *minor* children. Another reason is that most disabled persons are, or will be, eligible to receive state or federal benefits. In order to make best use of the private assets available for the care of a disabled child, it is essential to arrange the ownership and management of the assets with an eye toward government programs.

The interview in Chapter 3 introduces the unique concerns a lawyer faces when counseling parents of a disabled child. The Kennedys are an upper-middle-class family with four children. Dick Kennedy is 46 years old; he has a Ph.D. in chemistry and works for a drug company doing research and development work. Dick's annual income is currently $100,000. Mary Kennedy is 44; she is a registered nurse but she has worked at home since the birth of their first child 22 years ago. She is now contemplating returning to work outside the home. Dick and Mary have four sons: Scott, 22; Patrick, 19; David, 16; and Thomas, 11.

Scott is a senior at Downstate University. After he graduates he plans to begin a master's program in hospital administration. Pat is a freshman at City College. He is currently enrolled in a pre-med program and hopes to be a pediatrician. David is mentally retarded. He is a freshman at George Washington High School. His math and reading skills are at a second grade level. He has good verbal skills and his parents believe that he may make still further intellectual progress. Thomas is in the sixth grade at St. Catherine's School and is likely to pursue post-secondary education.

The Kennedys' assets are typical for a couple in their circumstances. They own their home as joint tenants. The market value of the home is $130,000, with a $35,000 mortgage. They have life insurance on the lives of both Dick and Mary covering the mortgage balance. They have a joint-tenancy savings account with a current balance of $23,000. They have two cars worth $6,000 and $9,000, both in Dick's name. We estimate the value of their furniture and personal property from the fact that it is covered by homeowner's insurance in the amount of $65,000. Dick has a retirement program through his employer; it has a death benefit currently worth $124,000; Mary is named as beneficiary; Dick's estate is contingent beneficiary. Dick has two privately purchased whole-life insurance policies with face amounts of $60,000 and $40,000; both policies have disability riders. Mary Kennedy is the beneficiary of the policies and the children are named as contingent beneficiaries.

Distilling what is found in bar association pamphlets on wills, there are three reasons for Dick and Mary Kennedy to have wills. First, when one of them dies, the intestacy statute may give some of the decedent's property to the children. This reason is the weakest of the three. It is true that a good many intestacy statutes give half or more of a decedent's estate to children, even when the other parent survives, thus invoking cumbersome, expensive guardianship protection against their being made the victims of their widowed parent. However, the Kennedys have all their cash in a survivorship bank account and their residential real estate is held in survivorship form as well. Almost all of the cash available to support the family following Dick's death will be life insurance (including retirement-plan death benefits) payable to Mary. What probate property there is will probably be eliminated by the family allowance or taken under a small-estate procedure. If Dick and Mary do not make wills, the Kennedy children stand to inherit a half interest in the cars and Dick's gardening tools.

The second reason for a will is that Dick and Mary may die together or in quick succession. If both Dick and Mary die intestate while the children are minors, their property will be available to the children, but half of it (David's and Tom's shares) will undoubtedly be placed in guardianship. Half of the life insurance proceeds will be included in the guardianship estates, either by inheritance from, or through, the survivor or by beneficiary designation, or in default of contingent beneficiary designations on the policies. Guardianships are cumbersome, expensive, inflexible, and unnecessary. A life insurance trust arrangement is less expensive, more flexible, and more likely to work if the Kennedy children are cared for out of state. The Kennedys need wills, or some equivalent, or both, if they want to see that their moderate wealth is used to maximum efficiency for their orphaned children. The emotional force of this can be enhanced somewhat by recalling that a widowed parent is invariably more concerned about wills than a parent whose spouse is living. (Consider, for example, the Gilley family, described in the Appendix.)

A trust arrangement will not entirely eliminate the need for guardianship; it will only confine guardianship to its proper and necessary ambit—the physical care of dependent and minor children. If both

Kennedys die during David's life, somebody will have to take care of David, and maybe of Thomas as well, and that somebody will be best advised to do so pursuant to appointment as guardian of their persons. That is the third reason for a will: The Kennedys can designate in it who this guardian is to be. The great value of this argument is not that it causes the Kennedys to make a will, but that it causes them to consider who is available to take care of their children and to discuss the situation with the persons they choose to be guardians.[1]

When the first of these three reasons, which is the least potent, is discounted, it is apparent that the reasons for the Kennedys to make wills bear almost no resemblance to the reasons for a couple with five million dollars to make wills. This project, in other words, is not a compact version of a "big" will. Dick Kennedy is no patriarch dispensing his largess evenly or capriciously to waiting relatives and friends. Disposition is the least of the Kennedys' problems. After their deaths, they must provide exactly what they are providing now—support for their children. It is not a matter of "estate planning," but rather of doing what they can to relieve a thoroughly horrible situation for their children. We call a lawyer's work for such clients "non-estate planning."

The Kennedys need a will to designate a person to act as guardian of the person for their younger children and a trust to provide a mechanism to manage the property they leave to their children. Both of those basic concerns—personal care and financial well-being—take a particular twist here because David is mentally retarded. Thomas will need a guardian only until his 18th birthday. David will probably need a personal guardian for some purposes throughout his life; he will also need assistance in managing his money. His situation, and that of his family, is similar to that of mentally ill children, and some physically handicapped children, and their families. The essence of the situation is a dependence that may not disappear by the time the child is of legal age—that may even last all of the child's life.

B. THE GENERAL SCHEME

All "estate planning" projects begin with a review of the clients' needs and an examination of the resources available to meet those needs.

---

1. "Annie's Mailbox" had a letter from "Loving Sister–To–Be (Again)," June 5, 2003, that dramatically illustrates that the choice of guardianship for a child is often more sentimental than thoughtful:

"Last week, my father called to tell me his wife, my stepmother, is pregnant. At first, I was thrilled. But I could tell from the tone of my father's voice that he was shocked....

"Annie, I'm 20 years old and in college. I know a baby will be a huge financial burden for my father, not to mention Dad will be 65 by the time my newest sibling graduates from high school. My father and his wife both smoke.... Neither of them is in the best of health.

"I know it sounds selfish, but I'm afraid that Dad is going to ask me to be the baby's legal guardian if something were to happen to him or his wife. Annie, I plan to wait until I am married with a good job before I even think of having children. I doubt I will have the financial resources or time to raise my youngest sibling.

"Do you think I should share these concerns with my father?"

Planning for parents who have a child with a disability differs from planning for parents of non-disabled adult children in three ways: First, a disabled child's financial needs are likely to be greater than those of a non-disabled adult child; second, potential resources available to the child include governmental assistance; and third, the disabled child may have unique and continuing management and personal-care needs. But planning for parents of a disabled child resembles planning for parents of minor children in many respects. Before addressing the unique concerns arising from David's disability, we will look at the issues that arise in all planning for dependent children, whether the dependency arises by virtue of the child's age or from disability.

There are three issues that are fundamental in planning for the care of children in a family such as the Kennedys, whether or not the family includes a disabled child: (1) What is the better fiduciary vehicle for management of children's property—guardianship or trust? (2) Since our answer to the first question, and, we hope, yours, is that a trust is better, which form of trust best serves their needs—an inter-vivos trust or a trust in a will (testamentary trust)? (3) How do non-probate assets (life insurance, death benefits under retirement plans, and property held by survivorship) fit into the fiduciary scheme?

1.   GUARDIANSHIP OR TRUST?

If the Kennedys die without wills or if they draft simple wills leaving all of their property to each other and upon the death of the survivor of them outright to the children, their property will pass to the persons they wish to benefit. However, if both Kennedys die while the two younger children are minors, a guardian of the estate (called a conservator in some states) will be appointed to manage each minor child's share. There are several disadvantages to this.

First, if the Kennedys do not have wills, the property passing to the children via the state's intestate succession laws will be equally divided among the four of them. Equal division into relatively inaccessible shares is a disadvantage in any family, since any family has children of disparate talents and varying good fortune. In this family, equal division disregards the fact that David has greater needs than any of his brothers, and that Thomas has greater needs than his two older brothers. In a family with a disabled child the disadvantage is acute. Whether the property is given to the children by their parents' wills or through the intestacy statute, or through beneficiary designations in life-insurance contracts or employment arrangements, each child's share must be separately managed, and a guardian has no authority to use the property of one child for the benefit of another, even if the other child has insufficient property to meet his needs, and even when the same person is guardian for both.

Second, guardianships end when a minor child reaches the age of majority, age 18 in most states. That means that each child's share will be distributed to him at age 18, and the child will then take over independent management of his assets. Although Dick's and Mary's estates are not large ones, one quarter of their combined estates is likely to be larger than they would comfortably hand over to an 18–year-old.

It is unlikely that David will ever be capable of properly managing such a sum of money. Because of his mental retardation, it may be possible to prevent the termination of David's guardianship at age 18; however, even if it is likely that such an extension would be granted, the process for obtaining the extension may be damaging to David. Increasingly, the law discourages the establishment of guardianships on the basis of a person's status, such as the status of being a mentally retarded person, and instead requires proof that the person needs a guardianship. In other words, an adult, whether or not mentally disabled, is presumed competent to conduct his or her affairs until a judge says otherwise. For persons such as David, who can understand the court proceeding, a judicial determination of incompetence may be more than embarrassing. It may undermine his self esteem and sense of competence to handle other matters that are clearly within his capabilities. It is also important to bear in mind that disabled people are often no more frozen into their situation than people without mental or physical disabilities are: Disabled people grow, acquire new skills, adapt to changing circumstances, become better and worse, just like the rest of us. Down's Syndrome children, for example, vary widely in mental and physical ability, notably as the result of training (or lack of it).[2]

Third, in spite of efforts to reform guardianship laws, in most states a guardianship estate is still more cumbersome and expensive to administer than a trust. A guardian is a court-appointed and court-supervised property manager. Because appointment of a guardian entails deprivation of the ward's rights, there are safeguards built into the guardianship procedures to help insure that the process is not misused. The actual appointment usually involves a hearing in open court, with notice to all interested parties. The court must approve the guardian's activities and makes many, if not most, discretionary decisions. Most jurisdictions require a guardian to file annual or other periodic accountings. Such court supervision is not only time consuming but expensive; it involves the apparatus of litigation: pleadings, dockets, judicial orders, time in the courthouse—all lawyer activities that are carried out with the meter running. A guardian of the estate normally is required to obtain a fiduciary bond to insure protection of the ward's assets. Furthermore, in

2. A person with Down's Syndrome has extra genetic material located at the twenty-first chromosome. The presence of the extra genetic material causes the physical and mental characteristics of persons with the condition. Physical characteristics may include slanting eyes, a flat bridge of the nose, a large tongue, and short fingers. Mental development is retarded. It was at one time assumed that all such children had relatively short life expectancies; while that may still be true in many cases, it can no longer be assumed to be true. Differences in condition, in care, and in the capacities of medical science mean that many such children will live into old age.

order to provide maximum protection of a ward's assets, guardianship laws often restrict the kinds of investments that may be made with a ward's assets. As a result, property placed in a guardianship often produces less income than trust investments. All of these safeguards entail expense that may be unnecessary if another adequate protective device can be arranged.

A fourth, serious objection to the use of guardianship as an asset management tool is that guardianship property is, or is deemed to be, the property of the ward. That could be a drawback for David, for at least three reasons:

(a) David's disability may qualify him for state-provided care or services. However, David's assets, including any assets held by a guardian for him, will be available to the state to reimburse it for the cost of such services. Furthermore, David's ownership of the guardianship assets could disqualify him for certain government programs for disabled persons who are financially needy. In short, assets that Dick and Mary leave to David in this manner may provide him little, if any, benefit. The assets will be used to provide him with care and services that would otherwise be provided by the public at no cost to David. This issue will be discussed more fully when we look at the particular planning challenges that arise when a disabled child is involved.

(b) David's property will produce income, which income will belong to David. Some governmental programs for handicapped citizens have income guidelines; David may have investment income that will keep him from being eligible for those benefits.

(c) David's property will pass to other owners when he dies; if he owns his property in the fee-simple sense, passage of that property to others will require a probate estate for him. Property that has been placed in a life-estate arrangement will become possessory in other owners, at David's death, without the necessity of probate administration. (In some cases the disabled child lacks testamentary capacity; she is not able to make a will, which means that her fee simple property will pass without "estate planning." A lawyer is bound to think that may not be a sound arrangement for the family.)

Fifth, guardianship steadily becomes even less reliable as a long-term planning tool for disabled persons. To a substantial extent, the federal representative-payee system for Social Security retirement and disability payments and Supplemental Security Income payments has supplanted guardianship. There is a trend away from overly restrictive treatment of disabled persons. There is an emphasis on providing disabled persons with the skills necessary to function in society. Current practice calls for placement of disabled individuals in the community whenever possible. The more independent the child becomes in his or her ability to conduct daily affairs, the less appropriate guardianship will be.

The trend toward greater independence for disabled persons, along with the trend in some states to review the need for guardianship annually, decreases the likelihood that guardianship as a protective form will provide lifelong assistance for a particular person. This trend, when it matures, will leave the disabled child nearer the position of a "normal" minor child when she or he reaches the age of majority; in both cases, in most American middle-class families, the child is legally competent but remains economically dependent. (There was a time when lawyers preparing wills and trusts put determinative significance on the age of majority—which was then 21—but that is no longer the case.)

To avoid the inflexibility and expense of a financial guardianship (or conservatorship), most lawyers suggest that parents of minor children create a contingent trust that will come into existence, or be funded, only if both parents die while the children are minors. "Minor" is a term defined in the trust, keyed (i) to an age that can be older than the age of majority for drinking, driving, and voting purposes, or (ii) to an event, such as graduation from college—either or both. In David's case such an "age" may be specially defined, or the trust may specify that David is to be considered, for trust purposes, in effect, a minor for the rest of his life; but a trust can be flexible in providing for the economic consequences of "minority" and disability. (See, e.g., Article IV in Form 4A in this chapter.)

The Kennedys need wills to appoint a guardian of the person who will assume responsibility for the actual care of David (and, maybe, of Thomas), and to add whatever property they leave in their probate estates to a trust for David and his siblings. The trust can be set up as, in form, a declaration of trust or a contract with the trustee, made during the life of the clients; or it can be provided for in one or both of the clients' wills. In either case, transfers of property are made, at or after the clients' deaths, to the trustee as legal property owner.

2. INTER–VIVOS OR TESTAMENTARY TRUST?

The Uniform Testamentary Additions to Trusts Act, its statutory progeny (Statutory Appendix), and its case-law equivalents have increased the use of inter-vivos trusts for clients such as the Kennedys. In most states it is safe to use trusts that are unfunded when established, and contingent as well. "Contingent" means they go into operation when and if the person or persons who set up the trust die leaving orphaned, minor children (or, in the case of children such as David, dependent adult children). The trustees of these trusts are able to be beneficiaries of life insurance and retirement plans. In the usual case these insurance and employment benefits, collected by the trustee, will be the principal assets in the trust when and if it is funded. Bank trust departments in most communities will accept these contingent trusts without fee while they are unfunded—that is, usually, during the settlor-insured's life. The wills of both parents can be drawn so that probate assets "pour over" into the trust arrangement. The arrangement can be planned so that there is only one trust, either an inter-vivos trust established by both parents, or a testamentary trust in the will of the second to die.

Contingent, inter-vivos, revocable life-insurance trusts are easily amended and are more flexible than testamentary trusts. For one example of relative flexibility, amendments to trust provisions in a will have to satisfy testamentary formalities. For another and more significant example, trust provisions in a will are invalid if the will is invalid, and are not in effect until the will is admitted to probate. Testamentary trusts are also subject to the fate of will-contest litigation if the will is challenged for failure to observe statutory formalities, or lack of testamentary capacity, or undue influence, or fraud. An unfunded inter-vivos trust usually goes into actual operation at the death of the survivor parent, so that insurance and any other funds made payable to the trust—including survivor benefits under employer-provided retirement plans—are available to the children without the delay and expense of probate. Such a trust does not, of course, eliminate the need for a will.

Exercise 10.1

10.1.1. Please explain why clients such as the Kennedys, if they use an inter-vivos, contingent, revocable life-insurance trust, will still need to make wills.

10.1.2. Can you think of a way to set up the Kennedys' ownership so that no property will pass under either will?

This approach involves the creation of an inter-vivos trust that exists at first only on paper. The Kennedys appoint a trustee during life but leave the trustee without funds. They each write a will that gives their property to the other (and they use insurance, retirement, and joint-and-survivor arrangements that have the same effect without probate), but in the event that the other does not survive, and they leave dependent children, all goes to the trustee: Joint-and-survivor property goes into the trust through the will of the second to die, as does property owned by that parent; beneficiaries on the life insurance contracts and for the death benefit under the pension plan are changed so that, if Mary does not survive Dick, the proceeds are paid to the trustee of the trust. This is the so-called "pour-over" trust (a misnomer because the wills and insurance contracts do the pouring; the trust is pouree). As the trust is usually constructed, it is contingent because it will come into existence, if at all, only if both parents die while at least one child is a minor. In the Kennedys' case, because David's disability will continue beyond his minority, the trust is contingent only on Thomas being a minor and on David's surviving both of his parents.

Such an arrangement, while now common, offends traditional ideas of what a trust is: It undermines the concept of a trust. A trust is not a piece of paper, not a contract, but an arrangement for the management of property—an arrangement under which the trustee is legal owner of property, but bound to administer the property for purposes other than her own. Conceptually, historically, a trust has always involved property. There is no trust until there is a trustee who owns property.

This conceptual difficulty is a legal difficulty and an obstacle to the use of the contingent inter-vivos trust *unless* trust law in the Kennedys' jurisdiction has clearly resolved it. (Jurisdictions that purport to resolve the difficulty have attempted to do so in different ways, some of which are inadequate.) What we want for our clients is this: The trustee of the revocable, contingent, life-insurance, pouree trust owns no property. The trustee owns no insurance policies; the settlors keep those. The trustee owns no assets from which to pay insurance premiums; the settlor pays the premiums. All the trustee has is the bare fact that it is secondary (contingent) beneficiary on some policies of insurance and under a pension plan, and that is a status the trustee can lose if the insured writes letters asking his insurance company and his employer to change the beneficiary designations. The consequence of all of this is that, within the traditional understanding of a trust, an unfunded life insurance trust is not a trust. Yet, the life insurance and pension-plan contracts instruct the insurance company to pay proceeds to the trustee of this "trust" and the insured's will instructs the executor of his or her estate to pay the probate assets to the same "trustee."

Because an unfunded life insurance trust is, at common law, a dubious entity, it is important that local statutes clearly authorize *both* insurance pour-overs *and* probate pour-overs into such trusts. In addition, the statute should be consulted to determine whether it authorizes pour-overs into trusts established *after* the will is executed, and whether it authorizes pour-overs into trusts established *before* the insurance is purchased. Finally, it is important to determine whether the statute makes adequate provision for jointly established pour-over trusts; and for a surviving co-settlor to have power to amend the trust.

Exercise 10.2

10.2.1. Consider, for example, Dagwood and Blondie Bumstead's family, in their old-fashioned, single-family residence in the suburbs, an American family with two college-bound, minor children, Cookie and Alexander. They have (for purposes of simplicity) five assets:

(1) Their house in the suburbs, owned as tenants by the entirety;

(2) Blondie's half-interest in a catering firm;

(3) A savings account in Dagwood's name;

(4) Life insurance on Dagwood's life, which Dagwood owns, with power in Dagwood to name primary and secondary beneficiaries;

(5) Dagwood's "401(k)" retirement plan, related to his employment at Dithers Construction Co.[3]

Assume that these clients want all five of these assets to be owned solely by the survivor of them; all of their property to go to their adult children, outright, after the survivor dies, and a single, contingent, revocable, inter-vivos trust arrangement for the children if, when the survivor dies, one or both children are minors ("majority" being, our clients say, age 25 or graduation from college, whichever is earlier). Explain the ownership and planning arrangements you will make so that transitions in ownership of each of the five kinds of property will occur as the clients want them to occur, in all possible orders of death.

10.2.2.   Assume your jurisdiction has a statute identical to the Indiana pour-over statute in the Statutory Appendix. Would inter-vivos trust arrangements for the Bumsteads be secure under this state of the law?

Many lawyers find the payment of life insurance proceeds to a *testamentary* trustee an attractive alternative, eliminating the need for an inter-vivos trustee and concentrating all economic resources in the testamentary trust. The insurance proceeds themselves and the retirement-plan benefits, although made contingently payable to the testamentary trustee, should not be subject to probate. In most cases, the only delay the device entails is the delay before testamentary trustees are qualified to serve. However, because there may be some lingering problems arising from the fact that at the moment of a testator's death, the moment at which the obligation to pay insurance proceeds arises, there is no trustee, this device is safe only if state law clearly authorizes payment of insurance proceeds to a *testamentary* trustee. (See the Statutory Appendix.)

Exercise 10.3

Review the first question in the exercise, just above, on the Bumstead family: Suppose, in your work for these clients,

---

3.   T. Gallanis, A. Dayton, and M. Wood, *Elder Law* 189 (2000): "A qualified cash or deferred arrangement under Sec. 401(k) of the Internal Revenue Code allows an employee to elect to have a portion of his or her compensation (otherwise payable in cash) contributed to a qualified profit-sharing, stock bonus, or ... money purchase pension plan. The employee contribution is most commonly treated as a pretax reduction in salary." When the employee dies before retirement, some or all of the balance in the account is payable to designated beneficiaries.

> that you have all decided that it would be best to use
> testamentary-trust wills for both clients, and that you have
> taken all steps necessary to make that arrangement work.
> Assume your jurisdiction has a statute identical to the New
> York testamentary-trust statute in the Statutory Appendix. Is
> the Bumsteads' testamentary-trust arrangement safe under
> this state of the law?

An inter-vivos trust has some particular advantages over a testamentary trust for clients such as the Kennedys. An inter-vivos trust can provide a structure for asset management for the parents in the event of their own incapacity, a structure that can offer financial assistance not only to the parents but also to the children. Asset-management trusts are often used as will substitutes for clients who are at or near retirement and need contingent guardianship substitutes in the event they become unable to manage their estates. (See Chapter 11.) When a trust is needed only for property management during the minority of the orphaned children, the usefulness of the trust may be more theoretical than real. Ordinarily the children become adults long before the parents reach the advanced ages at which the likelihood of a period of incapacity becomes high. However, in situations such as the Kennedys', where it is likely that David will always need property management for large sums of money, so that the need for a contingent trust for David will continue into the Kennedys' old age, an inter-vivos trust has advantages the testamentary trust does not have. For example, the protective provisions for the child can become effective at the earlier of the parents' deaths *or* their own incapacity.

3. SURVIVORSHIP OWNERSHIP?

The Kennedys hold their residential real estate and their cash in survivorship form. Joint ownership is an alternative to "simple wills" to the extent that each of the Kennedys gives his or her "estate" to the other. Nineteenth-century practitioners called joint-and-survivor ownership (joint tenancy or tenancy by the entirety) "the poor man's will." All significant family, investment, and business property passed "automatically" from the first to die to the survivor. (In common-law theory it did not "pass" at all; it was the survivor's all along and death of the first to die was not a passage of ownership but the removal of an obstacle to exclusive possession.) Each spouse had a "simple" will giving all of the property to descendants if the testator were the surviving spouse. Life insurance, if any, was made primarily payable to the surviving spouse and contingently payable to children.

Modern "estate planners" typically advise clients *not* to use survivorship forms of ownership. One of them gave an "estate planning" talk years ago, when the elder of your authors was young and impressionable, called "Beware of Dangerous Joints." But there are no convincing reasons against survivorship ownership for two people like the Kennedys who are harmoniously married and who have no federal estate tax problems. The device may even carry with it substantial state death-tax advantages, as well as some amount of immunity from the creditors of either spouse. They should keep their bank account as it is, although a look at the signature card and an inquiry into the circumstances of its execution to make certain that it is what it appears to be is advisable. They should probably keep their residential real estate in joint tenancy, and when they purchase a new car, they should take title as joint owners.

Survivorship ownership, insurance designations in favor of one another and contingently to the trust, and the widow's allowance or small-estates statute ordinarily will avoid probate, in the traditional sense, when one of the Kennedys survives the other. Wills are almost a formality in such a case. If the Kennedys die together, wills and trusts—for David and for Thomas if he is then still a "minor"—become essential; that reflection implies, of course, that each spouse ought to have the same sort of arrangement. What is suggested for the Kennedys is a children-centered arrangement. The "poor man's will" of survivorship ownership and life insurance will just about take care of everything else. The interview questions in Chapter 3 that set up these arrangements are these: (1) What is to happen after one of us dies? (2) What is to happen when both of us are dead, if we leave dependent children? (And dependent here typically means "minor" as the family defines it; in the Kennedys' case it means "minor" in that sense *plus* David. The appropriate notion of dependence for the Kennedys covers all of their children, adult, minor, and "minor"[4]; non-disabled and disabled.) (3) What is to happen when both of us are dead if all of the children are then independent?

C. PLANNING FOR A FAMILY WITH A DISABLED CHILD

We turn now to the aspect of our work for the Kennedys that has to do with David. First we will consider the nature of David's disability; then his legal situation; and finally resources available for his care after both of his parents are dead.

1. DISABILITY CLASSIFICATIONS

Before a lawyer can begin the planning process with parents who have a child with a disability, the lawyer needs to understand the disabling condition that affects the child. There are three general factors having to do with the disabling condition that must be considered in order to develop a plan: first, the mental competency of the child; second, the child's physical impairment; and third, the possibility of change in the child's condition.

---

4. By "minor" we mean subject to the definition of the word in a will or trust–i.e., not under the legal age (18) but under the age the testator or settlor specifies (the Kennedys chose 21).

Mental competency is not used here in a narrowly legal sense. In fact, for planning purposes, "capacity" is a better word than "competency." What is important is the mental capacity of the child to function in society and to make and communicate responsible decisions about his own life and welfare. In recent years the legal community has come to recognize that competency is not an all or nothing affair. A mentally retarded person may be competent (have the capacity) to handle his own wages, to live in a group home, and to enter into contracts for personal goods or services, but may lack the capacity to manage a large inheritance or comprehend complicated business transactions. It is important to avoid categorical or stereotypical responses and to determine the particular individual's ability to function and make decisions.

The term "mentally retarded" may be applied to anyone with an intelligence quotient of less than 68–70 (in some states the threshold is higher). However, there are enormous variations in the functioning levels among those designated as mentally retarded. Persons at the upper end of the scale may be able, with proper supportive services, to live independently in society. Plans for such a person should be significantly different from plans for a person on the lower end of the scale, who may never learn basic care skills. Prior to developing an "estate plan," a lawyer must obtain information about the particular child's needs, skills, limitations, and prognosis. The lawyer should ask the parents to provide current professional, medical, educational, and vocational evaluations of the child. The lawyer should also have information relating to the child's employment skills, interests, and hobbies, and the names and relationships of persons, other than the parents, who are close to and interested in the disabled person.

A physical impairment, either in itself or accompanying a mental disability, affects a person's ability to care for herself in a more or less independent manner. Physical impairment giving rise to a need for physical care and protection may arise either from a physical disability or from a mental disability. A person may be so mentally disabled by reason of mental retardation or mental illness that he or she is incapable of self care and is, therefore, physically impaired. Evaluation of the degree of the child's physical impairment is needed to determine both care alternatives and the amount of financial assistance that may be needed. If a child is physically impaired, but not mentally impaired, a lawyer must be careful to develop a plan that recognizes the child's mental capacity.

The final factor to be considered is the possibility of change in the child's condition. Mental retardation is a relatively stable condition. Although functioning levels among mentally retarded persons vary enormously, each person who is mentally retarded can be expected to function within a fairly predictable range for the duration of his or her lifetime. However, it is important to remember that a mentally retarded person is capable of progress and that environment and opportunities for stimulus and growth will determine that person's ultimate functioning level, just as they will for any other person.

Persons who are mentally ill, rather than mentally retarded, or who have physical disabilities, may experience, or may be expected to experience, significant fluctuations in their condition. With many kinds of mental illness, it is difficult to predict the duration of the condition or the likelihood of recovery or recurrence. When a child's prognosis is uncertain, the plan needs to be flexible and yet also include a structure for control and protection in anticipation of the child's continued or future incapacity.

2.   EMERGING LEGAL RIGHTS

In addition to understanding the type and extent of the disability affecting a client's child, a lawyer who represents parents who have a disabled child needs a general understanding of the legal rights of persons with disabilities—rights that have changed profoundly in recent years. Parents may not be aware of some of the legal rights their child has, such as the federally mandated right to education or benefits payable under her parents' Social Security accounts, or as a disabled person under the federal Supplemental Security Income program. Once parents are aware of their child's rights, they usually look around for ways to enforce those rights.

Recent changes in the law on education and health care, for the most part, have been based upon two interrelated concepts, individualized treatment and normalization. The concept of individualized treatment encourages disregard of stereotypes and allows a person with disabilities as much freedom as is consistent with her capabilities. Normalization, in broad strokes, means that a disabled person should have the opportunity to develop and live as normally as possible. Normalization may require, for example, that a disabled child should be placed in a regular classroom with tutorial assistance, rather than in a special-education classroom; or that an individual should live in her own home or in a group home rather than in an institution. The effect of these concepts on the law is the growing recognition by courts and legislators that restrictions on a disabled person's liberty should be as limited as possible. For example, a petition for full guardianship may be denied if proper care and support can be provided in some less restrictive way. The concept of normalization also means that a presumption of legal competency extends to persons with disabilities and that incompetency must be proved before restrictions are placed on a disabled person.[5]

---

5. The statutory standard for legal competency—which is traditionally the once-and-for-all, single fact that is established before a guardian or conservator is appointed for an adult—usually refers to the person's ability to manage his or her affairs. An example of the more flexible, modern approach is U.P.C. Art. 5, Part 3. Section 5–306(a) directs the appointing court to "exercise ... authority ... so as to encourage the development of maximum self-reliance and independence ... and make

Awareness of the changing law also emphasizes the fact that flexibility is important to any plan. Flexibility is important to accommodate change both in the personal condition of the child and in further refinement of the laws that provide benefits to persons with disabilities. It is standard to advise clients to seek periodic review of their wills and trusts, to insure that change in either their circumstances or in the law does not adversely affect their plans. The extent to which planning for a disabled child is interwoven with ever changing government benefit plans makes such periodic reviews all the more critical.

3. RESOURCES AVAILABLE

The planning process must include not only a review of the needs of the clients, but also an examination of the resources available to meet those needs. When dealing with clients such as the Kennedys who, although they have a relatively good income, have moderate family wealth, it is clear that assets will not be sufficient to provide total financial security for their disabled child for the remainder of his life. This will be so even if the Kennedys increase their wealth through the purchase of additional life insurance, a step many planners would recommend that they take.[6]

Because very few parents have sufficient resources to provide adequate care and support for a disabled child for the remainder of his life, the child's eligibility for governmental assistance should be explored and coordinated with the parents' plan. There are three basic types of governmental benefits for which the disabled child may be eligible. (Some of these are also available for non-disabled minor children.)

First, there are entitlement or insurance programs that provide benefits based upon contributions into the program rather than upon the recipient's need. Social Security is the best example of an entitlement program. A child who is disabled prior to the age of 22 will be eligible for Social Security benefits by reason of his disability, if one of his parents is covered by Social Security and subsequently retires, dies, or becomes disabled. (It is also possible, although not as likely, that the child may become eligible for Social Security benefits on the basis of his or her own contributions into the system.) The amount of the Social Security benefit is determined by reference to the insured person's average earnings and is not reduced or affected by earnings or other assets of the beneficiary, so long as the beneficiary continues to be "disabled" as defined by federal law. Our estimate is that David would be paid about $900 a month after

---

... orders only to the extent necessitated by ... mental and adoptive limitations or other conditions...."

6. Dick, who is at present the principal wage-earner in the family, could purchase $500,000 of term life insurance for an annual premium of $700–$900. Continuation can be guaranteed for as long as 20 years, probably subject to a change (upward) in the premium. Robert B. Treaster, "Term Life: The Safety Net Comes at a Higher Price," The New York Times, March 19, 2000, p. BN 13, col. 2.

the deaths of both parents. If and when David becomes eligible for survivor's Social Security benefits, he will be eligible for Medicare coverage (see Chapter 11), after an initial waiting period (two years as we write). When he is covered by Medicare, he will not require Medicaid coverage for most medical expenses, but Medicare will not pay for long-term institutional care.

The second type of governmental program for which a disabled person may be eligible provides financial or medical assistance based on need. The largest governmental assistance program for which an adult disabled person may be eligible is the federal Supplemental Security Income program (S.S.I.). A person may be eligible for S.S.I. even if he or she has never worked. Eligibility is based upon a showing that the claimant is either 65 years of age or older, blind, or disabled, *and* that the claimant is financially needy. Financial need is demonstrated if the claimant's resources and income fall below specified levels. If the disabled child is eligible, S.S.I. would provide monthly cash payments. (Our estimate for David: about $600 a month–without regard to survivor Social Security benefits–e.g., when one of his parents is living.) The child may also be eligible for state and federal programs providing benefits such as medical assistance, rehabilitative training, housing, and social services.

The third type of governmental program is available to all persons who fall within specified categories, without regard to ability to pay. For example, state institutional care is available in many jurisdictions to mentally disabled persons; the charge for care varies with the individual's income and assets. In this third type of program, eligibility for participation in the program is not based on need, but on the individual's own assets and the assets of relatives who are responsible for him or her. These assets may have to be used to pay the cost of the assistance received.

When it is possible that a disabled child will be eligible for an assistance program, one of the main concerns in planning is to integrate the potential governmental benefits with the financial resources of the parents, to provide the maximum level of comfort and security for the child. To accomplish this, care must be taken to structure any bequests to the child so that they do not render the child ineligible for need based programs such as S.S.I. If a gift to a disabled person results in a loss or reduction of government benefits equal to the value of the gift, the inheritance has provided no net benefit to the disabled person. Only the government has reaped the benefit. A related concern is to structure the gift so that the assets are insulated from claims of creditors, including the state, which may make claims for reimbursement for goods and services provided to the child. In many states parents cease to be financially responsible for their disabled child when the child reaches adulthood. In such states, the parents' estates would have no liability for state services provided to their adult child. However, if the parents' property is left to the child, so that the child owns it, the property may become subject to claims for reimbursement for past and current support on the basis of the child's own liability for his or her care. Claims for reimbursement are especially significant if the child is already institutionalized or if institutionalization is likely to be the only feasible alternative for care after the parents' deaths, because it is common for states to place liability for the cost of institutional care on the resident or his estate.

4. PLANNING ALTERNATIVES

Dick and Mary have two rather different planning concerns with regard to their children: (a) personal care of minor (or "minor") children, if that becomes necessary, and personal care of David; and (b) family resources available for David's support; and financial management of assets available to the other three boys (if management becomes necessary for them).

a. *Personal care*. The personal-care question is the more difficult of the two. Dick and Mary never considered placing David in an institution and are outspoken in their opposition to institutional care for mentally retarded persons. Although the Kennedys are capable and loving parents who are willing to care for and educate David, the daily work involved in raising him does create some strains on the family. Dick and Mary are unusual in that they assume that one of the other boys will take responsibility for David after they are dead. Many parents are reluctant to name one of their other children as guardian for a disabled child because they are hesitant to impose such an obligation. This can become poignant in conversations with clients: Parents who with one breath swear that their disabled child has been absolutely no burden will with the very next breath say they could not ask another child to act as guardian for the disabled child.

Parents are the natural guardians of their child during the child's minority. It is common for parents of a mentally disabled child to continue to act as *informal* guardians after the child has reached majority. During the parents' lifetimes this *de facto* guardianship arrangement often works quite well; the child is given significant support and protection without any judicial involvement. However, parents should be made aware that an adult child, whether or not mentally disabled, is presumed competent to conduct his or her own affairs until a judge orders otherwise; a *de facto* guardianship works only to the extent that the parents' right to act on behalf of the child is not challenged.

Parents are sometimes reluctant to initiate guardianship proceedings because of the stigma thought to be involved in the appointment of a guardian. However, when an adult disabled child is clearly not able to cope with the complications of daily life, or is vulnerable to exploitation, or when protection of the child is otherwise essential, it may be advisable for the parents to seek formal appointment as guardians for their disabled adult child. Judicial appointment of a guardian clarifies the child's status during the parents' lives and creates a structure to insure continuity of care after their deaths. In some states parents who have been appointed guardians for their disabled children may designate, during the parents' lives, a "standby guardian" who will assume the guardians' responsibilities immediately upon the death of the second parent. A standby guardian, unlike a guardian named in a parent's will, can be appointed by a court during the parents' lifetimes, thus insuring continuous protection at the parents' deaths.

The most common type of guardianship is a full guardianship of the person, or of the estate, or of both, in which the guardian is authorized to act on behalf of the ward in all aspects of the ward's personal or financial care (or both). Many states have recently authorized limited or partial guardianships. Limited guardianship normally affects the property rather than the person of the ward, and, as the name implies, anticipates a protective device less restrictive of the ward's legal power than full or plenary guardianship; it is not predicated upon a judicial finding of total incompetence. Guardianship, especially full guardianship, is a drastic device: It places pervasive restrictions on the legal power of the ward. A person under full (or plenary) guardianship may be deprived of his or her legal power to vote, marry, make contracts, and consent to medical treatment.

Guardianship is an unnecessary structure for a large majority of mentally disabled persons. Of all those persons classified as mentally retarded, approximately 89 per cent are classified as mildly retarded. (Such classifications, now out of vogue, are used here because of their shorthand value.) A mildly retarded person, with proper education and training, can be expected to live a fairly normal life in the community, to be employed in a basic skilled or unskilled job, and to live independently, or with her family, or in a group home. In such instances the total restriction inherent in a traditional guardianship is inconsistent with the mildly retarded person's capabilities.

David is more than mildly retarded and Dick and Mary are correct in assuming that he will probably need the protection offered by guardianship. Fortunately for David, however, David's alternatives are not only an institution or the household of one or more Kennedys, and David may well want an alternative. He will watch his brothers leave the Kennedy household for college and pursuits beyond; his *mental* retardation does not mean that he is *emotionally* retarded. He will probably reach a point, likely in his mid-to-late twenties, when he, too, will want to leave his parents' home. He may be able to do so: David has the potential to live well in a group home for mentally retarded persons. He will by adulthood have learned everyday self care and social skills. He probably will be able to make a fairly smooth transition from his parents' home into an arrangement in which he will be able to enjoy some of the independence of adult life.

Although the Kennedys do not think that David will want to leave their home, their discussion of operating their own group home reveals that they believe David eventually will need a social group larger than his immediate family. But they are not happy with any of the alternatives offered by local agencies; hence their discussion of operating their own group home. Understandably, they want to create the best situation possible for David, just as they want to give their other sons full opportunities to develop themselves. David's lifelong dependence makes more poignant every parent's fear over who will care for their children after their parents' deaths. But it does not seem to us that Dick and Mary have sufficient assets to set up and fund a group home that could continue to operate after their deaths for the remainder of David's lifetime. We are going to assume that this became apparent to them as our planning with them proceeded, that we talked with them about it, and that they decided to plan on the assumption that David's options will be to live with someone in the family or in a group home that is more or less like those they know about in their community.

Even if Scott assumes guardianship for David at some point in the future, he may not be the person who tells David that it is time to go to bed. Moreover, although it is now difficult for the Kennedys to envision Thomas as capable of serving as guardian for David, he too will reach adulthood and may be more interested in serving as guardian than Scott. If none of David's brothers is willing to become his guardian when he needs one, there may be other family members willing to take on the role. Dick and Mary have 12 nieces and nephews. One or more of David's cousins may be better suited by nature or inclination to assume responsibility for him.

In some communities there are volunteer guardian programs, where individual citizens volunteer and are specially trained to become legal guardians for mentally retarded persons in the community who do not have family members available or willing to assume the tasks of guardianship. In fact, Dick serves as a member of two boards of directors affiliated with a local agency that provides services to persons with mental disabilities. One of those boards sponsors a volunteer guardian program. Dick is aware that the individuals who choose to become guardians for unrelated adults do so because they have love they want to share with others; they undertake the role with enthusiasm.

The same board that recruits and trains the volunteer guardians also has a corporate guardianship program. The board of directors becomes guardians for mentally retarded adults who have no one to assume that role for them. The board formally makes decisions about the care of its wards and hires a staff to provide ongoing personal attention. Dick and

Mary naturally hope that one of their sons will be willing to become David's guardian, but their fears about what would happen to David if all of David's brothers were unwilling to do so are lessened by their awareness of other available resources within the community.

Exercise 10.4

We use the family name Kennedy for our clients in this chapter because we remember a moving documentary film, made in the 1970s, about a Kennedy family in Albuquerque which had two non-disabled daughters, Nancy and Tracey, and a Down's Syndrome eleven-year-old named David. Our Kennedy family is not the same, but our use of their family name is a way to remember that other Kennedy family and to honor the family of the late president, which had a mentally retarded member and which has given generous material and moral support to the causes of mentally retarded citizens.

Nancy Kennedy, of the Albuquerque Kennedys, was five years older than David. After the film was distributed, she wrote an essay in *Seventeen* magazine (April, 1979, p. 80) in which she talked of her love for her little brother. It is clear in that essay that Nancy thought about caring for David if or when her parents could not do so; in the film, the issue is significant and is not resolved.

Nancy's parents do not want to insist that she be ready to take on this burden (Nancy is, in the film, still in high school), but they feel confident that she could do it. They seem to feel that such an arrangement would be best for David, but they seem reluctant to say so. In the essay, Nancy says:

"I guess I've always known that he is part of me. When I was sixteen, I sat in on a panel discussion for the New Mexico Association for Retarded Citizens. A man in the audience asked me, 'What will become of your brother if something happens to your parents?'

"Without hesitation, I said, 'I would take care of him ... of course.' I had never given any thought to the possibility of losing my parents. And they had never asked me to assume responsibility for David. But I couldn't bear the thought of his being sent to an institution. I love my brother, and I feel that I *am* responsible for him."

10.4.1.   What should a lawyer say in such a case?

10.4.2.   A lawyer normally interviews only the parents for legal work such as we are explaining in this chapter, and the interview is normally done in the law office. Should the interview in this case include Nancy? Should it be done in the

Kennedys' home—and then include David and Tracey (who was five years old at the time of the film)?

10.4.3. If the interview includes Nancy, should the lawyer talk to her out of her parents' presence?

10.4.4. Should the lawyer offer his opinion on whether to nominate Nancy as David's guardian?

These are counseling questions for a situation in which the clients need help in making a choice for themselves and their family. If counseling in law practice is on a spectrum from providing information to resolving hang-ups, this situation is on the hang-up end of the spectrum. One way for law students to "discuss" it is to form a group and have members of the group play the roles of the people in this real-life drama.

10.4.5. There are a number of relatively easier planning decisions that may need to be made here. They are easier because they are consequent on the choice the clients, or the clients and Nancy, will make as to her role in David's future care. For example: What would you do by way of drafting a means for Nancy to be offered guardianship but not pressured to take it? What can be done by way of providing flexibility to fit the facts of Nancy's and David's future? (Nancy may be a wife and mother in middle age before this becomes an issue for her. David may be a relatively independent adult, or, to consider a worse case, he may be more dependent than he is now.)

10.4.6. Assume Nancy is to be the guardian of David's person: Is it a good idea that she also be guardian of his estate?

10.4.7. If the answer to that question is yes, is it a good idea to get all possible eggs into one basket and make her trustee of her parents' trust?

10.4.8. Consider the opposite situation: Suppose David is able to live in a group home and the guardian of his person is a volunteer from the local Association for Retarded Citizens. What are the pros and cons of Nancy's being guardian of David's estate in that case? Trustee of their parents' trust? Both?

In some states, when community resources are unavailable, there are statutory provisions for state or public guardianship. The public guardian, a state officer, becomes guardian for people who have no one willing or able to assume that responsibility. State or public guardianship serves a useful function, but it should be considered a last resort, because, when the state assumes the role of guardian, the state often is also the ward's provider of services. For example, if a state ward is a resident of a public institution, the state (or one of its departments) provides services to the ward while also serving as guardian. The conflict of interest is apparent. It is important that the guardian for an institutionalized person be an unequivocal advocate for the ward *vis-a-vis* the institution. Even if the ward is not institutionalized, public guardianship has obvious limitations. The ward's real contact is with social workers; it is a fairly impersonal system in which lack of continuity is likely to be the norm rather than the exception.

Although guardianship provides a structure for personal care and financial assistance, it does not fit the situations of all disabled individuals. The key question is whether it is necessary to protect the particular child involved. It is useful when considering that question to ask what the child is being protected from.

b. *Financial management.* Financial management is the easier of the two questions in planning for the Kennedys because it is the one we lawyers are more familiar with and the one we feel more competent to resolve. We will consider, first of all, forms of transfer of property ownership to or for the benefit of a child who is (i) a *minor,* or (ii) a "*minor*" (that is, legally of age but, in his parents' opinion, not yet ready to own significant amounts of wealth), or (iii) indefinitely *dependent* on his family, as David is. We will end up, of course, preferring a trust arrangement and will then turn to details of the trust. The considerations in preparing a contingent trust for minor, or "minor," children, and in preparing a trust for a disabled dependent child, are similar.

(i) Gift outright to child. An outright gift to any of these three kinds of children has obvious disadvantages. Even if the child is generally able to provide for herself, the inheritance from the parents' estate may be too large or complex for her to handle. Also, any property in the child's name is available to the child's creditors and the existence of the inheritance may make her a target for the unscrupulous. If the child is institutionalized or otherwise being provided services by the state, the state as creditor may seek to attach the child's property for reimbursement for the services it has provided the child; the child's property may have to be consumed before she becomes eligible for need-based governmental assistance programs.

(ii) Gift outright to a third party. Sometimes, rather than giving the child's portion of the property directly to him or her, parents give that child's share to a relative with whom the parents have an informal agreement that the property will be used for the benefit of the child. Such an arrangement is common, because it is simple and inexpensive, and because people trust their relatives. There are clear dangers to this approach. First, the third party probably has no legal obligation to use the money for the benefit of the disabled child. There is some traditional law on "equitable charges" that might reach such an arrangement, and in some states it is possible, given availability of the right evidence, to establish an express "oral" trust or a constructive trust on facts such as these—but these remedies are doubtful and, in any event, rarely practical where the amount of the gift is small. (Consider, for example, the *Koziell* case we discussed in Chapter 5.) Even if the client has no doubt that the third party would use the property for the benefit of the disabled child, the possibility of death of the third party before the disabled child dies, or of the third party's divorce or insolvency, creates a danger that the money will no longer be available to the child. The arrangement may also have adverse income-tax consequences for the third party who will be taxed on any income earned by investing the property but who may feel an obligation to use the before-tax dollars for the "beneficiary."

Such a plan does not offer adequate financial protection. If a family member is available to act as trustee, without fees, and state law (as is now typical) does not require that trusts be docketed or supervised by judges, even a small amount of money should be put in trust—on the theory that the smaller the amount available to a child, the more every dollar, and protection for every dollar, is needed. The trust instrument in such a case need not be elaborate: A letter signed by the donor of the gift will establish the trust in all jurisdictions; after that, planning is a matter of what the letter tells the trustee to do.

Fortunately for those parents who have insufficient resources to establish a bank-managed trust for a disabled child, and who have no family members or friends willing or able to take on the responsibilities of trustee of a trust for their child, alternatives are appearing. The Association for Retarded Citizens of Indiana, for example, has established a "Master Trust" under which parents may create sub-accounts for their disabled children. A bank acts as trustee and A.R.C.I. acts as consultant, or trust adviser: to maintain contact with key people in each beneficiary's life, to serve as the point of entry for disbursement requests, to consult with the trustee on disbursement requests, and to maintain individual records for each beneficiary. The Master Trust provides for a sub-account that may be attractive to parents who do not have sufficient assets to establish an individually managed bank trust; a sub-account may be established for as little as $15,000. An additional advantage of the Indiana scheme is that the A.R.C.I., in its consultant role, provides some personal care when there are no family members available to do so.

c. *Trusts.* A trust offers several advantages over other forms of personal care and financial assistance. Because a trustee manages the trust assets without regard to the competence or incompetence of the trust beneficiaries, a trust does not trigger an inquiry into the competency of a disabled trust beneficiary. The trust operates for the disabled child in the way it operates for minors or "minor" children. Also, assuming that the disabled child owns no property other than that passing from his or her parents' estates, a trust can provide complete management of the disabled child's property while imposing little or no restrictions on the other aspects of his life. Such an arrangement is consistent with the prevailing view that a disabled person should be allowed to be as independent as possible.

A trustee's legal power to act on behalf of a trust beneficiary is limited to management of the trust property. For example, a trustee has no authority to consent to medical treatment on behalf of a beneficiary or, if the beneficiary is confined to an institution, to object to living conditions in the institution. Therefore, if the child's functioning level is such that he clearly needs someone available to speak on his behalf, the existence of a trust will not eliminate the need for a guardian of the person. However, a trust can be structured to provide financial support for significant personal care protection which in some instances will eliminate the need for a guardian of the person.

When there are other children in the family and there is not much family wealth, most parents prefer to use a trust, rather than guardianship, for their disabled child because the trust may be structured to allow benefits for other children. If any of the children are minors at the parents' deaths, a single trust may be structured to provide for the children during their minority and for the disabled child for the remainder of his or her life. If all of the non-disabled children are adults at the parents' deaths, or when they become adults after the parents' deaths, the trust can be structured to benefit primarily the disabled child, and the other children in special situations.

The trust instrument can also provide for distribution of the remainder interest in the trust following the death of the disabled child. With a guardianship, a ward's property passes to the ward's estate at his or her death and, to the extent applicable, is subject to estate and inheritance taxes as well as claims of creditors. If the ward lacks testamentary capacity, the ward's estate is ultimately distributed to his intestate heirs. Typically a trust instrument provides for distribution of the remainder interest to the disabled child's brothers and sisters. (Such a distribution scheme assumes that the disabled child will not marry and have children of his or her own. While the likelihood of the disabled child's having children depends to a large extent on the degree and nature of the disability, parents should be encouraged to consider the possibility that their disabled child will some day have a family of his own.)

The chief advantage of the trust is its flexibility, which is important for three reasons: First, a trustee can be given flexibility that will allow the trustee to attempt to meet the child's needs even in the face of changing personal, social, or legal conditions. Second, a trustee's powers over income and principal may be structured to insulate the trust assets from claims of the state for reimbursement for support provided to the beneficiary and to prevent the trust estate from being counted among the child's resources when determining the child's eligibility for public assistance. This second advantage is especially important to parents with small-to moderate-sized estates, when it is anticipated that the assets available to the child, including benefits available to him through Social Security and other insurance programs, will be insufficient to provide complete financial assistance for the remainder of the child's life. Protecting trust assets from state claims and maintaining the disabled child's eligibility for public assistance may also be important to parents with more sizeable estates who are concerned about their disabled child's financial security but who are also interested in preserving some portion of their estates for the benefit of their other children.[7]

Third, the trustee can be put in the position of a surrogate parent in making distributions among all of the members of the family—the disabled child and his siblings, grandchildren, and spouses of children and grandchildren. (When a contingent trust is drawn for a family such as the Bumsteads [Exercise 10.2, *supra*], there are temporal limits to the number and nature of beneficiaries. But a trust for the Kennedy family may continue for 50 or 60 years, and by then....)

A trust for the benefit of a group of beneficiaries that includes a disabled child will have multiple objectives. These objectives influence an evaluation of the usefulness of a trust when the probable costs of administration are high and the potential corpus is small. Although there is certainly some minimum level below which such a trust is not feasible, one must remember that the trust may be used as a device for insuring continued personal assistance. Thus creation of a trust for the benefit of a disabled child may be justified even though the probable size of the corpus would not appear to justify it for a child who is not disabled. The trust can be available to receive additions from contributors other than the settlor-parents. In David's case, for example, additions to a trust for him could be made by gift or legacy from grandparents, aunts, uncles, and siblings. For the reasons stated above, guardianship is a poor planning device for such family donors; additions to an existing trust are preferable to outright gifts from such donors, or even to their establishing separate trusts for him—provided, of course, that the trust provisions are acceptable to the donors who provide the additions.

(i) *Structuring the trust.* The parents' purpose is to supplement the support provided to their disabled child by various government programs. Given the concern for insulating the trust property from claims for support and for preserving the child's eligibility for public

---

7. The remainder in a trust for a disabled child may become vulnerable to claims of public agencies that have provided benefits to the child.

assistance, the structure of the trust is extremely important. The variations in the powers of a trustee over the distribution of income and principal are limited only by the creativity of the drafter. Trusts do, however, fall into familiar patterns.

One such pattern is the simple *mandatory* trust: a trust that imposes a duty on the trustee to distribute all of the income to the beneficiary. The trustee of a mandatory trust has no discretion to choose who will receive the income or the amount to be distributed. The beneficiary possesses an interest in the trust that may be alienated either voluntarily or involuntarily and is available to creditors for the beneficiary's debts.

A trust that directs the trustee to distribute only so much of the income or principal or both as is necessary for the support and mainte-nance of the beneficiary is commonly referred to as a *support* trust. Because the settlor of such a trust intends that the trust be used specifically for the beneficiary's support, both voluntary and involuntary alienation of the beneficiary's interest are ordinarily prohibited. One recognized exception to this rule provides that the beneficiary's interest can be reached by creditors to satisfy an enforceable claim against the beneficiary for support—*i.e.,* for necessary services or supplies furnished to her (and, perhaps, to her dependents).

A trust that gives the trustee complete freedom to distribute any amount of income and/or principal or none at all is a *discretionary* trust. A purely discretionary trust includes no standard in the trust instrument against which the trustee's exercise of discretion may be evaluated. A beneficiary of a discretionary trust has no realizable interest in the trust until the trustee exercises discretion to distribute from the trust. The limited nature of the beneficiary's interest in a discretionary trust has the effect of making trust assets unavailable to the beneficiary's creditors—at least until the trustee distributes those assets to the beneficiary. Because the beneficiary cannot compel payment of trust assets to herself, or application of them for her own benefit, and because creditors' rights are derivative from the beneficiary's, the beneficiary's creditors cannot com-pel the trustee to pay anything to them.

Unfortunately, for purposes of analysis, trusts often are neither purely support nor purely discretionary. Typical trust language may mix phrases that traditionally connote a discretionary trust with language commonly used to establish a support trust. *Discretionary support* trusts may now be sufficiently common that they should be recognized as analytically distinct from both the discretionary trust and the support trust.

Spendthrift trusts expressly prohibit the voluntary and involuntary alienation of a beneficiary's interest. Where recognized, spendthrift provisions protect trust assets from claims of ordinary creditors. Like support trusts, however, spendthrift trusts are subject to the claims of certain creditors; typically a beneficiary's interest may be attached by creditors who provide the beneficiary with necessaries. The ability of a trust to protect a beneficiary's property depends to a very large extent on pertinent state law. State law governing whether certain types of trusts will be protected from particular kinds of claims or classes of claimants varies significantly, and the laws of the relevant state should be consulted before recommending any specific trust arrangement. The laws in some states are sufficiently ambiguous to make it difficult to predict the ultimate outcome. (See our discussion in Chapter 5.)

In a few states statutes have been passed that take the guesswork out of whether a trust estate will be insulated from state claims for support and reimbursement. Texas has a statute that provides that, for purposes of fees, maintenance, and support of a mentally retarded person in a residential care facility:

> if the resident is the beneficiary of a trust that has an aggregate principal of $250,000 or less, the corpus or income of the trust for the purposes of this subchapter is not considered to be the property of the resident or the resident's estate, and is not liable for the resident's support, maintenance, and treatment regardless of the resident's age.[8]

The Texas statute has limitations: It applies only to mentally retarded beneficiaries; it does not address the question of preserving eligibility for public assistance when the mentally retarded person does not reside in a state facility; and it does not protect trust estates in excess of $250,000. In spite of its limitations, the statute is important. It takes the gamesmanship out of the structuring of a trust for a mentally retarded person who resides, or is likely to reside, in a state facility. Without such a statute, the structure of a trust for a disabled child is often determined primarily by the need to protect the trust property from state claims.

Both California and Wisconsin have statutes that generally make a beneficiary's interest in trust assets available to reimburse the state for public support furnished to the beneficiary; trust provisions intended to insulate the trust assets from state claims are ineffective. However, both statutes restrict the state's right to reach trust assets if the beneficiary has a disability that substantially impairs the beneficiary's ability to provide for his or her own care or custody.[9] The legislative history of the California statute states that the provision was "intended to encourage potential settlors to provide in a trust for the care or support of a disabled person without the risk that the benefits of the trust will be taken to reimburse a public agency for a minimal level of support provided by the public agency."

8. Vernon's Texas Code Annotated, Health and Safety Code, Sec. 593.081(a).

9. California Probate Code, Sec. 15306(b); Wisconsin Statutes Annotated, Sec. 701.06(5m).

To the extent that it is possible to generalize, in those states where there are no such clear statements of policy, the safest approach appears to be to establish a trust under which distributions for the benefit of the disabled beneficiary are left to the *absolute* discretion of the trustee—a purely discretionary trust; the trust document should not say that distributions can be made for the maintenance, care, or support of the beneficiary.

A simple *mandatory* trust is not recommended because the beneficiary's income interest in such a trust is available to creditors, including the state. In many states, *spendthrift* restrictions on the beneficiary's interest do not now mean what they say. If all of the trust income is paid to reimburse the state, the corpus of a modest size trust may be rapidly depleted by the trustee's discretionary use of corpus to provide the beneficiary with supplemental assistance. Even if the trust beneficiary is not indebted to the state for services previously rendered, or is not chargeable for services currently being provided, the income from a trust may result in ineligibility for, or reduction in, payments from need based programs such as Supplemental Security Income. If any distributions from a trust result in an equal reduction in the amount of the S.S.I. payment, the trustee cannot improve the beneficiary's standard of living unless the trust is large enough to make monthly distributions that exceed the maximum S.S.I. benefits (and would make the child ineligible for S.S.I.).

A trust for *support* also should be avoided when the parents' objective is to have the beneficiary's basic needs supplied by the government and to have the trust provide "extras." A state's claim against a trust for reimbursement of the costs of maintaining the disabled person is more likely to succeed if the trust contains language indicating that trust assets are to be used for support: The state's right to reimbursement from the trustee for support furnished to the beneficiary may be dependent upon the beneficiary's right to compel distribution from the trust: The beneficiary of a support trust has an enforceable claim to support. Support standards impose a duty on the trustee to exercise its power to distribute or apply assets, leaving to the trustee's judgment only the extent or manner of doing so. Because the beneficiary can compel distribution from the trust of amounts needed for his or her support, and the state is a creditor that has furnished necessary support, the state may reach trust assets to the same extent as the beneficiary.

Because the parents hope to insure that their disabled child will continue to have proper support, even if government support for the disabled disappears, some lawyers use a support trust but narrow its scope in order to protect its assets from reimbursement claims and to retain eligibility for government programs. We do not recommend that: Some courts have held that the state may reach support trust assets even when the trustee is given "absolute" or "sole" discretion over distributions for the support and maintenance of the beneficiary. Likewise, instructing a trustee to take into consideration other resources available to a beneficiary does not sufficiently attenuate the beneficiary's interest. A beneficiary of such a support trust has a right to trust distributions only to the extent that they are needed to supplement other resources available to him, so that outside resources and the trust distributions together provide at least minimal support. Some courts have held that a trust provision for support is meaningless if a trustee is permitted to consider the availability of support at public expense when determining a beneficiary's need for trust distributions.

We recommend a discretionary trust, but that recommendation alone is imprecise. There are two types of discretionary trusts that should be considered: first, and probably most commonly used, a purely discretionary trust with language *prohibiting* the trustee from using trust income or principal to support the disabled beneficiary; second, a purely discretionary trust that neither prohibits nor authorizes the trustee to use trust assets to support the beneficiary. There is a risk in using this first type of discretionary trust, in stating that the trust *may not be used* to provide primary support for a disabled beneficiary. If public assistance is discontinued or seriously reduced in the future, the trust will be unable to provide primary support and the beneficiary will be left without any means of support. However, many lawyers now recommend such trusts, presumably on the assumption that it is more likely that an imprecisely drafted trust will render a particular beneficiary ineligible for assistance than that all such assistance will be eliminated.

A purely discretionary trust that *neither authorizes nor prohibits* the use of trust assets to support a beneficiary may increase the risk that the beneficiary will be ineligible for public assistance, but it allows the trust to function as a safety net if the beneficiary's public assistance is discontinued for any reason. The risk here arises from the fact that the intent of the settlor, gleaned from the language of the trust and the circumstances surrounding its establishment, are factors that are considered when determining whether the trust assets are available for the support of the beneficiary. Some cases have held that where it appears that the settlor intended to provide for the general benefit and support of the disabled beneficiary, the trust may be vulnerable to state claims, whether or not the trust is a true support trust. (This risk may be waning in some states. Some cases have held that discretionary support trusts, an even riskier type of trust, do not render the beneficiary ineligible for governmental assistance.)

Exercise 10.5

Narrow the options, for purposes of discussion, and advise the Kennedys on which of three types of trusts seems best for their family: (i) the discretionary trust with a prohi-

> bition on use of trust assets for support; (ii) the purely
> (simply) discretionary trust; and (iii) the sort of trust that was
> held to be effective in insulating trust assets from public
> eligibility requirements in several states. The lawyer-client
> conversation in which this issue is discussed should include
> the question: What is the worst thing that can happen? If the
> clients are not thinking in those terms, perhaps their lawyer
> should—and perhaps their lawyer should ask them to do so.

Some lawyers argue that a discretionary trust should also include a strong spendthrift clause to prevent attachment of the trust assets by creditors of the beneficiary. A spendthrift clause prevents the voluntary or involuntary alienation of the estate by the beneficiary before actual distributions of income or corpus are made to the beneficiary. Of course, a spendthrift clause does not protect the assets from attachment once distribution is made to the beneficiary. A spendthrift clause does not bar the claims of certain classes of claimants, notably those who provide necessaries. Combining discretionary-trust provisions with spendthrift provisions is conceptually redundant: If the beneficiary has no enforceable interest (and that is the concept which supports the use of discretionary trusts), then he has nothing he could voluntarily alienate or that a creditor could reach. Those who favor spendthrift clauses in discretionary trusts use the argument that an old-fashioned mother uses when she feeds chicken soup to her sick child: It can't hurt....

> (ii) *Making trust distributions.* Although properly structuring a
> trust requires attention to a significant amount of detail and careful
> coordination with the rules and regulations governing eligibility for
> the public assistance programs most likely to benefit the disabled
> child, such efforts constitute only half the battle. The other half of the
> battle is proper administration and distribution of trust assets. Even
> if a trust is structured so that its property is not counted among the
> beneficiary's resources, or available for reimbursement for public
> agencies, unless the trustee is mindful of the income limits, exclu-
> sions, and exemptions of the various programs, distributions from
> the trust may render the beneficiary ineligible for public benefits
> because he or she will have too much income. The purpose of the trust
> is to provide the disabled child with amenities that he or she would
> not have if the child's sole means of support were public assistance.
> Supplementing the bare necessities provided by the government will
> improve the quality of the child's life.

If a discretionary trust is used, the trust instrument should contain a statement of the settlor's intent and a description of appropriate trust uses. A trust is least likely to be counted as a resource of the beneficiary and render the beneficiary ineligible for public assistance, or be subject to creditors' claims, if the trust instrument states that trust income and principal are not to be used to provide the beneficiary's primary support. Whether or not such a statement should be included in the trust depends in part upon how strongly the parents feel about the availability or unavailability of the trust as a safety net in the event that government support of disabled persons is sharply decreased. It depends also upon the functioning level of the child and the programs from which it is most likely that the child will receive assistance. Before including language precluding the trustee from furnishing the beneficiary with in-kind support, it is important to examine the effect such a restriction might have upon the beneficiary's ability to live independently or with family members.

We do not recommend use of language prohibiting distributions for David Kennedy's support: David may be able to live semi-independently, and Dick and Mary dislike the living arrangements currently offered through the local agencies and not-for-profit organizations. We recommend a purely discretionary trust.

Regardless of the type of discretionary trust used, the trustee should be directed to investigate all sources of support for the beneficiary and to take (and encourage the guardian to take) whatever steps are necessary to enroll the beneficiary for private or public assistance or insurance. It is possible that the trustee, especially an individual trustee, also may serve the disabled child in some other fiduciary capacity, such as "representative payee" for Social–Security Disability or S.S.I. benefits. (The representative-payee system in federal Social Security and veterans-benefit law is a statutory quasi-guardianship that is simply established and not subject to routine judicial supervision. Payments from the agency are made to a payee for the eligible recipient.)

The trust instrument should prohibit commingling of funds from other sources with the trust assets. Although commingling already may be prohibited by state or federal law, a clause in the trust to that effect reinforces the argument that the trust estate is not an asset of the beneficiary and reminds the trustee of her duty. (It may be advisable to arrange for payee payments to be added to the trust; in that case, though, the trustee/payee should be prepared to account separately for the use of payee funds.)

The trust should outline the purposes for which distributions are proper. The trust instrument should indicate that the trust income and principal are intended to be used to provide for the beneficiary those things that are not provided from other sources. Examples might include sophisticated medical or dental diagnostic work or treatment not covered by medical-benefit programs, private rehabilitative training, and supplementary educational aid. In addition, it should be made clear that expenditures that would enrich the beneficiary's social life are not only authorized but expected. In addition to authorizing expenditures for vacations and periodic outings for the beneficiary, the trust could authorize payments for a person to accompany the beneficiary or to bring siblings who live at some distance to visit the beneficiary.

If it is expected that the disabled child will need S.S.I. benefits, or if the child lives in a state that provides medical benefits under the Medicaid program to all persons who are eligible for S.S.I., the trustee should become familiar with the financial eligibility criteria for S.S.I. If the child meets the severely limited income and resources guidelines of S.S.I., the child will be eligible for S.S.I. monthly cash payments.

At present, a single person who claims S.S.I. cannot have nonexcludable resources (as defined by regulations) in excess of $2,000. So long as the total value of these resources does not exceed the $2,000 limit, the trust estate can be used to furnish items such as television sets, radios, stereos, bicycles, and sports equipment—items that will generally make life more comfortable and enjoyable for the child. The exclusions—items that are excluded when determining an individual's resources—are perhaps of even greater significance in planning the type of property to be given to the trust beneficiary. A home owned and used by an S.S.I. claimant as his personal residence is an excluded asset regardless of the value of the home. One automobile is also excluded if it is necessary for the claimant or a member of the claimant's household for employment or medical treatment of a special or regular medical problem. Depending on the type of disability and the functioning level of the child, the trustee may be authorized to make distributions to acquire and maintain such assets in the beneficiary's name. In addition, the trust may purchase and retain assets in the name of the trust for use by the beneficiary, because assets used by the beneficiary but in which he or she has no right or title do not affect eligibility for S.S.I.

S.S.I. eligibility includes an income test as well as an assets test. An S.S.I. recipient is allowed only a small amount of earned and unearned income; income exceeding the allowances results in a dollar for dollar reduction of S.S.I. payments. The definition of income for S.S.I. purposes is very broad. Income is defined in a government publication as "anything you receive in cash or in-kind that you can use to meet your need for food, clothing, or shelter." However, a trustee may make *some* expenditures for a trust beneficiary that are not counted as income because they do not result in receipt by the beneficiary of food, clothing, or shelter, or of anything that could be used to obtain those items. For example, if a trustee pays an S.S.I. recipient's telephone bill or health insurance premium, the claimant does not receive income because the payment does not result in (i) receipt of food, clothing, or shelter, nor (ii) in the receipt of an item that may be sold and the proceeds used to purchase basic maintenance needs. Personal services performed for an S.S.I. claimant do not count as income. A trustee can pay for services, such as lawn care, housekeeping, meal preparation, or grocery shopping, without reducing the trust beneficiary's S.S.I. payments. The availability of such services might enable a trust beneficiary to continue to reside in his or her own home, rather than being institutionalized.

Provision of in-kind maintenance and support is treated differently than distributions of cash to an S.S.I. recipient. Although the rules and regulations are intricate and complicated, the basic rule is that when an S.S.I. recipient is given in-kind maintenance and support, his monthly S.S.I. check is reduced by only one-third even though the value of the support provided to him may far exceed one-third of the S.S.I. payment. If a trustee uses trust funds to pay rent and utilities and to purchase food and clothing for a beneficiary who is also an S.S.I. recipient, the recipient will suffer a one-third reduction in his S.S.I. benefits, even if the actual expenditures are far greater than that amount. In contrast, if the trustee distributed cash to the beneficiary to purchase or rent shelter or to purchase food and clothing, the full amount of the cash distribution would be income and reduce his benefits dollar for dollar.

In addition to familiarization with S.S.I. practices, the trustee should become conversant with the eligibility criteria for the Medicaid program in the beneficiary's home state. Medicaid provides medical assistance to poor persons who are aged, blind, or disabled or who are members of families receiving what was once called Aid to Families with Dependent Children (now Temporary Assistance to Needy Families). Medicaid may be even more important to a disabled person than S.S.I. For example, many adult, mentally retarded persons who do not live in their own homes, or in their parents' homes, live in "intermediate care facilities for the mentally retarded," as defined by Medicaid, a common form of which is a group home. Medicaid covers the cost of the group home for those persons who are financially needy enough to qualify for Medicaid.

The Medicaid program is administered by state governments, but it is funded jointly by the federal government and the states. The state rules vary widely within bounds set by federal statutes and regulations. Approximately two-thirds of the states provide Medicaid to all aged, blind and disabled S.S.I. recipients. The other third of the states use different and generally more restrictive criteria than are used for S.S.I. eligibility. Among the latter states, the usefulness of a trust as a supplement to Medicaid varies, and a careful examination of the state's statutory and regulatory eligibility criteria, as well as any interpretative case law, is necessary any time the use of a trust is contemplated for a disabled person who resides in one of those states.[10]

---

10. Under some state systems, a trust for David of the sort we describe here would not bar Medicaid eligibility. Those regulations (and the federal statute that mandates them) may not require that the remainder, after David's death, be available for Medic-aid reimbursement. If that requirement were in place, it would argue for considering either (i) a separate "David Trust" within the broad trust we propose in Form 4A, below, or (ii) a planning decision, now, to forgo Medicaid eligibility.

Exercise 10.6

If this planning works as well as we seem to think it might, David Kennedy, when he survives his parents, may receive maximum benefits under state and federal plans for disabled persons as well as the material comfort of being a member of an upper-middle-class American family. We justified planning that will keep David eligible for public benefits, when we talked about it early in this chapter. We said planning that would make David the responsible *owner* of family wealth would mean that his property would have to be used first, before he could take advantage of government programs. When a lawyer plans that way, we said, "Only the government has reaped the benefit."

But resources for government programs are limited. It is a bit abstract, perhaps, but hardly unrealistic to say that what is used to take care of David Kennedy is not available for a disabled child whose family has less for its children than the Kennedys have for theirs. Please talk about this with a wise elder or a sensitive friend or relative: Imagine how Dick and Mary Kennedy feel about it. Imagine how a welfare mother who has a child with exactly the same condition as David feels about it. Decide—you and your wise elder, sensitive friend, or relative—whether this is a moral problem and, if it is, whether the Kennedys' lawyer ought to mention it to her clients.

Our discussion has focused upon the considerations that are present when helping parents plan the disposition of their property for the benefit of their children, one of whom is disabled. As in all instances in which clients face the possibility of their deaths and their inability to continue to provide and care for persons who are dependent upon them, there are few clear-cut answers that will adequately respond to the range of human needs that are at issue; the presence of a disabled child simply makes that reality more stark. The planning tools are familiar: wills, inter-vivos trusts, and testamentary trusts. Boilerplate language and standard responses need to be carefully scrutinized and sometimes abandoned so that the documents used will accommodate the disabled child's special needs, and will supplement rather than supplant governmental assistance.

Throughout this chapter when discussing the non-disabled child in the Kennedy family we have tried to avoid the use of the term "normal children." We have done so because calling non-disabled children "normal" implies that the disabled child is not normal. Disabilities *are* a normal part of life. Planning for the Kennedys, or other families whose members include a disabled child, is more similar to planning for parents of non-disabled, minor children than it is dissimilar. The drafting work for the Kennedys needs an extra spin on the ball, but it is not a new ball game. The similarities should be apparent when comparing, in this chapter, the Jaramillo will and the Kennedy trust and "pour over" will.

D. GAY COUPLES AND THEIR FAMILIES

(First story:) The inveterate wordsmith and court watcher James J. Kilpatrick wrote in September, 2004, about a gay couple (male) who lived together on a farm in Oklahoma, raised three children (from a divorce one of them had gone through), and worked out an oral agreement under which the survivor took all property, along with wills ("neither witnessed nor notarized") under which each was beneficiary of the other. Both arrangements were contested by cousins of the first to die. The cousins won; Mr. Kilpatrick wrote, "A man who writes his own will had better not have covetous cousins"; when he wrote in 2004, the case was pending on the federal supreme court docket. We note in passing that if the couple had been married, much of the steam invoked by the covetous cousins would have been dissipated by the fact that the survivor would have had the claims of a surviving spouse that we discussed in Chapter 4, and most of the rest of it would have been dissipated if the couple had held their property in joint ownership. None of that spousal protection from covetous cousins would have depended on wills.

(Second story:) Dawn and Stephanie were a lesbian couple. They "shared joint finances and held themselves out to their families, friends, and community as a couple of a committed, loving relationship. [They] even participated in a commitment ceremony at which they proclaimed themselves to be committed domestic partners.... " They wanted children; Stephanie underwent artificial insemination (Dawn's brother was the sperm donor), and bore a child ("A.B."). For four years, both partners acted as parents; Dawn petitioned for adoption. But, while the adoption petition was pending, the couple split up. The child stayed with Stephanie; Dawn paid support and enjoyed visitation, for a while; then Stephanie "unilaterally terminated visitation and began rejecting Dawn's support payments."

Dawn filed a petition for declaratory judgment, seeking a court order saying she was A.B.'s "second legal parent." The trial judge dismissed the petition "for failure to state a claim." Stephanie appealed. The appellate court reversed. Judge Friedlander began the appellate opinion describing what we finally feel we need to notice in this part of our book on wills and trusts: "[T]he law will have to extend some form of recognition to gay and lesbian relationships to create a structure within which a myriad of legal issues emanating from such partnerships may be resolved, much as it has done with unmarried heterosexual couples." On the specific issue of A.B.'s parenthood, the controlling precedent was a 1994 decision in which the court invoked estoppel to hold that a child conceived by artificial insemination and born to a woman who was married to someone other than the donor was the child of the mother's husband. He was responsible, for example, for support of the child, because he had consented to the artificial insemination. The consent was a controlling because in both cases both partners sought the child: "When Stephanie agreed to bear and raise a child with Dawn, and, thereafter, consented to and actively fostered a parent-child relationship between Dawn and A.B., she presumptively made decisions in the best interests of her child and effectively waived the right to unilaterally sever that relationship when her romantic relationship with Dawn ended." (*In re the Parentage of A.B.*, 818 N.E.2d 126 (Ind. App. 2004). See also *In re Infant Girl W.A.*, 845 N.E.2d 229, (Ind. App. 2006), upholding the right of a same-sex couple to adopt a child who was not the natural child of either partner.)

The job of this chapter is to roll such stories back to the four years when Dawn and Stephanie and A.B. were a happy little family, as the family of five on the Oklahoma farm (three children, at least some of them minors) were, and to imagine them seeking a better set of law-office arrangements for their families than either family came up with. Lawyers, as a wise Hoosier judge once said, should try not to make things worse. And any lawyer who undertakes to do wills (and such) for people should realize that, while she cannot do much about death, she should be able to do something to prevent or moderate family fights over what is left behind. The immediate premise is that gay couples (and other kinds of domestic partners, cohabitants, and people in civil unions), and their children, should be able to provide in a private and thoughtful way for the orderly succession of ownership of their property and for the care and support of their children.

One approach, suggested by the veteran "estate planner" Frank S. Berall of the Connecticut Bar, is to use forms of agreement to make the gay couple as much like a heterosexual married couple as the law of contracts will allow. That approach necessarily invokes volatile legal and political developments (e.g., the federal "Defense of Marriage Act" of 2000; recent cases on gay marriage, and other state-level decisions that get indexed under "conflict of laws," along with what Mr. Berall calls "Gay rights: the breaking of the dam")–developments that those of us in the green-eyeshade, county-seat law practice do not let overwhelm us, especially when we do planning work for intact families. Mr. Berall's assumption is that the legal problems arising because of these developments should be resolved primarily through agreements between the partners. (He of course provides extensive advice on other arrangements, such as joint ownership, adoption, powers of attorney, and health-care agencies–the things we discuss in Chapters 11 and 12.) We are not as confident about the promise of agreements, especially when, as Mr.

Kilpatrick noticed, one of the partners has "covetous cousins," and when the political climate tends to produce decision makers less open-minded than the Indiana Court of Appeals was in the A.B. case.

We prefer and, with some regret, suggest an alternative approach. We suggest, in planning and drafting for gay couples, that lawyers regard the partners as if they were *not* married, but related as neighbors, business partners, and friends are; and to regard the children, when they are related to a gay parent neither biologically nor by adoption, as if they were, say, nieces and nephews (if only so that vindictive law will not regard them as illegitimate). This approach is not as hard-hearted as it may at first appear. It is merely evasive. It holds, as a matter of law-office practice, that our clients should be led to planning that is as secure and dependable as lawyers can make it; it suggests that clients need not be encouraged to turn their private family matters and their children into crusades for gay rights.

Consider, for example, devices we have outlined in this book (and will describe further in Chapters 11 and 12) that do not depend on a marital or parental relationship: legacies, trusts, life insurance and (most) employment benefits, durable powers, health-care agencies, life estates and remainders (etc.). And consider locating substitutes for those that seem to depend on marital or parental relationships. (R. Randazzo usefully points out that a joint representation agreement with their lawyer for the partners is particularly important when they are not married to one another; see also Shaffer's "My Client" piece.)

E.   FORMS FOR NON–ESTATE PLANNING CLIENTS

Form 3 is a will for Mr. Jaramillo; Mrs. Jaramillo will have a parallel will. Form 4A is an inter-vivos revocable trust for Dr. and Mrs. Kennedy, and Form 4B a "pour-over" will for Dr. Kennedy; Mrs. Kennedy will have a parallel will.

What we offer for study, then, are a form of testamentary-trust will for a family without disabled minor (or "minor") children (the Jaramillo family) and a form of inter-vivos revocable trust with pour-over wills for a family with minor children, "minor" children, and a handicapped child (the Kennedy family).

If the drafting assignment involves a family with a handicapped child who want to use testamentary-trust arrangements, parts of Forms 4A and 4B will need to be adapted for Form 3. If the drafting assignment involves a family without disabled children who want to use an inter-vivos revocable trust with "pour-over" wills, parts of Form 3 will need to be adapted for Forms 4A and 4B.

TESTAMENTARY-TRUST WILL

Mr. and Mrs. Jaramillo have two minor children, a jointly held home, one jointly held automobile, modest savings in a joint savings account, a loveable dog, and the usual suburban furniture and recreational property. Their key assets for planning purposes are insurance on Mr. Jaramillo's life and the death benefits in retirement programs from the Jaramillos' employment. Mr. Jaramillo's benefit is now vested at $200,000; it grows at the rate of about $15,000 a year.

Mrs. Jaramillo re-entered the employment market when her daughter Maria was old enough for school; she is now an assistant professor of Italian at Rollison College, a "tenure track" full-time job that has the promise of permanence. Her retirement benefits will begin to accumulate next year and will eventually be similar to Mr. Jaramillo's. At present she has as a fringe benefit a $50,000 group life insurance policy.

The Jaramillos have decided on a testamentary-trust arrangement. The key step in that arrangement is making changes in beneficiary designations on the life insurance and death benefits (a step that must be taken in correspondence with the companies that manage the insurance and retirement programs, *not* in the wills: see our discussion of the *Pavy* case in Chapter 5): The clients have decided on a plan that will make full transfer of all property to the surviving spouse and, in the will of the surviving spouse, to a trust for children if they are "minor," or outright to them or members of their families if neither is a "minor." So the Jaramillos' death-benefit designations, and the beneficiary designation on life-insurance policies, will be the surviving spouse (the contracts will probably define survival so as to provide a survival period of up to a month; if not the designation should provide it); and, if the spouse does not survive, to the trustees appointed in the will of the insured. Each of their wills will provide for a testamentary trustee who will probably never become active—first, because the testator of that will may not be the spouse who survives and second, because the children will probably be grown before both of their parents die. If a trust does go into operation, it will be the trust provided in the will of the spouse who (i) survives and (ii) dies while a child is "minor."

The key legal determination in using this device for these clients is a statute in the jurisdiction that permits payment of life-insurance and retirement death benefits to testamentary trustees *without* those benefits becoming part of the probate estate. (See the statutes in the Statutory Appendix.)

The drafting practice we recommend is to draft a will for one of the clients, submit it for study to both of them, revise and correct it, after discussion with the clients, and then, when the first will is all worked out, to make a parallel will for the other client. The saga proceeds through execution of the documents and changes in beneficiary designations in the insurance and benefits contracts. Beginning, then, with a draft for Mr. Jaramillo, this is the plan:

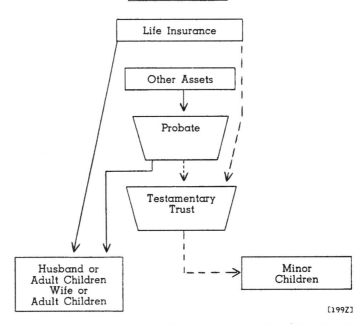

Husband and Wife

[199Z]

Considering the principal assets (insurance and the $200,000 in death-benefit proceeds under Mr. Jaramillo's retirement plan and the insurance and probable death benefit under Mrs. Jaramillo's Rollison College plan):

—   If Mr. Jaramillo dies first, his insurance and retirement-plan funds will have been paid directly (outside probate) to Mrs. Jaramillo. They or whatever she used them for will be in her probate estate and will be paid to adult children or into the trust for minor children, through provisions in her will. When Mrs. Jaramillo dies after Mr. Jaramillo, the Rollison College funds will be paid under the beneficiary designation (not through her will) into the trust established in her will.

—   If Mrs. Jaramillo dies first, her insurance and death-benefit proceeds will be paid, under the contracts, to Mr. Jaramillo. If she dies second, those funds will be paid to the trustee and will be available for minor children as soon as the will is probated and the testamentary trustees qualify—a couple of weeks in the normal case.

There is one possibility this arrangement does not cover: What if, at Mr. Jaramillo's death, after Mrs. Jaramillo dies, both children are adults? There is then no need for a trust, and, as we will see, his will does not pour probate assets into the trust if the children are adults. But the life insurance and pension-plan contracts provide that those contractual benefits be paid to the testamentary trustee.

There are two ways to provide for this possibility: (1) The beneficiary designations on the contracts could contain the additional contingency— *i.e.,* if Mrs. Jaramillo does not survive, and if the Jaramillo children are both adults, the benefits are to be paid to the children outright; if Mr. Jaramillo does not survive, and if either Jaramillo child is a "minor" at the death of Mr. Jaramillo, the proceeds are to be paid to the testamentary trustee. Or (2) the beneficiary designations can be left without this additional contingency and the trustee can be told that any such benefits he receives are to be paid over to the adult children. The first solution is preferable, but it depends on the willingness of the insurance companies and plan administrators to accept relatively complex beneficiary designations. Such agencies usually want clean, clear directions for payment; they do not want to have to investigate contingencies. They may not be willing to accept the designation we suggest above; they certainly would not accept the complex designation that would be required to make this provision for, say, the children of Dr. and Mrs. Kennedy. We invite your attention to the way Forms 3 and 4A deal with this problem.

When life-insurance or death-benefit proceeds are paid to testamentary trustees, they are not really paid *through* probate. The probate process here certifies that the will is valid; when the court does that, it establishes the authority of the trustee who is appointed in the will. The death benefit is then paid outside probate to the trustee. The proceeds are no more vulnerable to creditors than they would be if Mrs. Jaramillo were beneficiary of the death benefit; this would not be the case if the proceeds were paid to the probate estate.

This device has some unlikely difficulties. The difficulties are one reason some clients prefer to use an inter-vivos revocable trust and pour-over wills (Forms 4A and 4B). The fact that the difficulties are unlikely explains why some clients prefer the testamentary-trust will (Form 3), which gives them the convenience of being able to change their plan by changing their wills. Their ability to deal with their life insurance and retirement benefits is not affected by this (Form 3) plan, which is as "ambulatory" as the will is.

The unlikely difficulties in using a testamentary trust are consequences of the fact that it mixes legal concepts: We want the death benefit paid to a trustee appointed in a will, but we don't want the benefit to be subject to the probate process. A statute will tell us we can do this (contrary to case law), and it will tell us that its provisions include death benefits under retirement plans as well as life insurance. *If we don't find such a statute in the controlling jurisdiction we will not use this device.* But the statute probably will not solve all of the unlikely difficulties that arise from mixing concepts:

Suppose, for instance, that Mr. Jaramillo decided to bypass Mrs. Jaramillo and make his insurance and death benefit unconditionally payable to the testamentary trustee; suppose Mr. Jaramillo dies first and

Mrs. Jaramillo elects against his will: Does the elective property include the death benefit? (It might not, not even in some "augmented estate" jurisdictions, if it were paid to an inter-vivos trustee.) Suppose a child is born after the will is made: Is the death benefit, payable to a trustee for the older children, subject to the provisions of a pretermitted-heir statute?

Even if the testamentary-trust statute solves these difficulties, benefits payable to a testamentary trustee are subject to the normal delays of probate—and may be subject to the abnormal delays. A will contest (a jury-triable lawsuit over whether the will is valid) is an example: The will cannot be probated until the contest is resolved, and, until the will is probated, the trustees lack authority to collect the death benefit. Statutes on the subject commonly say that if the testamentary trust fails because of difficulties such as contest, the proceeds are to be paid to the testator's estate, which means they become subject to creditors and to all of the claims available in probate law (pretermitted heir claims, elections against the will, state inheritance taxes, etc.).

The testamentary-trust arrangement is open to publicity, since it will eventually appear in a probated will, and probated wills are in the public records. A revocable inter-vivos trust is not in the public records, and the pour-over will that directs probate assets to the trust need not say where benefits go or in what proportions. The testamentary trust may be subject to greater restriction and supervision than inter-vivos trusts are. (For example, other insured members of the family—the Jaramillo children's grandparents, say—may not be able to make their life insurance or retirement benefits payable to the same trust.)

Wise legal counselors and sophisticated clients nonetheless use the testamentary-trust scheme. But they do not use it—this bears repeating—unless (i) there is an applicable statute that permits payment of life-insurance proceeds to testamentary trustees; and (ii) the statute expressly includes death benefits under retirement programs. Assuming that the right kind of statute is in place, there are a number of reasons for preferring the testamentary trust:

— the inter-vivos revocable trust, as popular as it is becoming, has some unlikely difficulties of its own; those will appear in comments to Forms 4A and 4B, and in Chapter 11;

— middle-class clients may feel that "a simple will" is enough for modest people, or they may be in a culture that distrusts inter-vivos will-substitute arrangements;

— there remains an irrational practice in the profession of charging lower fees for wills than for trusts; there is no good reason for the disparity, but it tends to encourage lawyers to avoid inter-vivos trusts for middle-class clients, and it tends to enforce the inclination of clients to prefer "a simple will" without serious consideration of using trustees in the present instead;

— inter-vivos revocable trust arrangements require pour-over wills; they do not dispense with wills. So, with that arrangement you need both a trust and a will; with a testamentary-trust arrangement all you need is a will.

* * *

FORM 3. TESTAMENTARY TRUST, "NON–ESTATE" WILL, WITH COMMENTS

WILL OF EMILIO JARAMILLO[11]

I, Emilio Jaramillo, residing and domiciled in Marion City, Rollison County, Hoynes, declare that this is my will and revoke all other wills.

I. IDENTIFICATIONS AND DEFINITIONS

A. "My Wife" is Juanita Sanchez Jaramillo. We have two children, Luis Jaramillo and Maria Jaramillo, both of whom are minors at the time this will is written. In this will, "my Children" includes these two children and any other [lawful] children born to or adopted by me. "My Minor Children" includes all of my Children who are, at the time stated in the reference to them, under the age of twenty-six (26) years.

The limitation to "lawful" children is sometimes recommended for male clients, since spurious claims are possible and hard to disprove when the purported father is dead. This is for cases where the client does not *know* of any such children. Using "lawful" in a will for a gay parent–see Section "E," just above–may cause difficulties best avoided.

One advantage trust planning has over intestacy with guardianship for minors is that the clients can choose their own age of majority; the Jaramillos chose age 26.

B. "My Wife's Mother" is Rafaela J. Sanchez. "My Parents" are Hoenir M. and Micaela Jaramillo. "My Brother" is Ernesto S. Jaramillo, and "My Sister" is Julia Jaramillo Knox.

C. The following definitions obtain in any use of the terms in this will:

1. "Descendants" means the immediate and remote lineal descendants of the person referred to who are in being at the time they must be ascertained in order to give effect to the reference to them, whether they are born before or after my death or the death of any other person. The persons who take under this will as Descendants take by right of

---

11. The explanatory notes for forms in Chapter 9 (Forms 1 and 2) are not repeated with forms in this chapter; many of them— e.g., on the use of defined terms–are pertinent.

representation as that term is defined in the 1990 Uniform Probate Code, as amended through 1993. The term Descendants shall include adopted descendants only if they are legally adopted when they are under the age of fourteen years.

2. "Survive" is to be construed to mean that the person referred to must survive the event referred to by thirty days. If the person referred to dies within thirty days of the event, the reference to him shall be construed as if he or she had failed to survive.

II. APPOINTMENT OF FIDUCIARIES

A. I appoint my Sister executor of this will and trustee of the trust under this will, if one is established. If my Sister is unable or unwilling to serve in either or both of these capacities, I appoint my Brother to serve instead, in either or both capacities.

B. If it is necessary to appoint a guardian for any one or more of my Children, I nominate my Wife's Mother as guardian of each of my Children who requires a guardian. If my Wife's Mother is unable or unwilling to serve as guardian, I nominate my Sister.

> **Comment**. **The key feature of this will is that it provides *contingent* arrangements for minor children–a guardian to care for them and a trustee to care for their property. Parents typically have statutory power to "nominate" guardians for their children. The power should cover gay parents. Judges do the appointing. If–as is likely–the client and his wife survive the minority of their children, the provisions for guardian and trustee become unnecessary for cases in which none of the children is disabled.**

C. I recognize that a court in Hoynes may require that a resident coguardian be appointed when a nonresident is appointed guardian for a minor. If the appointment of a resident coguardian is required, I nominate John Morton, of Marion City, Rollison County, Hoynes, as the resident coguardian of any of my Children who requires a guardian. However, it is my desire that the custody of my Children and the management of their estates be committed to the care of the guardians nominated in paragraph B of this article. I request that my executor, my trustee, and the resident coguardian exercise whatever authority I am able to give them to that end.

> **Comment**. **Minor guardianship for property management, in its present statutory form in most states, is archaic, inefficient, and expensive; and the law's reduction of the age of majority to eighteen added a new reason to avoid even shaped-up**

guardianships. This form adheres to principle. There should be no need for guardianship management of property for the Jaramillo children–beyond possibly the approval of trust accounts, which should be done informally under paragraph C of Art. IX. The important function that those paragraphs serve is the designation of personal guardians; an obstacle to designation appears when the guardians are non-residents, which is often the case with mobile young families whose breadwinners work in ubiquitous industries or in a portable profession such as teaching. Where the local law or judicial custom require that non-residents may not be guardians without the appointment of resident coguardians, we recommend minimum compliance. One can hope for a change to permit non-resident guardians.

D.   I request that neither bond nor sureties be required of any fiduciary appointed under this Article.

III.   PAYMENT OF EXPENSES AND TAXES

I direct my executor to pay the following before any division or distribution under the following articles:

A.   all of the expenses of my last illness, funeral and burial and of the administration of my estate;

B.   all taxes payable by reason of my death. My executor shall not require my Wife as to any property, nor any beneficiary, as to property passing under the terms of this will, to reimburse my estate for taxes paid under this sub-paragraph.

C.   any mortgage debts on residential real estate passing to my Wife under this will or by right of survivorship, or not to do so, as my Wife may elect. I direct my executor not to pay mortgage debts on real estate given to devisees or cotenants other than my Wife.

IV.   NON–RESIDUARY LEGACIES

Comment.   **These paragraphs are for specific legacies. These will "abate" last—i.e., they will have to be used to pay debts, expenses, and taxes only when the residuary estate is all used up. When the client has a lot of these, and they represent most of his wealth, provision should be made for the order in which they abate, as compared with one another.**

A.   I give to my son Luis, if he survives me, the piano which was given to me by my mother.

B.   I give all of my other personal effects and household goods and the like not otherwise effectively disposed of, such as jewelry, clothing, furniture, furnishings, silver, books, pictures, and recreational vehicles, together with unused premiums on policies of casualty insurance thereon which are unpaid at my death and any proceeds of policies of casualty insurance thereon which are unpaid at my death, to my Wife if she survives me, or if she does not survive me to the trustee for my Minor Children appointed in Article II, above. If at my death I am not survived by my Wife and have no Minor Children, I give the property described in this paragraph to those of my Children who survive me, in shares of substantially equal value, to be divided as they shall agree, or if they fail to agree within five months after my death, as my executor shall determine.

Comment.   Consider here the use of lists, outside the will, to give tangible personal property (furniture, jewelry, antiques, heirlooms). The Uniform Probate Code version of the authorization of this is quoted in the comment to IV–E, Form 2, *supra*.

C.   Real or tangible or intangible personal property conveyed by me during my lifetime shall not be considered advancements. No adjustment of my estate shall be made on the basis of such inter-vivos gifts.

V.   RESIDUARY ESTATE

A.   "My Residuary Estate" is all of my property, real and personal, after the payment of debts and taxes under Article III, above, and after the gifts made in Article IV, above, including property as to which effective disposition is not otherwise made in this will, property as to which I have an option to purchase or a reversionary interest, and property over which I have a power of appointment.

B.   I give my Residuary Estate to my Wife if she survives me.

C.   If my Wife does not survive me and I am survived by one or more Minor Children, I give my Residuary Estate to my trustee, in trust, for the benefit of my Minor Children, according to the directions stated in Article VI, below.

D.   If my Wife does not survive me and I am not survived by any Minor Children, I direct my executor to divide my Residuary Estate into equal shares and to distribute those shares:

1.   one share to each of my Children who survives me;

2.   one share to the surviving spouse of each of my Children who fails to survive me but who leaves a spouse who survives me; and

3.   one share to the Descendants of each of my Children who neither survives me nor leaves a spouse who survives me.

Comment.   Clients have to decide whether or not to include spouses of deceased children. The lawyer's duty

is to see that the client thinks about it. This may be an almost ridiculous decision when made with reference to the widowed spouse of a child who has not even started kindergarten. (One young mother, who had a two-year old son, was asked about providing for her son's wife, thought a moment and said, "Her? No!") However, one important thing this will should do is survive–both as a sufficient expression of intention a generation into the future, and as a better-than-nothing will in case the Jaramillos fail to update their planning when they should.

E.   If my Wife does not survive me and none of my Children survives me, and none of the persons described in paragraph "D" of this article survives me, I direct my executor to divide my Residuary Estate into two equal shares and to distribute those shares as follows:

1.   one share to my Wife's Mother, if she survives me; if she does not survive me, my executor shall distribute this share under paragraph "2" of this paragraph; and

2.   one-half share to each of my Parents, or all of one share to the survivor of my Parents, if they or either of them survive me; if neither of my Parents survives me, my executor shall distribute this share:

   (a)   one-half share to my Brother and one-half share to my Sister, or all of one share to the survivor of my Brother and my Sister, if they or either of them survive me;

   (b)   and if none of the persons described in this subparagraph "2" survives me, my executor shall distribute this share under subparagraph "1" of this paragraph.

F.   If none of the persons otherwise benefitting under this article survives me, I give my Residuary Estate in equal shares:

1.   one share to the persons who would have taken my estate, and in proportions in which they would have taken it, under the law of Hoynes effective at my death pertaining to the intestate distribution of personal property, if I had died without a will; and

2.   one share to the persons who would have taken my Wife's estate, and in the proportions in which they would have taken it, under the law of Hoynes effective at my death pertaining to the intestate distribution of personal property, if she had died without a will, possessed of this share, on the date of my death.

3.   I do not intend that the State of Hoynes be a beneficiary under either of the preceding two subparagraphs. If it is impossible to distribute under either subparagraph without distributing to

the State of Hoynes, I direct that the share to which that subparagraph pertains be distributed under the other subparagraph. If it is impossible to distribute under either subparagraph without distributing to the State of Hoynes, I give my Residuary Estate to the Salvation Army of Marion City, Hoynes.

> **Comment.** **It is important that one's client understand the scheme of distribution in these paragraphs. No client will want it all, and every client will want it to be different than it is here. Many lawyers, reaching the ultimate contingency of paragraph "F," suggest that clients think about their synagogues or parish churches. See Section B–7, Chapter 9.**

G.   The executor and my trustee shall have the power to apply income and principal payable to any beneficiary who is under legal disability or who is, in the opinion of the executor or trustee, incapable of managing his or her affairs. In carrying out this power, the executor or my trustee may distribute income or principal directly to the beneficiary, to the guardian or parent of the beneficiary, to a bank account in trust, to a trust or custodianship for the beneficiary, or to a person with whom the beneficiary resides. The receipt of the beneficiary, guardian, parent, bank, custodian, trustee, or person shall discharge the executor or my trustee from responsibility for the proper expenditure of income or principal. The executor or my trustee may also accumulate income and withhold distributions of principal, in carrying out this power, to the extent permitted by law, until the beneficiary's legal disability is removed or until the beneficiary dies or, in the opinion of the trustee or executor, becomes capable of managing his or her affairs, at which time all amounts payable to the beneficiary shall be paid to the beneficiary or to the beneficiary's estate.

> **Comment.** **The principal purpose here is to provide for flexibility for payments not covered by the trust. A minor or incompetent person cannot give the executor or trustee a receipt for distributions made to him or her. If something like this is not in the will, the prudent executor will require the appointment of a guardian for the child, who is able to give the estate a receipt. (Under this will a distribution to a grandchild would be an example.) Guardianship is an expensive and inflexible process in this situation.**

VI.   ADMINISTRATION OF TRUST

A.   The primary purpose of the trust established in the event I am not survived by my Wife but am survived by any of My Minor Children is the support and education of My Minor Children. To that end, the trustee may accumulate income to the extent permitted by law. She shall pay or apply such income as she elects not to accumulate to or for the use of My Minor Children until the termination of the trust.

B.   If the income and other funds available to My Minor Children are insufficient for their support and education, my trustee may pay to or apply for the benefit of one or more of My Minor Children so much of the principal of the trust as she considers necessary. The trustee need not distribute either income or principal from the trust in equal shares. The trustee may exhaust the entire income and principal of the trust for the benefit of one or more beneficiaries, to the exclusion of the others, subject only to the primary purpose stated in Paragraph "A" of this Article.

C.   If the primary purpose of the trust is not impaired by doing so, the trustee may also apply income and invade principal for the support and education of any one or more of the following:

1.   those of my Children who are not My Minor Children (either because they were not among My Minor Children at my death or because they attain the age of twenty-six years after my death but before termination of the trust);

2.   the surviving spouse of each of my Children who either fails to survive me or dies during the administration of the trust; or

3.   the Descendants of my Children.

Applications of income and principal under this paragraph need not be made equally. The trustee may distribute to any one or more of the persons described in this paragraph to the exclusion of the others, subject only to the standards stated in this paragraph and to the primary purpose of the trust stated in paragraph "A" of this article.

Comment.   **A contingent trust for children is probably the most convincing reason for Mr. Jaramillo to have a will. The trust is the heart of this scheme, and directions on distributions are the heart of the trust. Contingent trusts for children should direct *all* resources to the rearing of minor children. They should direct *no* resources to such middle-class frills as graduate education, nice weddings, and starts in business, until the minor children are as secure as they would be if their father survived their minorities. There is nothing modest about the undertaking. A contingent trust confined to minor support is not conservative at all, but it is realistic. The common form-book alternative is a will that divides property among children and holds only the minors' shares in trust. That alternative for the Jaramillos is as**

pretentious as a yacht or a vacation in Tahiti would be. Not a cent of their money should be distributed to adults until the minor children are certain of food, shelter, medicine, and education. Their lawyer ought to tell them that; their lawyer ought, at least, to prevent their having the pretentious alternative without the opportunity to decide on it for themselves. The rigid-shares alternative is dynastic. A lawyer who routinely puts such estates into dynastic arrangements, in which a 25–year-old is treated as a five-year-old is treated, is only doing what a primitive computer could do better.

D. The trustee may have been named beneficiary on policies of insurance on my life, or under other contracts that pay benefits after my death, but not otherwise have trust duties under this will. If that occurs, the trustee is to collect these proceeds and to distribute them as if the trustee were my executor, and as if these proceeds were part of my estate. I do not intend, however, that any of these proceeds become part of my estate, nor that these proceeds become subject to the payment of creditors or taxing authorities to any greater extent than they would be if the trustee had duties beyond collection and distribution. I do not intend to impair the trustee's or executor's power and duty to hold, manage, and apply distributions from life insurance proceeds under paragraph "G" of Article "V," above.

Comment. A key part of this plan is that life insurance proceeds and other death benefits be paid to the trustee. But it may turn out to be the case that the trustee will have no management duties, because there will no longer be any minor children. In that case it is important that the trustee act as a collector of proceeds, so that the proceeds do not go into the probate estate (where they are subject to the claims of creditors and taxing authorities).

It might appear that this device is a sham to keep insurance proceeds immune from creditors and taxing authorities but otherwise make it like a part of the probate estate. Some legal scholars make that argument. We don't agree. Life insurance immunity is a creature of insurance, not of trusts, and the result, we suppose, of populism and life-insurance lobbies in state legislatures. This paragraph takes advantage of the law in no more outrageous a way than other beneficiary designations do, certainly in no more outrageous

a way than payment to an inter-vivos trustee for children does, and, *ex hypothesi*, we have a statute permitting us to make a testamentary trustee the life-insurance beneficiary. (See the Statutory Appendix.) In fact, the valuable power to hold and manage and apply for incompetent beneficiaries, coupled with the trustee's duty to collect and pay over, are good reasons to use an intermediate trustee here. All of these things are more commonly done by trustees than by executors.

VII.   TERMINATION OF TRUST

When there are no Minor Children living, the trustee shall distribute the remainder of the principal and accumulated income of the trust as follows:

1.   one share to each of my Children then living;

2.   one share to the then living surviving spouse of each of my Children who is not then living; and

3.   one share to the Descendants of each of my Children who is not then living and whose surviving spouse is not then living.

If distribution cannot be made under this paragraph because none of the beneficiaries described here is living at the time for distribution, my trustee shall distribute the principal and accumulated income of the trust to the persons described, and in the shares described, in Article V, above, applying that article as of the time for trust distribution and not as of the time of my death.

VIII.   POWERS OF FIDUCIARIES

I give to my trustee and, as to my executor, give to my executor and incorporate by reference, and to their successors in office, the fiduciary powers granted trustees in the Uniform Trustees' Powers Act, as that act provides on the date of execution of this will.

IX.   OTHER PROVISIONS

A.   My trustee may resign by giving written notice, specifying the effective date of the resignation, to the then current income beneficiaries of the trust, and, as to any beneficiaries under legal disability, to their guardians, or to the persons with whom they are residing.

B.   In the event the trustee resigns or is otherwise unable to continue to serve, I request that those of my Children who are then living and who are not then under legal disability nominate a successor trustee and that the nominee they choose be appointed to succeed the trustee. The successor trustee, whether appointed pursuant to their nomination or not, may accept the administration of the trust without examination or review, without liability for doing so, and may act without the necessity of conveyance or transfer.

Comment. **The purpose here is not to protect the stranger who may become successor trustee; it is to make it possible to obtain a competent successor, especially in case Mr. Jaramillo's sister proves inefficient or worse and gets the trust into a mess.**

C. The trustee shall render annual accounts of income and principal to each beneficiary who is not under legal disability, and to the guardian of each beneficiary who is under legal disability. The written approval of a beneficiary or of his or her guardian shall be binding on the beneficiary as to all matters and transactions covered by the account. The written approval of all beneficiaries to whom accounts are rendered under this paragraph, whether given personally or through guardians, shall, as to all matters and transactions covered by the account, be binding on beneficiaries who become entitled to principal or income after the last date for which the account is rendered.

Comment. **Local law varies a good deal on the workability of a non-judicial accounting clause; it typically makes a difference that the trust is testamentary, many jurisdictions keeping closer control over testamentary trusts than over inter-vivos trusts. If this is analyzed as a set of conditions on ownership, the non-judicial accounting provisions are valid. If it is analyzed as an attempt to oust courts of their jurisdiction, they are not. The theory behind this provision, and the theory behind such legislative provisions as the non-judicial accounting procedure in modern trust codes, is to eliminate the expense of formal accountings where nobody has a complaint. In that situation, the accounting consumes time, trouble, and money. (Anyway, when nobody has a complaint, the surveillance exercised over accounts by judge and guardians ad litem rarely goes beyond a look at the cover sheet.) If there is a complaint, the non-judicial accounting will turn it up. If it cannot be resolved, the problem will be presented in an adversary accounting proceeding, in which everybody involved will pay attention.**

[C. To the extent that it is possible for me to waive such requirements, I request that the trustee not be required to qualify before or be appointed by any court, nor, in the absence of breach of trust, to account to any court, nor to obtain the approval of any court in exercising power or discretion under this will. No person dealing with the trustee in good faith need see to the proper application of money or property given to the trustee.]

> **Comment.** **This alternative paragraph is a broad attempt, found in many bank forms, to eliminate accounting altogether. If the non-judicial accounting alternative won't work, this one won't either. In fact, this one may not work even where non-judicial accounting will work. To the extent that this alternative invites the trustee to proceed without rendering accounts, it seems to us a bad provision; and we are not convinced by trust officers who say it doesn't matter because they render informal accounts anyway, under local practice, or statute, or banking regulations. The protection of third parties is arguably useful in encouraging transactions, but we wonder if third-party surveillance ought not to be left intact.**

D.   At approximately the same time, my Wife and I are executing similar wills in which each of us is the recipient of the other's bounty. However, the wills are not the result of any contract or agreement between us, and either will may be revoked at the discretion of its testator.

> **Comment.** **The possibility of family quibbles on this point may seem remote, but several appellate cases suggest that the clause is a useful precaution.**

I, EMILIO JARAMILLO, sign my name to this instrument this 14th day of March, 2___, and being first duly sworn, declare to the undersigned authority all of the following:

1.   I execute this instrument as my will.

2.   I sign this will willingly.

3.   I execute this will as my free and voluntary act.

4.   I am 18 years of age or older, of sound mind and under no constraint or undue influence.

_____

Emilio Jaramillo

WE, THE WITNESSES, being first duly sworn, sign our names to this instrument and declare all of the following:

1.   The testator executes this instrument as his will.

2. The testator signs it willingly.

3. Each of us, in the conscious presence of the testator, signs this will as a witness.

4. To the best of our knowledge, the testator is 18 years of age or older, of sound mind and under no constraint or undue influence.

_____ residing at _____

_____ residing at _____

* * *

INTER–VIVOS NON–ESTATE TRUST AND POUR–OVER WILL

Our clients Dr. and Mrs. Kennedy decided not to set up a *funded* inter-vivos trust now for their children. After discussion with us they also decided against the testamentary-trust device, for some of the reasons mentioned in our introduction to Form 3. They decided on what are coming to be the most common "estate planning" devices for middle-class families with dependent children, the *revocable, unfunded,* and *contingent* inter-vivos trust and pour-over wills.

This plan is, like the plan for the Jaramillos, an all-to-the-surviving-spouse plan. After the death of the first to die of the Kennedys, all of the family property will be owned by the surviving spouse: Their home and most of their investment property will pass to the survivor "automatically," because it is jointly owned; life insurance proceeds and death benefits under retirement plans will be paid, pursuant to contract, to the survivor. And whatever probate property there is will be distributed, under the will of the first to die (Form 4B), to the survivor as sole legatee.

The inter-vivos trust probably does not *do* anything until the survivor of the two clients dies. Until then it will probably exist only on paper. Dr. and Mrs. Kennedy will appoint a trustee now but leave the trustee without funds. After the survivor of them dies, the will of that parent *may* convey to the trustee whatever property she or he dies owning (Form 4B); this will include, in the form of cash or investments, whatever is left of the proceeds of life insurance or retirement-plan death benefits that were paid after the first spouse died. If the children are of age and not dependent, the surviving parent's life insurance proceeds, and death benefits under the survivor's retirement plans, may be paid to the trustee outside the probate process.

We say these payments to the trust *may* be made; they may not be: If no children are living who are also dependent at that time, the trust will not ever be funded and both probate property and death benefits (including life-insurance proceeds) will be paid to children who are not dependent, or to their families. The trust is, in that way, *contingent.* If, after the second parent dies, any living child is dependent, the trust goes into operation—primarily to take care of dependent children; secondarily to take care of children who are not dependent, spouses of children, and grandchildren. If David Kennedy is not living when the survivor of his parents dies, and if, at that time, Thomas is of age, there is no need for trust administration. In that case, why have the insurance and death-benefit proceeds paid to the trustee? This problem is the one we discussed earlier in this chapter and in comments to Form 3, with respect to the Jaramillo family. Here, as there, we will assume that the trustee will collect those proceeds, in any event, even when the only duty of the trustee may be to pay them over to adult children–and then only if beneficiary designations have not been used to avoid payment to the trustee.

This is the way the plan looks:

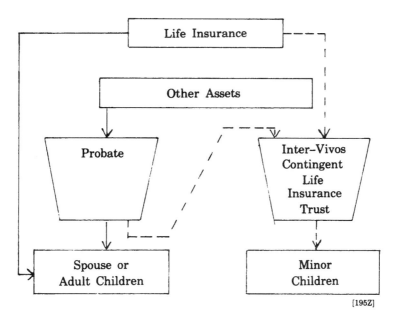

[195Z]

There is a largely historical, conceptual difficulty with this plan that is a consequence of the fact that the trust is only on paper until orphaned dependent children are identified. This is not much of a problem any more, but it has been a very serious problem in the past, and lawyers who use the device should stop and think about whether it could become a problem again: The problem is that the trust is nothing but a piece of paper when it appears as the primary object of the testator's bounty in a probated will, and appears as well as the beneficiary of life insurance and retirement benefits. Is such an unfunded, contingent trust capable of receiving those distributions—or, to put that question another way, do insurance-payment law and the statute on will execution permit property to be distributed through a secondary instrument such as this? (See our discussion of the *Farkas* case in Chapter 5.)

The answer to the conceptual difficulty is, probably, yes, although the legal authority behind the answer will differ from state to state, and clients who benefit from having the device available now owe a lot to the broken fortunes that were put at issue in the reform and cultural change that removed the difficulty. Most states have "pour-over" statutes (see the Statutory Appendix). If the drafter pursues the inquiry far enough, she will find that lawyers in states with inadequate statutes (and unpromising case law) use wills that pour over into revocable, unfunded, contingent trusts and seem not to worry about clear legal warrant for doing so. As we all learned when we studied title searches in the office of the county recorder of deeds, it is probably sound to rely (to some extent) on local custom where the statute is not as clear as a lawyer would like.

The best of these statutes—the Uniform Testamentary Additions to Trusts Act (in "Pour–Overs" part of the Statutory Appendix), for example, and statutes allowing life insurance payment to unfunded trusts—are comprehensive. But others are limited, even fragmentary, even nebulous. Some do not expressly permit the amendment of a jointly established trust (such as the one we are using here) after one spouse dies. Some do not *say* that the trust into which probate assets and insurance proceeds are paid need not be funded (although lawyers in states that have such statutes do use unfunded trusts). Some statutes seem not to permit testamentary pouring over into a trust established after the will is executed; some do not expressly permit pour-over of insurance proceeds into a trust established before the insurance is purchased.

Where there is no statute authorizing testamentary payments into an unfunded, contingent, revocable inter-vivos trust, the case-law theories behind using the device are (i) that the pour-over will can incorporate the trust by reference, or (ii) that the pour-over will can refer to facts of independent significance (and that the inter-vivos trust is such a fact). The first theory does not seem to contemplate—and may not permit— amendment of the trust after the will is made; the second may stumble on the argument that a trust that exists only on paper is not a fact of independent significance. (See our discussion of these issues in Chapter 5.)

Despite such academic misgivings, the plan our clients, the Kennedys, are using is in use all over the country. We are going to proceed on the assumption that it is safe in Hoynes, but we will leave the reader to trace how we arrived at that conclusion.

Finally, we recommended that the Kennedys have an inter-vivos trust and pour-over wills, rather than wills with testamentary trusts, because an inter-vivos trust may be used to provide property management for the Kennedys themselves in the event that one or both of them become incompetent, and it can be used to provide continuing assistance to David during any time that his parents may be incompetent. (See the discussion in Chapter 11 concerning the use of durable powers to fund inter-vivos trusts after a settlor becomes incompetent. Note that the trust in this chapter, Form 4A, is not drafted with attention to the Kennedys's possible need for Medicaid coverage for the cost of nursing home care for themselves. See the discussion of that issue in Chapter 11.)

FORM 4A. THE KENNEDY CHILDREN'S TRUST

This is a trust agreement executed by Richard John Kennedy and Mary Margaret Kennedy, husband and wife (the "Settlors"), who reside and are domiciled in Marion City and Rollison County, Hoynes, and Roberta Kennedy McCarter (the "Trustee").

The Settlors own and are insured under existing policies of life insurance, and expect to obtain additional policies of life insurance, on which they have caused or will cause the Trustee to be named as primary or contingent beneficiary. One or both of the Settlors have as part of their savings and retirement programs potential death benefits payable to survivors on which they have caused or will cause the Trustee to be named as primary or contingent beneficiary. The proceeds of these policies and benefits, and other property conveyed to the Trustee by the Settlors, either during the Settlors' lives or by their wills, shall be held by the Trustee as trust property and be devoted to the purposes described in this agreement.

> **Comment**. **Residence, domicile, and identification here serve the same purposes as in the opening paragraph of Form 1, Chapter 9. The clients may decide to name a sister or brother trustee, or they may choose a bank. Some lawyers suggest a relative as guardian of the children and trustee of the trust but provide that a bank is to become co-trustee if the trust becomes operative. In most circumstances that practice appears to evidence an underlying ambivalence. It says to the individual trustee, in effect, "We trust you if you have nothing to do, but if you have anything to do, we want bankers to watch you do it." It may be that the true underlying agenda is to relieve the family member of the burden of managing financial matters, thus freeing him to devote his time and attention to the personal care of the children. If that is the motivation, it is probably preferable to name the relative as guardian and make the bank *sole* trustee. If that is unsatisfactory because the clients want involvement of a family member in distribution decisions, a bank can act as trustee and a family member can be named trust adviser. (See, Comment, *Trust Advisers*, 78 Harvard Law Review 1230, 1965.) Or the family member can act**

as sole trustee but be given authority to use trust assets to hire investment advisers, accountants, and any other professionals needed to assist in the financial management.

In families with disabled children, such as the Kennedys', the recommendation that a family member serve as co-trustee with a bank is even more common. In such instances, the recommendation is based on an assumption that financial institutions are generally unfamiliar with the special needs of disabled beneficiaries and the intricate eligibility criteria associated with the various governmental aid programs. The family member co-trustee is included on the assumption that the family member will expend the time and effort needed to become familiar with the beneficiary's personal needs and with the public assistance programs. If a family member is capable of learning the ins and outs of the financial eligibility criteria for S.S.D., S.S.I., and Medicaid, that same family member also would be capable of hiring and supervising investment advisers and accountants, the cost of which is likely to be lower than a bank's trust-administration fee, and the cumbersome co-trustee device is avoided. Dick's sister Roberta has agreed to serve as trustee of this trust. She has the most contact with David of any of the Kennedy parents' siblings and is both capable and willing to undertake the duties of trustee.

There are some alternative styles for instituting inter-vivos trusts, reflecting a certain professional indecision about whether the instrument resembles a contract (as here), or an assumption of equitable duties (a declaration of trust by the trustee), or an imposition of equitable duties by the settlor. A trust can be any of the three. If you prefer the declaration form, the instrument would start: "(The Trustee) declares that (the Settlors) own and are insured under existing policies...." The concluding formalities are then much simpler, since only the trustee need execute the document. In some few states, however, trusts must be signed by *the settlor* to be valid; in many

**states this is true if the trustee holds real estate
or is likely to receive real estate in a pour-over
will.**

**If the imposition form is used, the document
resembles a will: "I (the settlor), residing and
domiciled in ... intend to make (the trustee), as
trustee under this transfer in trust, and contingent beneficiary of existing policies of life insurance and of policies I have obtained and expect to
obtain. The proceeds of these policies...." The
formalities of conclusion are similar to those in
this form; the trustee signs so that the document
will demonstrate the trustee's acceptance of the
trust.**

I.   AMENDMENT AND REVOCATION

A.   Each Settlor individually retains power to withdraw from the
trust any property he or she has transferred to the trust, including his or
her interest in any property jointly transferred to the trust.

B.   The Settlors, during their joint lives, may jointly revoke this
Trust in whole or in part, and may jointly alter any of its provisions. If one
of the Settlors becomes incompetent, the other Settlor may alter or amend
the trust, with the written consent of the incompetent Settlor's attorney-
in-fact, or guardian, or conservator, if any. If the incompetent Settlor does
not have an attorney-in-fact, a guardian, or a conservator, the other
Settlor, acting alone, may alter or amend the trust. If both Settlors
become incompetent, the trust becomes irrevocable and it may not
thereafter be altered, amended, or revoked. After the death of either of
the original Settlors, the survivor may revoke or amend the trust.

C.   Upon revocation the Trustee shall distribute the trust property
to the Settlors, giving each Settlor a share of the trust property having a
value that bears the same ratio to the total value of the trust property at
the time of revocation as the value of the property contributed to the trust
by each Settlor bears to the total value of property contributed to the
trust. If, however, the trust is revoked after the death of one of the
Settlors, the Trustee shall distribute all of the trust property to the
surviving Settlor.

D.   For purposes of this instrument, incompetence shall be determined by a Settlor's personal physician who shall inform the Trustee in
a signed writing that the physician has examined the Settlor and in the
physician's opinion the Settlor is incompetent to handle financial affairs
and to make decisions regarding the disposition of his or her property.

**Comment.   Clear provision of revocability and partial revo-
cability is required in many states and advisable**

everywhere. This trust is jointly established by Dick and Mary because they agree on how their property should be used for, and distributed to, their children after they are dead. There is no need for two trusts.

Since the trust is constructed on the assumption that Dick and Mary agree, the rights to amend are joint. Granting either of them the right to amend or modify the trust without the consent of the other could prove divisive. In contrast, each of them retains the right to independently withdraw any property he or she has given the trustee. At first blush those two provisions may appear inconsistent. However, if the durability of the trust and the harmony of the Kennedys' marriage are seen as the linchpins, the provisions are consistent. Although still agreeing upon the general scheme, either Dick or Mary may at some point regret the transfer of a particular asset to the trust and the ability to easily withdraw it may avoid interpersonal friction and preserve the trust.

The trust further provides that if a settlor becomes incompetent, the competent spouse can alter or revoke the trust, with the consent of the incompetent spouse's attorney-in-fact or guardian or conservator. Requiring a settlor to work with the representative of an incompetent settlor appears more cumbersome than it is likely to be in reality, because quite often the attorney-in-fact or the guardian will be the incompetent person's spouse, in this case the other settlor. If the surrogate for the incompetent settlor is not the settlor's spouse, that may be some indication, by either the settlor or a court, that it is advisable to have another person working in conjunction with the spouse.

The provision that incompetence is to be determined by a physician is as curious as it is common. Such a determination is functional rather than medical, but physicians commonly make such determinations and they are convenient "outsiders" who allow the smooth functioning of such provisions, bypassing the need for a court determination. Some clients and some law-

yers may find "personal" in paragraph "D" ambiguous. Some may wish to modify "physician" with a degree requirement (M.D. or D.O.). Some lawyers like to have the signatures of two physicians, on the apparent assumption that it is more difficult to arm-twist two physicians than one.

II. TRUST PROPERTY

A. The principal items of "Trust Property" will be proceeds of life insurance, proceeds of death benefits under the Settlors' retirement and investment plans, property conveyed to the Trustee by the personal representatives of the Settlors, any proceeds of any of this property, and income from trust assets.

> **Comment. A working definition of "trust property" avoids constant repetition of and entanglement in distinctions between income and principal. Those distinctions are less important here than in other trusts because principal is available to income beneficiaries.**

B. The owner of each life insurance policy on which the Trustee is beneficiary retains for his or her life all rights and powers conferred by the policies, including the right to change the beneficiaries of the policies and the right to assign incidents of ownership in the policies. During the owner's life, the Trustee has no responsibility with respect to these policies of insurance, except the duty to keep safely copies of contracts that the Settlors deliver to the Trustee. At the death of a Settlor, the Trustee shall either collect the net proceeds of all policies on which it is effective beneficiary or exercise optional modes of payment of these proceeds. Payment to and the receipt of the Trustee shall discharge insurance companies that have issued policies on which the Trustee is effective beneficiary.

C. Policies on which the Trustee has been or is being made beneficiary at the time this agreement is executed are listed in the schedule of policies that appears at the end of this agreement. The Settlors will notify the Trustee of additional designations of the Trustee as beneficiary and will cause legally sufficient conveyances to be made of other trust property.

D. The Trustee is not required to pay premiums or assessments on policies of insurance.

> **Comment. There is no reason for the clients to deliver policies to the trustee, but good reason for them to advise the trustee on which policies show the trustee as beneficiary. It may be that a zealous trust officer will get his hands on the policies**

anyway, in which case the trustee has to have a duty to keep them safely. Generally, though, the trustee has nothing to do until the settlors' deaths. This is what keeps this arrangement simple and keeps banks from charging fees for it during the settlors' lives. If this trust comes to be used as a funded "retirement" trust for either settlor, management of insurance policies, and transfer of assets to the trust, can be handled through durable powers of attorney. (See Chapter 11.)

E.   If at any time prior to a Settlor's death, property is transferred to the Trustee to be held as trust property, then during the Settlors' lifetimes, the Trustee shall:

1.   Except as provided in Paragraph 2, below, pay to, or apply for the benefit of the Settlors so much of the trust income and principal as the Settlors request in writing. In the event that the Settlors' requests for distributions are inconsistent or conflicting, the Trustee shall notify the Settlors of that fact and request that they prepare a joint request for distribution. If, within 30 days after the Trustee notifies the Settlors of the conflict, the Settlors are unable to agree upon a plan for distribution, the Trustee shall thereafter, and until such time as the Settlors do agree, make only such distributions as the Trustee in her sole and absolute discretion decides to make, which may include distributions for the benefit of David.

2.   During any period in which a Settlor is, in the judgment of the Trustee, unable to properly administer any payments made to the Settlor, the Trustee may distribute for the benefit of that Settlor so much of the trust income and principal as the Trustee in her absolute discretion determines is desirable to provide for the health, maintenance, and support of that Settlor, taking into consideration the Settlor's resources known to the Trustee. During that same period, the Trustee may distribute to or for the benefit of David, so much of the trust income and principal as the Trustee in her absolute discretion deems advisable. In making distributions to or for David under this Article, the Trustee shall be guided by the purposes and intentions expressed in Article IV of this trust. In making a determination as to whether a Settlor is unable to properly administer payments made to the Settlor, the Trustee may consult with the other Settlor, the Settlors' Children, and the Settlor's physician. The Trustee may conclusively rely on the physician's written medical opinion.

III. BENEFICIARIES AND DEFINITIONS

A. Scott Edward Kennedy ("Scott"), born February 11, 1978; Patrick John Kennedy ("Patrick"), born November 21, 1980; David Riley Kennedy

("David"), born January 29, 1984; and Thomas Hull Kennedy ("Thomas"), born July 12, 1988, and any other children born to or adopted by the Settlors are the "Settlors' Children." References to the "Settlors' Minor Children" include any of the Settlors' children, excluding David, who are, at the time stated in the reference to them, under the age of 21.

David, who is age 16 at the time of this agreement, is mentally retarded. Because of his disability, David is likely to need, to a greater extent than others of the Settlors' Children, both personal and financial assistance throughout his lifetime. As a consequence, different, but not separate, provisions are made in this trust for David, and David is specifically excluded from the class referred to as the Settlors' Minor Children.

B. Katherine Riley Hull is Mary Kennedy's mother. Jean Hull Donovan is Mary Kennedy's sister. Roberta Kennedy McCarter, Deborah Kennedy Fernandez, and Jeanne Kennedy Slade are Richard Kennedy's sisters. Neither of the Settlors has any brothers.

C. David and the Settlors' Minor Children are the primary beneficiaries of this trust. The other persons mentioned in this article, and the Settlors' Descendants and their spouses, are the secondary beneficiaries of the trust.

D. "Descendants" means the immediate and remote lawful, lineal descendants of the person referred to who are in being at the time they must be ascertained in order to give effect to the reference to them, whether they are born before or after the death of the Settlors or of any other person. The persons who take under this trust as Descendants shall take by right of representation, in accordance with the rule of *per stirpes* distribution and not in accordance with the rule of *per capita* distribution. "Descendants" includes adopted descendants only if they are legally adopted when they are under the age of fourteen years.

> Comment. **The question of whether to include or exclude adopted adults, when they have been adopted by members of the family other than the testator or settlor, deserves a thoughtful pause. Consider, for example, a gay couple in which adoption has been considered or used in order to make one partner the legal heir of the other: In order to accomplish the disposition of his own property, and for other purposes, an adult gay man adopts his partner, whom he is not allowed to marry. One question would be whether the family of the client wants to include the partner among possible legatees. If so, the age–14 limitation is in the way. It was adopted in earlier editions of this book without regard to the gay-partner situation,**

but with attention to appellate cases in which a grandchild had added an heir or legatee to the family by adoption, and cases of clients from other cultures in which adoption of adults was used as a sort of will substitute.

E. Survival of an event, such as the death of a Settlor or the termination of the trust, is to be construed to mean that the person referred to must survive by thirty days. If the person referred to dies within thirty days of the event, the reference to that person shall be construed as if that person had failed to survive.

Comment.   **The rationale for descriptions and definitions is made in some detail earlier in this Chapter, and in comments to Form 1, Chapter 9. Our definition of "descendants" here (Forms 4A and 4B) is different than the one we use in Forms 1, 2, and 3. The drafter has a choice. This one does not require consulting the Uniform Probate Code.**

It has become common to use an age older than the voting or selective-service age of 18 for the definition of minor children in a trust for children. Typically such trusts terminate when there are no more "minor" children. At termination the assets are distributed to the beneficiaries. Many parents prefer to delay distribution of trust assets until such time as it is likely that the youngest child will have finished college or post-secondary job training and the children have the maturity to properly manage the property.

Here we have defined "minor" children as those under the age of 21. Because the trust will continue for David's life, there will be no distribution of substantial amounts of trust principal to a 21- or 22-year-old child, except in the unlikely event that David dies before all of the other children reach 21. Treating the children who attain the age of 21 as adult beneficiaries makes them secondary beneficiaries and may require them to bear financial responsibility for the completion of their own post-secondary education or training. Given that the Kennedys' resources are not unlimited and that David may need some support from the trust for the rest of his life, support of the other children until age 21

is, in our opinion, a sound compromise. It was of course arrived at by our clients.

IV. TRUST PURPOSES AND ADMINISTRATION

A. The primary purposes of this trust are to support and educate the Settlors' Minor Children, and to supplement public assistance available to David. To those ends, the Trustee may accumulate income from the Trust Property to the extent permitted by law. The Trustee shall pay or apply income not accumulated to or for the use of David and the Settlors' Minor Children, until the termination of the trust.

B. If the income and other funds available to the Settlors' Minor Children are insufficient for the support and education of any one or more of them, the Trustee may pay to or apply for the benefit of one or more of them so much of the principal of the Trust Property as the Trustee considers necessary. The Trustee need not distribute either income or principal in equal shares. The Trustee may exhaust the entire income and principal of the trust for the benefit of one or more beneficiaries, to the exclusion of others, subject to the primary purposes stated in Paragraph A of this article.

C. David suffers from a developmental disability that substantially impairs his ability to maintain and support himself independently. During the Settlors' lives it is their intention to supplement the public assistance benefits that may be available to David because of his disability through such programs as Supplemental Security Income, Medicaid, Social Security Disability Insurance, and other state and local programs. It is the Settlors' intention that this trust continue to supplement the public assistance benefits available to David after the Settlors are no longer able to do so by reason of their own incompetence or deaths. It is not the Settlors' intention that the income or principal of this trust be used to supplant or replace public assistance benefits.

The Trustee may pay to or apply for David's benefit, for the duration of his life, such amounts from the principal of the trust as the Trustee in the exercise of its absolute discretion deems advisable for David's welfare. In making such distributions to David, the Trustee shall take into account all other resources available to David, including any benefits to which he is or may be entitled through public assistance, and the Trustee shall seek support and maintenance for David from all available public resources.

In exercising the discretionary powers conferred on the Trustee in this paragraph and in paragraph A of this Article, the Trustee shall be guided by the following statement of the Settlors' purposes and intentions: The Trustee is authorized to make trust distributions to or on David's behalf that will enrich and make his life more enjoyable, including the provision of recreational and vacation opportunities for him. The Trustee is authorized to use trust property to procure more sophisticated medical and dental treatment than may otherwise be available to David and to pay for private rehabilitative and educational training for him. The Settlors desire that David be able to maintain contact with his brothers and other family members and the Trustees are authorized to expend trust income and principal for transportation costs for David or other family members to facilitate such contacts and, if advisable, to provide a travel companion for David. The Trustee should exercise the discretionary powers conferred on her in a manner that will provide flexibility in the administration of the trust under conditions from time to time existing, and in exercising such powers, the decision of the Trustee shall be conclusive as to the advisability of any distribution of income or principal, and as to the person to or for whom such distribution is to be made, and the same shall not be subject to judicial review.

D. If the primary purposes of the trust are not impaired by doing so, the Trustee may also apply income and principal for the support and education of any one or more of the following:

1. those of the Settlors' Children, excluding David, who are not the Settlors' Minor Children (either because they were not the Settlors' Minor Children at the time this trust is first funded or because they attain the age of 21 years after the funding of the trust but before the termination of the trust);

2. the surviving spouse of each of the Settlors' Children who either fails to survive the Settlors or dies during the administration of the trust; and

3. the Descendants of any of the Settlors' Children.

[Alternative: Omit sub-paragraph 2 and re-number sub-paragraph 3.]

Applications of Trust Property under this Paragraph need not be made equally. The Trustee may distribute to any of the persons described in this Paragraph to the exclusion of others, subject to the standards stated in this Paragraph and to the primary purposes of the trust stated in Paragraph A of this Article.

E. The Trustee shall have the power to apply income and principal payable to any beneficiary who is under legal disability or who is, in the opinion of the Trustee, incapable of managing his or her affairs. In carrying out this power, the Trustee may distribute directly to the beneficiary, or to the guardian or parent of the beneficiary, to a trust or custodial savings account, or to the person with whom the beneficiary resides. The receipt of one of these distributees shall discharge the Trustee from responsibility for the proper expenditure of trust property. The Trustee may accumulate income and withhold distributions of principal, in carrying out this power, to the extent permitted by law, until the beneficiary's legal disability is removed or until the beneficiary dies or becomes capable of managing his or her affairs, at which time all amounts payable to the beneficiary shall be paid to the beneficiary or to the beneficiary's estate. [The power conferred in this paragraph shall terminate no later than 21 years after the death of the last to die of the Settlors and those of the Descendants of the Settlors who are living at the date of this agreement.]

Comment. **Paragraph B is standard language for an orphaned minor's trust. (See the Jaramillo testamentary trust, Form 3, Article V–G.) David is excluded from the class consisting of the Settlors' "minor" children because the support language in Paragraph B would entitle him to support from the trust and could adversely impact his eligibility for governmental support. If the Kennedys both die while Patrick and David are "minors," the importance of David's eligibility for public assistance is heightened. The other sons will need assistance from the trust to "raise" them to the age of 21. If trust funds also are used to provide David's basic support, they will quickly be exhausted and there will be no funds left to supplement the minimal subsistence provided for David by the public programs.**

Many lawyers, including one of the authors writing in another place, recommend that the paragraph outlining the use of trust property for the disabled child (Paragraph C) state that the Trustee *cannot* use the trust property to provide primary support for the disabled child. Prohibiting the use of trust assets for the beneficiary's support makes it less likely that the trust assets can be taken to reimburse the state for support supplied to the beneficiary or that the trust assets will make the beneficiary ineligible for need based public programs. Use of such a provision carries the obvious risk that if public assistance is discontinued or seriously reduced in the future, the beneficiary will be left without any means of support. However, most lawyers conclude that it is more likely that an imprecisely drafted trust will render a beneficiary ineligible for assistance than that all such assistance programs will be eliminated.

Paragraph C contains no such prohibition because David is, to use the jargon of mental-retardation professionals, "high functioning"

and, with proper social and financial support may be able to live "semi-independently." The ability of the trustee to pay David's rent and utilities or to purchase a home for him could make the difference between David having the financial resources to live on his own rather than in a group home or in the home of one of his relatives.

V. TERMINATION

A. This trust shall terminate upon David's death, if there are no Minor Children of the Settlors living at that time. If there are Minor Children of the Settlors living at the time of David's death, this trust shall continue until there are no Minor Children of the Settlor living, at which later time the trust shall terminate. Upon termination of the trust, the Trustee shall then distribute the remainder of the Trust Property as follows:

Comment. **State Medicaid regulations, and federal law compelling such regulations, may put significant restraints on what can be done with the remainder in a special-needs trust that is not counted for resource purposes and is not subject to reimbursement claims for benefits provided by the Medicaid program. These restraints may not burden the sort of trust we draft here for David Kennedy when this trust is set up by David's parents: Such provisions change in the winds of politics. We are not confident that the restraints will exempt this sort of trust. We therefore insert a bit of warning here and at other places in our discussion and in these forms.**

If the restraints were in place, trust amounts available for David, during his life, would not count as resources for Medicaid qualification purposes. But, by way of *quid pro quo*, whatever remained in the trust at David's death would be vulnerable to Medicaid reimbursement claims. That would argue for separate trust shares in this form–one, relatively small, for David, the other for the other children. Only the remainder in David's share would then be vulnerable for reimbursement. That would, of course, put some hard choices to our clients, in deciding how much to set aside for David. They might, faced with such hard choices, decide to forgo Medicaid as a possible benefit for David; but, even then, they

would have to keep an eye on changes in qualification rules for other programs, notably including the S.S.I. program. There is some case law that would impose a division of the trust into shares and treat only part of the trust as for David. See, for example, dicta in *Shaak v. Pennsylvania Dept. of Public Welfare*, 747 A.2d 883 (Pa. 2000).

The regulations (and the federal mandate) may exempt *testamentary* trusts. If the regulations were to include inter-vivos trusts, such as this one, in their restraint on trust remainders, and if there were to be a testamentary-trust exemption, our clients might want to provide for this trust in their wills.

1. one share to each of the Settlors' then living Children;

2. one share to the then living surviving spouse of each of the Settlors' Children who is not then living; and

3. one share to the Descendants of each of the Settlors' Children who is not then living and whose surviving spouse is not then living.

[Alternative to sub-paragraphs "2" and "3":

2. one share to the Descendants of each of the Settlors' Children who are not then living.]

B.   If distribution cannot be made under paragraph A of this article, because none of the beneficiaries described there is living at the time for distribution, the Trustee shall divide the Trust Property into two equal shares and distribute those shares:

1. one share to Katherine Riley Hull, if she then survives; if Katherine Riley Hull does not then survive, the Trustee shall distribute her share to Jean Hull Donovan, if she then survives; if neither Katherine Hull nor Jean Hull Donovan then survives, the Trustee shall distribute this share under Subparagraph 2 of this Paragraph; and

2. one share divided equally among those of the following persons who are living at the time for distribution: Roberta Kennedy McCarter, Deborah Kennedy Fernandez, and Jeanne Kennedy Slade; if none of those persons survives, the Trustee shall distribute this share under Subparagraph 1 of this Paragraph.

3. If neither share can be distributed because none of the persons benefitting under this Paragraph survives until the termination of the trust, the Trustee shall distribute the remainder of the

Trust Property to the Rollison County Center for Retarded Citizens Inc.

Alternative. [B. If distribution cannot be made under Paragraph A of this Article because none of the beneficiaries described survives until the time for distribution, the Trustee shall divide the Trust Property into equal shares and distribute one share to each of the following persons who survives until the time for distribution: Katherine Riley Hull, Jean Hull Donovan, Roberta Kennedy McCarter, Deborah Kennedy Fernandez, and Jeanne Kennedy Slade. If distribution cannot be made under this paragraph because none of the persons benefitting under this paragraph survives until the termination of this trust, the Trustee shall distribute the remainder of the Trust Property to the Rollison County Center for Retarded Citizens.]

C.   The Settlors and Trustee intend this trust to be funded, and the Trustee to assume duties beyond the custody of the policies, only in the event that David is living at the death of the survivor of the Settlors or there are Minor Children of the Settlors living at the death of the survivor of the Settlors. If David is not living at the death of the survivor of the Settlors and if there are no Minor Children of the Settlors living at the death of the survivor of the Settlors, the Trustee shall terminate the trust. The Trustee may have been named beneficiary on policies of insurance on the lives of the settlors, or under other contracts that pay benefits after their deaths, but not otherwise have trust duties. If that occurs, the Trustee is to collect these proceeds and to distribute them under the provisions of this Article. This provision does not impair the Trustee's power and duty to hold, manage, and apply distributions from life insurance proceeds under paragraph "E" of Article "IV," above.

VI.   THE TRUSTEE'S POWERS

[Introductory form for states that lack comprehensive trustee-power legislation:

The Trustee and her successor have the following fiduciary powers, which are to be construed in the broadest manner consistent with the validity of this trust and with the duties of the Trustee. The powers stated here are not intended to be exclusive, but are in addition to those granted by law. These powers are....]

Comment.   **The powers listed in Form 1, Chapter 9, can be inserted here; they are drafted so as to be applicable to an inter-vivos trustee without editing; the drafter should note comments made on those powers in deciding which of them to use here.**

[Introductory form for states that have an imposed-powers form of comprehensive trustee-power statute:

The Trustee and her successors have the fiduciary powers provided in [The Uniform Trustees Powers Act], except those powers enumerated in Sections.... The powers listed in Sections ... are limited, so that the Trustee does not have power to.... In addition to the powers in this statutory list, as limited in this paragraph, the Trustee and her successors have the following fiduciary powers....]

[Introductory form for states that have an incorporation-by-reference form of trustee-power statute:

The Trustee and her successors have the fiduciary powers provided in (the incorporation by reference statute, or the list in the recorder's office, or the stone tablet on the courthouse lawn) except that this incorporation does not include those powers listed in Sections ...; and, in addition, the Trustee and her successors have the following powers....]

Comment. The rationale for powers is developed in the comments to Forms 1 and 2, Chapter 9, and in Chapter 5.

VII. OTHER PROVISIONS

A. The Trustee may resign by giving written notice, specifying the effective date of the resignation, to a Settlor if one or both of the Settlors are then living, or if neither of the Settlors is then living, to the then current income beneficiaries of the trust and, as to any beneficiaries under legal disability, to their guardians or to the persons with whom they are residing.

B. In the event of the death, resignation, or incapacity of the trustee, then Deborah Fernandez shall automatically be, and hereby is, appointed as the first successor trustee. In the event of the death, resignation, or incapacity of Deborah Fernandez, after the death of the Settlors, those of the Settlors' Children who are then living and who are not then under legal disability shall nominate a successor trustee, who shall, when nominated, succeed the first successor trustee. Successor trustees, including the first successor trustee and any successors nominated by the beneficiaries, may accept the administration of the trust without examination or review, without liability for doing so, and may act without the necessity of conveyance or transfer. Incapacity, for purposes of this article, may be determined not only by a legal adjudication of incompetence or incapacity, but also by a writing signed by the trustee's or successor trustee's personal physician, stating that the physician has examined the trustee or successor trustee and in the physician's opinion the trustee or successor trustee is not able to discharge the duties of trustee under this trust.

C. The Trustee shall render annual accounts, after both of the Settlors have died, to each beneficiary who is not under legal disability, and to the guardian of the estate of each beneficiary who is under legal disability. The written approval of such a beneficiary or of a beneficiary's guardian shall be binding on the beneficiary as to all matters and transactions covered by the account. The written approval of *all* beneficiaries for whom accountings are required under this paragraph, whether given personally or through guardians, shall, as to all matters and transactions covered by the account, be binding on all beneficiaries who become entitled to principal or income after the last date for which the account is rendered.

D. Legal questions, if any, arising under this indenture shall be governed by the law of Hoynes.

> **Comment. One of the benefits of an inter-vivos trust—a benefit that reaches diminishing returns in these days of model and uniform acts, though—is that the law of conflict of laws permits the settlors to designate the law which will control questions under the instrument. They need not even, in the orthodox view, confine themselves to the law of the jurisdiction in which the settlors live.**

This indenture of trust is signed this ___ day of _____, ___.

———————————————————

Richard John Kennedy, Settlor

———————————————————

Mary Margaret Kennedy, Settlor

———————————————————

Roberta McCarter, Trustee

State of Hoynes   )
)   SS:
County of Rollison   )

Richard John Kennedy and Mary Margaret Kennedy, known to me, and known by me to be the persons designated Settlors in this Trust Agreement, and Roberta McCarter, known to me, and known by me to be the person designated Trustee in this Trust Agreement, appeared before me, a Notary Public in and for this County and State, on the ___ day of _____, ___, and acknowledged their signatures on this Trust Agreement.

———————————————————

(signature)

———————————————————

(printed signature)

Notary Public

My Commission Expires: _____   (Seal)

Comment. Closing formalities. This is the orthodox mid-western form, including a notary's jurat so that the indenture is recordable in case the trustee receives real estate. Clients go through these steps without significant resistance or curiosity, which is just as well because, we suspect, most of us lawyers would be hard put to explain the purpose of it all if we had to.

When the trustee is to hold real estate, local law may require a line in which the preparer of the document is identified, or a statement saying Social Security numbers have been redacted, or both. (We do not suggest Social Security numbers in these forms, but the statement may still be required.)

The schedule of insurance policies should be appended to the trust or Art. II, para C omitted.

FORM 4B.   POUR–OVER NON–ESTATE WILL

This will parallels the testamentary trust will, Form 3, above, in most particulars. It is tedious of us to repeat the will terms here, but we have done it on the theory that repetition is defensible if it means the reader will not have to flip back and forth as she drafts. We have not repeated the comments, though—on the theory that it is all right to ask the reader to flip back and forth as he thinks.

The comments and theories on the wills in Chapter 9 and in this chapter pertain to this short "pour-over" will. The purpose here is to distribute the probate estate if no contingent trust becomes necessary, and to nominate a guardian and pay probate assets to the inter-vivos trustee (see Form 4A) if a trust does become necessary. Little or no property will pass under this will if Mrs. Kennedy survives; most of what she gets will be paid by survivorship, insurance distribution, and pension and Social Security payments. What little probate property there is can probably be distributed to her as widow's allowance or under the small-estate statute. (More assets will pass under the pour-over will when the partners are not married.)

The old common law sustained the pour-over which is used here contingently, on the theory that the will incorporated the trust by reference (arguably making it a testamentary trust). More recent statutes and cases provide that this sort of will may pay to an inter-vivos trustee because the trust—even an unfunded life-insurance trust—is a fact of independent significance. The newest statutes such as the Uniform Testamentary Additions to Trusts Act do not require a theory. The law-office counseling which goes into the device is discussed in this chapter and in Chapter 5; representative statutes are in the Statutory Appendix.

This form is simpler than a will with testamentary trust—even if it is similar. The appointment of fiduciaries is simpler; the powers are much shorter, and are set out here without the alternatives for use in states with modern powers legislation. The dispositive provisions are shorter. We have eliminated from the ultimate (remote possibility) distributions the alternatives which use intestacy statutes and which are set out and explained in Form 3, above.

WILL OF RICHARD JOHN KENNEDY

I, Richard John Kennedy, residing and domiciled in Marion City, Rollison County, Hoynes, declare that this is my will and revoke all other wills.

I. IDENTIFICATIONS AND DEFINITIONS

A. "My Wife" is the former Mary Margaret Hull. We have four children, Scott Edward Kennedy, born February 11, 1978; Patrick John Kennedy, born November 21, 1980; David Riley Kennedy, born January 29, 1984; and Thomas Hull Kennedy, born July 12, 1988. References to "my Children" include these four children and any other lawful children born to or adopted by me. References to "my Minor Children" include all of my Children who are, at the time stated in the reference to them, under the age of twenty-one years.

B. My son David is mentally retarded. Because of his disability David is likely to need, to a greater extent than my other children, both personal and financial assistance throughout his lifetime. As a consequence, Article IV of this will provides that if my Wife does not survive me, but David does survive me, my residuary estate shall be given to the trustee of the inter-vivos trust identified there, even if David and all of my other surviving Children are twenty-one years of age or older.

C. "My Wife's Mother" is Katherine Riley Hull. "My Wife's Sister" is Jean Hull Donovan. "My Sisters" are Roberta Kennedy McCarter, Deborah Kennedy Fernandez and Jeanne Kennedy Slade.

D. "Descendants" means those immediate and remote lawful, lineal descendants of the person referred to who are in being at the time they must be ascertained in order to give effect to the reference to them, whether they are born before or after my death or the death of any other person. Descendants shall take by right of representation, in accordance with the rule of *per stirpes* distribution and not in accordance with the rule of *per capita* distribution. The term Descendants includes adopted descendants only if they are legally adopted when they are under the age of fourteen years.

E. "Survive me" means that the person referred to must survive me by thirty days. If the person referred to dies within thirty days of my death, the reference to that person shall be construed as if that person had failed to survive me.

II. APPOINTMENT OF FIDUCIARIES

A. I appoint my Sister, Deborah Fernandez, executor; if she is unable or unwilling to act, I appoint the Old Solid National Bank and Trust Company of Marion City, Rollison County, Hoynes.

B.   If it is necessary to appoint a guardian for any of my Children, I nominate my Sister Roberta Kennedy McCarter, as guardian of the person and estate of each of my Children who requires a guardian. If my Sister Roberta Kennedy McCarter is unable or unwilling to serve, I nominate my Sister Deborah Kennedy Fernandez as guardian of the person and estate of each of my Children who requires a guardian.

C.   I recognize that the law of Hoynes requires that a resident coguardian be appointed when a nonresident is appointed guardian for a minor. If at the time of my death the appointment of a resident coguardian is required, I nominate Charles J. Jones of Marion City, Rollison County, Hoynes, as resident coguardian of the person and estate of any of my Children who requires a coguardian in either capacity. However, it is my desire that the custody of my Children and the management of their estates be committed to the care of the guardians nominated in paragraph B of this article, and I direct that my executor, my trustee, and the resident coguardian exercise whatever authority I am able to give them to that end.

D.   I request that neither bond nor sureties be required of any fiduciary appointed under this Article.

III.   PAYMENT OF EXPENSES AND TAXES

A.   I direct my executor to pay the following before any other division or distribution:

1.   all of the expenses of my last illness, funeral, and burial and of the administration of my estate;

2.   all taxes payable by reason of my death. I direct that all such taxes be equitably apportioned among those persons receiving property by reason of my death either under the terms of this will or outside it. My executor shall be entitled to collect from the recipients of property passing outside this will the portion of the taxes allocable to that property.

B.   I direct my executor, before any division or distribution under the following articles, to pay any mortgage debt on residential real estate passing to my Wife under this will [, as community property,] or by right of survivorship, or not to do so, as my Wife may elect. I direct my executor not to pay mortgage debts on real estate distributed to devisees or cotenants other than my Wife.

[*Specific or general or distributive legacies:* See Forms 1 and 2, Chapter 9, above.]

IV.   RESIDUARY ESTATE

A.   I define my Residuary Estate as all of my property after the payment of debts and taxes [and legacies] under Article III above, including real and personal property whenever acquired by me, property as to which effective disposition is not otherwise made in this will, property as to which I have an option to purchase or a reversionary interest, and property over which I have a power of appointment.

B.   I give my Residuary Estate to my Wife if she survives me.

C.   If my Wife does not survive me, and I am survived by my son David or by one or more of my Minor Children, I give my Residuary Estate to Roberta Kennedy McCarter, trustee under a trust agreement executed by me and her, as trustee, dated ___, as amended before my death.

D.   If my Wife does not survive me and I am not survived by my son David or by any of my Minor Children, I direct my executor to divide my Residuary Estate into equal shares and to distribute those shares:

1.   one share to each of my Children who survives me;

2.   one share to the surviving spouse of each of my Children who fails to survive me but who leaves a spouse who survives me; and

3.   one share to the Descendants of each of my Children who neither survives me nor leaves a spouse who survives me.

[*Alternative to subparagraphs 2 and 3:*

2.   one share to the Descendants of each of my Children who does not survive me but who leaves Descendants who survive me.]

E.   If my Wife does not survive me and none of my Children survives me, and none of the persons described in paragraph D of this article survives me, I direct my executor to divide my Residuary Estate into two equal shares and to distribute those shares:

1.   one share to my Wife's Mother, if she survives me; if my Wife's Mother does not survive me, my executor shall distribute her share to my Wife's Sister if she survives me; if neither my Wife's Mother nor my Wife's Sister survive me, my executor shall distribute this share under subparagraph 2 of this paragraph;

2.   one share to be divided equally among my Sisters who survive me; if none of my sisters survive me, my executor shall distribute their share under subparagraph 1 of this paragraph.

[E. If my Wife does not survive me and none of my Children survives me, and none of the persons described in paragraph D of this article survives me, I direct my executor to divide my Residuary Estate into equal shares and to distribute one share to each of the following persons who survives me: my Wife's Mother, my Wife's Sister, and my Sisters.]

F.   If none of the shares can be distributed because none of the persons benefitting under this Article survives me, I give my Residuary Estate to the Rollison County Center for Retarded Citizens, Inc., to be used for its general purposes.

V. POWERS OF EXECUTOR

My executor shall have the following powers, which are not intended to be exclusive, but shall be in addition to those granted by law, and shall also pertain to administrators who succeed my executor:

1. to take possession of property, keep it safely, and segregate it from other property;

2. to sell, exchange, lease, rent, mortgage, pledge, give options upon, and partition real and personal property, at private or public sale, on whatever terms she finds advisable, without notice or order of court;

3. to render liquid my estate, in whole or in part, and to hold cash or readily marketable securities of little or no yield for such period as she finds advisable;

4. to borrow in the name of my estate, upon whatever terms she finds advisable, for the purpose of preserving property held by her;

5. to pay, compromise, or abandon claims held by her, and claims asserted against her, on whatever terms she finds advisable, without court authority;

6. to distribute in cash or in kind, in divided or undivided interests, even though distributive shares may as a result be composed differently;

7. to employ attorneys, accountants, and other professional assistants;

8. to enter into transactions with other fiduciaries, including executors or trustees of estates and trusts in which the beneficiaries have an interest and including herself as fiduciary for other estates and trusts;

9. to pay herself reasonable compensation for her services.

I, RICHARD JOHN KENNEDY, sign my name to this instrument this ___ day of _____, ___, and being first duly sworn, declare all of the following:

1. I execute this instrument as my will.

2. I sign this will willingly.

3. I execute this will as my free and voluntary act.

4. I am 18 years of age or older, of sound mind and under no constraint or undue influence.

_____

Richard John Kennedy

WE, THE WITNESSES, being first duly sworn, sign our names to this instrument and declare all of the following:

1.   The testator executes this instrument as his will.

2.   The testator signs it willingly.

3.   Each of us, in the conscious presence of the testator, signs this will as a witness.

4.   To the best of our knowledge, the testator is 18 years of age or older, of sound mind and under no constraint or undue influence.

_____ residing at _____

_____ residing at _____

REFERENCES AND BIBLIOGRAPHY

F. Berall, "Estate Planning Considerations for Unmarried Same or Opposite Sex Cohabitants," 23 Quinnipiac Law Review 361 (2004)

J. Burda, "Estate Planning for Same–Sex Couples," G.P./Solo (American Bar Association, 2004)

F. and N. Croke, Family Trusts (1998)

L. Frolik, "Discretionary Trusts for a Disabled Beneficiary: A Solution or a Trap for the Unwary?" 46 University of Pittsburgh Law Review 335 (1985)

L. Frolik, "Estate Planning for Parents of Mentally Disabled Children," 40 University of Pittsburgh Law Review 305 (1979)

T. Gallanis, "Inheritance Rights for Domestic Partners," 79 Tulane Law Review 55 (2004)

L. Greider, "Unmarried Together," A.A.R.P. Bulletin, October, 2004, p. 14

C. Harp, "Estate Planning for the Disabled Beneficiary," Probate and Property, March/April 1997, p. 14

V. Held, "The Ethics of Care," in David Copp (ed.), The Oxford Handbook of Ethical Theory (2006), at 537

M. Jasper, Rights of Single Parents (2005)

J. Mero, "Estate Planning for Incompetency," 25 Tax Management Portfolios (1987)

C. Mooney, "Discretionary Trusts: An Estate Plan to Supplement Public Assistance for Disabled Persons," 25 Arizona Law Review 939 (1983)

R. Owens and R. Jordan, "Estate Planning for Parents of Mentally Disabled Children," Trusts and Estates (September 1987)

M. Palermo, A.A.R.P. Crash Course in Estate Planning, ch. 10 (2005)

R. Randazzo, "Elder Law and Estate Planning for Gay and Lesbian Individuals and Couples," 6 Marquette Elder's Advisor 1 (2004)

J. Rosenburg, "Supplemental Needs Trusts for People with Disabilities: The Development of a Private Trust in the Public Interest," 10 Boston University Public Interest Law Journal 91 (2000)

T. Shaffer, "My Client the Situation," Res Gestae (Indiana State Bar Association), October 2005, p. 24

K. Shulman, C. Klyman, and A. Weber, "Planning for the Incapacitated Child," vol. I, Ch. 4, in Massachusetts Continuing Legal Education, Inc., Estate Planning for the Aging or Incapacitated Client in Massachusetts (1998)

Social Security Administration, A Guide to Supplemental Security Income for Groups and Organizations (2006).

R. Spain, "Estate Planning for a Disabled Beneficiary," The Practical Lawyer, October 1991, p. 29

P. Tobin, "Foresight: Planning Ahead for Special Needs Trusts," Probate and Property, May/June 1997, p. 56

R. Volkmer, "Identity of Settlor of Special Needs Trust," 25 Estate Planning 428 (1998)

A. Wernz and C. Mooney, "Planning for the Disabled Child," a study prepared for the Northwestern Mutual Life Insurance Company (1989)

A. Wernz, "Estate Planning for the Mentally Retarded," 1 Notre Dame Estate Planning Institute 265 (1976)

Chapter 11

PLANNING FOR DISABILITY AND OLD AGE

We can't take it with us ... that much we know.
My trouble's keeping the stuff 'til I go.

Evelyn Ryan*

Increased life expectancy is a mixed blessing. Along with the opportunities afforded by more years comes the likelihood that clients will spend some portion of those years mentally or physically incapacitated and the virtual certainty that both their incomes and their personal independence will decline.

Long-term care for incapacitated persons, young or old, is becoming more institutionalized. Recent statistics indicate that approximately one in four older persons will spend some time in a nursing home. Nursing home care, costing an average of about $50,000 per year in some sections of the country, can rapidly deplete the life savings of even upper-middle-class persons. The onset of a debilitating illness can quickly make the problems of middle-class clients resemble the problems of poor clients.

These changes help explain why "estate planning" lawyers have expanded their horizons beyond drafting wills and trusts. This expansion includes planning for the possibility of future poverty, disability, or incompetence. In order to serve clients competently, lawyers now need to be familiar with the Social Security, Supplemental Security Income, Medicare, and Medicaid programs; living wills, health care agencies, durable powers of attorney; life-care contracts, and nursing home contracts. Lawyers need to know about ways to increase their clients' income, as well as the traditional "estate planning" tools of wills, trusts, and pension plans.

In the past four decades a new subgroup of attorneys has grown up—the "elderlaw" attorneys—and there is now a National Academy of Elderlaw Attorneys. Many of these lawyers have backgrounds in legal services or similar programs that serve low-income clients. In those programs they learned the ins and outs of categorical assistance programs, knowledge that is becoming essential for lawyers who have aging clients, as most of us do. And, of course, the knowledge possessed by the old-fashioned "probate" lawyer remains part of our toolboxes.

Our work with the Kennedy family in Chapter 10 illustrates the interconnectedness of "estate planning" and public benefits law, areas

* Terry Ryan, The Prize Winner of Defiance, Ohio 228 (2001).

304

traditionally seen as unrelated and as the realms of entirely different types of lawyers. In this chapter we hope to convince you, depending on your perspective, that you cannot be a good family lawyer without at least a rudimentary understanding of public benefits, along with a working knowledge of trusts and estates. We will also dip into the complexities of the changing law on public support for medical care.

* * *

Joe and Maria Villalobos are at the age, or maybe a little beyond it, when they should begin preparing for the possibility that one or both of them may need physical and financial assistance. Joe is 70 and Maria is 72. They are older clients, but may not (yet) think of themselves as *elderly* clients. Clients such as Mr. and Mrs. Villalobos, those at or near retirement age, need a legal checkup. They probably know that, and probably know, too, that planning for the possibility of future incapacity is psychologically easier for the clients when they are still planning extended vacations, or even contemplating a new post-retirement business or part-time job, than when they have begun to slow down. (In 1950, a fifth of the male labor force was over 65; the figure had risen to half in 2006.)

When Joe and Maria Villalobos married, Joe was in graduate school in engineering. Maria was a high school math teacher, but she quit shortly before the birth of their first child and did not return to teaching. When the children were in high school Maria took a part-time job as a bookkeeper. She continued with part-time jobs until Joe retired, at the age of 62. The small engineering company he worked for had been acquired by a larger company and that company was acquired by an even larger company. Each time, of course, there were upper management changes at Joe's company. The comraderie and sense of shared mission so central to Joe's professional happiness started to erode following the first acquisition and was, in his opinion, non-existent after the second one. Maria felt that since the first acquisition the company hadn't properly recognized or valued Joe's contributions. Joe decided to take early retirement rather than stick it out for a few more years. The company hired three young engineers to take Joe's place.

Mr. and Mrs. Villalobos are both in good health. Joe still swims a mile a week, a habit he began in his early fifties as the work pressures mounted and so did his blood pressure. Like most Americans their age, they watch the amount of salt and cholesterol in their diet, and Maria walks a mile or two a day to keep in shape. Joe still paints the house inside and out, and plants a vegetable garden every year. Maria does all of the household chores.

The three Villalobos children are married; they are all educated professionals and are scattered across the country. Their older son is in California; he and his wife have two children. Their younger son is in

Florida; he has no children. Their youngest child, a daughter, lives and works in Manhattan; she has two children. The children keep in as much contact with their parents as distances permit. They try to come home at least once a year, and Joe and Maria use the freedom of their retirement to visit each of their children at least once a year.

Mr. and Mrs. Villalobos live in the same house in which they raised their children. They hold title to the house as joint tenants with right of survivorship. The current market value of the house is approximately $150,000. The mortgage was paid off before Joe retired, and thanks to Joe's constant attention it is in excellent repair. They also own a small lake cottage in an adjoining state. They hold title to the cottage as tenants by the entirety; it has a current market value of $60,000. Although Joe and Maria personally use the cottage only a couple of weeks each summer, they want to hold on to it because their children and grandchildren also vacation there yearly. Joe and Maria believe that continued ownership of the cottage helps keep their growing clan together.

Joe's pension pays them $1,200 a month, and their combined monthly Social Security retirement benefits are $2,200. Upon retirement Joe selected a joint and survivor payment option under his pension plan, meaning that the pension will continue for Maria, at a slightly lower amount, if Joe dies before she does. They were able to continue health coverage under the group plan at Joe's former place of employment provided they also pay Medicare Part B insurance premiums, which they do. They have so far elected not to participate in the new "Part D" Medicare prescription drug scheme, and, so far, the management of the group health plan has not insisted that they do so. They do not have long term care insurance.

Mr. and Mrs. Villalobos saved a bit for their retirement. They have $20,000 in a joint money-market account; they have $2,100 in a regular joint checking account. They have $30,000 in treasury bonds in both of their names with maturity dates varying from two to ten years from now. Joe owns 100 shares in the Fidelity Magellan mutual fund and 1,000 shares of common stock in Campbell Soup. They have $30,000 in paid-up life insurance each.

Joe and Maria haven't totally ignored their legal affairs over the past decade: The wonders of modern medicine have made triple bypass surgery almost routine but also have raised burdensome questions about the not so bright line between life and death. Joe and Maria executed living wills at the time of Joe's retirement. Shortly after Joe's retirement, Joe and Maria attended a seminar about retirement planning where they became concerned about the possibility of becoming unable to manage their financial affairs. They have executed documents giving one another and their oldest child general powers of attorney. (But see the Uniform *Durable* Power of Attorney Act in the Statutory Appendix.) As a result of that seminar, they became concerned about the high cost of nursing home care and about the fact that Medicaid will not cover the cost of a nursing home until they consume virtually all of their savings. Having worked hard for all they have accumulated and wanting to make sure that they will be able to leave something for their children, they announced to their children that if either of them went into a nursing home, they would immediately deed their house over to the children. The children protested and told their parents that they shouldn't assume that everything they heard at the seminar is good advice and that they should speak with their attorney before making decisions.

It is possible that Joe or Maria, or both of them, will experience some period of physical or mental disability that will interfere with their ability to care for themselves and manage their affairs. They learned at the seminar that they should consider ways to provide a substitute decision-maker as well as ways to finance their care. Executing living wills and powers of attorney was only a beginning (and, perhaps, as we will see, not a very good one).

Although planning with a client for the possibility of the client's future incapacity is similar to the planning done for David Kennedy in Chapter 10, there are important differences. Because David Kennedy is mentally retarded, even when he reaches legal age he may not be competent to make certain decisions. Thus, because David has never been fully competent, has never been able to form opinions or make decisions about his own care, his ability to delegate authority to others is limited. For example, if a decision must be made about David's medical care, a decision he may not be competent to make, it probably has to be made for him by a relative or guardian, who generally must do what is in his best interest—an *objective* standard. Joe and Maria, being competent to make a wider range of decisions about their lives, are able to delegate greater power to a substitute decision-maker. They can empower a substitute decision-maker to make the same decisions they would make for themselves—a *subjective* standard. They can preserve in this way their right to make idiosyncratic decisions. ("Idiosyncratic" and "subjective" in the sense that a loved one can make decisions, rather than a judge or a guardian who must answer to a judge. And in the sense that Joe and Maria can plan now for the decisions and for the personal and even unique dimensions that should go into them. See, for example, the discussion in Chapter 12 of planning in health care agencies.) Furthermore, they can choose the person(s) who will act as substitute decision-maker(s); David probably has to be content with one or both of his parents, one or all of his brothers, or with a decision-maker chosen for him by a judge.

As was true of David's parents' concern for their son, Mr. and Mrs. Villalobos would like the government, through the Medicaid program, to help with the cost of long term care if they ever need it. However, there are differences here too. Medicaid is a program for the poor; only persons who meet stringent financial eligibility criteria can receive assistance from the program for long-term care. David Kennedy has virtually no property of his own other than his clothing and sports equipment, and it is unlikely that he will ever accumulate any sizeable amount of property other than by gift or inheritance. With proper legal advice and cooperation from the state and federal legislatures, as they constantly revise the eligibility criteria for governmental assistance, transfers from David's relatives for his benefit can be structured so that they supplement rather than supplant government benefits.

Mr. and Mrs. Villalobos already own property. They have not accumulated an amount of property that calls for tax planning, but they have a nice nest egg to see them through their retirement years, assuming that neither of them suffers from an illness requiring long term custodial care. They are concerned not only that a protracted stay in a nursing home for one of them would leave no inheritance for their children, but also that it could leave the other of them, the "well spouse," impoverished. The Medicaid program can cover the cost of nursing home care, but they are concerned that they would have to consume most of their savings before they would be eligible for Medicaid. Because the Medicaid laws limit the ability of a person to give her assets away in order to qualify for Medicaid, Joe and Maria cannot set up trusts for themselves that resemble the trust the Kennedys have set up for David. Their plan to transfer their home as they go (or one of them goes) into a nursing home is almost certainly ill-advised.

* * *

An article by Claire Berman, in the November 1997 *Family Circle*, summarizes the concerns we talk about in this chapter, in three categories pertinent for middle-aged people: (i) ability to act, (ii) money, and (iii) health care: "Watching your parents grow older and more in need of assistance," she says, "makes you think: Is there anything I should be doing to prepare for my own old age? You probably hope to maintain a comfortable standard of living but may wonder, if it becomes necessary down the road, whether or not you'll be able to afford options such as expensive in-home care, relocation to an assisted-living facility, or a stay in a nursing home."

A. POWERS AND TRUSTS

Ms. Berman imagines these questions: "What can I do to insure that my affairs will be handled responsibly if I'm unable to act on my own behalf?" And, assuming an answer to that question, an answer we must discuss further, "How can I go about selecting the right person to have my power of attorney?" If a lawyer were to answer the second question, she would want to know more about what the client's concern is, and what her client understands by the phrase "power of attorney." And she would want to consider an array of options, including some that are not about powers of attorney.

1. POWERS OF ATTORNEY

The power of attorney documents that Mr. and Mrs. Villalobos have executed giving one another and then their oldest child power of attorney would probably not be of any assistance should either of them otherwise need to be put into guardianship. A power of attorney creates an agency relationship. At common law an agent's authority to act on behalf of the principal ceases when the principal becomes incompetent. It is common for an elderly person who is starting to have difficulty paying his bills to give power of attorney to a trusted friend or younger family member to allow that person access to bank accounts or authority to sign checks. It is also common for the attorney-in-fact (i.e., the agent) to continue to use that power even after the principal ceases to be able to act on his own behalf. But the ability of the attorney-in-fact to continue to use the power of attorney after the principal has become incompetent turns on luck, good will in the community, and other undependable factors.

In short, powers of attorney become useless when they are most needed, when the principal becomes incapacitated. That an attorney-in-fact's (agent's) power ceases when the principal becomes incompetent also means that a power of attorney may be ineffective, even when the principal is not disabled, because a third party may be unwilling to transact business in reliance upon the power unless the attorney-in-fact furnishes evidence that the principal is still competent. Statutes and case law in many states attempt to address that problem by stating that a third party may rely upon a power of attorney unless the third party has actual notice of revocation or of the incapacity of the principal. It is such doctrines, together with a legal principle that says a person is presumed competent unless he or she is adjudicated incompetent, that sometimes make it possible for an attorney-in-fact to continue to use a power of attorney after the principal has ceased to be capable of acting on her own behalf.

In the mid 1960s the idea developed of allowing powers of attorney to survive a principal's incompetence, that is, to be *durable*. In 1969 the National Conference of Commissioners on Uniform State laws first suggested that a power could be made *durable* when the instrument creating the power contains language showing that the principal intends the agency to remain effective even if the principal later becomes incompetent. Today all states have legislation permitting durable powers of attorney. (See the Uniform Durable Power of Attorney Act in the Statutory Appendix.) Many lawyers today would say that if the power of attorney Mr. and Mrs. Villalobos have given to their son is not durable, it should be.

Durable powers have, from this point of view, become an integral part of planning for the possibility of future disability or incompetence. Durable powers are often an alternative to guardianship, but a principal must be competent at the time a power of attorney is signed. A durable power cannot be used in place of a guardianship for a person who never has been competent, such as a severely retarded person, or some developmentally disabled persons, or for a person who, although competent during part of her life, has become incompetent. In contrast, a court confers upon a guardian or conservator the power to act on behalf of a person who is incompetent at the time guardianship is sought. When a durable power is used as a planning device (along with a will, for example), it needs to be executed before it will be needed.

One of the primary questions that must be answered when creating a durable power is whether the power should be effective to give the attorney-in-fact power as soon as the document is signed (a *present power*), or whether the power should come into effect only when the principal becomes incompetent (a *springing power*). Statutes commonly permit springing powers and they are attractive to those clients who do not wish to give a third person control over their affairs at the time the power is executed. Springing powers present a few complexities, though. The first is drafting the triggering mechanism. What are the conditions that the client wants to trigger the power? Usually incompetence; but who will determine that the triggering event has occurred—the client's physician, or two physicians, or attorney(s) plus named family members? The second is whether a springing power will be honored by third parties after the triggering event has occurred and the attorney-in-fact tries to use the power. Third parties are likely to ask for evidence that the power is effective. Documents may need to be presented with the power to prove that the spring has been sprung.

To circumvent the latter problems, sometimes a present power is executed—that is, a power that purports to give the attorney-in-fact power to act immediately—but the document is not delivered to the attorney-in-fact. Instead, it is delivered to a third party (another agent) who is given written directions as to when it is to be delivered to the attorney-in-fact. That is, rather than triggering the effectiveness of the power, the event triggers delivery of the document to the attorney-in-fact. The third party who holds the document for later delivery to the attorney-in-fact may be the lawyer who prepared the power.

Similar problems occur with the need for successor attorneys-in-fact. The person first named to act as attorney-in-fact herself may become incompetent or die; thus it is desirable to have a successor. Here too, manipulation of delivery to the successor is a common solution.

Exercise 11.1

11.1.1   Draft a clause that would cause a springing power of attorney to become effective if, and when, the principal becomes incapable of managing his business and financial affairs. Keep in mind that one of the reasons for using a durable power is to avoid the court proceeding needed to appoint a guardian or conservator. A court proceeding for that purpose, or to resolve a dispute about whether the event that causes a power of attorney to spring has occurred, is expensive, public, embarrassing, and painful. The springing mechanism should attempt to keep down cost and embarrassment, yet still achieve the client's objective of making the power effective only when needed.

11.1.2   Will the same clause work in the instructions to a "delivery" agent if you decide to use a present power and manipulate the delivery? Can the triggering mechanisms be more complex when they trigger delivery of the document to the attorney-in-fact than when they trigger effectiveness of a springing power, because the attorney-in-fact will not have to prove to third parties that the triggering events have occurred? Can the delivery option provide more discretion for the person who is charged with the decision?

11.1.3   Some attorneys act as the delivery agent for their clients who want to delay the ability of the attorney-in-fact to use the power but who prefer to write a clean, present power of attorney. What factors should a lawyer consider before agreeing to act as the delivery agent for a client?

Mr. and Mrs. Villalobos have already executed a (non-durable) power of attorney naming one another or their oldest son to be attorney-in-fact. That power is a present power; they appear to be comfortable giving their son authority to act and trusting that he will not use that power unless and until necessary. In fact, although we think that springing powers (however accomplished) may sometimes be advisable, in most instances we hope that a client is comfortable with the person selected as attorney-in-fact, so that a present power may be given directly to the attorney-in-fact, even when it is contemplated that it may never be used. On the other hand, principals who are advised to execute general powers—especially when the powers are durable—should realize that their attorneys-in-fact may be able to undo all of their business arrangements, impoverish them, and commit them to a nursing home.

These risks suggest a second major question: What powers should be given to the attorney-in-fact? The types of decisions that can be delegated can be broken into three categories: business, financial, and personal. In some instances it may be a good idea to give one person power to make all three types of decisions; in other situations it may be more advisable to divide the responsibilities—for example, naming a business partner to make the business decisions, a family member to make financial decisions, and perhaps a different family member to make personal decisions. Durable power statutes typically allow an attorney-in-fact to delegate, and that is one way to divide duties. (There are some powers that are not delegable and cannot be given to another. These may include the power to write a will, to vote, to contract marriage, or to seek dissolution of marriage through divorce or annulment.)

In some communities there are statutory forms that may be used to give a person general durable power of attorney, with the option of eliminating specific categories of enumerated powers. In other places each document needs to be individually drafted. And local custom in some places is to use two documents—one "financial," one for health care—while in other places (e.g., the forms used here), lawyers combine these functions into one power.

* * *

FORM 5.   DURABLE POWER OF ATTORNEY

Here, from the first category, is a part of the form promulgated by the Indianapolis Bar Association: (used here with the kind permission of the Association).

I.   POWERS I give to my attorney-in-fact the powers herein specified to be used on my behalf. I am incorporating by reference herein those powers which comply with my wishes in accordance with the manner prescribed by Ind. Code § 30–5–5. The powers given herein shall be considered limited so that my attorney-in-fact shall not have any power which would cause my attorney-in-fact to be treated as the owner of any interest in my property and which would cause that property to be taxed as owned by the attorney-in-fact, it being my intention not to grant any beneficial interests in my estate by this instrument. My attorney-in-fact shall have the following powers:

(initial appropriate powers):

☐   Real Property. Authority with respect to real property transactions pursuant to Ind. Code § 30–5–5–2.

☐   Tangible Personal Property. Authority with respect to tangible personal property pursuant to Ind. Code § 30–5–5–3.

☐   Bonds, Commodities and Shares. Authority with respect to bonds, commodities and shares pursuant to Ind. Code § 30–5–5–4. This authority

(select appropriate provision): (shall) (shall not)

exclude any power to purchase commodities, any power to sell short or to initiate a margin transaction and any power to purchase put or call options. This authority shall include the power to purchase United States Government obligations which are redeemable at par value in payment of estate taxes imposed by the United States Government....

* * *

☐   Gifts. Authority with respect to gift transactions pursuant to Ind. Code 30–5–5–9; however, this authority shall:

(select appropriate provision)

☐   include the power to make such gifts to my spouse as are needed to accomplish the minimization of income, gift and death taxes, even though my spouse may be serving as my attorney-in-fact hereunder; OR

☐   exclude the power to make non-spousal gifts in excess of the amount excluded from gifts under section 2503(b) of the Internal Revenue Code of 1986, as amended, or any successor thereto; OR

☐   exclude the power to make gifts to spouses of descendants....

* * *

II.   GUARDIAN If it becomes necessary to secure the appointment of a guardian of my person or estate or if protective proceedings are filed on my behalf, I hereby request the appropriate probate court to appoint _____ as my guardian or as the person to act on my behalf.

III.   FEES My attorney-in-fact

(select appropriate provision): (shall) (shall not)

be entitled to a fee for services provided as my attorney-in-fact....

* * *

V.   EFFECTIVE DATE AND INCAPACITY

A.   This power of attorney shall be effective:

(select appropriate provision)

☐   as of the date it is signed

☐   as of the ___ day of _____, 200 ___.

☐   upon the determination that I am disabled or incapacitated, or no longer capable of managing my affairs prudently. My disability or incapacity, for this purpose, may be established by the certificate of a qualified physician stating that I am unable to manage my affairs.

B.   My disability or incompetence

(select appropriate provision): (shall) (shall not)

affect or terminate this Power of Attorney.

* * *

Redacting and Recording. A pervasive durable power—such as the Indianapolis Bar Association form we quote from—will likely authorize the attorney-in-fact to act for the principal in deals involving real property. Dealing with real property responsibly often involves submitting the transaction's documents for recording in a public office. Title examiners and other bureaucrats will, when tracing such things as chains of title through the documents in the public office, look for the authority of the person who signed the documents. And so the responsible attorney-in-fact will offer the durable power to the recorder. Which brings us to two modern requirements, one of which requires that the document show who prepared it, and another of which requires that the preparer state that the document had no Social Security numbers in it, or that, if they once had Social Security numbers in it, they have been "redacted." (See, e.g., Indiana Code Sec. 36–2–11–15.) The first requirement traces, so far as we can tell, to concerns over the unauthorized practice of law (by, say, real-estate brokers). The second requirement seems to trace to concerns about identity theft and the possibility that bad guys will comb through the documents in the recorder's office seeking whom they may devour, as Scripture says. The second requirement may demand an "affirmation statement" whether or not the document has ever had in it a Social Security number, and it imposes perjury on the signatory who appends the "affirmation statement" but does not "redact" the numbers. Both requirements have to be put up with or the clerk in the recorder's office will refuse the document(s).

* * *

Durable powers of attorney are preferable to guardianships for a number of reasons, the first of which is that the principal decides who will make decisions on her behalf if she becomes incapable of doing so. A relatively new development is that in some states a durable power may be used to nominate a guardian or conservator for the principal if one becomes necessary. (Note that provision in the Indianapolis form.) This is important because appointing an attorney-in-fact will not always obviate the need for a guardian or conservator. If a guardian or conservator is appointed, an attorney-in-fact is accountable to the guardian or conservator, as fiduciary, and the fiduciary may have the same power to revoke or amend the power that the principal would have if she were not incapacitated. If the principal has the power to nominate a guardian or conservator, that power is often used to nominate the attorney-in-fact or someone compatible with the attorney-in-fact.

* * *

Tom Shaffer's old law firm (called Barnes, Hickam, Pantzer, and Boyd when he was there, now called Barnes and Thornburg) wrote clients last year about powers of attorney. (Two partners in the firm, Kristin Fruewald and John W. Houghton, made similar points in an article in the April 2004 *Indiana Lawyer*.) The letter to clients, in part:

> Powers of attorney have become an integral and routine part of an overall estate plan. Recently, some Indiana case law has ques-

tioned the validity of transactions involving powers of attorney. In particular, these cases raise a presumption of undue influence if the attorney-in-fact benefits from the transaction—even if the attorney-in-fact is not aware of the transaction. If you have a power of attorney or are named as an attorney-in-fact, you should be aware of these cases and understand not only the risks to the principal but also the responsibilities of the attorney-in-fact.

Two common situations come to mind. First, the principal undertakes actions that benefit the attorney-in-fact without the attorney-in-fact's knowledge or participation. For example, he names his second wife as his attorney-in-fact, buys her an expensive birthday present, and dies shortly thereafter. Children from a prior marriage can raise the presumption of undue influence. Second, the principal empowers the attorney-in-fact to make annual exclusion gifts to the principal's children. After the principal's incapacity, the attorney-in-fact makes gifts to the members of this class, including himself. These gifts are then challenged by a subsequent spouse. The presumption of undue influence could be raised in this instance and, if not overcome, could render the gifts void. Independent actions by the principal may be voidable because of the existence of the power of attorney and actions foreseen and intended by the principal may be thwarted if the presumption of undue influence cannot be overcome by clear and convincing evidence.

Under the current state [of the] law, what if anything, should you do if you currently are a principal or an attorney-in-fact? Go right on as in the past? Drop the power of attorney or resign as attorney-in-fact? Certainly, the power of attorney has its proper place in an estate plan. Its benefits outweigh its risks. But recent ... decisions suggest that, if you have a power of attorney, you and your named attorney-in-fact should be aware of some basics of the fiduciary relationship created by the power of attorney. First, the attorney-in-fact should be a person in whom you have the utmost confidence and trust. Second, you should realize that you bestow no favor on your appointed attorney-in-fact.

What about gifts of your property while the power of attorney exists or through use of the power of attorney? This is the area now fraught with the most unpleasant results. Your well-laid plans may go awry if, in the future, you or your attorney-in-fact plan to make gifts to the attorney-in-fact or members of his or her family. Before those plans are carried out, you should seek the advice of counsel. Counsel can then advise you of steps that may be taken to develop evidence to avoid or overcome the presumption of undue influence. For example, you can sign a transmittal letter stating why the gifts are being made or the gifts could be made by you in the presence of an independent third party.

Diane L. Liptack, an Indianapolis lawyer writing in the May 1999 *Res Gestae*, monthly magazine of the Indiana State Bar Association, sounded warnings to her fellow lawyers about the routine use of durable powers for clients such as Mr. and Mrs. Villalobos:

"As a result of the broad authority a principal can readily delegate to the attorney-in-fact and the lack of judicial oversight" when compared with a guardianship, which is subject to reporting requirements and routine judicial supervision, she wrote, "opportunities for self-dealing are apparent. While [the] law does require an attorney-in-fact to use due care for the benefit of the principal and to act in a fiduciary capacity, absent is a safeguard to insure the inept or mischievous attorney-in-fact is fulfilling the duties imposed in furtherance of the principal's best interest."

The law, she writes, "is not without remedies where the exercise of the agent's powers are brought into question. If transactions made have benefitted the agent, the law imposes a presumption of undue influence and fraudulent transfer. The burden of proof shifts to the agent who must demonstrate by clear and unequivocal evidence that he or she acted in good faith and did not take advantage of his or her trusted relationship...."

"Legal authority looks helpful in theory, but is not, practically speaking, effective to halt what are believed to be widespread violations of our growing elderly population. Since it is understandable that an injured party may never recognize the wrongful acts committed or be reluctant to initiate legal proceedings against an attorney-in-fact who is an immediate family member, or equally likely that the misappropriated assets may have been immediately dissipated by the agent and, therefore, not recoverable, the possibility of an untrustworthy agent is best addressed in the planning stage."

It is possible to undo a durable power without litigation, if the principal remains competent until the time for undoing. And it is possible, using the remedies Ms. Liptack mentions, to bring a misdealing agent to book. But undoing a power is difficult, even when the principal is competent to revoke the power; it involves locating all third parties with whom the agent dealt, and it should involve getting the document back from the agent. And the fiduciary remedies depend on the principal's being able and willing to act—even to initiate a guardianship proceeding and petition the supervising court to order the power revoked and the agent to account. Ms. Liptack ventures the opinion that none of these difficulties is likely to be remedied by the legislature, considering the popularity of the durable power:

"Given the unlikelihood of legislative reform compromising the relative ease" of setting up a power, "the protection of the principal may depend in large part on the prudence of the attorney consulted" before the power is executed. "Clearly, preprinted bar association 'one-size-fits-all' forms are not always best for the principal and agent, and their casual use may, in fact, suggest to both that a power of attorney is less than a serious undertaking." A local one-size-fits-all form is, though, a place to begin.

"The conscientious attorney may consider the following on the drafting and interview checklist:

"— Confer with principal to determine capacity to enter into a contractual agency relationship. Response to a telephone request for a lawyer to supply a power of attorney [usually initiated by the person who proposes to become the attorney in fact] is unwise. Where the principal lacks a trusted and qualified relative or friend, consider other alternatives to an ill-conceived power of attorney, such as automatic bill paying from a commercial bank account or a funded trust with corporate fiduciary.

"— Exercise prudent selection of appropriate powers, including the power to make gifts. Consider a prohibition of agents from making gifts to themselves, their dependents and creditors. Alternatively, condition gift giving on the written consent of a third party with interest adverse to the agent or, at a minimum, impartial to the agent. Gifts might also be limited by a specified purpose or standard, such as grandchildren education or fulfillment of church pledge, consistent with prior pattern of prior gifts. Of course, restrictions on gift-giving authority must be balanced with the desirability of gifts for Medicaid planning [of which more below] and death-tax reduction.

"— Employ use of multiple agents who must act jointly. Multiple agents can be appointed and authorized to act only with the consent of each. While this arrangement may be inconvenient and poses the problem of potential conflict, it does provide a check on the uncontrolled agent."

A planning option here is to provide an alternative attorney-in-fact who can step in to act at the discretion of the agent, or in order to exercise certain powers (such as gifts to the agent), and who can then step out and return power to the agent. Most durable-power statutes permit this device.

"— Employ use of a springing power of attorney which becomes effective only when needed. Principals naturally cherish self-determination and do not want their attorney-in-fact to act until incapacity occurs. By its terms, the power of attorney can provide a mechanism to 'spring' into effectiveness only upon the incapacity of the principal, possibly as determined in writing by the attending physician. Delay of the effective date of the powers is not in itself a solution if the integrity of the agent is an issue, but it may give the principal an opportunity, while the principal is competent, to evaluate the agent's fitness to serve." Our suggestion, just above, for delaying delivery of the power to the attorney-in-fact is, perhaps, an alternative to making the power "spring."

"— Detail the agent's compensation arrangement. An agent is entitled to reasonable compensation under [most] statutory authority. The terms of the compensation should be spelled out specifically since, if funds are misappropriated by the agent, 'compensation' may be claimed as a defense.

"— Require that accountings be sent to the principal and to a back-up recipient for review (especially where principal is incapacitated or inattentive to details), accompanied by supporting data such as bank statements and checks. Perhaps the principal's accountant or bookkeeping service could serve in this role since transmittal of financial data is already required for the tax return filings." Local law may require periodic non-judicial accounting. And local law probably permits docketing of the power (in effect an equitable action for accounting) by the back-up reviewer who cannot come to terms with the attorney-in-fact.

"— Where evidence of trouble looms likely, advise parties of the existence of adult protective service agencies ... which investigate alleged financial and personal abuses of vulnerable citizens."[1]

2. REVOCABLE LIVING TRUSTS

Revocable living trusts also are commonly used in planning for the possibility of incompetence. Using the trust device gives the settlor of the trust the opportunity to build in greater flexibility and specificity in property management than is typical when using a power of attorney. A settlor can establish investment guidelines, accounting requirements, and distribution provisions not usually included in a power of attorney.

Revocable trusts are also popular as probate avoidance devices. In a typical revocable trust, the settlor of the trust confers on himself, as trustee, all beneficial rights in the trust property during the settlor's life, and the settlor is also beneficiary. Upon the settlor's death, or incompetence, the trust becomes irrevocable, and dispositive provisions of the trust direct a successor trustee to distribute the trust property as an executor under a will would do (or, after incompetence and before death, as a guardian would do). Quite often the dispositive provisions are identical to those found in the settlor's will, or as we discussed in connection with the Kennedys, the will pours probate assets into the trust. Any assets owned by the trust at the settlor's death are not part of the settlor's probate estate because title to those assets is held by the trustee, not by the settlor. Of course, probate is avoided only as to those assets held in the trust at the time of the settlor's death. An *unfunded* revocable trust does not avoid probate.

1. We add, a bit tongue in cheek, this from a comment published in 2005 on recent federal tax legislation: "The healthcare power becomes tax driven when it includes a provision providing that, in the event the client is on life support, he or she should be kept alive until the most advantageous date in the tax code." The example, contemplating the demise of the federal estate tax in 2010, was the client "in failing health and on life support" who might make provision in her durable power for health care that would, as applied, keep her going for another year.

Advocates of the "living trust" argue that avoiding probate is a good idea. (The device traces, as far as we can tell, to a paperback book, sold on airport book racks in the 1960s, called *How to Avoid Probate*.) The chief advantage of avoiding probate, they argue, is avoiding delays in distribution of assets. Even in moderate estates, final distribution may be delayed as long as two years after the date of death; in large and complex estates a longer delay is normal.

Avoiding probate may also save money, although not as much money as seems to be commonly assumed. Harold Weinstock, in the third edition of his book *Planning an Estate,* calculates that in a million dollar estate, using a revocable inter vivos trust rather than having the estate probated saves approximately $11,000. Although the cost of probating a million dollar estate is typically much higher than $11,000, there are several factors that balance comparative cost: First, probate expenses are deductible, either on the federal estate tax return or on the estate's income tax return, so avoiding probate costs does not result in a dollar-for-dollar savings. Second, there are after-death services (such as filing death tax returns) that need to be performed whether or not there is probate, but if there is a probate estate these services are usually covered by the statutory fees and commissions. Lastly, drafting, funding, and administering a funded trust costs money (more money than having a will and durable power prepared) that must be taken into account when determining the savings from avoiding probate.

Avoiding probate may allow a decedent to keep his plan for disposing of his property out of the public eye. When a will is probated it becomes public record. If a person's property is distributed according to the terms of an inter-vivos trust, the dispositive scheme does not usually become public. This is not likely to be a big factor for Mr. and Mrs. Villalobos; however, every family has reasons to favor a non-public disposition of property.

There are analogous drawbacks to *avoiding* probate. (See Mr. Esmont's essay, cited in References.) When there is a probate proceeding, the personal representative gives notice to the decedent's creditors that they must present their claims. If a general creditor fails to file its claims within the period set by the probate law, the decedent's assets are no longer subject to the claim. Without a probate proceeding, the shortened claim period is not available.

Exercise 11.2

In a videotaped continuing-legal-education program one of us watched last year, the lawyer on tape described a client whose mother had died seven months earlier leaving a hospital bill of five thousand dollars. The bill was not paid, and her mother left no assets to pay it with. The client had that day picked up from her late mother's mailbox a letter from a mutual insurance company saying they were paying her mother three thousand dollars for her mother's interest as a policy holder (a common event these days for people who are insured by mutual companies). The probate-code non-claim period for the hospital bill (statute of limitations) was nine months from the date of death. The lawyer talking on the tape said he told the client she could proceed under the probate code to collect the mutual-insurance money, but that she should wait a couple of months to do it—until the time from date of death was more than nine months and it was too late for a creditor to file claims. A lawyer in the audience (not visible but certainly audible) called out, "That is not ethical."

Avoiding probate should not be confused with saving taxes. To say that assets are not in a decedent's probate estate does not imply that the assets are not in a decedent's gross estate for federal estate tax purposes, or that they are not subject to state death taxes. Nor does placing assets in a revocable trust save death taxes or income taxes.

* * *

Our focus in this part of this chapter is anticipating and preparing for the possibility that a client may become unable to manage his or her own affairs. A revocable trust in which the trustee is not the settlor (or in which there is a successor trustee after the settlor becomes incompetent) may be better than a durable power of attorney for providing lifetime management of an incapacitated person's assets; probate avoidance is, from that point of view, an incidental benefit.

A trust instrument may include investment guidelines and accounting requirements not usually included in powers of attorney. In addition, because title to trust assets is in the trustee, third parties are often more willing to deal with a trustee than with an attorney-in-fact. If the trust is funded, and if the settlor is not acting as trustee, the client can observe and evaluate the trustee's investment and administration of the trust. If the client is satisfied with the trustee's performance, additional assets can be added to the trust. If the client is unhappy, he (*or* his attorney-in-fact) can change trustees or revoke the trust.

In the popular "living trust," the settlor acts as trustee. In those instances, the trust instrument provides that a successor trustee takes over at the death of the settlor or earlier if the settlor is unable to continue to administer the trust. The same sort of triggering mechanism used with springing durable powers is needed to replace the settlor/trustee with a successor trustee if the settlor becomes incapable of managing the trust. Whether or not the settlor continues as trustee until his death, the trust serves as a probate avoidance device, after it has served as a back-up management device. (See our discussion of *Farkas v. Williams* in Chapter 5.)

If a client decides to act as trustee of his own trust, it is necessary to make it clear to the client that the trust is not a fiction. Trust accounting books should be maintained; tax returns may be required; and the trustee generally should act as a trustee: The settlor/trustee may have a statutory obligation to make formal periodic accountings to the eventual beneficiaries of the trust, and, even where the law does not require periodic accounting, the practice helps remind everyone that the trust is more than a piece of paper.

Because it is at least mildly inconvenient to administer a funded trust, even if the settlor acts as trustee, revocable trusts, even those established to provide lifetime management in the event of the settlor's incapacity, are not always fully funded, and sometimes are not funded at all. If a client is hesitant to fund a trust, or wishes to avoid the expense of funding and administering a trust unless and until it is needed, an unfunded or standby trust can be used in combination with a durable power of attorney. The durable power should specifically authorize, and perhaps instruct, the attorney-in-fact to transfer the principal's assets into the trust in the event the principal becomes incapable of managing his property. When the durable power is a present power (and not a springing power), it should probably include a mechanism for determining the principal's incapacity. In this instance, incapacity might trigger funding of the trust even if it does not trigger the effectiveness of the durable power.

Whether a trust may be entirely unfunded until it is needed depends on both state law and the client's broader scheme. If the client's will directs that probate assets be poured into the trust, it may be necessary to make the trust at least a contingent beneficiary on a life insurance policy. A testamentary pour-over into an unfunded *life insurance* trust is valid in most states. (See our discussion of unfunded trusts and pour-over wills in Chapter 10.) If no pour-over is contemplated, or if a pour-over is used only if the trust is funded during the testator's lifetime, there is no conceptual reason why the trust cannot be totally unfunded until the triggering event. The inter-vivos trust will not come into existence unless and until the attorney-in-fact transfers assets to it.

* * *

FORM 6. SUGGESTED LANGUAGE FOR THE JOSEPH AND MARIA VILLALOBOS TRUST

Amendment and Revocation

1. Each Settlor individually retains power to withdraw from the trust any property he or she has transferred to the trust, including his or her interest in any property jointly transferred to the trust.

2. The Settlors, during their joint lives, may jointly revoke this trust in whole or in part, and may jointly alter any of its provisions. If one of the Settlors becomes incompetent, the other Settlor may alter or amend the trust with the written consent of the incompetent Settlor's attorney-in-fact, or if the Settlor does not have an attorney-in-fact, with the written consent of the Settlor's guardian or conservator, if any. If an incompetent Settlor does not have an attorney-in-fact or a guardian or a conservator, the other Settlor, acting alone, may alter or amend the trust. If both Settlors become incompetent, the provisions of this trust may be altered by the Settlors' attorneys-in-fact or, if none, their guardians or conservators. If only one of the incompetent Settlors has an attorney-in-fact, or a guardian or a conservator, that person, acting alone, may alter any of the provisions of this trust.

3. The Settlors intend that the provisions of this trust may be altered either by the Settlors or their representatives in any way, including making the trust irrevocable and unamendable and providing that distributions may continue for one of the Settlors and not for the other.

4. Upon revocation, the Trustee shall distribute the trust property to the Settlors, giving each Settlor a share of the trust property having a value that bears the same ratio to the total value of the trust property at the time of revocation as the value of the property contributed to the trust by each Settlor bears to the total value of property contributed to the trust. If, however, the trust is revoked after the death of one of the Settlors, the Trustee shall distribute all of the trust property to the surviving Settlor.

5. For purposes of this instrument, incompetence shall be determined by a Settlor's personal physician who shall inform the Trustee in a signed writing that the physician has examined the Settlor and in the physician's opinion the Settlor is not competent to handle financial affairs and to make decisions regarding the disposition of his or her property.

* * *

3.   LIVING WILLS AND HEALTH CARE AGENTS

In theory, trustees of revocable trusts serve as surrogate decision-makers only for property management decisions, but the fact is that people and property are not easily separated (see Chapter 1); a number of personal care decisions may be made by a trustee for an incompetent trust beneficiary. For example, a trustee may be able to sign a lease on an apartment for a beneficiary, or even a nursing home contract, and thus make decisions about the beneficiary's place of residence. Nonetheless, some decisions, such as giving or withholding consent to medical care, are clearly outside a trustee's power. Traditionally, a guardian of the person was needed to make medical decisions on behalf of an incompetent person who did not have family members able or willing to make such decisions. (See Chapter 12 and the Statutory Appendix.)

Joe and Maria Villalobos say they have both executed living wills. One question is whether the documents are properly executed. Some states require elaborate execution formalities and restrict the persons who may act as witnesses; in Indiana, the living-will statute is also the—perhaps the only—form for making a living will. If the documents accurately convey their wishes, they may prove to be useful, to mean what they say. However, they may not accomplish all that the couple wish them to do. By their very nature, living wills are advance directives. As such, the directions given in living wills usually are broad and vague. The imprecise terminology used in most living wills leaves open such questions as whether a patient's condition makes the living will operative and whether the proposed treatment is the type that the declarant wishes to have withheld. And even when the document is clear, recent behavioral research indicates that physicians often do not pay attention to living wills.

In addition to or instead of depending on their living wills, Joe and Maria should consider naming an agent to make medical decisions on their behalf should they become incapable of making their own treatment decisions. A *health care agent* (attorney-in-fact for health care or attorney-in-fact under an all-purpose durable power) can use her knowledge of the patient's personal desires as well as information about the patient's condition and the risks and benefits of proposed treatment to formulate a decision on the patient's behalf.

A number of states now authorize a person to name a health care agent. Some states have included in their living will statutes authorization to name an agent to make health care decisions. Other states have a separate health-care-consent statute that authorizes health care agents. Still other states have amended their durable power of attorney statutes to authorize an attorney-in-fact to make medical decisions. Even in states without specific legislative authorization many lawyers think a health care agent may be named by using a durable power of attorney. Many states provide statutory agents (relatives, guardians) who have "pull the plug" authority in the absence of an appointment by the patient. (See Chapter 12 and the Statutory Appendix.) If a client wants to have his attorney-in-fact make health care decisions, that authority should be clearly stated in the document creating the durable power of attorney. (Some statutes provide required language for this.) If a client has both a living will and a health care agent, care should be taken that the instruments are consistent.[2]

---

2. The list of documents that might be in play—(i) an all-purpose durable power that includes health care power (not included in our example from the Indianapolis Bar As-sociation form, Form 5, *supra;* (ii) a durable power of attorney for health care (only); and (iii) the agency authorized in the Health Care Decisions Act (Statutory Appendix),

Because the nature of the transactions differs, and because the third parties who rely on the documents differ, drafting durable powers of attorney for health care differs from drafting durable powers for financial matters. Here are a couple of examples:

Mr. Brown executes a springing power of attorney that gives his child Amanda Brown power to withdraw money from his bank account if Mr. Brown becomes incompetent to handle his financial affairs. If Amanda Brown enters a bank and hands a teller a copy of the durable power and asks the teller to withdraw $1,000 from her father's account, the teller is going to want some proof that Mr. Brown is incompetent, that Amanda Brown has authority to act under the springing durable power. Ordinarily, of course, Mr. Brown would not accompany Amanda on this trip to the bank, and even if he did, the teller would not feel comfortable evaluating his competence. (Of course, the teller might be glad to hand the money to Mr. Brown, if Mr. Brown appears as competent as ever and will sign a receipt for it.)

In the medical context, the scenario plays differently. Physicians and hospital administrators are the third parties who must be convinced health care authority given in a durable power is effective. The principal is in the care of these third parties. Moreover, physicians are accustomed to making determinations as to whether their patients are capable of making their own health care decisions. A physician's certification of incapacity (or of inability to communicate) often is the mechanism triggering the effectiveness of a durable power (or of a health care agency). Because the third party is in a position to evaluate the principal's ability to act for himself, and because the third party is usually willing to make that determination, the triggering mechanism in a health care agency is often less elaborate than the mechanism triggering effectiveness of, or delivery of, a financial durable power. A simple statement to the effect that "I intend to create a power of attorney for health care that will take effect whenever I am unable to make my own health care decisions and will continue during that incapacity" is sufficient in some states. We have heard of cases in which health care powers consist of notes made on hospital charts.

Second example: Amanda Brown is the party who initiates the transaction; she enters the bank and asks for money from her father's account. An attorney-in-fact named to handle financial or business affairs usually initiates the transaction with the third party and must convince the third party that the attorney-in-fact has authority to enter into the transaction on behalf of the principal. It is more likely that the bank will deal with Amanda if she has a present (not springing) power of attorney. For the same reason, successor attorneys-in-fact are often given present

discussed in Chapter 12. The practice in the Notre Dame Legal Aid Clinic is to recommend "(i)" and "(iii)."

powers and asked not to use the power until the prior appointed agent ceases to be able to act, or delivery of the successor's power is delayed until it is needed. So, rather than giving Amanda's brother a power that says he may have access to his father's account if his father becomes incompetent and if Amanda is unable to act on her father's behalf, her brother is given a present power and asked not to use it unless and until both his father and Amanda become incompetent.

In contrast, in the health care setting, it is often the third party—the physician or an employee of the hospital—who initiates contact with the agent. A decision must be made about care for a patient who cannot communicate, and the health care providers look for someone authorized to make the decision. Often decisions must be made quickly, and the unavailability of the first-named agent is sufficient reason to turn to a successor agent. Therefore, it is helpful for a single document to name all of the persons who are authorized to act on behalf of the patient and to allow the health care providers to deal with a successor whenever the prior named agent is unavailable or unable to act on behalf of the patient. A statement that "if the person named as my health care agent is not available or is unable to act as my agent, I appoint the following person(s) to serve in the order listed below" is common. (See Chapter 12 and the Uniform Health Care Decisions Act in the Statutory Appendix.)

Executing the documents is only the first step. Copies of the documents should be given to the agent(s), to other family members, and to the principal's physician. The principal should discuss with her health care agent as many health care issues as she thinks might possibly arise. Relevant issues might include do-not-resuscitate orders, artificial nutrition and hydration, hospice care, and nursing home placement. (Chapter 12 contains a sample.) In addition to talking with the agent, the principal should speak with her family members and with her physician about both her philosophy of care and about the delegation of authority to the named agent(s).

In Joe and Maria Villalobos's case, it is likely that they will name each other as primary health care agents and then one or more of the children as successor(s). Discussion with the children about the delegation of authority and the order chosen is important. The purpose of such a discussion is not only to eliminate confusion if at some time a child is called upon to make a decision for either Joe or Maria, but also to minimize feelings of jealousy, inadequacy, or rejection that might otherwise be experienced by a child whose name is low on the list. In many families the parents make it clear that they hope all of the children will be able to confer and reach a consensus decision, but that it is wisest to give authority to speak to one person so that a decision may be made even if not all of the children are available or if they do not agree. The order of priority among children often follows birth order, or geographic proximity to the parents' residence.

Exercise 11.3

Make a checklist of the questions you would want to ask Mr.
and Mr. Villalobos before you would feel ready to draft a
durable power or health care agency—either or both—for
them.

HIPAA. Thomas J. Murphy, an elderlaw specialist practicing in
Phoenix, advises against using springing durable powers, because, he
says, federal law bars access to medical evidence on incapacity, and: "A
person cannot become an agent under a springing POA until the requisite
showing of incapacity has been made," so that an agent will not "have
access to medical records … that may indicate incapacity until …
appointed as an agent." Some lawyers draft separate releases, effective
without springing, in an attempt to solve the "Catch 22," as Mr. Murphy
calls it. Other lawyers draft broad releases into their power documents
(see below). (See References and Bibliography for discussions by Mr.
Murphy and by Miriam R. Adelman of the New York Bar.)

HIPAA is the acronym for the federal Health Insurance Portability
and Accountability Act of 1996 (42 U.S.C. 1320) and consequent regulations issued by the Office of Civil Rights of the federal Department of
Health and Human Services. Medical providers, faced with drastic
federal criminal penalties, invoke these federal rules when relatives and
agents seek patient information. In the *Mougiannis* case (New York
Appellate Division, 2005) discussed by Ms. Adelman (see References and
Bibliography), the patient's agent had both of the powers we discuss in
this chapter and in Chapter 12 and was the patient's daughter besides,
but the hospital refused to release the patient's (mother's) records
because the patient was no longer a patient in the hospital. It took
litigation through two levels of the New York courts to get the records,
even in the face of a New York statute: "Notwithstanding any law to the
contrary, the agent shall have the right to receive medical information …
necessary to make informed decisions regarding the principal's health."
(Indiana's version of the Uniform Durable Power of Attorney Act gives the
attorney-in-fact "access to records, including medical records, concerning
the principal's condition.")

The Hospital lost the case in *Mougiannis*. Legislators seem to do
their best toward the same end, although the day may come when a
provider, or, perhaps, a federal bureaucrat will argue that state protection
is pre-empted by HIPAA. Meanwhile practitioners such as Mr. Murphy do
one of three things in the face of the federal privacy rule:

(1) They abandon such creative and useful devices as the springing
power.

(2) They consult the state of authorities and advise their clients, as Tom Shaffer's former firm did in 2005: "We do not believe a specific 'HIPAA authorization' is necessary."

Or (3) They give that advice and then say (as Tom Shaffer's firm did), "There are reports of hospitals, clinics, and doctors' offices not cooperating with healthcare representatives," and offer their clients an "HIPAA Authorization."

Here is some sample borrowed language being used in health care agencies drafted in the Notre Dame Legal Aid Clinic:

> I intend for my health care agent to be treated as I would be with respect to my rights regarding the use and disclosure of my individually identifiable health information or other medical records. This release authority applies to any information governed by the Health Insurance Portability and Accountability Act of 1996 (a.k.a. HIPAA), 42 USC 1320d-d-8 and 45 CFR 160-64.

> I authorize any physician, health care professional, dentist, health plan, hospital, clinic, laboratory, pharmacy, or other covered health care provider, any insurance company, and the Medical Information Bureau Inc. or other health care clearinghouse, that has provided treatment or services to me or that has paid for or is seeking payment from me for such services, to give, disclose, and release to my [health care agent or attorney-in-fact], without restriction, all of my individually identifiable health information and medical records regarding any past, present, or future medical or mental health condition, to include information relating to the diagnosis and treatment of HIV/AIDS, sexually transmitted diseases, mental illness, and drug or alcohol abuse.

> The authority given my [health care agent or attorney-in-fact] shall supersede any prior agreement that I may have made with my health care providers to restrict access to or disclosure of my individually identifiable health information. The authority given my [health care agent or attorney-in-fact] has no expiration date and shall expire only in the event that I revoke the authority in writing and deliver it to my health care provider.

Exercise 11.4

HIPAA drafting is an area in which, as a lawyer's experience grows, she tends to develop a *policy*.

(a) She may be impatient with bureaucratic responses to the agents her clients authorize in durable powers and health-care agencies, study the federal materials and state statutes (e.g., the New York statute at issue in *Mougiannis*), and decide, as many lawyers have, that HIPAA does not require special effort on her part.

(b) She may, as Tom Shaffer's firm did, offer an additional document and offer it to clients:

> Healthcare powers of attorney may also authorize the healthcare representative to have access to the principal's medical records and consent to their disclosure. Although we do not believe a specific "HIPAA Authorization" is necessary, there are reports of hospitals, clinics and doctors' offices not cooperating with healthcare representatives. To ensure that a healthcare representative can access medical records and authorize their disclosure, we have drafted a HIPAA Authorization to help alleviate these problems.

(c) But, in that case, what *is* the document? If it aims to do what the language-for-insertion, just quoted, aims to do, it may not meet Mr. Murphy's "Catch 22" concern—that the document authorizing disclosure is dependent on itself ...

(d) ... which may lead her, as it has some Hoosier lawyers, to draft a separate, free-standing HIPAA authorization that will depend on the fact that the client (patient) is competent when he signs both it and the springing durable power ...

(e) ... or even, in setting up the free-standing authorization, make herself, the lawyer, agent for purposes of unfreezing medical information that would be, we suppose, one way to make it more likely that the client (or her agent) will return. On the other hand, the problem may never even come up (see "(a)").

(f) She could, we suppose, write to her congressperson and ask for legislation that would make HIPAA and her powers practice mesh better.

B. MONEY

Mr. and Mrs. Villalobos are fortunate; they own a nice home, and they have a decent pension, Social Security income, and considerable savings. They have health insurance that, combined with Medicare, will adequately cover the cost of even catastrophic medical care. Their main financial concern arises from the possibility that one or both of them may need long-term custodial care as a result of a debilitating mental or physical illness.

Consider the major sources of retirement income—Social Security, qualified pension plans, savings, and other sources of retirement income (the lottery?). Each of these topics is complex. Our discussion is cursory but we fear that omission of these topics could lead to the incorrect impression that lawyers, or more particularly wills and trusts lawyers, need not concern themselves with their clients' incomes.

1. SOCIAL SECURITY

Joe and Maria are like most retired Americans: The federal Social Security program provides most of their income. At $2,200 a month, it would not support them, but they could hardly get by without it. They are relatively better off than most retirement Social Security beneficiaries. From an "estate planning" point of view, the largest disadvantage of this asset is that it cannot be used in planning; the most their lawyer can do is take it into account. On the other hand, it is a dependable benefit and it will—most of it will—continue, at a lower amount, during the widowhood of whichever of them survives.

Social Security retirement is not need-based, but it is retirement based. The modest nest-egg wealth of the Villaloboses, including Joe's pension, does not affect either their eligibility or the amount they receive. Nor will income from employment if either or both of them takes a job at Wal–Mart. They are qualified for the program because (i) they or one of them worked, and they and their employers paid payroll taxes, (ii) for a sufficient period of time, and (iii) at rates of pay proportional to the amount of retirement benefits they receive.[3] If they (or one of them) had not met these time and amount requirements, they would probably have qualified—or eventually might have qualified—for old-age benefits under a parallel federal welfare program, the Supplemental Security Income program, which is need-based and significantly stingier—but would be available only if they were impoverished and would be affected by pension income and employment.

Joe and Maria were eligible for maximum retirement benefits at age 65. (Congress has raised this retirement age—it will increase gradually and be 67 for persons born after 1960—but that change will not affect these clients.) They could have retired earlier (at age 62) at lower rates of pay. At age 65 each of them became eligible for Medicare, both parts, and, if they elected Part B Medicare, would have had their retirement benefits reduced to pay Part B premiums.[4]

Women do not do as well under Social Security retirement as men do. The A.A.R.P. Bulletin reported in January, 2006: "39.5 per cent of American women 65 and older are kept out of poverty by Social Security. Still, 12.5 per cent of older women are poor despite the benefit." Part of

---

3. The Social Security Administration reported, in February 1999, that 70 per cent of payroll taxes go to benefits for retired people and to some survivors of deceased insured people, 19 per cent to the Medicare program, and 11 per cent to benefits for insured disabled people and their dependents. Administrative expense, the government says, is less than one per cent. Funds collected but not currently needed are loaned to the federal government.

4. See Part C–1 of this chapter, *infra*.

the reason is life expectancy: "Women at 65 are likely to live 19 more years—three years longer than men. But they'll get less income if caregiving obligations force them to move in and out of paid jobs." And, of course, some aging mothers and grandmothers may never have been in paid jobs and therefore may not be covered by Social Security (but only by the stingier Supplemental Security Income program—and maybe not even by that).

Exercise 11.5

Widows have Social Security retirement coverage, but the coverage is limited. Here is a common question, asked and answered in the "Ask Our Experts" column in an issue of the A.A.R.P. Bulletin:

Q. I am getting Social Security benefits based on my deceased husband's record. If I remarry, will I lose my benefits?

A. It depends on your age. If you remarry before you turn 60 (when widows' benefits can begin), you are no longer eligible for your former spouse's benefits unless the remarriage ends. If you remarry after age 60, you can continue to collect your deceased husband's benefits as a widow or you can receive your current husband's benefits, whichever is higher. If you're eligible for benefits based on your own earnings and they are the highest, you will get those.

---

2. PRIVATE RETIREMENT PLANS

Private retirement plans, including income-tax-qualified employee and individual retirement plans, are an important part of many clients' retirement planning. (Consider the wealth of the Kennedys, in Chapters 3 and 10.) The topic of retirement plans is broad, technical, and detailed—all three. Even a summary of the tax-qualification requirements is more than we will include in this chapter. Suffice it to say that those requirements range from minimum participation and coverage rules, and rules prohibiting discrimination in favor of certain employees, to vesting rules, provisions for a surviving spouse of an employee who dies prior to retirement, and rules requiring continuing support for the surviving spouse of a retired employee.

Retirement plans take a variety of forms: There are profit-sharing plans, pension plans, employee stock ownership plans, and stock bonus plans. To the extent that we will focus upon any of these devices, we will look at pension plans both because that is what Joe and Maria Villalobos have and because they are common assets, at least for middle-class workers. Pension plans come in at least two main varieties. There are defined benefit plans and defined contribution plans (also known as money-purchase pension plans). A defined benefit plan is what it sounds like. Enough money is contributed to the plan to fund a predetermined retirement benefit that is paid to the retired worker, usually for the rest of her life after retirement. The amount of the retirement benefit often is determined by a combination of factors such as years of service and the employee's level of compensation at the time of retirement. With a defined contribution plan there is no fixed retirement benefit. As the label suggests, with a defined contribution plan both the employer's contribution and the employee's contribution—if any—are fixed. The level of contribution usually is based upon a percentage of the employee's compensation. The amount of benefits the retired worker will enjoy depends upon the investment experience of the fund at the time of the worker's retirement.

Qualified retirement plans receive favorable tax treatment. An employer's contributions to a qualified retirement plan are deductible by the employer on its federal income tax return. The maximum amount that is deductible varies, depending upon the type of plan. Actual employer contributions, as well as benefits payable, as distinguished from deductibility of contributions, are also limited; if the limits are exceeded, the plan will not be qualified. The amount that an employer contributes to a qualified plan on behalf of an employee is not included in the employee's taxable income in the year that it is contributed. The employer's contributions are taxed to the employee when the employee receives them, usually in the form of a pension upon retirement: The employee's income tax is deferred until retirement. Congress provides retirement tax-deferral devices for the self-employed and in addition to employer plans. Examples include various individual retirement accounts and "Keogh" plans.

Between the time of contribution of funds into a qualified plan and pay-out to retirees, the funds in a plan are invested. Earnings realized by investing the plan funds are not subject to income tax while they remain in the plan. This fact, of course, permits earnings to compound much more quickly than if income taxes were being paid yearly on the earnings. Like employer contributions, investment earnings on the funds are included in the employee's taxable income upon receipt. (Again, the tax is deferred.)

The news in 2006 is rife with reports of cut-backs in pension programs; the subject has become, in business, what *Newsday* columnist Marie Cocco calls "a lose-lose proposition for millions of workers." As we revise our book in 2006, legislation such as the "Pension Protection Act" is pending in Congress. There is some federal back-up protection for pensions but, generally, that does not protect workers from employers who do not have plans—or who have and then abolish, reduce, or convert their plans.[5]

3. MORE MONEY

Social Security and Joe's pension may not be enough; that seems unlikely on present facts, but it would not have seemed unlikely in the days of rampant inflation that were the setting of the first edition of this book—and those days may return. And, in any event, many of your clients will not be as well off as the Villaloboses. Ms Berman's article poses the question, from one of her readers: "I'm worried about maintaining my standard of living after I retire. What groundwork can I lay now to help meet future costs?" Ms Berman's answer, in part, quotes a book called *The Truth About Money* (Ric Edelman, 1996): "The most important thing to do is to start putting money away now so that you can draw from it later," an answer that would have pleased the Puritan Fathers and Benjamin Franklin, but not a useful answer for clients who are already retired and living on fixed income. For them, we notice (but do not necessarily recommend) three possibilities—use of the equity in their $150,000 home by way either of (i) a loan on it or (ii) a reverse mortgage and (iii) use of their $60,000 in paid-up life insurance.

a. A "Home Equity" Loan

Many home-equity loan arrangements are scams. We quote a few paragraphs from Michael Hudson's still valuable *Merchants of Misery* (1996): "[H]omeowners often have large chunks of equity built up in their homes, because they've spent decades paying their house notes and because real estate values have inflated rapidly in the past two decades. That equity ... makes a tantalizing target for loan brokers, tin men, second-mortgage companies, and banks."

Mr. Hudson quotes a legal-aid lawyer who tries to undo or frustrate such loan arrangements: "It's like finding a ten-dollar bill in the street and saying: This is mine, I'm going to take it. Their attitude is: 'It's there for the taking.' "

"One day recently," this legal-aid lawyer "had office visits from three ... women who came in for wills and other legal work not related to home-equity loans.

"As an experiment, he asked each if they owned their homes. All three said yes.

"Were the houses paid for, or almost paid for? They were.

"Were they getting calls from people who wanted to loan them money on their houses?

---

5. See Daniel Gross, "The Big Freeze," A.A.R.P. Bulletin, March 2006, p. 10.

"All three of them, we got the same answer. 'I get calls every day of the week, Monday through Friday, two and three times a day....'

"The deregulation of the mortgage industry set the stage for second-mortgage scams against these homeowners in much the same way that deregulation of savings and loans created the S & L scandal. Since the late 1970s, federal and state lawmakers have struck down almost all limits on second-mortgage interest charges or created loopholes that made it easy for creative lenders to skirt usury laws.

"At the same time, the federal government does nothing to regulate second-mortgage companies. It has left responsibility for policing the industry with the states, many of which take a hands-off approach. In Massachusetts, for example, second-mortgage companies have generally been able to charge whatever interest rate they want—as long as they notify the state attorney general's office if they intend to charge 20 per cent or more." Mr. Hudson's legal-aid colleague noted that the Georgia legislature "wiped out all laws limiting mortgage interest except for a 1908 loan-sharking law. It limits interest on loans to five per cent *per month*...."

Mr. Hudson gives a case: "Frank and Annie Ruth Bennett have owned their house on a tree-lined street in Atlanta since 1969. Over the past decade, they've made several attempts to fix it up. Each time, they've fallen a little more into debt to second-mortgage companies. Even so, they still had managed to hang onto more than half the equity in the house, which is worth nearly $50,000.

"Now, with a debt of around $28,000 ... plus about $7,000 left on their original house note, most of the value in their property belongs to someone else. His Social Security check and her wages as a cafeteria worker ... aren't enough to keep up. They have fallen behind and have had to pay delinquency charges.... 'It's just tight, I'm telling you,' Annie Ruth Bennett said.

"She said that when a man called recently trying to sell her storm windows, she told him: 'When I get ready, I'll get in touch with you.' He called again, and she put him off again. Then he had a woman—his wife or secretary—call them again.

" 'I just tell them I'm sleepy and I don't feel like talking,' [Mr.] Bennett said. 'I'm not signing no papers. I've learned my lesson.' "

Home-equity loan scams are outside the scope of our book, but one of us is a legal-aid lawyer, and another of us used to be. We have discovered that people such as the Bennetts, who seek to maintain or improve their homes, can often obtain free services from area agencies for the elderly, or no-interest or low-interest loans from local government housing agencies, or both, and avoid home-equity lenders. Still, the home is a tempting source of financial help. The New York Times reported in February 2006 (citing the Federal Reserve Bank) that "household net worth" hardly increased in 2001–2004. Savings dropped by 23 per cent, but the average value of a family home in the U.S. increased almost as much as savings dropped. What has declined in one category may be found in the other: The Associated Press reported in March 2006 that the median price of homes in 2005 rose more than 40 per cent in Phoenix and Orlando, and around 10 per cent in much of the Midwest.

It is within the scope of our book to notice that this solution for Mr. and Mrs. Villalobos is one that will not assure additional income for them for the rest of their lives; that, when used for short-term expenses, it will increase, not decrease, their monthly expenses;[6] and that there is a real danger that this loan will end up in foreclosure and that their home will not be available for them to live in, or to pass along to their children and grandchildren.[7]

b.   Property Tax Relief

The elderly client's problem may be taxes—not federal income taxes but old-fashioned, local, ad valorem real-property taxes. Here is a case from Karen Hube's "On the Money" column in the January–February, 2006, A.A.R.P. magazine:

> Mona Smithfield lives in a great neighborhood, and that's a mounting problem for the 83-year-old former librarian. While her two-bedroom Cape on a leafy street in Westport, Connecticut, has more than doubled in value, to about $700,000 in a decade, the bad news is that her property tax bill has soared as well. Last year it was just shy of the $8,400 she collects from Social Security. A widow with few other assets, she could sell the house, get an apartment, and have a nice cushion left over for living expenses. Yet Mona (we changed her name to preserve her privacy) can't imagine leaving the home she loves.

---

6.   A question put to Robert Bruss (see the next section) indicates the possibilities: "My husband is 81, and I am 78. We have a home-equity loan on our house for almost 50 per cent of its market value. The monthly payment of $732.84 for five more years practically wipes out our Social Security and pension incomes, not leaving much for food, medicine, and household expenses, but we want to stay in our home as long as possible. Is there any hope ...?" Mr. Bruss was not able to suggest much more than that they sell their home; as his title for the day indicates, a reverse mortgage was not available for this situation because the home-equity loan was too high. Robert L. Bruss, "Equity Loan Limits Chance at Reverse Mortgage," The South Bend Tribune, Jan. 22, 2000, p. C–4, col. 1.

7.   Reform efforts are in the air and in the business press. The reformers range from congressional committees, the Federal Reserve Board, and legislators in several states, to an array of organizations that seek governmental regulation of what they call "predatory lending practices." The reformers aim at abuses such as above-market interest rates, high initiation fees, high rates of default and foreclosure, aggressive and deceptive solicitation practices (particularly in low-income neighborhoods), and "respectable" institutional investment in abusive lenders. Reformers that regulate or influence investment banks point to the fact that respectable investors take assignments of home-equity mortgages at rates that are well above the conventional secondary mortgage market. A growing local remedy, suggested in the text, has been the development of local non-profit lenders that are able to finance home-improvement projects at relatively modest interest rates.

Mona's problem becomes more general and even more touching when Ms Hube invokes survey results showing that 95 per cent of Americans past age 75 want to stay in their homes. The solution in many states may be an inquiry to the local assessor's office, for information on tax freezes or tax deferments for the elderly. Ms Hube continues:

> Fortunately, there's help for homebodies like Mona. Most states have supplemental tax-relief programs for property owners who've reached age 65 (a few go lower). Typically, states increase the homestead exemption or offer a property tax credit to reduce the bite imposed by counties, cities, and towns. Some states freeze the assessed value of property when the owner reaches a specified age. And many states—as well as municipalities including Mona's Westport—let people with incomes under certain levels put off paying some or all the tax until their homes are sold, though they must pay interest on the deferred amount.

> That last option, available in about half the states and the District of Columbia, can serve as a safety net for homeowners with enough equity in their property. Mona qualified under Westport's rules because she's well past the minimum age of 65, lives in her home, and had less than $75,000 in income last year. The town will collect the tax plus 4 per cent in simple (not compound) interest per year whenever the home is sold.

> Even if maintenance costs, health care expenses, or difficulty living independently spur a move later, deferred payment can help make ends meet in the meantime. The critical question for the homeowner is, What will remain from the sale after paying the tax bill? (Some places cap deferrals at 75 per cent or 85 per cent of the home's market value.) For Mona, whose equity in her house is approaching $500,000, the virtues of the program are clear. Assuming her home's value climbs only 3 per cent a year (nationwide the average annual gain since 1968 has been 6.4 per cent), property taxes rise 4 per cent a year, and she moves out at 90, Mona stands to come away with more than $600,000 after paying the tax and what's left on her mortgage.

c.   Reverse Mortgages

Reverse mortgages are less dangerous than home-equity loans, and they can be made to last for life, but they are expensive.

Robert J. Bruss, a real-estate lawyer and broker who practices in the District of Columbia and writes a syndicated weekly newspaper column on property matters, often advises readers to consider reverse mortgages as a way to increase their retirement income. "Over 80 per cent of senior citizens own or are buying their residences," he wrote in 1996, "and 62 per cent of this group own their homes free and clear.... Eighty-four per cent of these seniors say they want to stay in their homes...."

"[M]any seniors are house rich but cash poor. Sixty per cent of [one lender's] reverse mortgage clients are women living alone, usually between 71 and 81, with a median income of only $10,400...."

Mr. Bruss then explains what he is talking about: "[A] reverse mortgage, just the opposite of a forward mortgage, pays the senior citizen homeowner. No repayment is required until the borrower either moves out of the home or dies. Then the home is sold and the reverse mortgage principal and interest are paid from the sales proceeds."

There are available reverse mortgages that pay the homeowner for a fixed time, rather than for life. "These loans are not very popular and are most often used by borrowers age 90 or older." There is another version that pays until the homeowner dies, so long as she or he resides in the home. And there is a third type—the most attractive, we think, for clients such as ours—that pays "lifetime monthly advances [that] continue as long as the homeowner is alive, even if the home is sold. This type involves purchase of an annuity at the time of reverse mortgage origination."

Any of these arrangements, although in form a secured loan, should be "non-recourse." That is, there should be no danger of a deficiency judgment against the homeowner, beyond the value of the home. "The borrower never has personal liability for repayment, even if the home declines in value and the loan balance owed is greater than the market value.... [I]f your home is worth $150,000 when you die, but your reverse mortgage principal and interest total $175,000, the lender gets all the home sale proceeds and incurs a loss."[8]

Reverse mortgages are complex to obtain, and may pay less than the homeowner may have hoped. But they are much safer than home-equity loans and, as Mr. Bruss points out, can provide income (not reduce income), and provide it for life (or, in the case of a couple, for two lives). At the time Mr. Bruss wrote, these arrangements were available from four lenders, two of which were affiliated with the federal government and therefore, presumably, regulated to protect consumers.

A bit of reading of the comparative charts in Ken Scholen's *Your New Retirement Nest Egg* (1996) indicates that Mr. and Mrs. Villalobos can add several hundred dollars to their monthly income with a reverse mortgage—at a very high expense as compared with the administrative

---

8. Robert J. Bruss, "The Pros and Cons of Reverse Mortgages for Senior Citizens," The South Bend Tribune, July 20, 1996, p. D–3, col. 1.

Reverse mortgages are not available for homes in retirement communities where the formal arrangement the "owner" has is not, as we lawyers say, "fee simple." Pat Caporicci, in "The Mail" section of the January–February 2006 A.A.R.P. Magazine (p.8):

"[We] wish we could get one ourselves. But because we live in a 55–and-over community where we lease the land on which our home is built, we are ineligible to apply for a reverse mortgage. Our home is the only asset we have, and the Department of Housing and Urban Development should consider helping seniors in this situation."

cost of their other sources of income, and at the loss of their home as an asset to give their children. The monthly income figures suggested for them range from about $200 to about $500, depending on many variables. Closing costs for a reverse mortgage on a home such as theirs will be about $2,000, plus "points" (another $1,500 to $3,000 in this case); these in effect reduce the lump-sum value on which their monthly income is computed. It is evident from this source, and from Mr. Bruss's many discussions of reverse mortgage, that this financial device is very profitable for lenders. If it is a good deal for older clients it is only because it is better for them than the available alternatives.

d. Life Insurance Viatical Settlements

Finally, our clients have $60,000 in paid-up life insurance. They can probably take out the "cash surrender value" of these policies, to increase their income, if they are willing to give up the insurance. (Most life-insurance policies held by older people are some form of "whole life" insurance that contains—to describe the arrangement roughly—both "term" insurance on their lives and a "savings account" that is available if the value of the insurance becomes more important than the insurance itself.) That step would require advice from a sophisticated insurance consultant; we keep handy the name and telephone number of a consultant who works with the area agency for the aging and does not charge for his advice.

One point such an advisor might cover is that a viatical settlement may net them more than surrender of their policies, for cash value, to their life-insurance companies. Reports from bar-association programs, as we write, point to purchase by viatical-settlement investors who pay as much as 120 per cent of cash value. The difference is increased where the insurance companies charge a fee to those who seek cash surrender on policies. Another alternative would be to borrow on the life insurance—a loan from the insurer to the insured, often at an attractive interest rate, which of course is to be paid back. (If it is not paid back, the loan balance is deducted from the proceeds of the policy when the insured person dies.)

A viatical settlement is the sale of life insurance, by the insured person, to an investor who is in effect betting on the seller's early death. The term "viatical" comes from the Latin word "viaticum." To the Romans, it meant money or provisions for a journey, but the term came to refer to the last rites—the eucharist or communion given to Christians who are dying or are in danger of death. The "settlement" part of the device amounts to an assignment of life insurance by the insured person.

Viatical settlements began as a response to the financial needs of AIDS patients. Many people dying of AIDS in the 1980s had little or no health insurance but were overwhelmed by medical bills. Often their only assets were life insurance policies. Such patients began selling their life insurance policies to viatical-settlement companies. These companies would pay the policy holder a lump-sum percentage of the policy's face value and take over its premium payments. In return, the company would become the policy's beneficiary. When the policy holder died, the settlement company would collect the policy's full face value and distribute to its investors the difference between its proceeds and what it paid the policy holder. An investor in viatical settlements hopes that the viator dies soon, because that means a greater return on his investment.

Conflicts of interest appear when viatical settlement companies have paid "finder's fees" to physicians or attorneys who have provided medical or legal advice to one whom the industry has come to call a "viator." Some states now have statutes prohibiting the practice; Wisconsin prohibits physicians from investing in the life-insurance policies of their patients. Twenty-four states regulate the industry by requiring licensing of viatical-settlement providers, state approval of the viatical-settlement contract form, an "informed consent" procedure for viators, and a standardized payment schedule based upon the viator's life expectancy. Some potential viators have lied to insurance companies regarding their health in an effort to buy life insurance policies. In one case a viator with HIV sent a healthy person in his place for the insurance company's medical examination. Based upon the imposter's good health, the viator obtained a life insurance policy which he promptly sold to a viatical settlement company.

Viatical settlements are not everywhere considered securities. In some states the companies do not need to follow the disclosure laws promulgated by the S.E.C. or by state-level securities regulators. Hoping to attract investors, the companies may invent a non-existent viator or fraudulently exaggerate a viator's medical condition. As we write, legislatures in several states are considering state-level securities regulation for sale of viatical settlements.[9]

e. Insurance

Our local daily provided, in December 2004 some wind-up and in-general advice that would be useful for our clients Mr. and Mrs. Villalobos, as they survey their insurance program. Title: "Insurance You Don't Need":

> Financial advisers will typically urge you not to ignore important things such as insurance. It's critical to make sure you have insurance—for your home, your health, your car and often your life. There are other kinds of insurance that can serve you well, too—such as disability insurance or long-term care insurance.
>
> But not all insurance is equally valuable. Don't be overinsured. Don't buy insurance you don't need. Consumer Reports magazine recently

---

9. See also *Security Trust Corp. v. Estate of Fisher*, 797 N.E.2d 789 (Ind. App. 2003), and *Accelerated Benefits Corp. v. Peaslee*, 818 N.E.2d 73 (Ind. App. 2004).

listed several kinds of insurance policies that most people don't need. Here's a recap of some of them:

— Mortgage life insurance. A cheaper way to pay off your mortgage if you pass on is through term life insurance.

— Credit card loss prevention insurance. Instead of forking over as much as $180 per year for this, bask in the knowledge that by law, your losses because of card theft are capped at $50 per card.

— Cancer insurance. For many of us, our regular health insurance plan will cover medical expenses related to cancer treatments. So don't buy this unless it's offering more than you have, at a reasonable price.

— Accidental death insurance. This costs around $600 annually, and you're extremely unlikely to die via an accident. Term life insurance is a more logical investment.

— Involuntary-unemployment insurance. This is designed to make minimum payments on your credit card or auto loan debt should you become unemployed. A better bet is simply to maintain an emergency fund that can cover your living expenses for three to six months or more....

— Flight insurance. Sorry, but you're extremely likely to survive every flight you take. If you're concerned about premature death, look into term life insurance.

— Life insurance. Even this can be unnecessary for some. If you're single and childless, for example, and no one depends on your income, skipping it may be best.

C. HEALTH CARE

1. MEDICARE

Medicare is a nationwide federal health insurance program for the elderly and for certain disabled persons. Like Social Security retirement, Medicare eligibility is not determined on the basis of an applicant's financial need. The program is administered by the Social Security Administration and by the Health Care Financing Administration, but the government contracts with private insurance carriers to handle the day-to-day local administration. Medicare is provided in three parts: Part "A" of the program pays for hospital services, "skilled care" services, and some home-health care, but it is limited, and may, as Congress continues to struggle over "reform" of the program, grow more limited. In the program as we write:

— Part "A" coverage is limited to a defined "spell of illness" that, as we write, covers no more than ninety days of coverage, sixty days in most cases. The Medicare managers impose or negotiate their own rates of pay, based on the patient's diagnosis, which the hospitals must accept if they accept Medicare patients. (These rates are significantly lower than non-Medicare patients pay; the pay-off for the hospitals is that they are assured of payment at the lower rates.) Even during the covered period, the Medicare beneficiary is required to make "co-payments," which, as we write, are $800 for each sixty-day "spell of illness," more if hospitalization lasts longer.

— Pay for care at "nursing facilities" that are usually affiliated with hospitals but offer less intensive care is even more restricted. Admission to such facilities is limited to particular levels of diagnostic complexity, which, as the Medicare rules have developed, distinguish between "skilled care" and such other versions as "intermediate care." Medicare pays only for "skilled care," which is a severely limited category, and then only for limited periods of time and at limited rates of coverage. The majority of patients in nursing homes do not require "skilled care"; almost no care in nursing homes qualifies for Medicare coverage.

Part "A" Medicare pays for hospice care, for dying patients, subject to "co-pay" provisions and other restrictions.

Part "B" Medicare is a low-cost insurance program that is available to Part "A" participants for a relatively low monthly charge. (Low because the government pays the portion of Medicare cost the patient does not pay.) Part "B" is for physician fees, diagnostic tests, medical supplies ordered by physicians, rental charges on medical equipment, ambulance charges, some kinds of physical therapy, and some of the home-health care that Part "A" Medicare will not pay for. Neither part of the Medicare program covers check-ups, most eye care, hearing aids, dental care, or long-term care in nursing homes. Neither part is generous in paying for preventive care. As we write, Part "B" pays only eighty per cent of the amount it approves for coverage.

Part "D" Medicare is the controversial prescription-drug program added since the fourth edition of our book and, as we write for the fifth edition, mired in controversy and in evident and predictable flux.

This slight survey demonstrates, we hope, that the Villaloboses— who are insured under Parts A and B of the Medicare program—need to think about supplementary medical coverage, if they do not already have it. They may decide they need, first of all, insurance that will pay what Medicare will not initially pay when they see a medical practitioner or go into a hospital, but for many patients the most significant gap in Medicare coverage is and will remain, despite "Part D," prescription medication. There are a variety of "medi-gap" policies commercially available that claim to meet these needs. These are, for the most part, regulated by federal and state authority. Premiums for them vary according to coverage, deductibles, and whether the medical providers are approved by government. In some cases, employers provide this supplemental coverage for retired employees, conditioned on the employees' being covered first by both parts of the Medicare program. Some coverage, both Medicare and under "medi-gap" insurance, is available from managed-care organizations.[10] These often eliminate some of the limitations of one or both Medicare programs, but at the expense of limiting available medical providers.

That supplemental coverage for relatively ordinary medical care is part of our clients' situation. The other and perhaps graver part arises from the chance that one or both of them will need to be cared for in a nursing home. (About one in four elderly Americans faces some time in a nursing home.) The Medicare program provides virtually no coverage for that risk, which is really two risks: (i) That the clients will not be able to pay nursing home charges, which may run as high as $5,000 per month; and (ii) that they will not be able to obtain payment for nursing home care from the Medicaid program (of which more below) until they impoverish themselves.

2. MEDICAID

For Joe and Maria Villalobos, the federal-state Medicaid program is a safety net available to one or both of them for long-term care in a nursing home, and for the possibility that they will not have "medi-gap" insurance and might be able to obtain, when they both continue to live at home, Medicaid assistance for medical care that Medicare does not cover. If they qualify for Medicaid, they will be covered by the broadest and most thorough form of medical insurance in the economy of the United States. But they will qualify for Medicaid only if they are impoverished. And they will be impoverished, eventually, if one or both of them requires nursing-home care, at an annual cost, as we write, of as much as $60,000 or more each. (About half of Americans who are in nursing homes have their expenses paid by Medicaid.) The way the system works, in broad effect, is, first impoverishment, then Medicaid.

Those two facts—the broad coverage under the Medicaid program and the fact that it is only for the very poor—describe the challenge of

---

10. Larry Katzenstein, writing in the New York Times (Feb. 16, 2000) summarizes the differences between H.M.O. Medicare and fee-for-service Medicare (useful advice still, but complicated now by "Part D" Medicare):

"Original Medicare may be preferable for those who

– have a comprehensive employer-provided retiree health plan or can afford supplemental coverage.

– want to choose their own doctors and hospitals.

– have homes in different parts of the country.

– qualify for assistance from Medicaid."

"A Medicare H.M.O. may be preferable for those who

– face high bills for prescription drugs.

– cannot afford supplemental insurance.

– are flexible about doctors and hospitals and are willing to switch H.M.O.s should theirs withdraw from Medicare.

– are satisfied H.M.O. customers or have a doctor who also participates in a Medicare H.M.O."

Medicaid planning. Part of that challenge is contemplating the possibility that one or both of our clients may become very poor. From a planning perspective, for families such as the Villaloboses, the more common part of the challenge is attempting to rearrange their property ownership so that they will be treated by the government as very poor when they are not very poor. Or, to put the second part of the challenge another way, planning so that they can obtain Medicaid assistance and still leave some of their wealth first for the surviving spouse and then for their children.

The Medicaid program is a *categorical welfare* program. That is, it is available only to certain categories of poor people, not to poor people in general. For our purposes the relevant categories are disability (see also Chapters 3 and 10) and old age (described roughly the same way as for Medicare). The program is also available to blind people, to disabled people of all ages, and, in some states, to a category called the "medically needy." The rules for qualifying for medical aid in these categories, and qualifying within each category, vary from state to state: The Medicaid program is paid for with both state and federal money (about two-thirds federal), and governed by both federal and state rules. The rules vary significantly from state to state.[11] The program is, everywhere, administered by local welfare agencies that are about as quirky as zoning commissions or school boards.

The planning challenge—as we saw when we discussed David Kennedy in Chapter 3 and Chapter 10—is a matter of owning property so that it does not count for Medicaid purposes. In David's case the challenge was more easily met than it will be for the Villaloboses, because the wealth provided for David's "special needs" trust will not be David's wealth. The wealth we might be able to "protect" for Joe and Maria is their wealth: If we can come up with something useful for them, it will be their own wealth they set aside in order to qualify for taxpayer-provided care that is intended for people who have no wealth. The challenge can be described in four steps:

First, in order to file a promising application for coverage by Medicaid (when, say, Joe would be referred by his doctor for nursing-home care that will cost $4,500 a month), Joe (assuming for the moment that he is widowed) cannot have assets worth more than, say, $1,500 ($2,000 in some places). (These figures change; they will no doubt always be low.) Assets aside, whatever income Joe has will have to be paid to the nursing home before Medicaid will pay anything. Some assets do not count (a small planning opportunity): Joe's application, for example, could disclose but not count a paid-up funeral and burial plan, ordinary amounts of personal property; in some circumstances, a home with its furnishings; and an automobile. Counting his home may depend on

---

11. Federal rules, of course, control, but federal rules allow states to choose whether to provide or to withhold certain significant benefits. About half the money spent on Medicaid in the late 1990s went for these optional benefits.

whether his doctor says Joe may return to it; if that hurdle is passed, Joe may also be able to retain a fund for maintenance of the home. There may be similar restrictions on not counting the automobile. If Joe's application succeeds, Medicaid will pay the difference between his income and his nursing-home bill, and even allow a small monthly amount for Joe to buy toiletries with. (The rate Medicaid pays the nursing home is set by the program; it is much less than what the nursing home charges paying customers. As is true of the Medicare program, except [sigh] as to "Part D," the government here acts, as a powerful collective-bargaining agent might, to negotiate or—since it is the government—impose low rates.)

Second, the situation changes if Maria is living and does not need care in a nursing home. Medicaid has complex sets of (federal and state) "well-spouse" rules that were designed, in federal legislation, to make it possible for the spouse who is not in an institution to continue a sort of lower-middle-class life outside. The administrators do an inventory of the family's property when Joe goes into the nursing home; they then divide it for Medicaid-qualification purposes. Whatever ends up on Joe's side of the ledger has to be spent for nursing-home care, before Medicaid takes over (with a couple of exceptions). Whatever ends up on Maria's side does not count for Medicaid-qualification purposes (until Maria has to follow Joe into the nursing home; see Step One). The division does not have to be a half-and-half division. Maria is allowed to retain—i.e., Medicaid will not count—a sizeable amount of cash (half, up to a stated maximum in the neighborhood of, say, $95,000 in 2005), the home, an automobile, furnishings, personal property, etc.

And Maria's continuing income does not count either, up to a modest, middle-class amount, but also *above* at least a very modest, *lower*-middle-class amount—so that Joe's income and, if need be, his income-producing wealth can be applied on Maria's side of the ledger until the floor is met. The legislation and regulations provide that all of these figures have built-in adjustments, some keyed to the Consumer Price Index, some keyed to the federal poverty level, and all are vulnerable to whatever Congress and state legislatures are up to when they propose to "reform" the Medicaid program.

The planning trick at this *second* level is to move as much as possible from Joe's side of the ledger to Maria's side of the ledger. The rules will specify how much income Maria can have without that income being counted on Joe's qualification for Medicaid. Income that can be moved from Joe's Social Security and pension checks to Maria's income will not have to be paid to the nursing home (Medicaid will pay more). If Joe's income for that purpose runs too low—and even, maybe, without regard to Joe's income—the value of what was assigned to Joe when the application was made can be moved to Maria's side of the asset ledger, until it produces enough income to come up to the floor. (This figure is keyed to the federal poverty guidelines; in 2005 it was $2,378 per month.[12])

The *third* step is to re-arrange property ownership so that assets, and income from assets, will not be counted toward Joe's qualification for Medicaid. (Anything that comes to be counted has to be spent before Medicaid will spend anything, so that, when Joe dies, his estate will have no assets Medicaid can reimburse itself from.) We suggested one example just above, when we noticed that Joe, in order to provide minimum income for his "well spouse" (Maria), is able to transfer income-producing assets to her, which assets are then regarded as hers and not his (for Medicaid purposes), during Joe's life and after his death.

When moving assets and income from the nursing-home spouse to the "well spouse" is taken care of (in an ideal situation), the nursing-home spouse is left without assets. Future "estate planning," then, is for the "well spouse."

Finally, the *fourth* step is to attempt a "special needs trust" for the Villalobos family (for Joe now, and maybe for Maria later), as we did for David Kennedy in Chapters 3 and 10, so that there is a source of support from the family for expenses not covered by the Medicaid program—a source of support that will not be counted for Medicaid purposes. Welfare and Medicaid "reform" legislation over the past several years has substantially reduced the opportunities for this fourth sort of planning. Your elder author can remember describing a plan, from a farming state, in the 1970s: The elderly grandparents owned a $4 million farm; their lawyer told them how that farm could be put into a "special needs" trust that would not count for Medicaid purposes, so that these millionaires could qualify for public assistance if (when) either of them went into a nursing home: The couple transferred the farm, "in fee," to their children, who then transferred it to themselves as "special needs" trustees for their parents. It is now virtually impossible, in our opinion, for a couple to set up a Medicaid-effective "special needs" trust for themselves. But some lawyers continue to think it can be done. We wish them (and their clients) well.

We turn next to Medicaid planning that focuses on the death of the surviving spouse, to transfer of the property our client or our client couple hope to preserve for their children as they also seek qualification for Medicaid: It is still possible to transfer property outside the scope of Medicaid, to the next generation, provided enough time passes between the transfer and the Medicaid application (three to five years, depending on circumstances, as we write). And it is still possible to transfer property

---

12. William J. Holwager, "Avoiding *Tannler* Transfers: Supplemental Needs Trusts and the Institutionalized Spouse," in Indiana Continuing Legal Education Forum, Recent Developments in Long Term Care (1998).

between spouses, which property would then evade the division made of the couple's patient's property at the time of Medicaid application, and would then be available for disposition to the next generation after the death of the surviving spouse.

Consider then a client whose assets are less troublesome than most: An elderly widow. She has an adult daughter, lives on Social Security retirement income and has Medicare, and has managed to pay off the mortgage on her modest home. She wants to leave the home to her daughter, but she also wants to be eligible for Medicaid for medical expenses that may become large and may not be covered by Medicare, including, especially, nursing-home care. The challenges here are two: (i) to get the home to her daughter without losing a chance at Medicaid eligibility; and (ii) to remove the home from her ownership, so that the state cannot reach it, after her death, to reimburse itself for what it paid for her care under the Medicaid program. (Virtually anything a person owned at death—even when it did not count as a Medicaid resource during life—can be reached under "estate recovery" provisions in state and federal law.)

It is not possible to do this with a will that gives the home to her daughter. Our elderly widow can, while she lives, qualify for Medicaid without having her home count as an asset—so long as she continues to live in it or is, in her doctor's opinion, able to return to it. But when she goes into a nursing home, and is likely to spend the rest of her life there, the value of the home will have to be applied to the nursing-home bills before Medicaid will begin paying those bills. And, even if the home did not count as an asset for purposes of eligibility (if, for example, she obtained Medicaid assistance for expensive prescription medicines but did not go into a nursing home), the home can be reached under "estate recovery" rules after she dies.

Prior to recent "reforms," there were several types of inter-vivos transfer that would preserve the home, permit Medicaid qualification, and put the home outside the "estate recovery" system. The client could, for example, put the home into joint-and-survivor ownership with the daughter, or she could transfer the home with a retained life estate. (Sometimes these devices worked because of regulatory provisions that said only "marketable" assets counted as Medicaid resources. Neither the survivorship interest nor the life estate would be marketable during the client's life; both would be gone at the client's death, and therefore not available for "estate recovery.") Those devices have been for the most part eliminated by recent "reforms."

Under the rules as we write, our client could transfer the home outright to her daughter and hope to live long enough to have it not count as a Medicaid asset. The critical factor in this device is time: Anything a Medicaid applicant has transferred for inadequate consideration counts as an asset, for a while, and then no longer, and therefore prevents

Medicaid coverage for a while. How long "for a while" is varies according to the form of the transfer and the state of "reform" rules at the time. If less than the specified time, it counts as if the applicant still owned it. If less than that and the application is for nursing-home care, the rules provide for a reduction in the amount counted as a Medicaid asset; the computation for this reduction consults the local cost of nursing-home care and the amount of time that has elapsed since the conveyance. The asset value is reduced, month-by-month, using the local nursing-home cost each month.

Transfers that are in trust, particularly transfers to an irrevocable trust in which the Medicaid applicant has retained an interest, are subject to special trust rules that, as we write, are in a state of confusion. Time was, for example, when a farmer could transfer the farm into an irrevocable trust (to a trustee other than himself) and retain the income from the trust property without having the principal of the trust count as a Medicaid asset. Congress thought it removed that possibility in the 1994 "reforms," but there remained an opinion among some lawyers that it was still available.

We would, after thinking about all of this, respect a lawyer who decided not to bother with Medicaid transfers at all and contented herself with recommending medi-gap insurance and, perhaps, long-term care insurance[13] to guard against the possibilities of estate depletion—all of that with the understanding that people have to be impoverished to get Medicaid, and that is the way things will probably be until the United States manages to provide adequate medical protection for all of its citizens.[14]

Exercise 11.6

In an exercise in Chapter 10 we asked you to consider the morality of establishing a special needs trust for David Kennedy, a trust that would allow him to qualify for public assistance programs designed for disabled persons who are poor and that, at the same time, would provide David with the advantages that his middle class parents would have pro-

---

13. It would cost Joe and Maria about $5,000 a year to buy long-term care insurance which would cap coverage at about $150,000, or about three years for each of them, and would pay less (by about $125 a month) than the cost of nursing-home care.

14. Meanwhile, some lesser developments are promising. Indiana, for example, now approves long-term care policies, sold commercially, that cover an amount of nursing-home cost that is equal to the value of the insured person's assets. If that insurance is in place, the assets are not counted for Medicaid eligibility: If Joe and Maria Villalobos buy $200,000 worth of such insurance, to cover $200,000 of their assets, Joe will be able to obtain Medicaid coverage at the nursing home from the day he enters, and, assuming both spouses are insured, that "estate" can go to the next generation without risk of "estate recovery." See Mary Ann Hack, "Long Term Care Insurance," in Indiana Continuing Legal Education Forum, Recent Developments in Long Term Care (1998).

vided for him if they were still alive. We pointed out that public funds spent on persons in David's situation are not available to assist other persons who may have greater financial needs than he has. The fact that David's parents may totally disinherit him and that David has no funds of his own and is unlikely to ever accumulate any may have influenced your response to our previous question.

Medicaid planning for middle-class people like Joe and Maria Villalobos may put a finer point on the moral issue, or at least may have before the amendments described above. The recent changes made by Congress that allow a community spouse to retain substantial assets and that protect much more income for a community spouse seem to indicate a shift in public policy, a shift that makes Medicaid look like a middle-class entitlement program. Does the new legislation change your attitude toward "planned poverty" in any way?

D. CONCLUDING THOUGHTS

As we said when we began this book, lawyers are inevitably counselors. Every client who walks into a lawyer's office comes with more than a legal question, especially when the client is trying to "arrange her affairs" for the possibility that she may soon experience a period of physical or mental disability. A lawyer who chooses to ignore the non-legal questions, feelings, and doubts that the client brings with her may draft a perfectly worded instrument but will seldom have a perfectly satisfied client.

If a client's property, and the hassles of managing it, are part of what keeps him alive, his lawyer ought to consider what the effect might be if a trustee bought and sold his securities, or if someone else mowed his lawn. (See the Eliot interview in the Appendix.) The older of your authors had a client many years ago—a man older and less healthy than Mr. Villalobos, with more money. He came to the office asking for an inter-vivos trust. His assets were in real estate for the most part, real estate he had selected, bought cheap, tended, and then pushed people around on. He had a coronary condition, but he was up early every morning looking after his investments, dreaming of new commercial horizons, and living as he had for 15 years of retirement. Your elder author, a relatively non-directive legal counselor, balked at the trust idea, maybe even urged against it a little. Finally the client talked himself out of the inter-vivos trust. He might not have lived as long (another 14 years as it turned out) or have been as well if he had used the trust. Today, with the advent of durable powers of attorney that can be used to fund a standby trust, he could have his trust (he may well have wanted it, sort of as another acquisition appropriate to his station in life) without needing to give up control of his property.[15]

REFERENCES AND BIBLIOGRAPHY

A. Barnes, L. Frolik and R. Whitman, Counseling Older Clients (1997)

K. Boxx, "The Durable Power of Attorney's Place in the Family of Fiduciary Relationships," 36 Georgia Law Review 1 (2001)

E. Clark, C. Kruse, and L. Sirico, "Symposium: Thoughts on Advance Medical Directives," 37 Real Property, Probate, and Trust Journal 537 (2002)

D. Clifford, Make Your Own Living Trust (3d ed. 1999)

F. Collin, Jr., J. Lombard, Jr., and A. Moses, Drafting the Durable Power of Attorney: A Systems Approach (2nd ed. 1987)

J. Crain, "HIPAA—A Shield for Health Information and a Snag for Estate Planning and Corporate Documents," 40 Real Property, Probate, and Trust Journal 357 (2005)

C. Dessin, "Acting as Agent Under a Financial Durable Power of Attorney: An Unscripted Role," 75 Nebraska Law Review 574 (1996)

The Economist, "Forever Young: A Survey of Retirement," March 27, 2004

Elder Law Advisory, "Re–Thinking Living Wills," June 2005; Rene H. Reixach, "Interspousal Transfer Limitations," September 2005; Milton A. Adelman, "Life Estates and Medicaid," November 2005; "New Medicaid Asset Transfer Rules Under the Deficit Reduction Act of 2005," March 2006

L. Ershow–Levenburg, "Guardianship Actions Against Individuals Who Have Selected an Agent as Power of Attorney: When Should the Courts Say 'No'?" 7 Marquette Elder's Advisor 84 (2005)

D. Esmont, "Revocable Living Trust–Traps and Pitfalls," Res Gestae, April 1993, p. 458

J. Fairbanks, "Lifetime Care Contracts—Are Senior Citizens Putting All Their Eggs in One Basket?," 4 Probate & Property 4 (March/April 1990)

W. Fatout, "Guardianship Medicaid Planning: Estate Planning from the Probate Court Perspective," Res Gestae, July 1999, p. 21

---

15. Among all of the things that change in ways that bear on this chapter are these statistics (among many in Floyd Norris's "Off the Charts" report in the Oct. 29, 2005, New York Times (p. B–3):

– By 2050, 21 per cent in the U.S. will be over 65. (It will be 34 per cent in Italy, 36 per cent in Japan.)

– At present, years of life expectancy for persons age 65 (U.S.), for men: 17, for women: 21.

– In 2004 (U.S.), 28 per cent of the labor force were ages 65–69.)

S. Fatum, "Living Will and POA for Health Care—Should a Client Have Both?" Illinois Bar Journal, February 1993, p. 105

L. Frolik and R. Kaplan, Elder Law in a Nutshell (3d ed. 2003)

T. Gallanis, A. Dayton, and M. Wood, Elder Law (2000)

D. Hoffman, S. Zimmerman, and C. Tompkins, "The Dangers of Directives or the False Security of Forms," Journal of Law, Medicine, and Ethics, Spring 1996, p. 5

A.H. Hook, "Mr. Hook, I Have Been Cued," Elder Law Advisory, Oct. 2000

M. Hudson, "Found Money: Need Cash? A Reverse Mortgage Might Be the Answer, But Make Sure You Know the Costs," A.A.R.P., November–December 2005, p. 36

V.L. Jarnagin, "A Call to Action for National Long–Term Care Reform: Indiana's Private–Public Cooperative as a Model," 29 Indiana Law Review 405 (1995)

L. Joire, "Ethical Problems in Limiting Medicaid Estate Planning," 12 Georgetown Journal of Legal Ethics 789 (1999)

J. Lemke and S. Moskowitz, "Protecting the Gold in the Golden Years: Practical Guidance for Professionals on Financial Exploitation," 7 Marquette Elder's Advisor 1 (2005)

L. Mezzullo, M. Woolpert, and A. Christopher, Advising the Elderly Client (1992)

J. Miller, "Voluntary Impoverishment to Obtain Government Benefits," 13 Cornell Journal of Law and Public Policy 81 (2003)

C. Mooney, Y. Asher, S. Bass, K. Hambleton, S. Kraskin and H. Prensky, "Alzheimer's Disease—Planning for Dementia," 2 Probate & Property 7 (November/December 1988)

D. Moy, Living Trusts: Designing, Funding, and Managing a Revocable Living Trust (1997)

T. Murphy, "Dealing With HIPAA: Powers of Attorney, Record Releases, Court Orders, and Subpoenas," 5 Marquette Elder's Advisor 183 (2004)

Practicing Law Institute, Representing the Elderly Client (1989)

L. Ray, "The Viatical Settlement Industry: Betting on People's Lives Is Certainly No 'Exacta,' " 17 Journal of Contemporary Health Law and Policy 321 (2000)

J. Regan, The Elderly Client and the Law (1990)

I. Schneider and E. Huber, Financial Planning for Long–Term Care (1989)

K. Scholen, Your New Retirement Nest Egg: A Consumer Guide to the New Reverse Mortgages (1996)

S. Shepherd, "Living Wills: Why a Patient's Last Wishes Are Not Always Respected," 34 Howard Law Journal 229 (1991)

D. Shilling, "Assisted Living Regulation," Elder Law Advisory, February 2006

B. Silverstone and H. Kandell–Hyman, You and Your Aging Parent (1975)

P. Strauss, R. Wolf and D. Shilling, Aging and the Law (1990)

M. Weatherford, "An Ethical Outlook on Attorneys Preparing Wills and Trusts," 23 Journal of the Legal Profession 391 (1999)

J. Zeleznik, F. Post, M. Mulvihill, L. Jacobs, W. Burton, and W. Dubler, "The Doctor–Proxy Relationship: Perception and Communication," Journal of Law, Medicine, and Ethics, Spring 1999, p. 13

Chapter 12

PLANNING FOR THE FINAL JOURNEY

To begin this, at the end, I (Tom Shaffer, writing by himself in this chapter for the fifth edition of this book) am in my own old age retired from the Notre Dame Law Faculty and a volunteer supervising attorney in the Notre Dame Legal Aid Clinic, in South Bend, Indiana. I supervise law students who have been "certified" by the Indiana Supreme Court to practice law under supervision. I get to be the supervision. We "do wills," just as county-seat lawyers wearing green eyeshades, in offices over the bank, have done in Indiana for decades. Even as the practice has changed: The bank buildings installed elevators, for one thing. For another, we and our sister and brother lawyers have discerned that "doing wills" these days involves more than doing wills. The last chapter provides several examples. This chapter provides another:

One of the student-lawyers I work with scheduled a house call to an elderly widow in South Bend. The agenda was to finish work on her will. I tagged along. It occurred to me later that what he and his client did that day is what should have happened years ago between Terri Schindler Schiavo and a lawyer in Florida, when Terri was well and could decide what she would want done for her when she appeared to be at the end of her life, capable of being kept apparently alive by medical technology, but not able to communicate with her doctor.

The newspapers in 2003–2006 were full of the case of "the brain-damaged Florida woman who [was] at the center of a major legal battle over whether she should remain on [a] feeding tube that [kept] her alive" (as the Catholic News Service described Terri in 2003). Her case went through every possible level of both state and federal courts, and was kicked around in both state and federal legislatures, before the feeding tube was finally withdrawn and Terri slowly died. My student-lawyer was, in his house call, seeking to plan to prevent that sort of legacy being given to his client and her family. After the will was signed, he asked his client what she would want done in a case such as Mrs. Schiavo's. Our client said, "No tubes."

Suppose the student-lawyer had not asked, and suppose his client had done nothing about "end of life decisions." Suppose she had then ended up in a coma with a tube or two or three to help keep her body alive. The law in that situation says that the patient has a constitutional right to refuse the tubes or to order them taken out. She also has a constitutional right to have someone give those directions when she cannot give them. She has those rights when she has done nothing. The Indiana

Health Care Decisions Act (a version of the Uniform Act; see the Statutory Supplement), and similar legislation elsewhere, specified, for every person, a substitute decision maker—usually a member of the family. Our client had a decision maker, whether she knew it or not, if she were to say nothing. Indiana's version was at issue *In the Matter of Sue Ann Lawrance*, 579 N.E.2d 32 (Ind. 1991). That was unclear in the Schiavo case, which meant that much of the wrangle there was in courts dealing with guardianship.

Back to our house call: There were two problems with the substitute provided by law. Her student-lawyer explained these to our client. The first problem was that she might have wanted a different decision maker than the one the Indiana statute provided.[1] The second comes up when the patient has done nothing about end-of-life decisions or nobody is around who knows she has a substitute to make decisions for her. (You would be surprised at how many people in hospitals don't know about substitute decision making; doctors and hospital people regularly want a patient's family to go to court for a guardian when one purpose of the Act and the public policy announced in the *Lawrance* opinion is to avoid trips to the courthouse.)

The way to solve the first problem is to avoid the Act's list of surrogates and appoint an agent to make end-of-life decisions. The agent will have the same authority the substitute under the Act would have had. The way to solve the second problem is for our client to make sure, while she is well, that her doctors and her hospital know that she has someone to act for her, without guardianship; to make sure these medical providers know to contact her agent (or to contact the substitute decision maker provided by law); to make sure her substitute decision maker is available when end-of-life issues are raised; and to make sure her substitute decision maker knows what she wants. (The situation seems to call for a family conference at the time the client's will is made. Or at least for a counseling session with the client and her agent, and then for a letter to the client.)

Richard Russo's novel *The Risk Pool* (1988) describes what happens when no one is around to act as or to ask about a health care agent. The narrator visits the hospital room in which his father, Sam Hall, just died:

> If he had been able to do it, he'd have spared himself two senseless operations during those final weeks, and God only knew how many indignities, the last of which was an heroic attempt to resuscitate him, in direct violation of the written instructions he'd placed on the

---

1. Indiana Code Sec. 16–36–1–5: "[C]onsent to health care may be given .. by a judicially appointed guardian ... or by a spouse, a parent, an adult child, or an adult sibling ... or ... by the individual's religious superior, if the individual is a member of a religious order...." The Indiana statute does not establish a priority among these. A health care agent would resolve priority questions and otherwise trump the list. Compare the Uniform Health Care Decisions Act (see the Statutory Supplement).

bedstand and which now were neatly folded somewhere in the same unmarked envelope that contained the anatomical gift he'd made of his remains.

* * *

Clients and their doctors and hospitals often think, as Sam Hall perhaps did, that the easy way out of these complexities is for their patients to sign living wills. The Indiana Living Will Act is the product of struggle through more than one session of the legislature as, among others, the Roman Catholic Bishops sought to forestall euthanasia. The signed document becomes effective when a doctor "certifies in writing" that the patient is incurably ill, that "death will occur within a short time," and that "the use of life-prolonging procedures would serve only to artificially prolong the dying process." If the doctor writes those things, the doctor is free to follow the patient's (the form's) direction to let her "die naturally." As a result (I am told) of negotiation with the Catholic Bishops, the Indiana form includes a set of choices, boxes to be checked, on nutrition and hydration: [i] insert the tubes, [ii] don't insert the tubes, [iii] let my legal decision-maker decide about tubes. My student-lawyer's house-call client would, I guess, have checked "[ii]," but maybe she did not know, yet, that she could have a friend to decide for her.

In any event, my student-lawyer's opinion was that a living will was not best for his client. There are three problems with living wills. The first is that doctors and hospitals often do not know they exist, and when they are known to exist, *two-thirds of the time they are ignored*. Tubes are installed because there is no one present, at the moment of decision, who knows the patient has a living will that says, No tubes. (Or, perhaps, no one is around who cares to say anything about tubes.) Perhaps it would help if someone who knows were around and announcing a decision she was empowered to make, a decision the medical provider was legally required to follow.

Another problem is that the living-will document is often too narrow in restricting effectiveness to incurable disease and death-within-a-short-time, as Indiana's statutory form does. And the third problem is that the patient has to guess, when she signs the form, what will be the matter with her when the form, if anybody looks at it, might come into play.

* * *

In any case, the student who was this elderly woman's lawyer advised against depending on the substitute decision-maker provided by law, and did not suggest a living will. He recommended (and drafted) appointment of an agent. Our client chose a friend to be her health care agent. That left the moral problem commentators on the Schiavo case argued about. Our client raised it. She asked me: "Would this health care agency, in this case, have been all right under Catholic teaching?" Our client, a faithful Roman Catholic, asked me that. She did not ask her (student-) lawyer. I suppose her choice of me was because I was manifestly older. I assume my student and I appeared equally pious. I suggested that she talk to her pastor. She said, "I don't want to talk to my pastor. I want to know what you think." I said I thought an Indiana health care agency (called a proxy in other states) is consistent with Catholic teaching.

[That part of the story, even when a bit theological, is hardly unfamiliar in county-seat law practice. The rest of these bracketed paragraphs may be: My colleagues on the Notre Dame law faculty, not all of them Catholics, have given significant attention to our client's moral question. You will be astounded to learn that we professors don't agree. My view, and the student-lawyer's view, was that nothing in the moral theology of complicity (to use a harsh old Catholic word) stands in the way of accepting the fact that the law gives the end-of-life decision to the patient and to a substitute decision-maker; and nothing stands in the way of appointment of an agent to take the place of the substitute decision-maker.

[The complicity argument assumes it would be immoral—it would be *euthanasia*—for the patient or her substitute to give orders that would directly result in her death. The complicity question is whether the lawyer who drafted a document or advised on a statute, long before the end-of-life crisis arose, is what lawyers might call an accessory to euthanasia. I am not persuaded by either argument. I feel, too, that answers to the harder moral questions the surrogate or agent may have (in a case like Mrs. Schiavo's) are in a couple of paragraphs from Pope John Paul II's encyclical "On the Value and Inviolability of Human Life" (1995):

[First, the Pope wrote that refusing what he called "aggressive medical treatment" (and the medical and legal evidence is that surgical installation and maintenance of feeding tubes is aggressive medical treatment) is not a kind of killing. "Certainly there is a moral obligation to care for oneself and to allow oneself to be cared for," the Pope wrote, "but this duty must take account of concrete circumstances. It needs to be determined whether the means of treatment available are objectively proportionate to the prospects for improvement. To forgo extraordinary or disproportionate means is not the equivalent of suicide or euthanasia; it rather expresses acceptance of the human condition in the face of death."

[Those are abstract guidelines. I think they come close, though—even for non-Catholics—to the unpredictable future that is before a patient and her lawyer when a health care agency is prepared, or a living will signed, or when a person decides that she need to do nothing about end-of-life decisions because the law will provide a surrogate for her when the time comes for end-of-life decisions.]

The harder moral job will come if the surrogate or agent is asked (as Mr. Schiavo was) to decide how such moral guidelines apply to a grim reality. And that is a matter of conscience for the patient or her decision maker, not a matter of law. A lawyer or supervisor of student-lawyers might point out that, as a matter of law, the substituted decision can belong to a person who cares about our client. That lawyer's work is, in my opinion, consistent with sound morals. (There are also, of course, analyses of the ethical question from Jewish and Protestant and Islamic thinkers. I keep a file.... [See References at the end of this Chapter.])

* * *

In any event, my student-lawyer and I, having opined (well, I opined) on the moral question, should not have left the matter with power in the friend, but no guidance for her. How will our client's friend know how best to decide? Our client said to us, "No tubes." But there are tubes and tubes and some are only minor therapy. (Think of how the dentist keeps your mouth cleared out so she can clean your teeth.) What about ventilators and blood transfusions and band-aids? The statutory authority of a surrogate or health care agent extends to "any care, treatment, service, or procedure to maintain, diagnose, or treat an individual's physical or mental condition" (Indiana). All the way down to band-aids, pats on the back, and therapeutic lollipops. How is the agent to know, aside from consulting what the Pope called "acceptance of the human condition in the face of the death," both what her friend wants and what will be (in every sense) best for her friend?

Our client and her friend ought to talk about that. Her friend might want to keep notes. Our client's lawyer might want to supply guidelines for the conversation. Many have been published. Here, for one example, is a device proposed by the American Bar Association Commission on Legal Problems of the Elderly (the A.B.A. Commission worked from a Veterans Administration booklet on "planning for future medical decisions"). We offer it as an aid to conversation; lawyers who suggest its use beyond that (as, say, some sort of written addendum to the appointment of the agent) need to make sure it will not dilute the agent's authority[2]:

* * *

---

2. Under Indiana Code Sec. 16–36–1–4(b), for example, the agent's power is curtailed when the person who has given the power "has indicated contrary instructions...."

What if You …	Definitely Want Treatment	← →		Definitely Do Not Want Treatment	
a. No longer can walk but get around in a wheel chair.	1	2	3	4	5
Comment _____					
b. No longer can get outside—you spend all day at home.	1	2	3	4	5
Comment _____					
c. No longer can contribute to your family's well being.	1	2	3	4	5
Comment _____					
d. Are in severe pain most of the time.	1	2	3	4	5
Comment _____					
e. Are in severe discomfort most of the time (such as nausea, diarrhea).	1	2	3	4	5
Comment _____					
f. Are on a feeding tube to keep you alive.	1	2	3	4	5
Comment _____					
g. Are on a kidney dialysis machine to keep you alive.	1	2	3	4	5
Comment _____					

What if You …		Definitely Want Treatment	← →	Definitely Do Not Want Treatment	
h. Are on a breathing machine to keep you alive.	1	2	3	4	5
Comment _____					
i. Can no longer control your bladder.	1	2	3	4	5
Comment _____					
j. Can no longer control your bowels.	1	2	3	4	5
Comment _____					
k. Live in a nursing home.	1	2	3	4	5
Comment _____					
l. Can no longer think or talk clearly.	1	2	3	4	5
Comment _____					
m. Can no longer recognize family or friends.	1	2	3	4	5
Comment _____					
n. Other.	1	2	3	4	5
Explain_____					

* * *

Suppose Sam Hall's wishes had not been hidden away where nobody found them—or, apparently, wanted to find them. Compare Carol Levine's mother (see References):

> Although in good health until age 89, she repeatedly told us she did not want to die like our father, after a grueling and ultimately failed research protocol for a lethal leukemia, or like her demented

sister, being shuttled back and forth between nursing home and hospital. She trusted me as her health care proxy to protect her from a painful and dehumanized death. Our discussions, backed up by the papers … gave her a sense of security and comfort.… She reached her 90th birthday, her final goal. I held her hand and whispered the "Shema," the Jewish prayer that is supposed to be the last words a person utters, as she died peacefully at home.

* * *

Form for Health Care Agency

This is a form of appointment of health care agent under the Indiana version of the Health Care Decisions Act. The "If at any time" language was imposed by the Indiana General Assembly for durable powers that include health care authority; it probably applies as well to an appointment such as this one. (See Ch. 11 for discussion of the HIPAA provisions.)

FORM 8.   APPOINTMENT OF A HEALTH CARE REPRESENTATIVE

I Ann Boleyn Tudor voluntarily appoint my daughter, Mary Tudor, of 121 West Camelot Street, Indianapolis, Indiana, whose phone numbers are 555–555–5551 and 555–555–5552 (cell), as my health care representative, and I authorize her to act for me in all matters of health care in accordance with the law of Indiana on health care consent.

I authorize my health care representative to delegate decision-making power to another person.

I authorize my health care representative to make decisions in my best interests concerning withdrawal or withholding of health care, as that term is defined in the law of Indiana.

If at any time, based on my previously expressed preferences and the diagnosis and prognosis provided, my health care representative is satisfied that certain health care is not or would not be beneficial, or that such health care is or would be excessively burdensome, then my health care representative may express my will that such health care be withheld or withdrawn and may consent on my behalf that any or all health care be discontinued or not instituted, even if death may result.

My health care representative must try to discuss this decision with me. However, if I am unable to communicate, my health care representative may make such a decision for me, after consultation with my physician or physicians and other relevant health care givers.

To the extent appropriate, my health care representative may also discuss this decision with my family, my friends, and my advisors, to the extent they are available.

I revoke any and all advance directives, health care powers and proxies, and any and all other such documents that I have signed or authorized prior to the date of the execution of this document. I do not intend, however, to revoke the durable power of attorney in favor of Mary Tudor that I am executing at about the time I sign this document.

This appointment is to be exercised in good faith and in my best interest.

This appointment becomes effective and remains effective, if I am incapable of consenting to my health care, unless I revoke this appointment by notifying my health care representative, my health care provider, or the physician attending me, which revocation may be made orally or in writing, provided that I am at the time capable of consenting to health care.

I intend for my health care agent to be treated as I would be with respect to my rights regarding the use and disclosure of my individually identifiable health information or other medical records. This release authority applies to any information governed by the Health Insurance Portability and Accountability Act of 1996 (a.k.a. HIPAA), 42 USC 1320(d) and 45 CFR 160–164.

I authorize any physician, health care professional, dentist, health plan, hospital, clinic, laboratory, pharmacy or other covered health care provider, any insurance company, and the Medical Information Bureau Inc. or other health care clearinghouse that had provided treatment or services to me or that has paid for or is seeking payment from me for such service to give, disclose and release to my health care agent, without restriction, all of my individually identifiable health information and medical records regarding any past, present or future medical or mental health condition, to include all information relating to the diagnosis and treatment of HIV/AIDS, sexually transmitted disease, mental illness and drug or alcohol abuse.

The authority given my health care agent shall supersede any prior agreement that I may have made with my health care providers to restrict access to or disclosure of my individually identifiable health information. The authority given my health care agent has no expiration date and shall expire only in the event that I revoke the authority in writing and deliver it to my health care provider.[3]

3. These paragraphs (from "I intend for my health care agent" to this point) are meant to meet the requirements of the federal "HIPAA" statute. See the discussion in the last chapter.

The use of this form, or other appointment of a health care agent, should be coordinated with a durable power of attorney (such as the power suggested in the last chapter). The usual expectation, where the client has both, is that the health care provision in the durable power will be used, if needed, to contract for treatment and that this agency (or proxy) will be used only when the client (patient) cannot communicate with the health care provider. Conflict is unlikely if the same person is both attorney in fact and health care agent. If that is not the case, each document should refer to the other and state which is to be con-

Dated this ___ day of _____, 2___.

_____

Ann Boleyn Tudor

I declare that I am an adult at least eighteen (18) years of age and that at the request of Ann Boleyn Tudor I witnessed the signing of this document by her on the date noted above.

_____   _____

Signature   Printed Name

Address and Phone Number:

_____

_____

_____

REFERENCES AND BIBLIOGRAPHY

A. Caplan, J. McCartney, and D. Sisti, The Case of Terri Schiavo: Ethics at the End of Life (2006)

Conference on the Law of Death and Dying (J. Kim, ed.), 37 Loyola University of Chicago Law Review 279 (2006)

E. de St. Aubin, S. Baer, and J. Miller, "Elders and End-of-Life Medical Decisions: Recommendations to Attorneys Serving Seniors," 7 Marquette Elder's Advisor 259 (2006)

M. Elon, B. Auerbach, D. Chazin, and M. Sykes, "Euthanasia and the Right to Refuse Treatment," in Jewish Law (Mishpat Ivri): Cases and Materials (1999), at 637–696

A. Goodnough, "Behind Life-and-Death Fight, A Rift that Began Years Ago," The New York Times, March 26, 2005 (Terri Schiavo)

R. Hamel, Making Health Care Decisions: A Catholic Guide (2006)

S. Haredin, M.D., and Y. Yusufaly, M.D., "Difficult End-of-Life Treatment Decisions," 164 Archives of Internal Medicine 1531 (2004)

S. Jacoby, "The Schiavo Factor: Now the States Are Rushing to Decide Who Decides," A.A.R.P. Bulletin, May 2005, p. 14

A. Johns, "Older Clients with Diminishing Capacity and Their Advance Directives," 39 Real Property, Probate and Trust Journal 107 (2004)

sulted—especially when the issue is treatment for terminal conditions when the patient (client) cannot make her own decisions.

J. Keenan, S.J., L. Cahill, P. McCormick, J. Paris, S.J., K. Himes, O.F.M., T. Shannon, and J. Walker, "Notes on Moral Theology" and "Questatio Disputanda" (both on end-of-life decisions), 67 Theological Studies 99–174 (2006)

C. Levine, "She Died the Way She Lived," The New York Times, December 6, 2005, p. D–5

B. Lo, M.D., and R. Steinbrook, M.D., "Resuscitating Advance Directives," 164 Archives of Internal Medicine 1501 (2004)

M. Rosenblatt–Hoffman, "The Schiavo Odyssey: A Tale of Two Legislative Reprieves," 7 Marquette Elder's Advisor 357 (2006)

S. Saad, Living Wills: Validity and Morality, 30 Vermont Law Review 71 (2005)

M. Schiavo, Terri: The Truth (2006)

R. and M. Schindler, A Life That Matters: The Legacy of Terri Schiavo—A Lesson for Us All (2006)

T. Shannon and J. Walter, "Assisted Nutrition and Dehydration and the Catholic Tradition," 66 Theological Studies 651 (2005)

D. Sinclair, "Patient Self–Determination and Advance Directives," VIII Jewish Law Association Studies 173 (1994)

M. Sternberg, "Death of a Living Will," Moment Magazine, June 1999, p. 42

Symposium, "Reflections and Implications of *Schiavo*," 35 Stetson Law Review 1–205 (2005) (13 contributors)

E. Waugh, "The Islamic Tradition: Religious Beliefs and Healthcare Decisions," Park Ridge Center for the Study of Health, Faith, and Ethics (not dated)

*

APPENDICES

STATUTORY APPENDIX

ACCOUNTING

INDIANA CODE, SECTIONS 30–4–5–12 TO 15:

SEC. 12. (a) Unless the terms of the trust provide otherwise, or unless [accounting is] waived in writing by an adult, competent beneficiary, the trustee shall deliver a written statement of accounts to each income beneficiary or his personal representative annually. The statement shall contain at least: (1) all receipts and disbursements since the last statement; and (2) all items of trust property held by the trustee on the date of the statement at their inventory value.

* * *

(c) Upon petition by the settlor, a beneficiary or his personal representative, a person designated by the settlor to have advisory or supervisory powers over the trust, or any other person having an interest in the administration or the benefits of the trust, including the attorney general in the case of a trust for a benevolent public purpose, the court may direct the trustee to file a verified written statement of accounts.... The petition may be filed at any time, provided, however, that the court will not, in the absence of good cause shown, require the trustee to file a statement more than once a year.

(d) If the court's jurisdiction is of a continuing nature ... the trustee shall file a verified written statement of accounts containing the items shown in [Section 13(a)] with the court biennially, and the court may, on its own motion, require the trustee to file such a statement at any other time provided there is good cause for requiring a statement to be filed.

SEC. 13. (a) A verified written statement of accounts filed with the court ... shall show: (1) the period covered by the account; (2) the total principal with which the trustee is chargeable according to the last preceding written statement of accounts or the original inventory if there is no preceding statement; (3) an itemized schedule of all principal cash and property received and disbursed, distributed, or otherwise disposed of during the period; (4) an itemized schedule of income received and disbursed, distributed, or otherwise disposed of during the period; (5) the balance of principal and income remaining at the close of the period, how invested, and both the inventory and current market values of all investments; (6) a statement that the trust has been administered according to its terms; (7) the names and addresses of all living beneficiaries and a statement identifying any beneficiary known to be under a legal disability; (8) a description of any possible unborn or unascertained beneficiary addresses of all the trustees.

(b) The court may, either on petition or on its own motion, require the trustee to submit such proof as it deems necessary to support his verified written statement of accounts. The court may accept the unqualified certificate of a certified public accountant in lieu of other proof.

SEC. 14. (a) With respect to the annual written statement required by [Section 12], a beneficiary or his personal representative will be deemed to have discharged the trustee from liability as to that beneficiary for all matters disclosed in the statement if he approves in writing the trustee's statement.

(b) In a proceeding in which the court has been requested by petition to approve a verified written statement of accounts, any person authorized by [Section 12(c)] to petition for an accounting may file an appropriate responsive pleading, and if he does so, he must file it within the period of time after notice that a responsive pleading is required to be filed after service of a prior pleading under the Indiana Rules of Procedure.

(c) When a responsive pleading filed under subsection (b) of this section includes objections to any matter contained in the trustee's statement, those objections must be specific unless the court orders otherwise.

(d) Upon request for approval of a verified written statement of accounts and the filing of objections, if any, the court shall determine the correctness of the statement and the validity and propriety of all actions of the trustee described in the statement and may take any additional action that it deems necessary.

SEC. 15. (a) Subject to the right of appeal, a judgment rendered by the court under [Section 14], either approving the statement or disapproving it and surcharging the trustee, is final, conclusive and binding upon all the parties to the action who are subject to the jurisdiction of the court.

(b) Entry of the judgment by the court finally disposes of the matter and the clerk may not tax or charge a service fee for any year beyond that in which the judgment is rendered.

PERPETUITIES

Kentucky Revised Statutes Annotated, Sec. 381.216

In determining whether an interest would violate the rule against perpetuities the period of perpetuities shall be measured by actual rather than possible events; provided, however, the period shall not be measured by any lives whose continuance does not have a causal relationship to the vesting or failure of the interest. Any interest which would violate said rule as thus modified shall be reformed, within the limits of that rule, to approximate most closely the intention of the creator of the interest.

Vermont Statutes Annotated, Tit. 27, Sec. 501

Any interest in real or personal property which would violate the rule against perpetuities shall be reformed, within the limits of that rule, to approximate most closely the intention of the creator of the interest. In determining whether an interest would violate said rule and in reforming an interest the period of perpetuities shall be measured by actual rather than possible events.

POUR OVERS

Uniform Testamentary Additions to Trusts Act (1991)

(a) A will may validly devise or bequeath property to the trustee of a trust established or to be established (i) during the testator's lifetime by the testator, by the testator and some other person, or by some other person including a funded or unfunded life insurance trust, although the trustor has reserved any or all rights of ownership of the insurance contracts, or (ii) at the testator's death by the testator's devise to the trustee, if the trust is identified in the testator's will and its terms are set forth in a written instrument, other than a will, executed before, concurrently with, or after the execution of the testator's will or in another individual's will if that other individual has predeceased the testator, regardless of the existence, size, or character of the corpus to the trust. The devise or bequest is not invalid because the trust is amendable or revocable, or because the trust was amended after the execution of the will or the testator's death.

(b) Unless the testator's will provides otherwise, property devised or bequeathed to a trust described in subsection (a) is not held under a testamentary trust of the testator but it becomes a part of the trust to which it is devised or bequeathed, and must be administered and disposed of in accordance with the provisions of the governing instrument setting forth the terms of the trust, including any amendments thereto made before or after the testator's death.

(c) Unless the testator's will provides otherwise, a revocation or termination of the trust before the testator's death causes the devise or bequest to lapse.

New York Estates, Powers, and Trusts law, Sec. 13.3.3

[In the part of this Appendix, under Trustee As Life Insurance Beneficiary, *infra*]

POWERS OF FIDUCIARIES

Uniform Trustees' Powers Act, Sections 3–7

SEC. 3. (a) From time of creation of the trust until final distribution of the assets of the trust, a trustee has the power to perform, without court authorization, every act which a prudent man would perform for the purposes of the trust including but not limited to the powers specified in subsection (c).

(b) In the exercise of his powers including the powers granted by this Act, a trustee has a duty to act with due regard to his obligation as a fiduciary, including a duty not to exercise any power under this Act in such a way as to deprive the trust of an otherwise available tax exemption, deduction, or credit for tax purposes or deprive a donor of a trust asset of a tax exemption, deduction, or credit or operate to impose a tax upon a donor or other person as owner of any portion of the trust. "Tax" includes, but is not limited to, any federal, state, or local income, gift, estate, or inheritance tax.

(c) A trustee has the power, subject to subsections (a) and (b):

1. to collect, hold, and retain trust assets received from a trustor until, in the judgment of the trustee, disposition of the assets should be made; and the assets may be retained even though they include an asset in which the trustee is personally interested;

2. to receive additions to the assets of the trust;

3. to continue or participate in the operation of any business or other enterprise, and to effect incorporation, dissolution, or other change in the form of the organization of the business or enterprise;

4. to acquire an undivided interest in a trust asset in which the trustee, in any trust capacity, holds an undivided interest;

5. to invest and reinvest trust assets in accordance with the provisions of the trust or as provided by law;

6. to deposit trust funds in a bank, including a bank operated by the trustee;

7. to acquire or dispose of an asset, for cash or on credit, at public or private sale; and to manage, develop, improve, exchange, partition, change the character of, or abandon a trust asset or any interest therein; and to encumber, mortgage, or pledge a trust asset for a term

within or extending beyond the term of the trust, in connection with the exercise of any power vested in the trustee;

8. to make ordinary or extraordinary repairs or alterations in buildings or other structures, to demolish any improvements, to raze existing or erect new party walls or buildings;

9. to subdivide, develop, or dedicate land to public use; or to make or obtain the vacation of plats and adjust boundaries; or to adjust differences in valuation on exchange or partition by giving or receiving consideration; or to dedicate easements to public use without consideration;

10. to enter for any purpose into a lease as lessor or lessee with or without option to purchase or renew for a term within or extending beyond the term of the trust;

11. to enter into a lease or arrangement for exploration and removal of minerals or other natural resources or enter into a pooling or unitization agreement;

12. to grant an option involving disposition of a trust asset, or to take an option for the acquisition of any asset;

13. to vote a security, in person or by general or limited proxy;

14. to pay calls, assessments, and any other sums chargeable or accruing against or on account of securities;

15. to sell or exercise stock subscription or conversion rights; to consent, directly or through a committee or other agent, to the reorganization, consolidation, merger, dissolution, or liquidation of a corporation or other business enterprise;

16. to hold a security in the name of a nominee or in other form without disclosure of the trust, so that title to the security may pass by delivery, but the trustee is liable for any act of the nominee in connection with the stock so held;

17. to insure the assets of the trust against damage or loss, and the trustee against liability with respect to third persons;

18. to borrow money to be repaid from trust assets or otherwise; to advance money for the protection of the trust, and for all expenses, losses, and liabilities sustained in the administration of the trust or because of the holding or ownership of any trust assets, for which advances with any interest the trustee has a lien on the trust assets as against the beneficiary;

19. to pay or contest any claim; to settle a claim by or against the trust by compromise, arbitration, or otherwise; and to release, in whole or in part, any claim belonging to the trust to the extent that the claim is uncollectible;

20. to pay taxes, assessments, compensation of the trustee, and

other expenses incurred in the collection, care, administration, and protection of the trust;

21.   to allocate items of income or expense to either trust income or principal, as provided by law, including creation of reserves out of income for depreciation, obsolescence, or amortization, or for depletion in mineral or timber properties;

22.   to pay any sum distributable to a beneficiary under legal disability, without liability to the trustee, by paying the sum to the beneficiary or by paying the sum for the use of the beneficiary either to a legal representative appointed by the court, or if none, to a relative;

23.   to effect distribution of property and money in divided or undivided interests and to adjust resulting differences in valuation;

24.   to employ persons, including attorneys, auditors, investment advisors, or agents, even if they are associated with the trustee, to advise or assist the trustee in the performance of his administrative duties; to act without independent investigation upon their recommendations; and instead of acting personally, to employ one or more agents to perform any act of administration, whether or not discretionary;

25.   to prosecute or defend actions, claims, or proceedings for the protection of trust assets and of the trustee in the performance of his duties;

26.   to execute and deliver all instruments which will accomplish or facilitate the exercise of the powers vested in the trustee.

Sec. 4. The trustee shall not transfer his office to another or delegate the entire administration of the trust to a cotrustee or another.

Sec. 5. (a) This Act does not affect the power of a court of competent jurisdiction for cause shown and upon petition of the trustee or affected beneficiary and upon appropriate notice to the affected parties to relieve a trustee from any restrictions on his power that would otherwise be placed upon him by the trust or by this Act.

(b) If the duty of the trustee and his individual interest or his interest as trustee of another trust, conflict in the exercise of a trust power, the power may be exercised only by court authorization (except as provided in sections 3(c)(1), (4), (6), (18), and (24)) upon petition of the trustee. Under this section, personal profit or advantage to an affiliated or subsidiary company or association is personal profit to any corporate trustee.

Sec. 6. (a) Any power vested in 3 or more trustees may be exercised by a majority, but a trustee who has not joined in exercising a power is not liable to the beneficiaries or to others for the consequences of the exercise; and a dissenting trustee is not liable for the consequences of an act in which he joins at the direction of the majority of the trustees, if he expressed his dissent in writing to any of his cotrustees at or before the time of the joinder.

(b) If 2 or more trustees are appointed to perform a trust, and if any of them is unable or refuses to accept the appointment, or, having accepted, ceases to be a trustee, the surviving or remaining trustees shall perform the trust and succeed to all the powers, duties, and discretionary authority given to the trustees jointly.

(c) This section does not excuse a cotrustee from liability for failure either to participate in the administration of the trust or to attempt to prevent a breach of trust.

Sec. 7. With respect to a third person dealing with a trustee or assisting a trustee in the conduct of a transaction, the existence of trust power and their proper exercise by the trustee may be assumed without inquiry. The third person is not bound to inquire whether the trustee has power to act or is properly exercising the power; and a third person, without actual knowledge that the trustee is exceeding his powers or improperly exercising them, is fully protected in dealing with the trustee as if the trustee possessed and properly exercised the powers he purports to exercise. A third person is not bound to assure the proper application of trust assets paid or delivered to the trustee.

TRUSTEE AS LIFE INSURANCE BENEFICIARY
Indiana Code, Sec. 27–1–12–16

A. The terms "proceeds" and "proceeds of life insurance" and similar phrases used in this section mean and include any and all benefits payable by the insurer by reason of the death of the insured under any "life insurance," "policy of life insurance," "insurance policy," "policy," or "annuity contract" providing for benefits on the death of the insured, including individual ordinary life policies, certificates issued under a group policy, annuity contracts, and accident or health policies....

B. Proceeds of life insurance policies heretofore made payable to a trustee or trustees named as beneficiary or hereafter to be named beneficiary under an inter vivos trust shall be paid directly to the trustee or trustees and held and disposed of by the trustee or trustees as provided in the trust agreement or declaration of trust in writing made and in existence on the date of death of the insured, whether or not such trust or declaration of trust is amendable or revocable or both, or whether it may have been amended, and notwithstanding the reservation of any or all rights of ownership under the insurance policy or annuity contract; subject, however, to a valid assignment of any part of the proceeds. It is not necessary to the validity of such trust agreement or declaration of trust that it be funded or have a corpus other than the right, which need not be irrevocable, of the trustee or trustees named therein to receive such proceeds as beneficiary.

C. A policy of life insurance or annuity contract may designate as beneficiary a trustee or trustees named or to be named by will if the designation is made in accordance with the provisions of the policy or contract whether or not the will is in existence at the time of the designation. The company shall, within sixty days after receipt at its home office of proof of probate of the will, pay the proceeds of such insurance or contract to the trustee or trustees designated in the insurance policy or annuity contract, subject to a valid assignment of any part thereof and any other provisions of the policy or contract, unless prior to the actual payment by the company it shall have received at its home office written notice of the filing or pendency of (1) objection to the probate of said will, or (2) a suit to contest the validity of said will or of the testamentary trust or trusts created therein to which such proceeds are payable, or (3) petition for the construction of that part of the testamentary trust designating the trustee or trustees: Provided, however, That if the company makes any payment or payments of proceeds to such trustee or trustees in accordance with the terms of the policy or contract before receipt at the home office of such written notice, said trustee or trustees shall give full acquittance therefor to the company and such payment shall fully discharge the company from all claims and liability to the extent thereof. Provided, further, That if such written notice is received by the company, payment by it of any unpaid proceeds may be delayed during the pendency of said objections, suit, or petition for construction for not to exceed one [1] year from the date of death of insured, and thereafter the company may pay any and all unpaid proceeds due by reason of the death of the insured to the clerk of the court wherein the probate proceeding is pending by depositing them with such clerk who, as such clerk, shall give full acquittance to the company for all proceeds so paid and the company shall be fully discharged from any and all liability and claims by or on behalf of any other person or persons whomsoever to the extent of the amount so paid and deposited. The clerk shall thereafter hold and disburse said proceeds in accordance with the order of said court to the party or parties and in the amount or amounts provided in said order upon receiving proper receipts therefor; all Provided, however, That the procedure provided for herein shall not preclude the company from interpleading or being interpleaded in any appropriate proceeding or filing a bill of interpleader in any court of competent jurisdiction.

D. If no claim to proceeds is made by any trustee designated as the beneficiary in any policy of insurance or annuity contract within one year after the death of the insured or if satisfactory evidence is furnished the insurance company within the one-year period showing that there is or will be no trustee qualified to receive the proceeds, payment may be made by the insurance company to those thereafter entitled.

E. The proceeds of insurance collected by the trustee or trustees are not part of the testator's estate and are not subject to the debts of the insured or to transfer, inheritance, or estate taxes to any greater extent than if the proceeds were payable to some named beneficiary or beneficiaries other than to the estate of the insured or executor or administrator thereof....

Illinois Compiled Statutes, Ch. 755, Section 5/4–5

A person having the right to designate a beneficiary of benefits payable under any insurance, annuity or endowment contract (including any agreement issued or entered into by an insurance company in connection therewith, supplemental thereto or in settlement thereof), or the right to designate the beneficiary of benefits payable upon or after the death of a person under any pension, retirement, death benefit, deferred compensation, employment, agency, stock bonus or profit sharing contract, plan, system or trust, may designate as a beneficiary a trustee named or to be named in his will whether or not the will is in existence at the time of the designation. The benefits received by the trustee shall be held and disposed of as part of the trust estate under the terms of the will. If no qualified trustee makes claim to the benefits within 18 months after the death of the decedent or if within that period it is established that no trustee can qualify to receive the benefits, payment shall be made to the representative of the estate of the person making the designation, unless it is otherwise provided by a beneficiary designation or by the policy or other controlling agreement. The benefits received by the trustee shall not be subject to claims or other charges enforceable against the estate or to estate or inheritance taxes (including interest and penalties thereon) to any greater extent than if the benefits were payable to a named beneficiary other than the estate of the person making the designation, and in the case of benefits which otherwise qualify for exclusion from the gross estate for federal estate tax purposes, such benefits shall not be used by or for the benefit of the estate of the decedent.

New York Estates, Powers, and Trusts Law, Sec. 13–3.3

(a) The proceeds of thrift, savings, pension, retirement, death benefit, stock bonus and profit-sharing plans, systems or trusts, of life, group life, industrial life or accident and health insurance policies and of annuity, endowment and supplemental insurance contracts (hereinafter referred to as "proceeds") may be made payable to a trustee designated as beneficiary in the manner prescribed by this section and named as:

1. Trustee under a trust agreement or declaration of trust in existence at the date of such designation, and identified in such designation, and such proceeds shall be paid to such trustee and be held and disposed of in accordance with the terms of such trust agreement or declaration of trust, including any amendments thereto, as they appear in writing on the date of the death of the insured, employee or participant. It shall not be necessary to the validity of any such trust agreement or declaration of trust that it

have a trust corpus other than the right of the trustee as beneficiary to receive such proceeds.

2. Trustee of a trust to be established by will, and upon qualification and issuance of letters of trusteeship such proceeds shall be payable to the trustee to be held and disposed of in accordance with the terms of such will as a testamentary trust. A designation which in substance names as such beneficiary the trustee under the will of the insured, employee or participant, shall be taken to refer to the will of such person actually admitted to probate, whether executed before or after the making of such designation.

(b) If no qualified trustee claims such proceeds from the insurer or other payor within eighteen months after the death of the insured, employee or participant, or if satisfactory evidence is furnished to the insurer or other payor within such period showing that there is or will be no trustee to receive such proceeds, such proceeds shall be paid by the insurer or other payor to the personal representative or assigns of the insured, employee or participant, unless otherwise provided by agreement with the insurer or other payor during the lifetime of the insured, employee or participant.

(c) Except to the extent otherwise provided by the trust agreement, declaration of trust or will, proceeds received by the trustee shall not be subject to the debts of the insured, employee or participant, to any greater extent than if such proceeds were payable to the beneficiaries named in the trust, and for all purposes including transfer or estate tax purposes they shall not be deemed payable to or for the benefit of the estate of the insured, employee or participant.

(d) Proceeds so held in trust may be commingled with any other assets which may properly become part of such trust.

(e) Nothing in this section shall effect the validity of any designation heretofore made of the trustee of any trust established under a trust agreement or declaration of trust or by will.

(f) This section shall be construed as declaring the law as it existed prior to its enactment and not as modifying it.

TRANSFERS TO MINORS
Uniform Transfers to Minors Act (excerpts)

§ 3. Nomination of Custodian

(a) A person having the right to designate the recipient of property transferable upon the occurrence of a future event may revocably nominate a custodian to receive the property for a minor beneficiary upon the occurrence of the event by naming the custodian followed in substance by the words: "as custodian for ___ (name of minor) under the [name of Enacting State] Uniform Transfers to Minors Act." The nomination may name one or more persons as substitute custodians to whom the property must be transferred, in the order named, if the first nominated custodian dies before the transfer or is unable, declines, or is ineligible to serve. The nomination may be made in a will, a trust, a deed, an instrument exercising a power of appointment, or in a writing designating a beneficiary of contractual rights which is registered with or delivered to the payor, issuer, or other obligor of the contractual rights.

(b) A custodian nominated under this section must be a person to whom a transfer of property of that kind may be made under Section 9(a).

(c) The nomination of a custodian under this section does not create custodial property until the nominating instrument becomes irrevocable or a transfer to the nominated custodian is completed under Section 9. Unless the nomination of a custodian has been revoked, upon the occurrence of the future event the custodianship becomes effective and the custodian shall enforce a transfer of the custodial property pursuant to Section 9.

§ 4. Transfer by Gift or Exercise of Power of Appointment

A person may make a transfer by irrevocable gift to, or the irrevocable exercise of a power of appointment in favor of, a custodian for the benefit of a minor pursuant to Section 9.

§ 5. Transfer Authorized by Will or Trust

(a) A personal representative or trustee may make an irrevocable transfer pursuant to Section 9 to a custodian for the benefit of a minor as authorized in the governing will or trust.

(b) If the testator or settlor has nominated a custodian under Section 3 to receive the custodial property, the transfer must be made to that person.

(c) If the testator or settlor has not nominated a custodian under Section 3, or all persons so nominated as custodian die before the transfer or are unable, decline, or are ineligible to serve, the personal representative or the trustee, as the case may be, shall designate the custodian from among those eligible to serve as custodian for property of that kind under Section 9(a).

§ 6. Other Transfer by Fiduciary

(a) Subject to subsection (c), a personal representative or trustee may make an irrevocable transfer to another adult or trust company as custodian for the benefit of a minor pursuant to Section 9, in the absence of a will or under a will or trust that does not contain an authorization to do so.

(b) Subject to subsection (c), a conservator may make an irrevocable transfer to another adult or trust company as custodian for the benefit of the minor pursuant to Section 9.

(c) A transfer under subsection (a) or (b) may be made only if (i) the personal representative, trustee, or conservator considers the transfer to be in the best interest of the minor, (ii) the transfer is not prohibited by or inconsistent with provisions of the applicable will, trust agreement, or other governing instrument, and (iii) the transfer is authorized by the court if it exceeds [$10,000] in value.

§ 7. Transfer by Obligor

(a) Subject to subsections (b) and (c), a person not subject to Section 5 or 6 who holds property of or owes a liquidated debt to a minor not having a conservator may make an irrevocable transfer to a custodian for the benefit of the minor pursuant to Section 9.

(b) If a person having the right to do so under Section 3 has nominated a custodian under that section to receive the custodial property, the transfer must be made to that person.

(c) If no custodian has been nominated under Section 3, or all persons so nominated as custodian die before the transfer or are unable, decline, or are ineligible to serve, a transfer under this section may be made to an adult member of the minor's family or to a trust company unless the property exceeds [$10,000] in value.

§ 8. Receipt for Custodial Property

A written acknowledgment of delivery by a custodian constitutes a sufficient receipt and discharge for custodial property transferred to the custodian pursuant to this [Act].

§ 9. Manner of Creating Custodial Property and Effecting Transfer; Designation of Initial Custodian; Control

(a) Custodial property is created and a transfer is made whenever:

(1) an uncertificated security or a certificated security in registered form is either:

(i) registered in the name of the transferor, an adult other than the transferor, or a trust company, followed in substance by the words: "as custodian for ___ (name of minor) under the [Name of Enacting State] Uniform Transfers to Minors Act"; or

(ii) delivered if in certificated form, or any document necessary for the transfer of an uncertificated security is delivered, together with any necessary endorsement to an adult other than the transferor or to a trust company as custodian, accompanied by an instrument in substantially the form set forth in subsection (b);

(2) money is paid or delivered to a broker or financial institution for credit to an account in the name of the transferor, an adult other than the transferor, or a trust company, followed in substance by the

words: "as custodian for ___ (name of minor) under the [Name of Enacting State] Uniform Transfers to Minors Act";

(3) the ownership of a life or endowment insurance policy or annuity contract is either:

(i) registered with the issuer in the name of the transferor, an adult other than the transferor, or a trust company, followed in substance by the words: "as custodian for _____ (name of minor) under the [Name of Enacting State] Uniform Transfers to Minors Act"; or

(ii) assigned in a writing delivered to an adult other than the transferor or to a trust company whose name in the assignment is followed in substance by the words: "as custodian for _____ (name of minor) under the [Name of Enacting State] Uniform Transfers to Minors Act";

(4) an irrevocable exercise of a power of appointment or an irrevocable present right to future payment under a contract is the subject of a written notification delivered to the payor, issuer, or other obligor that the right is transferred to the transferor, an adult other than the transferor, or a trust company, whose name in the notification is followed in substance by the words: "as custodian for _____ (name of minor) under the [Name of Enacting State] Uniform Transfers to Minors Act";

(5) an interest in real property is recorded in the name of the transferor, an adult other than the transferor, or a trust company, followed in substance by the words: "as custodian for _____ (name of minor) under the [Name of Enacting State] Uniform Transfers to Minors Act";

(6) a certificate of title issued by a department or agency of a state or of the United States which evidences title to tangible personal property is either:

(i) issued in the name of the transferor, an adult other than the transferor, or a trust company, followed in substance by the words: "as custodian for _____ (name of minor) under the [Name of Enacting State] Uniform Transfers to Minors Act"; or

(ii) delivered to an adult other than the transferor or to a trust company, endorsed to that person followed in substance by the words: "as custodian for _____ (name of minor) under the [Name of Enacting State] Uniform Transfers to Minors Act"; or

(7) an interest in any property not described in paragraphs (1) through (6) is transferred to an adult other than the transferor or to a trust company by a written instrument in substantially the form set forth in subsection (b).

(b) An instrument in the following form satisfies the requirements of paragraphs (1)(ii) and (7) of subsection (a):

"TRANSFER UNDER THE [NAME OF ENACTING STATE] UNIFORM TRANSFERS TO MINORS ACT

I, _____ (name of transferor or name and representative capacity if a fiduciary) hereby transfer to _____ (name of custodian), as custodian for _____ (name of minor) under the [Name of Enacting State] Uniform Transfers to Minors Act, the following: (insert a description of the custodial property sufficient to identify it).

Dated: _____

_____

(Signature)

_____ (name of custodian) acknowledges receipt of the property described above as custodian for the minor named above under the [Name of Enacting State] Uniform Transfers to Minors Act.

Dated: _____

_____

(Signature of Custodian)

(c) A transferor shall place the custodian in control of the custodial property as soon as practicable.

§ 10. Single Custodianship

A transfer may be made only for one minor, and only one person may be the custodian. All custodial property held under this [Act] by the same custodian for the benefit of the same minor constitutes a single custodianship.

§ 11. Validity and Effect of Transfer

(a) The validity of a transfer made in a manner prescribed in this [Act] is not affected by:

(1) failure of the transferor to comply with Section 9(c) concerning possession and control;

(2) designation of an ineligible custodian, except designation of the transferor in the case of property for which the transferor is ineligible to serve as custodian under Section 9(a); or

(3) death or incapacity of a person nominated under Section 3 or designated under Section 9 as custodian or the disclaimer of the office by that person.

(b) A transfer made pursuant to Section 9 is irrevocable, and the custodial property is indefeasibly vested in the minor, but the custodian has all the rights, powers, duties, and authority provided in this [Act], and neither the minor nor the minor's legal representative has any right, power, duty, or authority with respect to the custodial property except as provided in this [Act].

(c) By making a transfer, the transferor incorporates in the disposition all the provisions of this [Act] and grants to the custodian, and to any third person dealing with a person designated as custodian, the respective powers, rights, and immunities provided in this [Act].

§ 12. Care of Custodial Property

(a) A custodian shall:

(1) take control of custodial property;

(2) register or record title to custodial property if appropriate; and

(3) collect, hold, manage, invest, and reinvest custodial property.

(b) In dealing with custodial property, a custodian shall observe the standard of care that would be observed by a prudent person dealing with property of another and is not limited by any other statute restricting investments by fiduciaries. If a custodian has a special skill or expertise or is named custodian on the basis of representations of a special skill or expertise, the custodian shall use that skill or expertise. However, a custodian, in the custodian's discretion and without liability to the minor or the minor's estate, may retain any custodial property received from a transferor.

(c) A custodian may invest in or pay premiums on life insurance or endowment policies on (i) the life of the minor only if the minor or the minor's estate is the sole beneficiary, or (ii) the life of another person in whom the minor has an insurable interest only to the extent that the minor, the minor's estate, or the custodian in the capacity of custodian, is the irrevocable beneficiary.

(d) A custodian at all times shall keep custodial property separate and distinct from all other property in a manner sufficient to identify it clearly as custodial property of the minor. Custodial property consisting of an undivided interest is so identified if the minor's interest is held as a tenant in common and is fixed. Custodial property subject to recordation is so identified if it is recorded, and custodial property subject to registration is so identified if it is either registered, or held in an account designated, in the name of the custodian, followed in substance by the words: "as a custodian for _____ (name of minor) under the [Name of Enacting State] Uniform Transfers to Minors Act."

(e) A custodian shall keep records of all transactions with respect to custodial property, including information necessary for the preparation of the minor's tax returns, and shall make them available for inspection at reasonable intervals by a parent or legal representative of the minor or by the minor if the minor has attained the age of 14 years.

§ 13. Powers of Custodian

(a) A custodian, acting in a custodial capacity, has all the rights, powers, and authority over custodial property that unmarried adult owners have over their own property, but a custodian may exercise those rights, powers, and authority in that capacity only.

(b) This section does not relieve a custodian from liability for breach of Section 12.

§ 14. Use of Custodial Property

(a) A custodian may deliver or pay to the minor or expend for the minor's benefit so much of the custodial property as the custodian considers advisable for the use and benefit of the minor, without court order and without regard to (i) the duty or ability of the custodian personally or of any other person to support the minor, or (ii) any other income or property of the minor which may be applicable or available for that purpose.

(b) On petition of an interested person or the minor if the minor has attained the age of 14 years, the court may order the custodian to deliver or pay to the minor or expend for the minor's benefit so much of the custodial property as the court considers advisable for the use and benefit of the minor.

(c) A delivery, payment, or expenditure under this section is in addition to, not in substitution for, and does not affect any obligation of a person to support the minor.

§ 15. Custodian's Expenses, Compensation, and Bond

(a) A custodian is entitled to reimbursement from custodial property for reasonable expenses incurred in the performance of the custodian's duties.

(b) Except for one who is a transferor under Section 4, a custodian has a non-cumulative election during each calendar year to charge reasonable compensation for services performed during that year.

(c) Except as provided in Section 18(f), a custodian need not give a bond.

§ 16. Exemption of Third Person From Liability

A third person in good faith and without court order may act on the instructions of or otherwise deal with any person purporting to make a transfer or purporting to act in the capacity of a custodian and, in the absence of knowledge, is not responsible for determining:

(1) the validity of the purported custodian's designation;

(2) the propriety of, or the authority under this [Act] for, any act of the purported custodian;

(3) the validity or propriety under this [Act] of any instrument or instructions executed or given either by the person purporting to make a transfer or by the purported custodian; or

(4) the propriety of the application of any property of the minor delivered to the purported custodian.

§ 17. Liability to Third Persons

(a) A claim based on (i) a contract entered into by a custodian acting in a custodial capacity, (ii) an obligation arising from the ownership or control of custodial property, or (iii) a tort committed during the custodianship, may be asserted against the custodial property by proceeding against the custodian in the custodial capacity, whether or not the custodian or the minor is personally liable therefor.

(b) A custodian is not personally liable:

(1) on a contract properly entered into in the custodial capacity unless the custodian fails to reveal that capacity and to identify the custodianship in the contract; or

(2) for an obligation arising from control of custodial property or for a tort committed during the custodianship unless the custodian is personally at fault.

(c) A minor is not personally liable for an obligation arising from ownership of custodial property or for a tort committed during the custodianship unless the minor is personally at fault.

§ 18. Renunciation, Resignation, Death, or Removal of Custodian; Designation of Successor Custodian

(a) A person nominated under Section 3 or designated under Section 9 as custodian may decline to serve by delivering a valid disclaimer [under the Uniform Disclaimer of Property Interests Act of the Enacting State] to the person who made the nomination or to the transferor or the transferor's legal representative. If the event giving rise to a transfer has not occurred and no substitute custodian able, willing, and eligible to serve was nominated under Section 3, the person who made the nomination may nominate a substitute custodian under Section 3; otherwise the transferor or the transferor's legal representative shall designate a substitute custodian at the time of the transfer, in either case from among the persons eligible to serve as custodian for that kind of property under Section 9(a). The custodian so designated has the rights of a successor custodian.

(b) A custodian at any time may designate a trust company or an adult other than a transferor under Section 4 as successor custodian by executing and dating an instrument of designation before a subscribing witness other than the successor. If the instrument of designation does not contain or is not accompanied by the resignation of the custodian, the designation of the successor does not take effect until the custodian resigns, dies, becomes incapacitated, or is removed.

(c) A custodian may resign at any time by delivering written notice to the minor if the minor has attained the age of 14 years and to the successor custodian and by delivering the custodial property to the successor custodian.

(d) If a custodian is ineligible, dies, or becomes incapacitated without having effectively designated a successor and the minor has attained the age of 14 years, the minor may designate as successor custodian, in the manner prescribed in subsection (b), an adult member of the minor's family, a conservator of the minor, or a trust company. If the minor has not attained the age of 14 years or fails to act within 60 days after the ineligibility, death, or incapacity, the conservator of the minor becomes successor custodian. If the minor has no conservator or the conservator declines to act, the transferor, the legal representative of the transferor or of the custodian, an adult member of the minor's family, or any other interested person may petition the court to designate a successor custodian.

(e) A custodian who declines to serve under subsection (a) or resigns under subsection (c), or the legal representative of a deceased or incapacitated custodian, as soon as practicable, shall put the custodial property and records in the possession and control of the successor custodian. The successor custodian by action may enforce the obligation to deliver custodial property and records and becomes responsible for each item as received.

(f) A transferor, the legal representative of a transferor, an adult member of the minor's family, a guardian of the person of the minor, the conservator of the minor, or the minor if the minor has attained the age of 14 years may petition the court to remove the custodian for cause and to designate a successor custodian other than a transferor under Section 4 or to require the custodian to give appropriate bond.

§ 19. Accounting by and Determination of Liability of Custodian

(a) A minor who has attained the age of 14 years, the minor's guardian of the person or legal representative, an adult member of the minor's family, a transferor, or a transferor's legal representative may petition the court (i) for an accounting by the custodian or the custodian's legal representative; or (ii) for a determination of responsibility, as between the custodial property and the custodian personally, for claims against the custodial property unless the responsibility has been adjudicated in an action under Section 17 to which the minor or the minor's legal representative was a party.

(b) A successor custodian may petition the court for an accounting by the predecessor custodian.

(c) The court, in a proceeding under this [Act] or in any other proceeding, may require or permit the custodian or the custodian's legal representative to account.

(d) If a custodian is removed under Section 18(f), the court shall require an accounting and order delivery of the custodial property and records to the successor custodian and the execution of all instruments required for transfer of the custodial property.

§ 20. Termination of Custodianship

The custodian shall transfer in an appropriate manner the custodial property to the minor or to the minor's estate upon the earlier of:

(1) the minor's attainment of 21 years of age with respect to custodial property transferred under Section 4 or 5;

(2) the minor's attainment of [majority under the laws of this State other than this [Act]] [age 18 or other statutory age of majority of Enacting State] with respect to custodial property transferred under Section 6 or 7; or

(3) the minor's death.

HEALTH CARE AGENCY

UNIFORM HEALTH CARE DECISIONS ACT

Sec. 1: ... "health care" means any care, treatment, service, or procedure to maintain, diagnose, or otherwise affect an individual's physical or mental condition.

Sec. 2: ... (b) An adult or emancipated minor may execute a power of attorney for health care, which may authorize the agent to make any health-care decision the principal could have made while having capacity.

(c) Unless otherwise specified in a power of attorney for health care, the authority of an agent becomes effective only upon a determination that the principal lacks capacity, and ceases to be effective upon a determination that the principal has recovered capacity.

Sec. 5: ... (a) A surrogate may make a health-care decision for a patient ... if the patient has been determined by the primary physician to lack capacity and no agent or guardian has been appointed or...is not reasonably available.

(b) An adult or emancipated minor may designate any individual to act as surrogate by personally informing the supervising health-care provider. In the absence of a designation, or if the designee is not reasonably available, any member of the following classes of the patient's family who is reasonably available, in descending order of priority, may act as surrogate:

the spouse, unless legally separated;

an adult child;

a parent; or

an adult brother or sister.

(e) If more than one member of a class assumes authority to act as surrogate, and they do not agree on a health-care decision and the supervising health-care provider is so informed, the supervising health-care provider shall comply with the decision of a majority of the members of that class who have communicated their views to the provider. If the class is evenly divided concerning the health-care decision ... that class and all individuals having lower priority are disqualified from making the decision. (From *Comment*, after Section 5: When such deadlock arises, it may be necessary to seek court determination of the issue....)

DURABLE POWERS OF ATTORNEY

UNIFORM DURABLE POWER OF ATTORNEY ACT (1979 ACT AS AMENDED THROUGH 1999)(EXCERPTS)

§ 1. Definition.

A durable power of attorney is a power of attorney by which a principal designates another his attorney in fact in writing and the writing contains the words "This power of attorney shall not be affected by subsequent disability or incapacity of the principal, or lapse of time," or "This power of attorney shall become effective upon the disability or incapacity of the principal," or similar words showing the intent of the principal that the authority conferred shall be exercisable notwithstanding the principal's subsequent disability or incapacity, and, unless it states a time of termination, notwithstanding the lapse of time since the execution of the instrument.

§ 2. Durable Power of Attorney Not Affected by Lapse of Time, disability or Incapacity.

All acts done by an attorney in fact pursuant to a durable power of attorney during any period of disability or incapacity of the principal have the same effect and inure to the benefit of and bind the principal and his successors in interest as if the principal were competent and not disabled. Unless the instrument states a time of termination, the power is exercisable notwithstanding the lapse of time since the execution of the instrument.

§ 3. Relation of Attorney in Fact to Court-appointed Fiduciary.

(a) If, following execution of a durable power of attorney, a court of the principal's domicile appoints a conservator, guardian of the estate, or other fiduciary charged with the management of all of the principal's property or all of his property except specified exclusions, the attorney in fact is accountable to the fiduciary as well as to the principal. The fiduciary has the same power to revoke or amend the power of attorney that the principal would have had if he were not disabled or incapacitated.

(b) A principal may nominate, by a durable power of attorney, the conservator, guardian of his estate, or guardian of his person for consideration by the court if protective proceedings for the principal's person or estate are thereafter commenced. The court shall make its appointment in accordance with the principal's most recent nomination in a durable power of attorney except for good cause or disqualification.

§ 4. Power of Attorney Not Revoked Until Notice.

(a) The death of a principal who has executed a power of attorney, durable or otherwise, does not revoke or terminate the agency as to the attorney in fact or other person, who, without actual knowledge of the death of the principal, acts in good faith under the power. Any action so taken, unless otherwise invalid or unenforceable, binds successors in interest of the principal.

(b) The disability or incapacity of a principal who has previously executed a power of attorney that is not a durable power does not revoke or terminate the agency as to the attorney in fact or other person, who, without actual knowledge of the disability or incapacity of the principal, acts in good faith under the power. Any action so taken, unless otherwise invalid or unenforceable, binds the principal and his successors in interest.

§ 5. Proof of Continuance of Durable and Other Powers of Attorney by Affidavit.

As to acts undertaken in good faith reliance thereon, an affidavit executed by the attorney in fact under a power of attorney, durable or otherwise, stating that he did not have at the time of exercise of the power actual knowledge of the termination of the power by revocation or of the principal's death, disability, or incapacity is conclusive proof of the nonrevocation or nontermination of the power at that time. If the exercise of the power of attorney requires execution and delivery of any instrument that is recordable, the affidavit when authenticated for record is likewise recordable. This section does not affect any provision in a power of attorney for its termination by expiration of time or occurrence of an event other than express revocation or a change in the principal's capacity.

EXCERPTS FROM THE INDIANA POWER OF ATTORNEY ACT

[Indiana Code Sec.] 30–5–4–1. Requirements for validity. To be valid, a power of attorney must meet the following conditions:

(1) Be in writing.

(2) Name an attorney in fact.

(3) Give the attorney in fact the power to act on behalf of the principal.

(4) Be signed by the principal in the presence of a notary public.

30–5–4–2. Date power of attorney effective. (a) Except as provided in subsection (b), a power of attorney is effective on the date the power of attorney is signed by the principal.

(b) A power of attorney may:

(1) Specify the date on which the power will become effective; or

(2) Become effective upon the occurrence of an event.

30–5–10–1. Revocation. (a) Except as otherwise stated in the power of attorney an executed power of attorney may be revoked only by a written instrument of revocation that:

(1) Identifies the power of attorney revoked; and

(2) Is signed by the principal.

(b) A revocation under subsection (a) is not effective unless the attorney in fact or other person has actual knowledge of the revocation.

(c) If an executed power of attorney was recorded under IC 30–5–3–3, the revocation of the power of attorney must:

(1) Be recorded; and

(2) Reference the book and page or instrument number where the instrument creating the power of attorney is recorded.

30–5–10–2. Termination date and time. If a power of attorney specifies a termination date and time, the power of attorney terminates at that date and time.

30–5–10–3. Termination by incapacity of principal. (a) Except as otherwise stated in the power of attorney, a power of attorney is not terminated by the incapacity of the principal.

(b) The incapacity of a principal who has previously executed a power of attorney that terminates on the principal's incapacity does not revoke or terminate the power of attorney as to the attorney in fact or other person who, without actual knowledge of the incapacity of the principal, acts in good faith under the power. Unless otherwise invalid or unenforceable, an action taken under this subsection binds the principal and the principal's successors in interest.

ADDITIONAL CLIENTS

PAULINE BULLOCK GILLEY

Mrs. Gilley's husband died eight months ago. He was psychological counseling director at Hoynes University, a professional position there. He was only 36 and his death was a sudden and difficult tragedy for his wife and four small children. Mrs. Gilley is 35.

Dr. Gilley had very little property aside from a modest amount of life insurance. There has been no probate administration for his estate. Here is an outline:

A. Benefits from Hoynes University

    1. $10,000 in continued salary, payable to Mrs. Gilley in four quarterly installments, two of which have been collected.

    2. $12,000 in widow's benefits, payable in six monthly installments, all of which have been collected.

    3. Social Security, maximum entitlement, being paid currently.[1]

B. Life insurance proceeds paid on the life of Dr. Gilley; all of these are being held by the companies for payment on Mrs. Gilley's order. She is sole beneficiary.

    1. Gigantic Insurance, ordinary life, $80,000; settlement options available.

    2. Midwest Mutual, term, $20,000; settlement options available.

    3. Death benefit under annuity from Professors Annuity Association of America; $6,700; already collected.

    4. $900 death benefit from University Equities Fund (a variable annuity); payable in a lump sum; already collected.

C. Life insurance in force on life of Mrs. Gilley: $21,000, Prudence Insurance, ordinary life, premiums payable to age 65. Benefi-

---

1. Our estimate is that, in 2006, Mrs. Gilley would be paid $2,074 per month for her and her children. Substantial amounts would continue to be paid to her until her youngest child reaches age 16. Benefits con-tinue for each child until the child reaches age 18 (or age 19 if the child is still in high school), and beyond that if the child is disabled.

ciaries are children of the marriage, as secondary beneficiaries. Premiums are $80 per year per $10,000 of coverage.

D. Joint savings account, Society National Bank of Cleveland, $4,000; Mrs. Gilley has already transferred the account into her name solely.

E. Joint checking account, Old Hoynes National Bank, Robertsville, Blakey County, Hoynes; Mrs. Gilley has also transferred that account. Average balance since Dr. Gilley's death: $825.

F. Chevrolet two-door sedan; held jointly; Mrs. Gilley has transferred ownership to herself. No liens.

G. No real estate; personal effects of nominal value.

No estate administration was opened for Dr. Gilley and neither federal nor state death-tax returns were made. He had no will. Mrs. Gilley has no will.

Mrs. Gilley's concern is, of course, for the care of her children if she dies while any of them is a minor. She has a sister and brother-in-law in Chicago; they have three children; her brother-in-law is a securities salesman. Her parents live in Cleveland and are in good health. Her other sister is unmarried and is a legal stenographer in Detroit. Dr. Gilley's parents are both dead; he had no brothers or sisters. Mrs. Gilley's family tree:

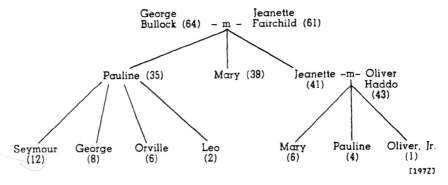

Mr. and Mrs. Richard (Martha) Golk are close friends in Robertsville, if the assistance of close friends is required. Mrs. Gilley says she has lived in Robertsville for six years and plans to remain here, although she wants minor children taken care of by Jeanette, in Chicago, if she dies while any child is a minor. She and her sisters are close; she has faith in Mary's business judgment and great affection for her parents. George Bullock will retire next year from a position as agent at an Amtrak station.

* * *

The companies that insured Dr. Gilley's life are holding the proceeds of the policies. Mrs. Gilley, who is beneficiary on all of the policies, can require that the companies pay her all of the proceeds, in cash. She also has available to her a range of "settlement options," provided in the contracts, which are explained by one company as follows:[2]

(1) Interest income. The company holds the proceeds as principal and pays Mrs. Gilley interest as well as withdrawals of principal as she requests.

(2) Fixed period income. The company holds the principal and makes periodic payments of both interest and principal in a specified amount. "The size of the payments depends on the amount of proceeds, the payment period, and the interest rate at the time the option is selected.... The Fixed Period Income option provides a guaranteed payment period. At the end of the payment period, payments will stop.... If you should die before the guaranteed period ends, the beneficiary of your choice may receive one of the following options: receive payments for the remainder of the period, receive a lump sum distribution, or select another settlement option with a lesser guaranteed period.... Keep in mind that once the Fixed Period option is selected, it cannot be changed later to another method of payment."

(3) Fixed amount [i.e., one of three types of annuity]. The company retains principal "plus interest, to pay you a specified monthly income for as long as the proceeds last. The larger the payment, the shorter the period of income." Arrangements similar to that for the Fixed Period income option if the payee (annuitant) dies before the period ends. Choice here, as there, is irrevocable.

(4) Fixed period and life [i.e., a second, lifetime type of annuity]. "[E]qual monthly payments are guaranteed to be paid to you for life.... On a 10–year settlement, for example, an absolute minimum of 120 monthly payments will be made. Payments will continue thereafter only if you are still living." If the payee (annuitant) dies before the fixed period ends, a beneficiary is given the options similar to those under the Fixed Period Income option. Choice here is also irrevocable.

(5) Joint and Survivor Income [i.e., a joint-and-survivor, third type of annuity]. Payments are guaranteed for the longer of two lives. "Income varies ... depending on the age and sex of the recipients." If both payees (annuitants) die before the fixed period ends, a beneficiary (third person) is given the range of options similar to those provided under the Fixed Period Income option. The choice is irrevocable.

---

2. American Family Life Insurance Company, "Your Guide to Settlement Options" (1997). These options vary from company to company, contract to contract. These are, we think, typical. This booklet does not specify interest rates, which are, in our observation, lower than those paid on other investments although larger than they were in insurance arrangements provided a generation ago.

JOHN CARL MARSHALL[3]

I. Personal data

A. John Carl Marshall, 39, born in Nashville, Tennessee. Served United States Navy; honorable discharge. Graduated public schools in Tennessee and attended Hoynes State University for two years. Left school to work in his father's business in Hoynes City. Returned from military service to his father's business in Hoynes City.

B. Present residence in Hoynes City.

C. Married Janet Marie LaTour in Chicago 20 years ago, while he was in the Navy. The couple had two children: a son, John Carl Marshall, Jr., and a daughter, Marie Anne Marshall. Both children are minors. (The age of majority in Hoynes is 18.) These children now reside with their mother in Indianapolis, Indiana. John (17) will graduate from high school there this year. Marie (14) is a student in high school.

D. Divorced Janet Marie LaTour Marshall ten years ago, by decree of the Family Court of Hoynes City, decreeing dissolution with (undefined) reasonable rights of visitation in the father and custody in the mother. (Janet Marie subsequently moved to Indianapolis, by permission of the Family Court taking the children with her.) This decree incorporated a separation agreement entered into by the parties, which provided:

1. Support payments for each child of $750 per month (modified five years ago, to $1,250 per month).

2. Division of property (long since accomplished).

3. Obligations on John Carl Marshall to carry medical insurance on each of the children (which he has done) and at least $50,000 in life insurance on his own life, payable to Janet Marie LaTour Marshall, or, if she predeceases John Carl Marshall, to the two children, share and share alike. (If Janet Marie remarries, she agrees that she will waive her right to contest a beneficiary change to the children.)

4. This clause: "John Carl Marshall further agrees that he will provide by will that two-thirds of his estate be distributed to the children of this marriage, namely, John Carl Marshall, Jr., and Marie Anne Marshall."

5. Mr. Marshall has kept all support payments current, provided insurance as required, and exercised his visitation rights by having the children spend two weeks of their summer vacations with him.

---

3. A series of interviews with Mr. Marshall is in Ch. 13 of Shaffer and Redmount, Legal Interviewing and Counseling (1980).

E. Married Inger Sollsen, a native of Norway, long since a naturalized citizen of the United States, six years ago, in Hoynes City. Mrs. Sollsen was a widow; she had one child, Henrik (no middle initial) Sollsen, born eleven years ago in Hoynes City. She brought no property of any consequence to her marriage to John Carl Marshall. Her parents are dead. She has one brother, living in Norway. She is now 37 and in good health. She is employed as a licensed real-estate salesperson by Imperial Realty Co., Inc., Hoynes City.

F. One child, Alexander Hamilton Marshall, born to John Carl Marshall and Inger Sollsen Marshall three years ago.

G. Parents, Francis Charles Marshall and Martha Washington Marshall, are both living and in good health. They are in no way dependent on the client and will almost certainly never be dependent on him. They had no other children.

H. Member of the Benevolent and Protective Order of Elks, the Hoynes City Unitarian Church, the American Civil Liberties Union, and the Democratic Party.

II. Business Data

A. Has been employed continuously in his father's business, Marshall Milling Corporation, which manufactures electrical parts and other automobile supplies for the large automobile companies. This was a sole proprietorship until 15 years ago, when the senior Mr. Marshall incorporated it.

1. Francis Charles Marshall is a director, President, Chairman of the Board, and chief executive officer.

2. Martha Washington Marshall is Vice–President and a member of the Board, but is not active in the business.

3. John Carl Marshall is Secretary–Treasurer and one of two other directors. The fourth director is Aaron Thomas Burr. Mr. Burr is an officer in the Hoynes City Bank and has no direct managerial connection with the corporation, other than his office as director.

4. Capitalization is 2,000 shares of no-par common capital stock. Twelve hundred shares are held by Francis Charles Marshall, 300 by Aaron Thomas Burr, 200 by Martha Washington Marshall and 300 by John Carl Marshall. These last were given to John Carl over a three-year period, 11–13 years ago, and valued at that time at $2,800 per share.

5. The book value of these shares (i.e., the result of dividing the total book value of the corporate assets by the number of shares) is $3,000 per share. No shares have been sold for the past three years, and none of the shares has ever been listed on an exchange or sold over the counter. Six years ago, one of the then shareholders, John

Jay, died. His estate sold his shares to Aaron Thomas Burr for $4,300 a share. The company has prospered and its annual earnings have increased since then. It pays (i.e., reports) income taxes under I.R.C. Subchapter "S."

B.   John Carl Marshall is occupied full time in duties for the corporation. He is paid an annual salary of $90,000 and may expect annual raises. He has benefits (retirement and widow's benefits, medical and disability coverage) and is covered by a profit-sharing plan, non-contributory, drafted to qualify for favorable income tax treatment, and cleared with the Internal Revenue Service, and his contributions to federal Social Security to date entitle him and his survivors to maximum Social Security benefits.

C.   Inger Sollsen Marshall works virtually full time as a real-estate salesperson, earning about $30,000 a year, without significant fringe benefits.

III.   Other Property

A.   Securities, all owned by John Carol Marshall

1.   Listed securities:

(a)   1500 shares, common stock, Sara Lee.

(b)   3,000 shares, common stock, General Motors.

2.   Unlisted securities: 300 shares, Marshall Milling Corporation (noted above).

B.   Other relatively liquid investments: ten $10,000 U.S. Treasury bonds, due five to ten years from now; those were obtained over a ten-month period, six years ago. They are owned by "John Carl Marshall or Inger Marshall."

C.   Real Estate

1.   House and lot at 110 Washington Street, Hoynes City, Hoynes, owned by "John Carl Marshall." This was mortgaged, but the mortgage debt has been paid and the mortgage released. Assessor's full valuation (cash value) last year was $225,000.

2.   Forty-acre farm and cabin in Montrose County, Colorado. Assessor's full valuation (cash value) five years ago, the year it was purchased, was $165,000. This farm is farmed by a neighbor and the profits split equally between Mr. Marshall and the active partner. There is no written agreement on this arrangement. The farm stands in the name of "Inger Marshall."

D.   Bank Accounts:

1.   Mr. and Mrs. Marshall have a joint-and-survivor savings account at the Story Trust Company in Hoynes City; current balance $12,400,

all of it contributed from Mrs. Marshall's earnings and from the couple's securities dividends.

2. Mr. and Mrs. Marshall have a joint-and-survivor checking account at the First National Bank of Hoynes City, with a current balance of $2,100. Deposits are from the earnings of both spouses.

E. Insurance

    1. On Mr. Marshall's life:

        (a) Policy No. 1123475, Indianapolis Life Insurance Company, income endowment policy, face value of $100,000 taken out nine years ago. Beneficiaries are Janet Marie LaTour Marshall, but if she remarries or dies before the insured, John Carl Marshall, Jr., and Marie Anne Marshall, share and share alike. Annual premiums $412.90.

        (b) Group Certificate 215, Policy 512A, term insurance under group plan issued to Marshall Milling Corporation by Mutual Insurance Company of New York. Face value $65,000. These premiums will go up steadily, and rapidly, in the next ten years, and Mr. Marshall will not be able to renew this insurance after his sixtieth birthday. Convertible to an "ordinary life" policy from the same insurer. No cash surrender value. Beneficiary: Mr. Marshall's estate.

        (c) $50,000 ordinary life, Indianapolis Life Insurance Company, Policy No. 2113608, payable to Inger Sollsen Marshall and then to the children born of the marriage of John Carl and Inger Sollsen Marshall. Last year, Mr. Marshall filed a revocable election on settlement options under this policy, under which a fixed monthly income computed on the company's annuity tables will be paid to Mrs. Marshall for the rest of her life and, if she dies within 20 years of Mr. Marshall's death, for the remainder of that twenty-year period to the children born of the marriage. When this was done, Mr. Marshall transferred ownership of this policy to Mrs. Marshall.

    2. On Mrs. Marshall's life:

        (a) $10,000 policy, Equitable Life Assurance Society of the United States, No. 502689, "ordinary life" with premiums payable to the date of death at steady rate of $78.00 annually. Beneficiary is Mr. Marshall if he survives, contingently to the children of their marriage.

        (b) Indianapolis Life Policy No. 2113608, noted above, is owned by Mrs. Marshall.

F. Personal property in the Marshall home is arbitrarily valued at $25,000.

IV. Miscellaneous

A. Mr. and Mrs. Marshall do not have wills.

B. Neither Mr. nor Mrs. Marshall has interest in trusts and neither has any powers of appointment. However, the wills of Francis Charles and Martha Marshall may contain provision for them, including, possibly, trust interests and powers of appointment.

C. Mr. Marshall is the business associate of his parents and their only child. He expects to inherit a controlling interest in the family business from them. However, he has no assurances to that effect and believes his parents may, in their wills, make direct provision for Janet, J.C., Jr., and Marie.

LEWIS ELIOT

Property and other data:

— 60,000 shares of Middlesex Land Corporation, a Hoynes corporation. This is all of the issued, outstanding stock of the corporation. The corporation's sole asset is a business building in downtown Paddington, which is owned free of encumbrances and is subject to a 50–year lease to the Dime Store Company, 28 years of which lease have not been used. The lease is renewable at the option of the lessee for an additional period of 50 years, at the stated rental amount. The building was extensively refurbished by the lessee. Rent is $107,000 per year, payable in quarterly installments, in advance. Taxes and insurance are borne by the lessee. All payments of rent and taxes are current. The assessed valuation of the land and building in 1996 was $560,000; assessments are generally one-third of market value. Mr. Eliot purchased these shares ten years ago for a single, block price of $815,000. The stock certificate is to "Lewis Eliot."

— 1,900 shares, common stock, Ford Motor Company; the stock certificate on these shares and on the three blocks of shares noted below is to "Lewis and Margaret Eliot, as joint tenants with right of survivorship and not as tenants in common."

— 520 shares, common, General Electric.

— 1100 shares, common, Sears.

— 3000 shares, common, Hewlett–Packard.

Note on Securities: All of the securities except the stock in Middlesex Land Corporation are pledged to the Old Hoynes Bank and Trust Company, securing a loan agreement entered into when Mr. Eliot discharged certain notes executed to pay for the Middlesex stock. This agreement calls for a balloon payment of $250,000 to the bank six months from now. The stock certificates are in the bank's possession; dividends are paid to Mr. Eliot, however.

Land contracts on seventeen parcels of residential real estate in Middlesex County, Hoynes—most of them in the city of Paddington. The total face amount of these is $650,000; the amount of principal due on them totals $423,000. They are all payable in monthly installments, at rates of interest ranging from 6.5 per cent to 10 per cent. None of them is currently in default, but several have been in default in the past. All of the contracts are on a printed form of agreement recommended by the Hoynes City Board of Realtors. Seventeen different vendees, some married. The vendor in each contract is listed as "Lewis Eliot" and record title (that is, the last warranty deed in each chain of title) is to "Lewis Eliot, married." Taxes are current; there are no extraordinary liens or encumbrances.

A vacant building site near the center of Paddington, Hoynes, on a busy street and in a desirable location. Not at present devoted to any useful purpose. Assessed valuation ten years ago was $22,000 (indicating a cash valuation then of about $66,000). Address: 112 South Wellington Avenue. No liens or encumbrances; taxes current. Last instrument in chain of title is a warranty deed to "Lewis Eliot and Margaret A. Eliot, husband and wife."

A vacation cottage on an island in the St. Joseph River near Niles, Michigan. This cottage was recently and extensively refurbished and (the building alone) is probably worth $70,000. The land on which the cottage stands was leased from Leonard March of Niles, Michigan, 26 years ago, for 30 years. The lease provides that all improvements on the land are the property of the lessee. The lease contains no provision for renewal. The lessee is "Lewis Eliot."

House and lot at 12 Churchill Place, Paddington; the last instrument in the chain of title is a warranty deed:

> "... to Lewis and Margaret Eliot, husband and wife, Lot No. 4 in Marlborough Acres, a subdivision of Middlesex County, Hoynes, as per plat thereof recorded at Plat Book 10, page 456, in the Office of the Recorder of Middlesex County, Hoynes."

No unusual liens or encumbrances; no mortgage. Assessed valuation five years ago was $110,000. (See above notes on assessments in Middlesex County.)

No life insurance; may be uninsurable (has had one stroke; advanced age).

No retirement plan.

No separate estate in Mrs. Eliot.

No children; no previous marriages for either spouse.

No interests in estates or trusts; no powers of appointment.

Mr. Eliot is 78 years old. Mrs. Eliot (Margaret Austin Eliot) is 74. Mrs. Eliot's widowed, childless sister, Charlotte Austin Luke, is 80. Mr. Eliot's widowed sister-in-law, Ann Simon Eliot, is 66 and has an adult son and four grandchildren.

Mr. Eliot wants to benefit his wife and his sister-in-law, Mrs. Luke. Ann Simon Eliot and her descendants do not need his property, in his opinion, and he does not want to benefit them or any other persons. Benefits after provision for Mrs. Eliot and Mrs. Luke are to be to the charities listed in his will of 13 years ago, and in the proportions there listed.

Mrs. Eliot has a will precisely parallel to Mr. Eliot's will of 13 years ago.

Mr. Eliot is a retired officer of the Old Hoynes Bank and Trust Company. He and Mrs. Eliot live on his investments, and on Social Security. He is not a veteran.

Mr. Eliot is not well but is nonetheless active, alert and optimistic. Mrs. Eliot has a chronic liver condition which has caused her hospitalization for two-or-three-week periods on four occasions in the last two years. Mrs. Luke is well for her age.

* * *

LAST WILL AND TESTAMENT OF LEWIS ELIOT

I, Lewis Eliot, being of sound mind and disposing memory do hereby make, publish and declare this as and for my Last Will and Testament, hereby revoking all other Wills and Codicils by me made.

I. I give, devise and bequeath to my sister-in-law, CHARLOTTE AUSTIN LUKE, the sum of Ten Thousand Dollars ($10,000.00).

II. The balance of my estate, real, personal and/or mixed, I give, devise and bequeath to my wife, MARGARET AUSTIN ELIOT, absolutely.

III. In the event my wife should predecease me, I give, devise and bequeath the balance of my Estate, real, personal and/or mixed unto my sister-in-law, CHARLOTTE AUSTIN LUKE.

IV. In the event my wife and my sister-in-law should predecease me, I give, devise and bequeath all of my property, real, personal and/or mixed as follows:

(a) Fifty percent (50%) to PADDINGTON COMMUNITY SCHOOLS, Paddington, Hoynes, with direction said sums to be placed in the Paddington High School Cumulative Student Loan Fund or in such other student loan fund the Paddington Community Schools may have established.

(b) Thirty percent (30) to THE AMERICAN LEGION.

(c) Twenty percent (20) to SIGMA CHI FOUNDATION, Evanston, Illinois.

V. I constitute and appoint my wife, MARGARET AUSTIN ELIOT, Executrix of this my Last Will and Testament. In the event my said wife, MARGARET AUSTIN ELIOT, should predecease me, I constitute and appoint my sister-in-law, CHARLOTTE AUSTIN LUKE, Executrix of this my Last Will and Testament. In the event my wife and my sister-in-law should both predecease me, I constitute and appoint THE OLD HOYNES BANK AND TRUST COMPANY, Paddington, Hoynes, the Executor of this my Last Will and Testament.

IN WITNESS WHEREOF, I have declared this instrument to be my Last Will and Testament, and have executed it by affixing hereto my hand and seal this 15 day of March, [13 years ago].

/s/ Lewis Eliot (SEAL)

The above and foregoing instrument, signed, sealed and acknowledged by the said LEWIS ELIOT, in our presence and we, at his request
and in his presence, and in the presence of each other, have hereunto
subscribed our names as witnesses thereto, and we do further certify that
on the day last aforesaid, we verily believed the same LEWIS ELIOT to
be of sound and disposing mind and memory.

/s/ Ronald Porson   /s/ Margaret March
510 Legal Building   1915 Harmony Lane
Paddington, Hoynes   Paddington, Hoynes

THE ELIOT INTERVIEW[4]

The lawyer has reviewed the file material prior to the interview.
When the interview begins, Mr. and Mrs. Eliot are in the lawyer's office,
having been seated there by the secretary; Mrs. Luke joins them later and
is shown in by the secretary, who brings her to the office door, which is
open. "C," in this interview, is Mr. Eliot, our client. "Mrs. E" is Mrs. Eliot
and "Mrs. L" is Mrs. Luke.

1 L: I've learned a little bit about this project, today, and
            you've sent along your old will and I've got a pile of
            papers here on your property, that I've been through.
            This is the first time that I've met Mrs. Eliot. And what
            I'd really like to do is set all that property information
            aside and just have you tell me a little bit about your
            family, and about Mrs. Luke, and what you want done
            with your property.

2 C: We'd like to have a will so drawn that the property
            would go to Mrs. Eliot on my death, and in the event of
            both of our deaths to my wife's sister, Mrs. Luke.

3 L: I see. Does Mrs. Luke live here in town?

4 C: Yes, she does.

5 L: I take it you spend quite a bit of time together?

6 C: Oh, yes.

7 L: Are you in agreement with that arrangement, Mrs.
            Eliot? Is that what you have in mind, too?

8 Mrs. E: Yes.

9 L: When you say "property go to," Mr. Eliot, I'm not sure
            I know exactly what that means. Now, you apparently

---

4. This interview appears in R. Redmount and T. Shaffer, *Legal Interviewing
and Counseling,* Copyright 1980 by Matthew Bender Co., and is used with
permission. That book, by the way, is made
up for the most part of law-office interviews
and analysis of them and includes several
"estate planning" cases.

spend a lot of your time looking after all this land that you own and these land contracts, these buildings, and so forth. Is Mrs. Eliot going to spend that time, also, after you've gone? (*Pause.*)

10 C: I don't believe so. No.

11 L: So we've got to think about some arrangement so she wouldn't have to do all the things you do.

12 C: Yeah, that's right.

13 L: What about Mrs. Luke? Is she likely to want to do those things?

14 C: No, I believe not.

15 L: You know, a lot of people use trusts in situations like this, where a trustee is doing all the work. Would that appeal to you? How do you feel about it—having some bank look after this property?

16 C: Then that would be set up more or less once and for all, wouldn't it? Carry on through the different successors of this property, right?

17 L: We sure could do it that way, and that would be—that would save having an estate—possibly here you could have three estates in a row within a very short period of time and that is expensive and time consuming.

18 C: I think that's very interesting.

19 L: I was talking to one of the young lawyers that's an associate of mine about this, and she said that she thought that what you ought to do is put all that property in a trust right now and not have to look after it anymore.

20 C: Surely it should be considered.

21 L: You could spend all your time fishing. How would you feel about living like that, without having anything to do—the bank would look after it all?

22 C: (*Pause.*) I would favor this.

23 L: You would? (*Pause.*) You know, that kind of surprises me. I didn't think you would. I figured you probably got a lot of fun looking after that stuff. I realize it's hard work, too, but I thought you probably enjoyed it.

24 C: One at my age isn't so ambitious as he once was.

25 L: Just as soon sit around a little more, huh? I was looking through those papers on that Dime Store Building, and you must have spent heaven only knows

how many weeks working that deal all out. That's a
very complicated deal. Well, let's set that question
aside. We could do that—if you want to—but maybe
there are some other things we ought to think about
first. How much control do you think the bank ought to
have over what Mrs. Eliot has to say about the property? (*Pause.*) Let's assume you die first, and she lives
for a while after your death, and we've got a trust, and
that means the bank is the legal owner of the property.
How much do you want the bank to do, and how much
do you want Mrs. Eliot to do?

26 C: Well, certainly she should be secured of her support. I
believe that probably the bank should have more or
less the control.

27 L: Control the support. You know, you can do that in a lot
of different ways. You can do that so the bank pays the
light bills and everything else. Or you can do less than
that. You can have the bank hold the investment
property and Mrs. Eliot take care of the house and
household, and so forth, so the bank just looks after the
investments and pays her monthly payments. I would
just kind of like to know how that strikes you, which
one of those models. (*Pause.*) You can go all the way the
other way, where Mrs. Eliot really looks after the
investments and the bank just kind of works as an
errand boy. She tells them what she wants done, and
then they do it.

28 C: Oh, I think Mrs. Eliot would favor taking care of her
own affairs to the extent of paying her own bills and
that sort of thing.

29 L: So she'd be independent in the house. How does that
strike you, Mrs. Eliot?

30 Mrs. E: That's fine. That's what I'd like to do.

31 L: Would you want to have more to say about the investments than that, or are the investments pretty much
up to the bank?

32 C: I think that if we have a reputable bank they could look
after that, the investments, and the business that way.

33 L: Mr. Eliot has been working with the—I was looking in
these papers here, I think it's the old Hoynes Bank,
here in town—if I can find it—well, the old Hoynes
Bank, and apparently your relationship with them has
been satisfactory.

34 C:	Yes.
35 L:	They have a good trust department. One of the things I worry about with a bank, when I have a client with so much of his investment in real estate as you do—they don't like real estate, you know, and they are going to be inclined to get rid of it, put the money in stocks and bonds.
36 Mrs. E:	Well, now, if they were handling all of our investments, say, even at this time, or if Mr. Eliot should happen to pass on and they'd be handling it for me, wouldn't they be required to consult us before they'd sell any of that real estate, or would they have the authority under this system we'd work out so that they'd just go ahead?
37 L:	We can make it either way.
38 Mrs. E:	(*To Mr. E.*) How do you feel about that?
40 C:	I think we should be in on a major deal; we should be notified.
42 Mrs. E:	The final word should come from us, if we'd prefer to sell or we wouldn't. I think that should be that way.
43 L:	I can understand that; many of those people who are on those land contracts are people you've known for years, done business with. You might like to keep that personal relationship with them, instead of having it turned over to an investment company of some kind.
44 Mrs. E:	I think so. Don't you?
46 C:	Seems right, yes.
48 Mrs. E:	Unless one of us should become seriously ill, or something, then we wouldn't be able to.
49 L:	Well, the trust could take care of that, too. One of the things these trusts can do is step in when you become seriously ill and then go all the way to the extreme of paying the light bills and everything else.
50 Mrs. E:	It could be set up in that manner.
51 L:	This device could also be used to save death taxes. One of the things that concerns me about the old wills is that they are—that form of will is very, very expensive from the death-tax point of view, because what happens there is that if Mr. Eliot dies first, then you, Mrs. Eliot, and then Mrs. Luke—it happens that way—oh, well, here's Mrs. Luke now.
52 Mrs. L:	Hello.

53 L: Hello, Mrs. Luke. How are you?

54 Mrs. L: Very well, thank you.

55 L: Oh, I don't know if you would remember me but my wife was a student of yours when you taught at Paddington Schools—Nancy Lehr—

56 Mrs. L: Did she have braids? Well, you wouldn't remember that.

57 L: I would never have married her if she had had braids.

58 Mrs. L: Well, I think she had braids with little bows in them in the third grade.

59 L: Well, I think it's fine that you remember. I won't suggest to you how long ago that was.

60 Mrs. L: No, don't. Please don't.

61 L: Well, we were talking—I assume Mrs. Luke joined us, Mr. Eliot, because you wanted her to.

62 C: Sure enough, sure enough.

63 L: We were talking about the Eliots' wills, and, as you know, you figure prominently in those, Mrs. Luke.

64 Mrs. L: Well, I sort of understood that that was so.

65 L: If you don't mind, we'll just keep on going from where we were, and you chime in whenever you like.

66 Mrs. L: Thank you.

67 L: We were talking about death taxes in these old wills. If it happened that you died in the order one-two-three, Mr. Eliot, Mrs. Eliot, and Mrs. Luke, there would be three probate estates, there, of approximately—the first would be over $2 million—this is very rough, but it's the idea—the first would be over $2 million, the second would be maybe about a million and a half, the third would be more than a million and there would be death taxes imposed by both the state and federal governments in each of them—lawyers' fees, probate court costs, and a fair amount of delay. And your thought was that, aside from taxes, this trust arrangement—it might be nice for your family—and I was going to say that the trust arrangements can also be made to reduce those taxes, now, and, in effect, what the trust would be doing, is saying to the trustee, "Take care of Mrs. Eliot, then take care of Mrs. Luke, then give what's left to the charities," and you won't have those three estates. You would only have one estate,

and that will be yours, Mr. Eliot. And I figure the tax savings in that can be as much as half a million dollars and the other costs also—some savings in dollars.

68 C: That's very interesting.

67 L: Well, we're leaving aside this question of whether we want to set this up during your life, or just in the will; but, if that sounds all right to you so far, I can get some idea of what kind of document we're going to draft.

68 C: Yes, I believe that's all right. What do you think about that, Mrs. Eliot?

70 Mrs. E: That sounds like a good plan to me.

71 L: If we set it up during Mr. Eliot's life, when Mr. Eliot dies, there really won't be too much probate business. Maybe a little. When Mrs. Eliot dies there should be none at all; and when Mrs. Luke dies there should be none at all. So that we keep the estate together as well as we can—of course, you realize, people with so much property as you have, pay some death taxes inevitably. (*Pause.*) Now let's talk a little more about that: One of the principal ways you save death taxes is the federal-estate-tax marital deduction, which allows you to deduct out of the tax, what's given to—if it's given to a surviving spouse. Now, how do you put that situation together with what you want—a trust arrangement to take care of Mrs. Eliot? The short answer to that is that there are lots of ways to do it. One way is to give Mrs. Eliot the power, at her death—after your death—to give the property to anybody she wants.

72 C: I would favor this plan.

73 L: Now, we should be candid about it; it's not just a formality. If Mrs. Eliot wanted to give this property to somebody other than Mrs. Luke she could.

74 C: Well, I'm sure she should have the choice, too. Her opinion—

75 L: Of course, she would now, under your old wills, wouldn't she? Because she would get the whole estate and she could give it to anybody she wanted. Mrs. Luke in that situation would take the property only if Mrs. Eliot gave it to her. So that sounds all right to you, roughly?

76 C: It sounds all right to me.

77 L: How does it sound to you, Mrs. Luke?

78 Mrs. L: Very fine.

79 L: You folks are easy to get along with.

80 C: I feel I should be a little more objectionable about this maybe, but I'm starting to get to be an old man, and I think I've got to think seriously as an old person about this.

81 L: Well, so are we all. (*Pause.*) There is still the question here about whether to do this during your lifetime, and—by the way—I don't think we need to hurry on this. As soon as I get some idea of what you want, I'll draft up some documents. I'll try to make them clear and understandable, and all three of you can have some time to look at them, and we can talk about them. We don't have to be in a big hurry.

82 Mrs. L: Well, do you know that we're going to Florida next week?

83 L: Oh. All three of you going to Florida?

84 Mrs. L: Yes. You didn't know about that?

86 C: I wouldn't worry about that. I expect to live another ten years at least and be able to do business. I think this should be considered.

88 Mrs. L: Well, Margaret and I were talking about it—we sort of feel—before we go away—we were sort of hoping that if we were going to do it, you could do it by the end of next week.

90 Mrs. E: Would that be possible? Could we expedite it a little?

91 L: We can, certainly. But I'm not sure that we want to. The existing wills, the old wills, are not bad as a stopgap arrangement, and these tax disadvantages I was talking about—if it should happen that the plane crashed or something like that—why, we could work it out. We could do some salvaging. In other words, the situation would not be horrible, and maybe it isn't worth doing a hurried-up job. I sometimes do this with clients when they're going on trips. It's funny how often people come talk to you about wills just before they're going on a trip. You are very kind to give me a week. A lot of people come in when they're going in about an hour.

92 C: I don't think we need to hurry this thing. I think ladies tend to want to hurry these things up. I think we have plenty of time.

94 Mrs. L: Well, you just don't know about those planes. You've been hearing about the crashes and the close calls. I just don't think that you can expect to live forever.

96 C: Well, surely we can stand some good advice here.

98 Mrs. L: And take more time. Is that right?

100 C: Take a little more time.

101 L: I'd like to—even if we did a hurry-up job—I'd still want to go back over it later after you got back from your trip, because I don't think this permanent arrangement can be hurried, Mrs. Luke. My advice is that your present wills would suffice in an emergency.

102 Mrs. L: We just have to pay all the taxes. I mean we would save on taxes the other way.

103 L: Well, of course, if you're talking about dying in a plane crash, there won't be any taxes, because it will all go to the charities.

104 Mrs. L: Oh, I see.

105 L: The taxes become difficult here. (*To Mrs. Eliot*) Actually they become most difficult when you die after Mr. Eliot's death. At his death, you have this marital deduction, because he's giving all the property to you, assuming you survive. Then at your death there is no marital deduction and the tax impact there could be enormous. The bracket that you'd be in could take a good third of the estate. At Mr. Eliot's death, if you survived, the tax impact would be all right. (*Pause.*) I wanted to ask a little about these assets, and then, if we decide we can, come back. I don't want to wear you out today, because we can talk about this again.

106 C: Right.

107 L: I had a couple of questions on this property. This Dime Store Building is part of your financial arrangement to buy all of it, Mr. Eliot. You put that thing in the corporation, and you now own the entire corporation, all the stock in it?

108 C: That's right, yes.

109 L: I wonder why we want to keep that corporation. It could be that part of this process—if you keep the corporation like that, where you own it all, you have a duty on yourself to keep up the—you have to go through the formalities of having a board of directors, and the board of directors meetings. Most people, and if

I read your papers right, you are included, don't do that, even though you're supposed to. You're supposed to file yearly reports with the Secretary of State—

110 C: That's right, yes.

111 L: That's a lot of trouble, and I don't see any benefit, to tell you the truth. It made good sense back when its ownership was divided between you and your sister-in-law, but I don't think it's necessary anymore.

112 C: Well, when I was more active I wouldn't have had it any other way.

113 L: Well, a lot of people think it gives an investment more status, if it's in a corporation, but I don't agree with that, and I think it might be better to dissolve that corporation. That was the only question I had about that. That's a good, free, clear asset, and you've got this debt on it that I assume you've arranged to pay back. You don't feel insecure about being able to pay back this debt?

114 C: No.

115 L: Let's see. That's in your name. The common stocks are all in joint tenancy. I've been through all those. A lot of lawyers, when they get that joint tenancy property in an estate like yours, want to undo it and put it all back in your name. My advice would be not to worry about that. There isn't that much in it, here. It's not a large amount of property. These land contracts are really what I had in mind when I asked you if you wanted to tell the bank to hold onto the real estate, because I think they will want to get rid of those—but we can tell them not to—and as I understand it you want to keep some control over selling the land contracts.

116 C: I'm sure we will.

117 L: This vacant building is what we call a tenancy by the entirety in this state; that is, you own it as joint owners. Figuring on renting that? To somebody?

118 C: Well, yes, I hope to.

119 L: Okay, so that may be becoming more valuable, and you may get some more income from it. Your house and lot is all clearly straightforward. As I understand it, you don't have any life insurance.

120 C: No, don't have any.

121 L: And your company didn't have a retirement plan?

122 C:	No.	
123 L:	And you don't own anything in your own name, Mrs. Eliot?	
124 Mrs. E:	No.	
125 L:	Well, that leaves only this one asset. I assume you know what it is, this vacation cottage in Michigan where you have got a lease on that little island in the river and you built a cottage on it. You use that in the summer for vacations, is that what that is?	
126 C:	Yes, vacations.	
127 L:	You know, you're going to lose that land pretty soon under that lease. You've only got about four years under that lease.	
128 C:	You think it would be well to sell the cottage before the lease runs out?	
129 L:	Well, I haven't seen it. Of course, you know what it's like. I would think moving a cottage off an island in the river would be fairly difficult, when the lease runs out. You're entitled to do that under this lease. Maybe you could get the lessor to buy the cottage or renew your lease. I guess that doesn't have a lot of problems for us in estate planning, but it's going to have some other problems. I'll be happy to help you with that.	
130 C:	It's a real fine cottage.	
132 Mrs. E:	We really don't use it much anymore.	
134 C:	It's a real fine cottage. I think I ought to get a good bundle out of that.	
135 L:	Probably a nice place to fish.	
136 C:	I'll make you a good deal on it.	
137 L:	They've started to clean out that river. They've got fish in it now. (*Pause.*) Now your old will gave $10,000 outright to Mrs. Luke if Mrs. Eliot survives—otherwise, everything to Mrs. Luke. Do you still want to retain that outright $10,000?	
138 C:	No, I don't believe so.	
139 L:	Get it all under the trust arrangement?	
140 Mrs. L:	If he died from a plane crash, $10,000 is what I would get, is that right, under the old will?	
141 L:	Yes, under the present will.	
142 Mrs. L:	That's what I thought.	

144 C: Well, that's good. (*Pause.*) But under the trust arrangement it would all be maintained and taken care of.

146 Mrs. L: Yes, but that's not going to be before the trip. That's not going to be done now—he says he can't do it before we leave next week.

148 C: Well, there's a little chance we might not crash.

149 L: The stewardess always says it's the safest part of your trip. (*Pause.*) The old will made Mrs. Eliot executrix and Mrs. Luke executrix if Mrs. Eliot didn't survive, and—only if neither of the ladies was able to do it—the bank. If you are going to have a trust with the bank, it would be my advice to make the bank executor also. That simplifies the transfer of assets from the estate to the trust. Unless there is some reason I don't understand about having family members appointed executrix, I would advise you to make a bank executor.

150 C: Oh, I think that's very good.

151 L: Okay, fine. Now the other question I want to get an angle on before I try some drafting on you, is whether you want to transfer all your property now for this arrangement, as my associate thought you might want to, in which case, you see, the bank begins to manage these assets now, while you are alive. When you die—it's not like a will exactly, because the bank just continues to manage it. It's not that sharp of a transition. That's one advantage of the thing.

152 C: Well, I contemplate living a little while. I'd like to think about it just a little bit.

153 L: You may not want to give up all that work.

154 C: That's right. I'm pretty active. I can do quite a little yet.

155 L: I suspected that was the way you would feel, and I attributed my associate's suggestion to her youth. (*Pause.*) Well, we could do it either way, but actually the drafting is not that much different. The form of the trust is different. But the content of it is not much different than a will would be.

156 C: I see.

157 L: So, now one other unpleasant subject, and that's my fees. I usually, on this kind of work, just charge for my time, and my time is billed at $150 an hour. I hesitate to estimate how long it will take, but I wouldn't think more than 20 or 30 hours and probably quite a bit less

than that. So the rough estimate I'll give you is something between $3,000 and $5,000 for this job; it may be a little less, if we don't run into any great difficulties.

158 C: Golly, that kind of money I can buy another end of the Dime Store Building.

159 L: Buy some more Dime Store, yes.

160 Mrs. E: One square foot. (*Pause.*)

161 L: Well, generally, is that all right? I don't want you to be surprised when you get my bill.

162 C: Well, let's see. Mrs. Eliot is going to have to get in on this. (*To her*) Shall we—think that's all right?

164 Mrs. E: Yes, I think so. (*Pause.*)

165 L: Well, costs go up all over, don't they?

166 C: Now, that will be all right.

167 L: All right. Thank you, Mr. Eliot. (*Pause.*) Well, my next step—and I hope you have a very nice trip—my next step will be to have in your hands, by the time you get back—this is—what would you say?—a two-week trip?

168 Mrs. L: No, we are going to be down there three weeks, three and a half weeks.

170 C: Yeah. But I might hurry them up a little.

171 L: So it's approximately a month to five weeks from now. I'll have something drafted so you can think about it by that time, and we may want to get together and talk again.

172 C: All right.

173 L: Well, thank you very much for coming in.

174 C: Very good, I appreciate it. Thank you.

175 L: Goodbye. Goodbye, Mrs. Luke.[5]

---

5. Many lawyers would see in this interview, and in Andrew's presence in the Striker interview, just below, a couple of "ethical problems": First, since both Mr. and Mrs. Eliot are clients, is there a potential conflict of interest in talking with and acting for both of them? (Note the exchange at 71–72 in the Eliot interview and imagine present and future tensions there, as well as with regard to the provisions for Mrs. Luke.) This representation-of-spouses issue is mentioned in note 2, Ch. 3, with regard to Dr. and Mrs. Kennedy as clients. The issue has become a bit vivid lately, after the American Bar Association "deleted" R.P.C. Rule 2.2 and some states—notably Indiana—decided not to comply. See T. Shaffer, "My Client the Situation," Res Gestae, October, 2005, p. 24. Second, the presence of a third party (Mrs. Luke, Andrew) may affect the attorney-client privilege, should testimony from the lawyer here be sought after the death of the client(s).

ROSE STRIKER

This interview is conducted, by appointment, in the client's home. The client consulted the local legal services office on a Social Security matter and asked, while talking to a lay advocate in that office, about having her will made. The lawyer was assigned to help her with the will. A third party—Andrew—lives in Mrs. Striker's house and is present for most of the interview. The interview as it appears here has been slightly condensed.

1 L: Mrs. Striker, I told you earlier I'm here to—you know—talk to you and I understand that you are interested in having a will drafted and, first of all, I would like to sit and talk with you and learn a little bit about you, and discuss some of your problems, and maybe this will help us better understand your wishes in drafting your will. Is that okay with you?

2[6] C: That's all right.

3 L: All right. Won't you tell me a little bit about yourself? Where you're from. Where you were born and raised.

4 C: I was born in Paddington, 1801 Charles Street, and I have lived in this house 50 years. My husband and I made it and he died when he was 55; and I lived here alone until I had to put an ad in the paper, and had these roomers come in.

5 L: I see.

6 C: And I never had a child, which I wish I had.

7 L: I see. Well—

8 C: But, now I'm happy I haven't got any.

9 L: Uh huh. Where did your husband work, Mrs. Striker?

10 C: He worked for Greenview Laundry for 29 years; then they folded up and he went out to Bendix. He was in the Navy four and a half years, and he was a tailor until after the laundry folded up, then he went to Bendix. He died of cancer.

11 L: And you've lived in the Paddington area all of your life, then?

12 C: Right here. In the same house. Oh no! When we first

6. Even numbers are used for the client; odd numbers for the lawyer.

408

got married, and we lived at 122 Kensington Street, and then I wanted a bungalow on the hill; so my husband and I worked together to make this home.

13 L: I see. Then did you work throughout your life?

14 C: Oh, very much. I worked in the laundry. I worked at Ball Band. And then I worked after that—no, before that—I worked at Swiss Laundry. I used to check out laundry. I liked that because it was book work and you had to figure. I really like that. So then I got so thin. I wish I was that way now.

15 L: (Laughs.)

16 C: My husband made me quit. Then he died, and that's the whole story.

17 L: Well, um, now you talked about—you know—your assets. You say that this is the only thing you own—is your home?

18 C: That's right.

19 L: Do you have any banking accounts, checking accounts, savings accounts—

20 C: Oh, I put money in the bank to pay my taxes. I think right now in the bank, I've got $193, because I've got to save for that, and then I buy my own food, because I got a bad heart and I got high blood pressure, and I'm supposed to diet, and that diet food really costs you, you know it?

21 L: Oh, it certainly does. It really does. It is very expensive.

22 C: You ain't so slim either.

23 L: Pardon me?

24 C: You are not so slim either.

25 L: Well—

26C: I'll bet you like food, don't you?

27 L: Oh, I like to eat. Yes ma'am, I certainly do. Uh. Uh. (Pause.) Do you have any—uh—U.S. savings bonds or any—

28 C: Nothing. Not at all.

29 L: Stocks?

30 C: All I get—I have—is Social Security, and Medicare, and—uh—that's about all. Oh, I've got a lot to use when I die, where I am to be buried—beside my

husband—and I got an insurance policy that's paid up. That's all I got.

31 L: You say you have your burial plot—uh—

32 C: Yeah. It's in Riverview Cemetery. Beside of my husband.

33 L: That's real wonderful. Uh. Let's—uh—talk a little bit more about your family now. You were—how many in your family, Mrs. Striker?

34 C: Nine.

35 L: Nine kids. How many boys and girls?

36 C: Two boys and seven girls. And they're all dead and I'm the youngest one living. And I'm 71.

37 L: So you are the only one in your family of children still living?

38 C: No, I have two other sisters.

39 L: Two other sisters are living.

40 C: Mary is eight years older than I am and Peggy is four years older than I am.

41 L: Now you mentioned one of them that you don't really care for, now—

42 C: Peggy.

43 L: And she is 75?

44 C: Now wait. Yeah. Her birthday is in November. I think she was 75. And Mary was—she's eight years older— and she was 79 the 20th of April.

45 L: Do you mind if I smoke?

46 C: No, go ahead. Help yourself.

47 L: Uh. Where does Peggy live, Mrs. Striker?

48 C: Washington Heights Apartments. She has two children in—uh—California....

49 L: Now, her only two children are out in California, then?

50 C: Uh huh. She could have come here and lived with me but her and I wouldn't get along. I was—When we was kids I was always roller skating and doing something and every time I went some place my mother insisted on me taking Peggy and she could never make friends or anything. She just wanted to boss everybody.

51 L: Uh huh. Well, she was older than you, right?

52 C: Uh huh.

53 L: Three—four years older?

54 C: Uh huh.

55 L: And—uh—so, actually, your dislike for her started in—uh—childhood, then.

56 C: Who, me?

57 L: Yes, you and Peggy.

58 C: Oh, yeah. We used to do a lot of things together. Peggy always had an idea of being an interior decorator, and me I'd like to play jacks—jacks and hopscotch—and I wanted to be—uh—not fooling around; but I loved to go out in the kitchen with my mother and cook.

59 L: Uh huh. (Pause)

61 L: Now, Mrs. Striker—uh—you have another sister you say—Mary?

62 C: Uh huh.

63 L: Now where does Mary live?

64 C: She lives at 102 Moon Street right off of West.

65 L: And she's 79?

66 C: Uh huh.

67 L: Does she live by herself also?

68 C: No. She's got a husband. That's why she don't—uh, dislikes me having Andrew around here, because she said I should be living alone. And her husband's living. They've done a lot for me. See, when my husband died, I only got $50.40 from the government. I still get it. And then I broke my ankle and—well—I paid for all of that. And—she—when I was in the hospital, when I broke my ankle, Henry and Mary were there every day, and she did pay my taxes. But finally the doctor that took care of my ankle—it wouldn't knit—it knitted but it wouldn't heal—so he had to break it open. You can see the scars right here.

69 L: Yeah, I see them.

* * *

86 C: And another thing I'll tell you. After my husband died I didn't think I could live without him.

87 L: Uh huh.

88 C: And I spent $2,000 on booze. And my sister put me to

Beatty's [the state mental hospital]. And I even paid for that. And I was only getting $50.40. (Laughs.)

89 L: Uh huh. So, you—

90 C: So wasn't I a nasty girl?

91 L: (Laughs.) Well, not really.

92 C: Huh?

94 (Andrew laughs.)

95 L: In other words you say that you—uh—started drinking booze pretty heavy, huh?

96 C: Uh huh. Yeah.

97 L: And uh—

98 C: I didn't think I could live without him.

99 L: Uh huh.

* * *

116 C: Uh huh. And, when they put the roof on, we had to have $1000, and my husband and I made it. But it still took us 18 years to pay for this house. You just tell them boys that's studying to be lawyers that marriage and building—Everybody says you got to have a home. It takes a lot. My husband always said you had to—uh—sweat by the head of your brow to make a living, and make it good, to be right. He always said he wanted to die young; but when he was in and out of the hospital—he never called me Rose, he always called me Mommy—and he said, "Mommy, no. Mommy, no. Mommy. Mommy, no!" You could hear him all over that hospital. See how people cling to their lives, even when they are sick, when they know they are gone?

117 L: Uh huh.

118 C: He said he wouldn't be afraid to die, but he was.

119 L: Uh huh.

120 C: The last time I went to see him, I stayed with him all night, which the nurses, and this and that, said I could. He just grabbed my hand and squeezed it so tight. He couldn't talk. He just smiled. And that was it. But that guy was jealous. He loved me so much, and I did him too.

* * *

132 C: Sure. Like they tell me: I was the best looking Polack in the West End. But there is a lot of good-looking Polish people, you know it?

133 L: Oh sure. Mrs. Striker, how much did your house cost when you built it?

134 C: Ah, I think it was $5,430.

135 L: Uh. Did that include the price of the lot, or was the lot—$750 for the lot—included, or—

136 C: No. That was all included.

137 L: So. That's total?

138 C: Uh huh.

139 L: Do you have any idea what your house is worth today?

140 C: Well, Marshall—you know he's the Treasurer—he tells me that—uh—my taxes are going up because the improvements—we made improvements—we, uh—this is the second furnace we had. We had two roofs on the house. And we had siding put on it.

141 L: Uh huh. Aluminum siding?

142 C: No.

143 L: Just, uh—

144 C: A guy came over here and wanted to sell me some the other day. What am I doing—I've got one foot in the grave already. What the heck do I want with siding? I want to give this home to somebody that really appreciates it. I don't think my sister Mary can use it. Oh, God, she's got a cute bungalow. You don't believe me, you just go west to Moon Street. They work in that yard. But he won't let her drive the car.

146 (Andrew laughs.)

148 C: But they got a basement that's better than my front bed—uh—front living room.

149 L: I see.

150 C: But they've both worked all their life, too, that's—Mary was a saver for me when I was working. I believed in clothes. I worked as a telephone operator. I had to have decent clothes and go out and go to eat because from Williams Street to 1801 Charles Street, I couldn't make it in half an hour. Could you?

151 L: No, I don't think so. (Laughs.) Well, Mrs. Striker, do you have any idea how much your house is worth

	today—according to what Mr. Marshall told you or—
152 C:	About—well, the tax receipts are $3000, but I think this house is worth more than $3000, don't you?
153 L:	Oh, certainly. So you pay taxes—
154 C:	My taxes now—I got to pay them sometime this week—is $120.06. That's for six months.

* * *

172 C:	I bought a stepladder, and I bought a power lawn-mower, and I bought two TVs, and—
174 Andrew:	And you sit right there in front of the TV and watch Johnny Carson.
176 C:	And then I bought paint to paint this living room, and I bought paint for the kitchen, and paint for the bathroom and the hallway. Andy's supposed to paint that, but his eyes is bad.
177 L:	Uh huh. Uh—Mrs. Striker, you told me that you have no stocks or bonds?
178 C:	No. I haven't.
179 L:	You have—in checking accounts, you have $193?
180 C:	That's right. And 68 cents. But I got to draw 120 bucks out of it to pay my taxes.
181 L:	Do you have any savings accounts?
182 C:	No. That ain't checking. That's savings.
183 L:	Where is your checking account at, Mrs. Striker?
184 C:	National Bank. Here on the Avenue.
185 L:	How much Social Security do you receive a month?
186 C:	I'll have to go look. Uh, I think it's eight hundred—I've got it written down. I'll go look. Less $45.50 for Medicare—so, now, I get $858.00. Then I get a V.A. check, for $50.40. So that makes it $904.40.
187 L:	So you receive Social Security of eight hundred and—
188 C:	Fifty-eight.
189 L:	A month?
190 C:	That's right. And they're gypping me out of it, too. Because I get paid by the month and there are some days longer—some months longer—uh—than others, so they are getting that, but I'm happy to get this.
191 L:	So you get a V.A. check of $50.40.

192 C:	Yeah, everybody gets that.
193 L:	Per month?
194 C:	That was in service.
195 L:	I see.
196 C:	Funny they don't take that away from me.
197 L:	Right. Well—
198 C:	Because they give my husband a fishing license and by golly he had it about six months and they took it away from him.
199 L:	So the nine hundred dollars you receive per month you use to live on, to pay your bills, and—
200 C:	Yeah. Telephone, water bill—and the telephone bill is going up; electric bill is going up; and the water bill is going up. And—you just figure—well, you know, you're running a house. You're married. Does your wife work?
201 L:	Yes, ma'am, she does.
202 C:	Well, by God, you couldn't make it yourself.
203 L:	It would be awfully hard.
204 C:	You're doggone right. I might be a Polack and I don't know much—
205 L:	(Laughs.)
206 (Andrew laughs.)	
208 C:	But, by golly, how can we live on nine hundred, with the food prices, and me on a diet! You know what I pay for a loaf of diet bread, about this big? Two dollars and a quarter!
209 L:	It's—
210 C:	It's enough to drive anybody to drinking.
211 L:	Mrs. Striker, now we have talked about your financial position so the only thing that you have—
212 C:	Is this home.
213 L:	Is this home.
214 C:	Oh I got—And don't forget: Andy's here. He's got saws; he's got a lot of tools; and, when he leaves, if I die first, he's going to take them with him. And he's got some of his pots and pans and stuff.
216 Andrew:	Looks like I've got all the tools but then I just can't get work. You know what I mean?

217 L:	Uh huh. Well, we can't value those in your estate. That's his personal belongings.
218 C:	Uh huh.
219 L:	Uh—Mrs. Striker, you just said that you've got a will. Did you write the will yourself?
220 C:	No. Huh uh. Lawrence Preston did. I used to go to school with him.
221 L:	Where is it now?
222 C:	We tore it up. Because Mary said I was giving everything away. That Junior Striker never did nothing for me, but it was my husband's idea that, when I die, he'd get it.
223 L:	I see. Was this an attorney who wrote the will or just a friend?
224 C:	Me! I went up and saw him.
225 L:	So does he know that you tore the will up?
226 C:	No, I never told him. He don't even come over and see me. The last time I saw him was about five years ago—wasn't it?—in November.

* * *

237 L:	All right. So, Mrs. Striker, we have to—you know—in your will, we have to dispose of all your property, and we want to dispose of it to who you want to have it. Now, this home, as you say, is your only—uh—
238 C:	That's all I got.
239 L:	The only thing you have, of value. Now who do you want to have the home?
240 C:	Lester Stuart. He befriended me when I wanted a couple of bucks. Five dollars or so. He's just a friend.
242 Andrew:	Leslie Stuart. S–T–U–A–R–T.
243 L:	(Writing.) The home—
244 Andrew:	He's a bartender at the Alibi Inn.
245 L:	How do you spell his last name?
246 C:	S–T–U–A–R–T.
247 L:	A–R–T?
248 C:	Yeah.
249 L:	All right now. He's just a friend? A personal friend?
250 C:	Uh huh.

252 Andrew: His name is Leslie.

253 L: Not Lester?

254 Andrew: No. Leslie.

256 C: He's an Englishman.

258 Andrew: Yeah. He's a Limey.

260 C: He's got troubles, too. He's got a sick wife. But she's 52 years old and, if a guy needs a home, he does. He's got a home, but he don't like it where he lives because there's colored people on both sides of him. He says they don't bother him but he says, when he gets out to mow the lawn or do anything, why they speak and, that's it.

261 L: (Writing. Long Pause.) Thank you. Mrs. Striker, the first thing that your estate has to take care of is we have to pay your personal debts and your personal—

262 C: I haven't got any debts.

263 L: And your burial expenses.

264 C: Huh?

265 L: And your burial expenses.

266 C: I got money for that. That's what I was going to ask you. I got a thousand. The lot's paid for. I will be buried beside my husband. And my insurance is made out to my sister Mary. Now, would you just let it ride and let her bury me or leave it—the insurance—to Les, too?

267 L: Is it a life-insurance policy?

268 C: Yeah.

269 L: Who's the life-insurance policy with?

270 C: Prudential.

272 Andrew: I'm going to take a walk. See you later.

273 L: For how much, Mrs. Striker?

274 C: What?

275 L: How much is the life insurance policy?

276 C: A thousand.

277 L: And you bought that purposely to, uh—

278 C: Oh, I took that out when I was 20 years old, and it was only 26 cents; but—they expected me to die before I did, so now I get—uh—what do you call it?—dividends. But I don't get them: Whoever the policy is made out to, why they'll get it.

279 L: I see. Did you—uh—say your sister, which sister is the—

280 C: Mary.

281 L: Mary?

282 C: Carson.

283 L: What's her last name?

284 C: Carson. C–A–R–S–O–N.

285 L: What's Peggy's last name?

286 C: Schmidt. She married a Belgian. Schmidt.

287 L: Does she teach school at City High?

288 C: Oh, no. She's too dumb, by God, to blow her nose! They—her husband—had quite a nice job, and they had their name changed. But they had it changed because Peggy and her husband always said they were French, and that was just a big lie.

289 L: Okay.

290 C: Well what would you do? Would you change that insurance? See, I don't know when I'm going to die. We don't—you don't, either. Mary don't know when she's going to die. So then, if Mary dies, then I have to, or—uh—Les dies, we'll have to change all that again.

291 L: Well, Mrs. Striker, without, you know—uh—giving you any information in this regard, I would like to think about it, but it seems to me that you have no money in savings accounts to pay for burial expenses. Although your burial lot is paid for—

292 C: That's right.

293 L: Uh. That's in the Riverview Cemetery.

294 C: Uh huh. Out on Post Road. Not very far from the county farm where Andy's going to go. (Laughs.)

295 L: Ah—

296 C: It's right across from Masonic Cemetery. You know where it is?

297 L: Yes, ma'am. I know where it's at. It's real pretty out there. Your insurance policy seems to be the only money you will have coming in, you know, when you do die; and that's made out to your sister. It seems to me maybe it would be wise to change the beneficiary—to yourself—for the purpose of burying you.

298 C: I can't do that with this policy.

299 L: You can't change the beneficiary?

300 C: No. Huh uh. It's got to made to somebody that I say can—uh—use it.

301 L: Do you think your sister Mary would pay for your funeral?

302 C: With my insurance, yeah, because I told her that I didn't want no earrings, no wristwatch, no nothing, no glasses; and when they embalm me, I want to be covered up, and I don't want nobody to look at me; and I doubt that anybody will come to see me. (Pause.) Ain't that a funny way to feel about it?

303 L: Well—uh—

304 C: No. The reason that I want to make this: I got too many nieces and nephews; they'll all come in. I don't want— They never done nothing for me, and I don't want to give them nothing either. Even this house. But you know there's a lot of people that'd love to have this house, for free. If they got a $1000 to pay inheritance tax. (Pause.) You'd probably like it yourself, wouldn't you?

305 L: (Laughs.) Well, I wouldn't say that, Mrs. Striker. I—uh—

306 C: No, you got a better home than I got.

307 L: No. I'd love to have this home; but—uh—I think that, you know, this is your home. You've worked hard to pay for it and—

308 C: And I can do as I want to.

309 L: You can do what you want with it. And, like I say, if you want to give it to Mr. Stuart, that's your prerogative. Uh—uh—Now you say that Mary Carson will pay for the burial—

310 C: Uh huh.

311 L: —expenses, with this life insurance policy?

312 C: That's right.

313 L: (Pause. Writing.) All right now. Mrs. Striker—uh—

314 C: Call me Rose.

315 L: All right, Rose—uh—the furnishings in your house, you want them to stay with the house, or do you want to give those to anybody, any of your relatives?

316 C: No. Huh uh. It all goes. I got a vase out there that my

husband paid $25 for. Mary always says when I die she wants that; but how does she know who's going to die first or second or last; and—uh—whoever gets it, will get my home too. They can have everything.

317 L: Right.

318 C: And after I'm dead, they can dispose of it the way they want to.

319 L: All the furnishings to go to Mr. Leslie Stuart. (Writing.) Can you think of anything else, Rose, that you have that—uh—you would like to—uh—bequest to anybody. You know. Give it.

320 C: Give to somebody? No. We got it. Matthew and I made it ourselves, and there ain't nothing worth much. Now, if Les wants the furniture, and he wants to have an auction, let him sell it. Cause that's why I got all these covers made. It is all worn out. There ain't a decent thing in this living room. But I try to make it livable.

321 L: It's very comfortable. Very comfortable. So as I see it, Mrs.—or—Rose—

322 C: Well, my husband had a wristwatch he got in the laundry, for 29 years of work and I gave it to Matthew's nephew, to his boy.

323 L: Uh huh. So as I see it, Rose, everything that you have, all your personal belongings, you want to go to Leslie Stuart.

324 C: Uh huh.

325 L: And—uh—you don't want Mary or Peggy to have anything, or any of your nephews or nieces.

326 C: No.

327 L: Now you were talking about your nephews and nieces. Do you know all of them?

328 C: God, no. There's an Olek, there, lives at Dayton, and Nowackis; they got a bunch. And—uh—my older sister. There's Alice, there's Grace and John—he married a millionaire's daughter. He was a basketball player and—uh—he lives in Georgia. Huh uh. I remember them when they was little kids, but, don't forget, I'm 71 years old. I forget to remember.

329 L: Uh huh. (Pause.) When was your birthday?

330 C: 28th of July.

331 L: You're 71 years old.

332 C: Uh huh.

333 L: And you live at 1801 Charles Street. (Writing.) This is—uh—.

334 C: They call it Paddington.

335 L: Paddington.

* * *

347 L: Right. (Pause.) Rose, is there anything else you would like to tell me in regard to your—uh—estate, or do you have anything else to talk to me about?

348 C: No. I ain't got nothing. Just my body and soul.

349 L: Well, that's worth a lot.

350 C: I can't give that to you.

351 L: (Laughs.) Okay. Well, I think at this time we will close the interview and I will go and prepare the will for you, and then I'll bring it back here, and we'll sign it, and—uh—execute it, and have it ready to go. Okay?

352 C: Yeah.

*

TABLE OF CASES

References are to Pages.

TABLE OF STATUTES

INDEX

References are to pages

427

CREDIT CARD LOSS PREVENTION INSURANCE

CRYPTOLOGIST, THE

CURTESY

CY PRES

DEAR ANNIE